MANAGED LIVES

An inherent tension exists in the history of psychoanalysis and its applications between the concepts of freedom and security. In *Managed Lives*, this tension is explored from the point of view of therapeutic experience. Set against the background of Freud's contested legacy, the book examines ways of managing oneself under psychiatric supervision, in the analytic encounter and in the emotional and moral contexts of everyday life.

Through a series of detailed case studies, Steven Groarke addresses therapeutic experience as a formation of managed society, examining the work of Donald Winnicott on types of management, Colin Murray Parkes on bereavement and Anthony Giddens on the sociological appropriation of psychoanalysis. *Managed Lives* forms an original critical analysis of contemporary managerial culture and its self-reflexive project, as well as presenting the idea of management as a source of inner security and vital morality. Presented in three parts, the book addresses:

- the criterion of maturity;
- the reflexive norm;
- the managed society.

Together, the book's arguments provide a fresh and challenging perspective on post-Freudian uses of faith, the risks of critical rationality and the difficulties of living an ethical life under modern conditions.

Managed Lives is ideal for academics and research students working on psychoanalytic studies, social theory and mental health studies, as well as students and trainees taking courses in psychotherapy, psychoanalysis, counselling, social work and health and social care.

Steven Groarke is a reader in Social Theory at the University of Roehampton, a psychoanalyst of the British Psycho-Analytical Society and a member of the International Psychoanalytical Association. He currently works in private practice in London.

MANAGED LIVES

Psychoanalysis, inner security
and the social order

Steven Groarke

LONDON AND NEW YORK

First published 2014
by Routledge
4 Park Square, Milton Park, Abingdon, Oxon OX14 4RN
605 Third Avenue, New York, NY 10017

Routledge is an imprint of the Taylor & Francis Group, an informa business

© 2014 Steven Groarke

The right of Steven Groarke to be identified as author of this work has been asserted by him in accordance with sections 77 and 78 of the Copyright, Designs and Patents Act 1988.

All rights reserved. No part of this book may be reprinted or reproduced or utilised in any form or by any electronic, mechanical, or other means, now known or hereafter invented, including photocopying and recording, or in any information storage or retrieval system, without permission in writing from the publishers.

Trademark notice: Product or corporate names may be trademarks or registered trademarks, and are used only for identification and explanation without intent to infringe.

British Library Cataloguing in Publication Data
A catalogue record for this book is available from the British Library

Library of Congress Cataloging in Publication Data
Groarke, Steven.
Managed lives : psychoanalysis, inner security and the social order / Steven Groarke.
pages cm
1. Psychoanalysis. 2. Self-management (Psychology) 3. Social sciences--Philosophy. 4. Social sciences and psychoanlysis. I. Title.
BF173.G7197 2013
150.19'5--dc23
2013019594

ISBN: 978-0-415-69219-9 (hbk)
ISBN: 978-0-415-69220-5 (pbk)
ISBN: 978-1-315-88015-0 (ebk)

Typeset in Times
by GreenGate Publishing Services, Tonbridge, Kent

TO MY MOTHER AND IN MEMORY OF MY FATHER
WITH LOVE AND THANKS

    Nah ist
Und schwer zu fassen der Gott.
Wo aber Gefahr ist, wächst
Das Rettende auch.

Hölderlin, 'Patmos' (1803)

CONTENTS

Preface ix
Acknowledgements xiii

PART I
The criterion of maturity 1

1 The Winnicottian typology of management 10
The Freudian critique of culture 11
The primary maternal frame 15
Catastrophic disillusionment 20
Social management 24

2 Reclamation and the unthinkable 31
The failure–dissociation model 32
Therapy as an act of faith 35
The redress of psychoanalysis 39
The exigency of return 44
The paradox of reclamation 49
Holding 51

3 Society's permanent task 59
Revaluation of the value of war 60
The calculus of security 63
The antisocial imagination 67
Leave-taking 74

PART II
The reflexive norm   79

4 Norms and facts   84
Communities of care 84
Rules of method 89
The Durkheimian norm 97
Social medicine and health surveys 100

5 Illness and identity   107
Needs and norms 108
Family-centred model of treatment 110
Awareness that something is wrong 117
A duty to the dead 120

6 Vulnerability and trauma   126
The predictive–preventive strategy 127
The calculation of risk 131
Traumatic grief 135
The case of Henry 142

PART III
The managed society   149

7 Basic security   154
Social facts and reflexive norms 155
The crisis of trust 161
The social logic of identity 165
Faith and knowledge 171
Normative orders of conduct 175

8 The regulated life   182
Coping with anxiety 184
The narrative frame of reference 189
Utopian realism 195
The re-moralization of the social 200

Conclusion: The difficult task   210

References   218
Index   239

PREFACE

This is a book about forms of therapeutic experience; it is about ways of managing oneself in the psychoanalytic encounter, under psychiatric supervision, and in the emotional and moral context of everyday life. Set against the background of Freud's contested legacy, we focus on the way in which some of our most intimate experiences are constituted and framed by therapeutic norms and values. The principal aim of the book is to determine and to critique the therapeutic underpinning of normative theories in a series of related disciplines and practices. This in turn involves linking the administration of normality, as a defining feature of managed society, to the difficulty of living an ethical life under modern conditions. More than therapy itself, we focus on the role of therapeutic experience in general as a formation of managed society. And while the argument is set out in a series of case studies, the book is primarily a theoretical critique of managed lives. The first part of the book considers the norm as an expression of life itself, the idea of normative vitality as a psychosomatic experience. The second part discusses the reflexive norm in bereavement studies and psychiatric supervision. The third and final part of the book focuses on the reflexive project of self-regulation as a twofold process of normalization and re-moralization. In each case, I aim to draw out the irreducible antinomy of security and freedom in the post-Freudian context of secularized or secularizing modernity.

A century after the publication of *The Interpretation of Dreams* and *Three Essays on the Theory of Sexuality*, we have assimilated Freud to any number of interpretations and settings. And with the passing of the so-called 'age of Freud', the important question now is what psychoanalysis has become as a normative conception of our world. It is important not to assume that the controversies surrounding Freud are simply a matter for the endless wrangling of the psychoanalytic schools. That we are indebted to Freud, heir to a legacy of radical ideas and unsettling techniques, is evident in the ongoing modifications and appropriations of psychoanalysis. This is a debt which is no less apparent in the adamant refusal to credit the doctrine of the unconscious mind; in the resistance to the central concepts of psychoanalytic theory; and even, perhaps especially, in respect of the deliberate denigration and dismantling of the Freudian interpretation.

While room has to be made in the history of psychoanalysis even for those who find it fraudulent, the acculturation of psychoanalytic thinking to the contemporary mainstream needs to be no less broadly conceived. It is only in this way that the history of psychoanalysis may justifiably present itself as a psychoanalytic history. To be clear, the clinic is not the *locus* of attention in the wider cultural debate about psychoanalysis; clinical thinking occupies the many voices of the increasingly few whose first responsibility is to their analytic patients. And yet, it seems to me the 'climate of opinion' remains no less indebted to Freud than it was when, on the occasion of Freud's death, Auden wrote his commemorative poem. That we remain Freudian, that our language reflects the pervasive influence of psychoanalysis, is evident even in a culture where there has generally been scant regard for Freud, where in England his name has hardly been esteemed or his work given much credit.

In what sense, then, can it be said that 'we conduct our different lives' under the auspices of Freud? The claim no longer means for us what it meant for Auden. Given the deliberate and systematic dismantling of the National Health Service in Britain over the past thirty years or so, therapeutic thinking of any kind hardly seems like a welcome customer. Instead, the preoccupation with biological deficits, coupled with the vested interest of the pharmaceutical conglomerates, is bolstered by governmental polices for short-term cognitive behavioural therapies. The eradication of symptoms and the restoration of functional capacity seem to be the main objectives, indicative of a refusal to learn about human welfare from the nature of our suffering. The hubris that has given rise to this state of affairs is disheartening enough; further to which, however, versions of psychoanalytic thinking continue to operate in subtle and unexpected ways, often in tandem with the more conservative elements in the culture. That we are all living lives supervised and regulated by radically modified versions of Freudian techniques is symptomatic of the degradation of the situation of psychoanalysis itself.

Rather than an overview of this situation, the book is presented in the form of three detailed studies on the assimilation of the Freudian legacy in post-war Britain. I introduce the studies in greater depth at appropriate points throughout the book. Broadly speaking, however, I aim to demonstrate the revision, occlusion, and appropriation of psychoanalysis in the work of Donald Winnicott, Colin Murray Parkes, and Anthony Giddens.

I begin with Winnicott's contribution to psychoanalysis in the aftermath of World War II. Taking a detailed look at his innovative conception of management, I discuss Winnicott's tendering of hope against the background of social welfare reforms after 1945. The first part of the book is divided into three chapters: Chapter 1 provides an overview of intuitive, therapeutic, and social types of management. Chapter 2 discusses the management of regression, particularly in the case of early trauma, as a coherent post-Freudian model of analytic practice based on reclamation. Chapter 3 focuses on the treatment of antisocial behaviour as a type of personal management, but also as an historical and political formation of social defence. The main reason for beginning with Winnicott, besides his pre-eminence in English psychoanalysis in the second half of the twentieth century, is that his work clearly demonstrates the tension between independence and regulation which, it seems to me, is inherent in psychoanalysis. On the one hand, Winnicott posits the irreducibility of life; the primacy of creativity; and the moral dimension of inner security. On the other hand, in lending his voice to the permanent task of defence, particularly with respect to the disaffected and antisocial elements in society, Winnicott gives proof of the degree to which psychoanalysis has been co-opted on to the side of social governance. I trace the contours of this tension throughout the book, identifying the inherent conflict of interpretations in psychoanalysis in terms of the wider difficulties of modern ethics and politics.

In the second part of the book I examine the development of bereavement studies during the 1960s. It will be argued that, alongside Bowlby and others, Parkes's studies of grief in adult life represent the beginning of a new phase in the understanding of mourning and its relation to self and society. On the grounds that the death of a husband is more likely than other types of loss to result in psychological difficulties of one kind or another, the widow emerges as a new object of psychiatric concern in post-war Britain. In challenging the Freudian argument on the crucially important question of mourning, Parkes presents an alternative approach to therapy modelled on communities of care. Before turning to a consideration of this alternative model of therapeutic action, in Chapter 4 I discuss some of the theoretical and institutional obstacles to medical reform in the post-war period. I then go on in the following chapter to consider Parkes's attempt to overcome these obstructions on the assumption that health and personal identity are in some degree commensurate with illness. In the third and final chapter of Part II I examine the management implications of Parkes's psychosocial model as a type of therapeutic supervision. The central argument in these three chapters is that, with the emphasis on the rationally ordered life and, in particular, on the self-empowerment of the rational individual, bereavement studies represent a deliberate dismantling of the Freudian interpretation.

Apropos Winnicott's typology of management, Parkes comes down unequivocally on the side of social management as a type of reflexive medicine. But whereas Parkes advances the normative framework of reflexivity *contra* psychoanalysis, the sociologist Anthony Giddens appropriates psychoanalysis to the reflexive project of the self. With regard to our central theme of security and freedom, while a common preoccupation with the binding foundations of a good society runs through the work of Winnicott, Parkes and Giddens, in Giddens and Parkes the reflexivity of moral norms is divested of Freud's concept of the unconscious. This is hardly a new reading of Freud. The sociological revision of psychoanalysis has been attempted in various ways, according to different political and ideological objectives, in different historical and cultural contexts.

For his part, Giddens turns to psychoanalysis as a therapeutic model of civic culture: in a series of works dating from the mid-1970s through the 1990s, he aligns psychoanalysis with a calculative attitude towards the risks and opportunities of late modernity. In the third and final part of the book I examine the way in which Giddens uses Lacanian psychoanalysis, American ego-psychology, and selected readings in British object-relations theory in support of a new rationality of government. I focus in Chapter 7 on Giddens's theory of the securely founded self; the chapter includes a discussion of post-Freudian uses of faith and the so-called 'crisis of trust'. Chapter 8 examines the link between moral understanding and rational reflection in the governmental context of human welfare. I bring my argument to a close with the sociology of 'positive welfare' as a mechanism of self-regulation based, at once, on a neo-Durkheimian project of rational ethics and a coherent post-Freudian narrative of security.

The main argument of the book is that life-management reveals a fundamental conflict of interpretations after Freud, to take the measure of which requires a genuine interdisciplinary approach. This asks a lot of the reader who is prepared to follow our argument as it moves from psychoanalysis to psychiatry and sociology; from the therapeutic process to formations of political reason and the activity of government; and from psychology to morality and religion. We put a further charge on the reader in presenting three highly selective case studies, while at the same time making broad claims about emotions, ethics, and society. There is no gainsaying the obvious pitfalls in my approach. But if I succeed, first in extending the critique of managerial culture with respect to our intimate lives, and second in demonstrating that management is nonetheless a source of vital morality and inner security, then I shall have achieved what I set out to do in the book.

ACKNOWLEDGEMENTS

In various parts of the book, I have drawn on papers that first appeared in the following journals: 'Winnicott and the government of the environment', *Free Associations*, volume 8, part 2 (46): 74–104, 2000; 'Psychoanalysis and structuration theory: the social logic of identity', *Sociology*, volume 36 (3): 559–76, 2002; 'Autonomy and tradition: a critique of the sociological and philosophical foundations of Giddens's utopian realism', *Critical Review of International Social and Political Philosophy*, volume 7 (3): 34–51, 2004; 'Unthinkable experience: Winnicott's ontology of disaster and hope', *American Imago*, volume 67 (3): 399–429, 2010; 'The criterion of maturity', *Psychoanalysis, Culture and Society*, volume 13 (1): 35–52, 2012.

The Tree by D. W. Winnicott is reprinted by permission of The Marsh Agency Ltd on behalf of The Winnicott Trust.

Lines from *The Spirit Level* by Seamus Heaney and from various poems by T. S. Eliot are reproduced by kind permission of Faber & Faber.

I have benefited over the years from conversations with friends, teachers, students and colleagues. Too many to name individually, they will gather from what I have written how useful those conversations have been. My colleagues at Roehampton University enabled me to take a term of study leave in 2012 in order to complete a final draft of the book.

I am grateful to Kate Hawes at Routledge for commissioning the book and to the anonymous reviewers who provided helpful suggestions on my initial proposal. I am grateful also to Lyndsey Dodd for the project management of the book, to Cathryn Pritchard for indexing, and to the production team at Routledge for their excellent work. On a number of occasions David Denney's generous support of my work has been decisive. Josh Cohen and Peter Rudnytsky have also supported my writing. I am indebted to both of them: to Peter for accepting my work as editor of *American Imago*, and to Josh for the solidarity closer to home. I have Gustaw Sikora to thank for confirmation of the fact that the generosities of friendship run deeper and are more meaningful in their reach than the controversies of the Schools. But at the same time I am grateful to Josh Cohen, Francois Louw, Anne Patterson and Megan Virtue for helping me keep the historical realities of the controversies in mind as clinical realities.

ACKNOWLEDGEMENTS

The time I spent at the Tavistock Clinic and at Parkside Clinic was both a valuable and an enjoyable experience. The British Psycho-Analytical Society and the accompanying Institute of Psychoanalysis, alongside the rest of the profession, may have good reason to do some soul-searching from time to time. But I would not wish to trade my experience of training in the British Psycho-Analytical Society. In becoming the analyst I have it in me to be I remain indebted above all to my patients. Further thanks are due to those with whom I trained; to my supervisors Roger Kennedy and Susan Loden; and to my third consultant, Robin Anderson. That being an analyst is a particular way of being a person came home to me in the company of Michael Parsons.

Although he may not always recognize it in what I write, my brother is the first companion to my thoughts. Finally, I owe special thanks to Louise Allnutt, who provided loving encouragement throughout the writing of much of this book, and whose becoming a mother during the final draft graced our lives.

Part I

THE CRITERION OF MATURITY

As a psychoanalyst with an additional forty-odd years of experience in paediatrics and child psychiatry, D. W. Winnicott continued to believe that despite the most disastrous failure, there is still room for hope. By investing the symptoms of disaster ('breakdown') with a dynamic value, Winnicott placed hope itself, the vital wish to get well, in a *dialectical* relation with types of catastrophic reaction.[1] Further to the intrapsychic neurotic conflict in classical Freudian theory, Winnicott combined a deficiency model of ill-health with a dynamic concept of internal reality. The former is based on the relationship between the individual and the environment; the latter, on the relationship between living and non-living. My aim in the first part of the book is to reconstruct the dialectic of disaster and hope along these lines as a new formation of therapeutic and ethical thinking.

There is widespread agreement from clinicians and historians alike that Winnicott transformed the theory and practice of psychoanalysis in the second half of the twentieth century.[2] We explore the positive implications of Winnicott's contribution to psychoanalysis in terms of an innovative developmental series: innate maturational potential; primary creativity; pre-reflective intuition; the act of faith; and the living self. But this is only one side of the story: the way in which Winnicott's work has been used both in therapeutic settings and outside the clinic, exemplifies the way in which psychoanalysis is co-opted on to the side of social governance. In this respect, Winnicott's revision of classical Freudianism demonstrates the ambivalent position of psychoanalysis itself as an administrative schema as well as a type of psychological treatment.

We focus in the book on the inherent conflict of interpretations in psychoanalysis, starting in Part I with Winnicott's theory of 'management'. In *Human Nature* alone, Winnicott's unfinished and posthumously published *summa*, we come across upward of twenty different uses of the concept of 'management'. The list of applications includes: the 'practical management' of mother and baby at the beginning (1988: 111) and 'general management after birth' (1988: 114); 'management of the first feed' (1988: 103); 'management of the skin in infant care' (1988: 122) and overall 'body management' (1988: 123); 'quiet (unexcited) management' as the basis of embodiment (1988: 124); management and 'illusion' (1988: 136); and 'the management of the first triangular relationship' as the basis of health and maturity (1988: 49). On the other hand, the concept also covers adverse emotional development in terms of the 'early failure of management' (1988: 100) or 'chaotic management' (1988: 139).

And further to pre-reflective understanding (and its breakdown) in the context of the earliest relationship, the concept extends to therapy and rehabilitation, including, the 'suitable management [of] relatively healthy small children with a certain liability to neurotic illness' (1988: 38); the management of 'the compliant false self' (1988: 109); problems of management following adoption (1988: 29); and, paradigmatically, the 'skilful management' in the analytic setting of the transition from internal reality to the outside world (1988: 91).

We get a sense of the intricacy of Winnicott's model from this list of applications, which also gives us an idea of the complex trajectory of managed lives that the model generates. In Part I we set out the conflicted position of psychoanalysis against the background of this model. Starting with a general overview, we differentiate three types of management in Winnicott: the mother's *intuitive management* of her baby as an expression of love; the *therapeutic management* of regression in the analytic setting as a process of reclamation; and the continuity of *social management* in the case of antisocial action as a combined strategy of self-control and social defence. In the following chapters, we go on to detail the dialectic of disaster and hope, concentrating on the traumatic failure of life at the beginning (Chapter 2) and on deprivation as both a psychological and a social problem (Chapter 3). But before turning to the details of Winnicott's argument, I shall begin by way of introduction with some general comments on disaster and hope. This will allow me to say something about my general theoretical approach.

Foucault (1989: 8) famously divided twentieth-century thought into two philosophical formations, which, he suggested, 'have remained profoundly heterogeneous'; namely, phenomenology and epistemology. The opposition does not stand up to scrutiny. This is evident, not least of all, on the strength of Foucault's own contribution, where the shift from phenomenology to epistemology ('archaeology') is coupled with a further shift from epistemology to politics ('genealogy') and beyond to a philosophy of the subject. Here, as elsewhere, it is not a case of two opposing traditions of thought, but of a complex theory of subjectivity. Similarly, Badio (1993) makes the point that while Canguilhem, who is the exemplary figure in this debate, does not have an explicit doctrine of the subject, nonetheless, the subject arises at strategic points in Canguilhem's work through a series of ontological, methodological, and ethical 'discontinuities'. The historicity of the subject, on this reading at least, is determined in its dissatisfactions, infinite displacements, and errant trajectory.[3] It is precisely the freedom to move that characterizes the individual as a historicized subject, the vital drama and therapeutic implications of which are captured in Canguilhem's Preface to *Idéologie et rationalité dans l'histoire des sciences de la vie*: 'To err is human, to persist in error is diabolical' (1977: ix). In *New Reflections* on his 1943 *Essay*, Canguilhem (1966: 272–3) based the concept of disease itself on error, understood as 'the immoderacy of the organic response'.

We follow Canguilhem's lead, with respect to 'the value attached to life in a given society' (1966: 161), by approaching the epistemology of psychoanalysis and the social sciences as an historical and political reflection on society. As such, our aim is to determine a particular conceptualization of *security* in relation to normality and normalization. The category 'normal' applies across the human and social sciences, ranging from the nature of life to forms of social conduct. We discuss security as an internal and external norm, starting with the vital normativity of psychosomatic relations in the context of primitive emotional development. The irreducibility of psychosomatic norms forms the essential background to the dialectic of disaster and hope. For Winnicott, the normative issue is emphatically and solely the experience of living; the idea that the norm issues from life is central to his theory of human nature. Nevertheless, given the fact that we experience life in historical and cultural forms, the dialectic of disaster and hope is therefore endowed with moral and political meaning in a particular conjuncture.

In Britain the public reaction to World War II and to the domestic misery of its aftermath, was directly informed by contemporary developments in psychoanalysis and psychotherapy.[4] The experience of war inevitably precipitates developments in these fields of inquiry, developments that subsequently provide professional and administrative resources in the aftermath of the war. This is not to suggest that developments in post-war government can be explained simply, or primarily in terms of wartime events. The immediate events of the war need to be seen in a more broadly defined context. What Braudel (1972/3; 1980) calls the long time-span (*longue durée*) of social and economic history provides one way of seeing the irregularity of war in a wider perspective. In fact, Braudel shifts the focus away from events and episodes altogether, including outbreaks of war and more immediate examples of societal conflict. This approach downplays the notion of war as a great and sudden misfortune, if not the whole idea of calamitous events.

While Braudel's methodological pronouncements are useful and interesting, it seems important not to lose sight of the particularity of war and its significance in the twentieth century. The work of Foucault affords us another way of looking at the relationship between war and society, indeed, from the point of view of security. Foucault takes a different tack to Braudel in suggesting that episodes of military conflict are symptomatic of an underlying history of social and political warfare. Unlike Braudel, Foucault (1997: 162) describes 'a generalized war that permeates the entire social body and the entire history of the social body'. He pursued this line of inquiry with increasing rigour from the mid-1970s, starting with *Surveiller et punir* (1975; English translation: *Discipline and Punish*, 1979) and the lecture course he gave in 1976 at the Collège de France. For Foucault, the very ambivalence of modernity is evident in the phenomenon of 'total war' that runs counter to the Enlightenment idea of war as exceptional and barbaric.

The contrasting historical perspectives in Braudel and Foucault raise important, albeit difficult questions about the nature of warfare which remained high on the political agenda throughout the twentieth century. These questions have become no less urgent in the wake of the attacks of 11 September 2001, the underground tube attacks in London in 2005, the Madrid train bombing in Spain, and the counter-insurgency initiates in post-invasion Afghanistan and Iraq.[5] We are effectively in a post-war situation, where the so-called global war on terrorism has intensified debates about security policies and procedures, the defence of society, the mobilization of state power and the legitimate use of violence. Trying to decide historically whether war is an anomalous or a habitual phenomenon is an ambitious undertaking which lies beyond the scope of this book. Nevertheless, my analysis of the application of psychoanalysis to social problems is informed by the paradigm of war coupled with Foucault's critique of normalization and the rationalities of government.

Together with Canguilhem's general epistemological approach, what Foucault calls 'governmentality' provides a framework for our analyses of therapeutic management and its social applications in post-war Britain. We are interested primarily in the generalization of therapeutic reason rather than the contribution of psychiatry and psychology to the war effort. Further to the techniques Winnicott made available for the treatment of antisocial behaviour, we focus in Parts II and III on the normative effects of psychiatric supervision and social governance, respectively. Taken together, these social initiatives raise new questions concerning the type of power the state can or should exercise over the individual. Thus, starting in Part I with Winnicott's treatment of evacuated children and the use of residential management, we focus in subsequent chapters on the aim of making society more manageable.

On the basic assumption that the events of war give 'rise to new ways of construing institutional life in terms of "human relations" and "the group"' (Rose 1989: 15), we begin with a consideration of Winnicott's (Winnicott and Britton 1947: 59) attempt 'to discover the best form of management and treatment' for the most damaged and deprived individuals in society. The kind of treatment Winnicott proposed, particularly in the case of deprivation and delinquency, demonstrates something fundamental about new ways of governing in post-war Britain. In the aftermath of war, Winnicott rendered the problems of disaster and deprivation amendable to management, not only in the case of individual patients and families, but also at the level of social regulation and cohesion. The concept of management thus extends from clinical thinking to the general well-being, integration, and safety of the wider community.

Are we overstating the importance of psychoanalysis? Does social welfare, never mind analysis and psychotherapy, play such a decisive role in post-war reconstruction? The task of rebuilding social and moral relations in post-war Britain involved a sustained effort to reform and revitalize governmental policies and institutions. But Britain's decolonization during this period almost certainly had a deeper and more significant impact than the emergence of the welfare state.[6] Nevertheless, the reformation of social welfare provides an organizing principle in post-war Britain, even if the end of Empire remains the more profound transformation in the long term. Foucault's 1976 lecture course at the Collège de France (1997; English translation: *Society Must Be Defended*, 2003) clarifies this situation theoretically, identifying the articulation of class and race as the backdrop to the exercise of power. In the British context, while the victorious 1945 Labour government presides over an irreversible shift in global power at the level of Anglo-American relations, the Attlee project is nonetheless concerned with matters of national solidarity and security. These are precisely the kinds of concerns that Winnicott articulates with respect to residential care and the task of protecting the public from antisocial and disruptive elements. Again, while the Keynesian doctrine sets out the government of society in terms of 'the simultaneous manipulation of economic and social variables' (Donzelot 1993: 133), at the same time, the Freudian legacy is reworked as a mechanism of security at the mundane level of everyday life.

Notwithstanding the international developments throughout the 1940s, in which America continues to attack the 'power politics' of Britain and Old Europe, social reform provides an indispensable framework for domestic concerns, ranging from rationing and town planning to Bevan's establishment of the National Health Service. It is in this context, drawing explicitly on the paradigm of war, that Winnicott (1948: 73) came up with new ways of thinking about the aftermath of disaster: 'Can we make use, in peace, of the results of what was so painfully experienced in time of acute stress and awareness of common danger?' The strategic implications of Winnicott's ideas about management are contained in this question. Consistent with the general administrative task, in the aftermath of the war techniques of management were applied to problems of attachment and solidarity. Winnicott's question, therefore, is indicative of a shift in the activity of government and its objects of concern: from a governmental point of view, antisocial behaviour replaces revolts, sedition, and dissent as perhaps the single most persistent problem in the 'war' fought out in daily life. The 'antisocial tendency' may be seen in this case as a forerunner of the wider culture of disaffection in late capitalism.

More than an observer or commentator, Winnicott was instrumental in bringing about the new state of affairs that he identified. As we shall see, the generalization of defence in response to antisocial elements augments and consolidates ways of thinking about society that are characteristic of the managerial–administrative practices which emerged in the aftermath of the war. Again, Foucault's analysis of 'pastoral power' as the groundwork of modern governance is particularly instructive. In his 1978 lecture course at the Collège de France (2004; English translation: *Security, Territory, Population*, 2007) Foucault was careful to point out that the law, discipline, and security do not comprise a chronological sequence so much as a series of transformations in the exercise of power. New technologies of security do not displace, but revise and rework juridical and disciplinary mechanisms. Most important, society remains subject to a fundamental series of conflicts and shifting alliances that set the terms of reference for the ordinary relations of law and order. The point is that juridical power or the rule of law amounts to a secondary phenomenon, while human rights and respect for liberties derive from the more basic technological norms and imperatives of security.

How does the dialectic of disaster and hope operate in this wider historical–political field? The problem of managing hope in the aftermath of disaster reveals an underlying tension between social reformism and individual freedom. A tension between two sets of norms and values that accounts not only for the technical pliability in Winnicott's thought, but more important, for the ambivalent historical and political position of psychoanalysis itself. The culture of the mid-twentieth century is divided in ways that become apparent in English psychoanalysis, where the more radical pronouncements on creativity, aliveness, and potentiality, what Winnicott (1988: 29) called the 'inherent growth element', remain at odds with administrative programmes underpinned by science and technology. The problem of hope brings this ambivalence to the fore. Is hope an aspiration of the freedom to relate or part of a social contract between the individual and society? Are our hopes of maturing into independent individuals invested with political as well as personal ideals? Most importantly, perhaps, whose hopes are being managed in the treatment of antisocial behaviour and general disaffection?

The hope invested in children, together with the child's capacity to have faith, is particularly important when it comes to the basic tensions we shall be looking at throughout the book. Managing childhood demonstrates the extent to which the problem of hope is divided in complicated ways between systems of security and acts of freedom. Modelled on the residential care of 'difficult children', the management of hope becomes part of the administrative task, a permanent task of social defence; the problem of hope is therefore linked to the theme of government. On the other hand, Winnicott approaches childhood and regressed states in adult patients from the developmental perspective of health and the ideal of active living. The incompatibility of these two perspectives on management exemplifies an underlying ambivalence in the institution of psychoanalysis, if not in Winnicott's own thinking. A prescriptive stance towards the progress of modern society, what Donzelot (1993) calls 'the promotion of the social', is set against a framework modelled on a form of maternal care adequate to innate potential and the creative process of maturation. We discuss this basic conflict of interpretations in terms of reflexivity and spontaneity, respectively.

For Winnicott, hope comes into play as a therapeutic resource where there is an intolerance of life and a concomitant failure to mature. Lives that repeat themselves fail and, where repetition is chronic, the failure of life may be catastrophic. As such, hope marks a certain threshold in circumstances that are decisive for the individual, but also for the state of society and culture. What Winnicott (1956b: 123) calls the 'moment of hope' may be counted among the most intimate of human expressions on the order of the inner self. At the same time, seen against the background of profound disillusion, the moment of hope is not without historical resonance in the aftermath of war, but also in a humanist culture seemingly bereft of its religious faculty. We intend a broad, interdisciplinary field of inquiry, encompassing the cultural as well as the political context of managed lives, informed by the recent debate in social theory about faith and reason in 'post-secular' society.[7]

For Winnicott, the management of hope is inseparable from his views about illusion–disillusionment. He articulates hope on a number of levels as a problem of belief and, invariably, the figure of the child plays a decisive role. What is the child who reaches out and steals something hoping for? What does the child hope will come of the lies he tells, if not the sins he commits or the rules he breaks? According to the way in which Winnicott poses these questions, the management of hope emerges as a particular technique of intimacy on either side of the secular divide, indicative of an ambivalence that runs deep in the contemporary European imagination. Inevitably, Winnicott assumed his debt to Freud in the context of his own cultural and religious background; that is to say, he anglicized Freud on a number of counts.

For instance, Winnicott's attempt to grapple with hope may be compared with the way that Thomas Hardy's poetry 'manages a perfect balance between his unbelief and his nostalgia for the faith in which he had been reared' (Tomalin 2006: 278). Diana Athill (2009: 48) makes a similar claim for biblical narratives being 'engraved in my imagination so deeply that they can't be erased by disbelief'. Winnicott was notoriously reticent in acknowledging his sources, a reticence that applied to his use of scripture, allusions to which are nonetheless pervasive throughout his work. Certainly, the comparison with Hardy and the literary tradition of Protestantism that he inherits from Milton is far from incidental. The interplay of literature and religion, I shall argue, stands in back of Winnicott's notion of therapeutic management, his use of faith, and his concomitant investment in the values of hope and love. The idea that therapy is an act of faith epitomizes what we might call Winnicott's Christianized understanding of value, an understanding that seems to me to exemplify the religious heritage of psychoanalysis.

To widen the cultural context in another, albeit related direction, a common involvement in moral truthfulness traversed to a greater or lesser extent by the intimacies of lyricism, is characteristic of a community of feeling in Jane Austen, Hardy, and T. S. Eliot. Winnicott's close affinity with this tradition of English literature rests on his preoccupation with the question of faith, or the capacity to believe, in the earliest relationship. It is hard to imagine Winnicott finding much use for poets like Tennyson, Yeats or Wallace Stevens, poets who start with the sublime feelings of inwardness and work their way out towards different kinds of moral concern. Winnicott seems more at home with what awakens in us to begin with as innate morality, the moral contours of internal reality as the basis of ontological security. He credits the infant's inherent tendency to love, while at the same time the evolution of what he calls 'a personal superego' (1963b: 94) delimits a sense of security that starts with primary creativity at the breast and extends to poetic thinking and religious experience.

Starting with the basic assumption that the self is inseparable from its *concern*, Winnicott will be our critical and clinical guide to the uses of faith after Freud. In specifying the different meanings of management in a post-Freudian context, we shall take our bearings throughout the book from the Winnicottian model of psychotherapy. To the extent that the latter is underpinned by the Christian values of love, hope, and faith, by ethical as well as clinical thinking, an indication of the role of religion in Winnicott's life and work is therefore in order.[8] The 'capacity to have faith' was important for Winnicott (1961: 14) in terms of the way in which, according to his personal needs, he reworked the moral and religious background of the culture. Born into a family of churchgoers who belonged to a nonconformist Protestant denomination, the Wesleyan Methodists, Winnicott was in no doubt about the importance of his Christian upbringing. He acknowledged its value for him as late as 1967 in a letter to Bion: 'I have no desire to throw away all that I listened to over and over again and tried to digest and sort out ... It is not possible for me to throw away religion just because the people who organize the religions of the world insist on belief in miracles' (1987b: 170).

An independent attitude of mind towards religion was as important to Winnicott as the teachings, a point he made clear in a letter to the Jungian analyst Michael Fordham, from the mid-fifties: 'One must be able to look at religious beliefs and their place in psychology without being considered to be antagonistic to anyone's personal religion' (1987b: 74). He goes on in the same letter to describe himself as 'religious' in his 'own particular way'; his conversion to Anglicanism took place sometime between 1917 and 1920 while he was a medical student at St Bartholomew's Hospital in London.

Through the use of literary and biblical references, I shall draw out what I see as the characteristic discriminations in Winnicott's thought. This does not imply that his psychological arguments necessarily carry any theological weight, nor am I suggesting that Winnicott claimed sanction from poetry. The point is that while remaining preoccupied with the therapeutic imperative, Winnicott engages the available norms and values of the culture as authentic inspiration for his clinical thinking together with his understanding of human nature.[9] In the letter to Bion that we have just cited, for instance, Winnicott (1987b: 170) added that he was 'very interested in the way you bring in the Bible story in your paper on catastrophic change and also quite frequently'. We are interested in the way Winnicott himself 'brought in' principles of Christian conduct by way of the criterion of maturity.

To be clear about our own view, we believe that Winnicott's thought accords with a utopian gesture underpinned by faith that has more in common with Hardy's 'nostalgia' than it does with the promotion of social control as an administrative task. Nevertheless, the conflict of interpretations to which Winnicott's thought gives rise provides the background for our central theme, namely, the way in which Freud's legacy has been variously revised, occluded, and appropriated. To indicate the main source of conflict, Winnicott announced his utopian reading of hope under the heading of 'spontaneity'. A child is able to be spontaneous, according to Winnicott (1967a: 98), only so long as 'the security of the framework' holds up, by which he meant the ontological security afforded the child in a loving, responsive, and generative family environment. Life realizes its potential as creativity in a reliable situation is the point Winnicott was making.

The coupling of 'spontaneity' and 'security', which pertains across the entirety of Winnicott's work, is immediately complicated and involves irreconcilable developments in both theory and practice. As well as an original theory of human nature, Winnicott's thoughts on maturity gave substance to the wider governmental response to the war on at least three counts. First, Winnicott construed the immediate problem of evacuation in terms of the relationship between mothers and children. If, as Isaacs (1941: 3) maintained at the time, evacuation provided 'an opportunity to learn priceless lessons for future social service', it was Winnicott who brought these lessons home in the form of therapeutic management and the social provision. Second, the evaluation of the 'external factor' along these lines drew attention to separation and loss not only as clinical phenomena, but also as social problems. Third, the significance accorded to the environment not only in the development of infants, but also in the treatment of adult patients with 'early damage', anticipated important developments in post-war preventive mental health.

As we have indicated, it is not our intention to reduce Winnicott's clinical thinking to a series of governmental propositions or administrative categories. Winnicott was not an original political thinker, nor did he deliberately set about formulating a psychoanalytical model of government. His contribution to our understanding of human nature goes far beyond the limits of instrumental reason, and we learn more about unconscious processes than we do about anything else from his thoughts on democracy, freedom, and society. Moreover, while his notion of management lends itself to the administrative task, at the same time, the pre-eminence of Winnicott's theory of creativity in English psychoanalysis unsettles the sociological reading of his work.[10] The creative imperative upholds the promise of hope for its own sake. The idea that life is what matters, that living is reason enough and requires no further justification, lies at the heart of Winnicott's thinking. Creative living is presented as a description of what human beings are like, a description which identifies the conditions of creativity in the intuitive management of maternal love.

In sum, together with primary creativity and the act of faith, we shall discuss the utopian use of hope as a counterpoint to the sociological appropriation of psychoanalysis as a form of 'utopian realism'. However, we shall also address the extent to which Winnicott made it possible to link the problem of hope with the theme of government. The discussion in the first three chapters is therefore divided as follows: on the one hand, we consider love and the primary maternal frame as the cornerstone of Winnicott's work, and discuss new ways of thinking about time and experience from the standpoint of therapeutic management. On the other hand, we demonstrate the extent to which therapeutic thinking, including the reclamation of experience, is co-opted onto the side of social governance through the Winnicottian example. We draw out some of the main implications of the governmental argument in these initial chapters, before turning to a more detailed discussion of the assimilation of psychoanalysis to social management in psychiatry and sociology in Parts II and III, respectively.

Notes

1 For a comment on the dialectical nature of Winnicott's thought see Ogden (1992) and Widlöcher (2012).
2 See Ogden (1986), Hughes (1989), and Abram (2013).
3 Heidegger (1962: xv) confirms the complex historical position of the subject, contrasting the historicity of his own thought (*die Geschichtlichkeit des Denkens*) to the tradition of Descartes, Kant, and Husserl; and he argues in *Being and Time* that hermeneutics, as the interpretation of the being of Dasein, elaborates 'Dasein's historicity [*Geschichtlichkeit*] ontologically as the ontical condition for the possibility of historiography [*Historie*]' (1927: 62; translation modified).
4 See Riley (1983) for an outline of new developments in psychoanalysis and psychology in Britain at the end of the war, particularly with respect to women workers, mothers and babies.
5 As a direct consequence of these attacks, the question of religion has re-entered public debate. How to conceptualize the relation between faith and reason is now a matter of real concern, and we return to this question throughout the book.
6 See Kynaston (2007) and Clarke (2007) for contrasting accounts of Britain's history in the 1940s.
7 For a critique of the secularization hypothesis, see Habermas (2008; 2010).
8 See Parker (2012) for the most detailed discussion to date of Winnicott and religion. Parker's argument works free of Freud's view of the religious life through an integrated pattern of biography, exegesis, and critical evaluation that culminates in the intersection of Wesley's *imago Dei* and Winnicott's true self. Goldman (1993: 122) identifies what he sees as Winnicott's 'lingering religiosity', including the effect of the Wesleyan Methodist tradition on the form and content of his thought. Similarly, Hoffman (2004) discusses Winnicott's involvement in the Wesleyan church and Fairbairn's early schooling in Scottish Presbyterianism as formative, albeit contrasting experiences of Christianity; and, most importantly, she points to the influence of these early religious affiliations on the authors' respective developmental and clinical thinking.
9 While not in my view tantamount to an implicit theology, Winnicott's clinical thinking nonetheless fulfils the requirement of 'minimal' transcendence, according to Bilgrami's (2010: 163) definition: 'our responsiveness to *external* callings of one kind or another makes possible what it is to be an agent at all and therefore makes possible the most abstract condition for living an unalienated life'.
10 See Applegate and Bonovitz (1995) for a Winnicottian approach to psychosocial development and the institutionalization of 'coping capacities'.

1
THE WINNICOTTIAN TYPOLOGY OF MANAGEMENT

Freud paved the way for the sociological assimilation of psychoanalysis in his critique of religion and morality. The sociological themes of his argument are immediately evident in the views he expressed some six months after the outbreak of World War I. Against the background of the 'disillusionment' of the war, Freud (1915b: 283–4) drew attention to the 'transformation of egoistic into altruistic inclinations'. The transformation is brought about, according to Freud, by external as well as internal factors. He argued that the external constraints of socialization are combined with the willingness to sacrifice narcissistic pleasures for the advantage of being loved. The reference to egoistic and social instincts cuts across the disciplinary distinction between psychology and sociology. The same basic assumption underpins *Group Psychology and the Analysis of the Ego*, where, instead of applying psychoanalysis to the study of society, Freud (1921: 69) proposes that 'from the very first individual psychology ... is at the same time social psychology as well'.

Narcissistic and social phenomena alike are considered the proper subject matter of psychoanalysis, a proposition that is underpinned by the theme of identification. Presented between the first topography and the structural synthesis of *The Ego and the Id* (1923), *Group Psychology* announces the important link between identification and the Oedipus complex. None of this is straightforward, however. Freud (1921: 105) maintains that, as 'the earliest expression of an emotional tie with another person', identification 'helps to prepare the way' for the Oedipus complex. It appears that the little boy's wishing to 'be like' his father amounts to a primary identification prior to any sexual object-choice. On the other hand, identification with the father becomes 'the precursor of an object-tie with the father'; a libidinal attachment based on what the little boy would like to 'have'. Identification with the father, where the child takes his father as his ideal, underlines the complicated connection in Freud's argument between the differentiation of psychic structures and the internalization of authority. It is clear, however, that the developmental axis is located in the Oedipus complex and confined to libidinal attachments. Moreover, the argument in *Group Psychology* concerning primary identification is coupled with the idea that there is no society without paternal authority. For Freud, the cohesion of society is maintained by the investment of individuals in the objects that substitute for their paternal ego ideal.

As the argument extends to *The Ego and the Id* and beyond, it is the identification with the father in the Oedipus complex that results in the superego. Accordingly, Freud's critique of culture and society relies on his account of paternal identification and the notion of the superego. This does not amount to a fully developed programme of social reform any more than a coherent strategy of social defence. Nevertheless, alongside a preoccupation with the introjection of ideal models, including the 'libidinal ties' that characterize a social group, the sociological thematic of the Freudian interpretation comprises a critical analysis of religious belief and moral values. In the following section, we consider these two themes in turn: the regressive nature of religion and the refractory object of the moral life. Given that faith is a central theme of the book, it is important in this respect to compare the views of Freud and Winnicott, before going on to an overview of Winnicott's post-Freudian typology of management.

The Freudian critique of culture

The Freudian critique of religion is based on the idea that religious belief is an illusion brought about by an unconscious desire. Freud (1927: 31) states that 'we call a belief an illusion when a wish-fulfilment is a prominent factor in its motivation, and in doing so we disregard its relations to reality, just as the illusion itself sets no store by verification'. As such, the psychoanalysis of religion concerns an illusion that is at odds with reality in ways that remain hidden on account of desire. What lies hidden behind the illusion of religious belief, according to Freud, is the infantile wish for a father. The intuition of transcendence, indeed any truth proper to the religious life, is ruled out in this account by the underlying motive of human helplessness. Religious ideas, Freud (1927: 30) argued, 'are not precipitates of experience or end-results of thinking: they are illusions, fulfilments of the oldest, strongest and most urgent wishes of mankind. The secret of their strength lies in the strength of those wishes.' And Freud concluded that, insofar as the 'terrifying helplessness' of infancy remains active in adult life, we cling to the wish for a loving heavenly father. We cling to God, in other words, through a sense of psychological insecurity.

Looked at in this way, religious belief is an expression of the need for protection against the consequences of human frailty, an infantile longing for the father that renders us incapable of mature thought. This is essentially what *The Future of an Illusion* has to offer by way of a critique of culture. Although the maturing of the mind is implicit in Freud's secular argument, namely, his argument against reliance on a solicitous Providence in the form of an idealized father, the critique itself is nonetheless driven by the criterion of necessity *rather than* maturity. How does this compare with Winnicott's views? The point is not that Freud thought religious belief is illusion and Winnicott thought otherwise, but that Winnicott did not share Freud's view of illusion. Where Freud saw illusion negatively, as a failure to make the necessary sacrifices in the face of reality, Winnicott held a more positive view of illusion, indeed, as a precondition for making contact with reality. These represent two contrasting views of maturity and its relation to reality. Freud maintains that religious belief is illusion in which a wishful impulse has been mistaken for a perception of reality. By contrast, far from collapsing wish-fulfilment and the unverifiable together, Winnicott credits illusion itself as an inherent aspect of human experience. He saw both imaginative illusion and the capacity to believe as grounded in the earliest relationship between mother and baby.[1]

Initiating a relationship between the infant and the world on the basis of illusion involves the use of management as love. But what does it mean to say that love is the basic intuition of intuitive management? First, in meeting the 'sensory hallucinations' of the infant, the mother allows for the infant's illusion that it has created what it needs. Far from causing the infant to turn away from reality, the mother allows for illusion to the extent that she 'makes real just what the baby is ready to look for' (Winnicott 1968b: 100). As long as the mother allows for 'the illusion that there is an external reality that corresponds to the infant's own capacity to create' (1968b: 101), the infant thus experiences the world as he imagines it to be. In this way, the mother facilitates the infant's reach for meaning from the inside. The necessity for illusion is evident in the experience of omnipotence as a condition of creative living and emotional maturity alike. Freud continued to view illusion as an imaginary construct that conceals reality. By contrast, Winnicott does not equate illusion with false appearances, nor does he allow reality to answer for creativity. For Winnicott, illusion itself provides access to reality; genuine contact with reality presupposes an ongoing imaginary subjective identification with the world. Subjectivity is thus inscribed into the very kernel of objective reality. The argument is principally concerned with the infant as creator of the world, but applies no less to mature religious belief. For Winnicott (1968b: 101), it is only through a sufficient experience of the illusion of 'being God' that one may reach the 'humility proper to human individuality' and, we might add, thereby make 'a place where God is lodged' (Williams 2004: 325).

Second, Winnicott describes how 'transitional objects' – for example, a piece of cloth or blanket – give shape to the 'area of illusion' between mother and infant. It is what comes into play, through the use the infant makes of the illusion mother facilitates, that enables the transition from the infantile act of oral incorporation to 'the first not-me possession' (1953: 89). Again, Winnicott is not describing a break with illusion on the Freudian model of reality-testing. For Winnicott, the criterion of maturity is not underpinned by an apprehension of the limits of human illusion, or by the primacy of knowledge over faith. Rather, following the experience of illusion as omnipotence (the infant as creator of the world), 'transitional phenomena represent the early stages of the use of illusion' (1953: 95). Note the reference to the 'early stages'. The use of illusion is seen as coterminous not only with transitional phenomena, but also with the potential for human experience *per se*. Maternal love is not a prelude to disenchantment; the mother manages disillusionment not by dispensing with illusion, but by preparing for its transformation as imaginative and faithful living: 'This matter of illusion is one which belongs inherently to human beings and which no individual finally solves for himself or herself' (1953: 95). According to the use we make of it, illusion is 'retained in the intense experiencing that belongs to the arts and to religion and to imaginative living, and to creative scientific work' (1953: 97).

Religion may be seen, then, as an integral part of the culture, at the same time as our sense of reality proceeds from an original act of faith nurtured by love.[2] We shall say more about this in a moment. Freud, however, arrived at exactly the opposite conclusion, instructing us to overcome the father complex and venture into an inhospitable world with no illusions. There is an essential austerity about the way in which Freud (1927: 56) put his final verdict to his imaginary interlocutor: 'No, our science is no illusion. But an illusion it would be to suppose that what science cannot give us we can get elsewhere'. This is how things stand at the end of *The Future of an Illusion*: in an ironic reference to the twin gods *Logos* (reason) and *Ananke* (necessity), the image of truth is set out strictly along scientific lines and without further compromise. The austerity that runs through Freud's argument renders the value of knowledge itself as a kind of security, something to set against the vulnerability of infantile feelings.

When Freud turns to ethical life and inquires further into what lies hidden behind the ideal, he grants there is more to culture than the consolation that religious illusion affords us. Nevertheless, in the extension of the Freudian critique from the illusion of transcendence to the question of happiness, the contrasting worldviews of Winnicott and Freud are once again evident: whereas Winnicott continues to address the question of happiness from the standpoint of maturity, Freud's critique turns instead to the cultural formations of the death drive. Introduced initially to account for the inherent compulsion to repeat, the hypothesis of the death drive was subsequently contextualized as a cultural as well as a psychological phenomenon of destructiveness. Following the structural synthesis in *The Ego and the Id* (1923) and the new theory of the instincts in *Beyond the Pleasure Principle* (1920), Freud finally placed the destructive element in a cultural context. It is important to recognize the central role Freud assigned to death in his critique of culture, his attempt to sound out the death drive through an interpretation of hate and war. The context of war informed the work of Winnicott and Freud alike, although they came to understand the meaning of destructiveness in profoundly different ways.[3]

The cultural interpretation of the death drive relies on what Freud made of the 'sense of guilt' (*Schuldgefühl*). On the level of individual conscience, the sense of guilt connotes a split in the ego between accused and accuser, a split that comes down to a tension between ego and superego. Freud (1930) accounts for the harshness of the latter, the demands of conscience, as an aggressiveness turned inwards. The superego does to the ego what the ego would do to others in accordance with the destructive instinct of non-erotic aggression. Freud describes how the desire for aggression is internalized, appropriated by the critical faculty, and unleashed against the ego without reserve. 'The tension between the harsh superego and the ego that is subject to it, is called by us the sense of guilt; it expresses itself as a need for punishment' (1930: 123). The essential unhappiness attributed to the moral life is immediately apparent: '[I]t is precisely those people who have carried saintliness furthest who reproach themselves with the worst sinfulness' (1930: 126).

Freud rises to the occasion when it comes to an explanation of the cultural institution of guilt. In a defining move of modern discrimination, Freud proposed that the morality of the civilizing process consists of the use of guilt against the recalcitrance of the individual; against the sadism of the superego; or against the aggressiveness of the ego and its malignant narcissism. Morality itself is seen as prohibitive. Accordingly, culture assumes its task on behalf of civilization by deploying internalized aggression against external aggression. Society is mobilized therefore against 'the hostility of each against all and of all against each' (1930: 122). The Hobbesian worldview is given a new twist in Freud, where hostility itself comes to the defence of society. The cultural function of guilt thus marks a shift in the Freudian interpretation from a conflict between the agencies of the personality to the antagonism of mutually opposing instinctual forces. Indeed, Freud (1930: 132) struck a decidedly dramatic note in his descriptions of guilt as an expression of 'the eternal struggle between Eros and the instinct of destruction or death'.

What are our chances of happiness on these grounds? What are we to make of the good life? Freud (1927: 6) eschewed the distinction between culture and civilization. He saw culture as a way of managing the civilizing process, and, with the prohibitions of morality lodged in the renunciation of the superego, civilization itself seems inimical to personal well-being. The critique of culture extends to a critique of the moral life as such. The tendency is to view culture and the superego as two sides of the same process, while morality appears to lead inexorably to unhappiness. The implication is that the community benefits at the cost of its individual members, a price it seems we cannot afford not to pay.

Freud's (1930: 141) attempt to limit the struggle between the individual and society to 'the economics of the libido' is unconvincing. The Freudian interpretation of guilt identifies the institution of morality itself with the irreconcilable conflict of love and death, which is seen as characteristic of every attempt at human community. Social defence becomes a permanent task for Freud, where security depends on a compromise not only between the ego and the id, but also between the individual and society. There was an initial expectation in Freud's (1930: 145) argument that the vitality of life, 'eternal *Eros*', would make an effort to assert itself in the battle with its 'equally immortal adversary'. There is a case to be made for love as the original thesis in the final theory of the instincts (Loewald 1966: 62); the efficacy of which, however, does not accord with the verdict Freud deduced from history. In 1931, with peace in Europe again under threat, Freud qualified any optimism he might have had with respect to the developmental force of love. It was left to others, Winnicott foremost among his generation of English psychoanalysts, to take Freud's thoughts on love further; and in English psychoanalysis, at least, Winnicott's thoughts remain unsurpassed.

The primary maternal frame

Faith breaks repeatedly on the Freudian interpretation, where reality-testing amounts to a reduction of illusion. Consistently rigorous in his critique of religious belief and moral sentiment, Freud's interpretation is invariably aimed at the demystification of meaning rather than its reclamation. The emphasis on strengthening our sense of reality is set against our infantile dependencies. Basically, illusions derived from infantile wishes in the case of religious belief, are subject to critical exposition alongside the idea that unhappiness issues invariably from ethical life. Freud (1927: 48) called this 'education to reality'. While this interpretation gave rise to a generation of imitators, Freudian epigones armed with the so-called principle of reality, Winnicott's attitude to life was quite different, comprising a normative stance towards inner security and moral sentiment combined with a revaluation of illusion.

The shift in attitude from necessity to maturity precipitates tensions within psychoanalysis as a whole that are reflected in Winnicott's own thinking. To state our main argument: on the one hand, Winnicott used the religious and moral resources of the culture for the restoration of meaning; on the other hand, his work lends itself to the sociological appropriation of psychoanalysis and the concomitant mobilization of society. The criterion of maturity applies in both cases and, from the 1940s onwards, is combined in Winnicott's thought with the idea of the 'environment mother', a pre-object mother who facilitates development by managing the infant in loving and caring ways. Winnicott's revision of psychoanalysis is based on the idea of the primary maternal frame as a type of pre-reflective management. As the background to our critical discussion of the post-Freudian legacy, we set out the basic types of management, including intuitive management, in the present chapter. We concentrate in this section on maternal love as the cornerstone of Winnicott's work.

Disagreeing with Freud and Klein on the centrality of instincts in psychic life, particularly the idea that hate is an innate manifestation of the death drive, Winnicott argued instead that primitive emotional development relies on the mother's loving responsiveness to her infant's innate creative potential.[4] For Winnicott (1952), the 'environment-individual set up' precedes the individual ego. He describes a situation in which the mother makes experience available (or not) to the infant through a type of intuitive management that is in tune with the infant's life. This suggests that it is a loving world, which the infant finds lovable.[5] Love and the place where we live come together as organizing principles of psychic life prior to the matter of reality. While allowing for the basic Freudian insight that unconscious states of mind are at once real and comprehensible, Winnicott continues to privilege the loving nature of the external world as a condition of psychological growth. Freud (1911a: 220n4), when considering archaic or primitive forms of mind, does in fact refer to 'the care [the infant] receives from its mother', but the intimacies of infant feeding and management do not, as they do for Winnicott, form the groundwork of his thinking. Conversely,

Winnicott concentrates almost exclusively on the mother and ignores the infant's intimate bodily and affective contact with the father.[6]

Primarily concerned with living '*an experience together*' (1945: 152; emphasis in the original), Winnicott claims that inner psychic reality itself 'presupposes the existence of an inside and an outside' (1935: 129*n*2). However, instead of simply placing things inside or outside, Winnicott draws attention to thresholds, intermediate areas, transitional phenomena, and potential spaces in describing the infant's experience of the world. The widely repeated claim that 'there is no such thing as an infant' (1960a: 39) may be understood in this way with respect to introjections based on 'the *experience of reliability*' (1968b: 97; emphasis in the original). Winnicott makes it clear that the infant relies on the mother for its own enjoyment in being alive, and can make nothing worthwhile or meaningful for itself out of an unreliable experience. The infant finds satisfaction, Freud's (1900: 565–6) 'original experience of satisfaction', in what is actually and reliably available in the form of maternal love.

The primary situation of sensible beings one with another comprises a framing structure that Winnicott saw as the basis of psychological growth. In this case, the way to excel at being human is an altogether spontaneous matter and requires nothing in the way of training or the regulation of appropriate aptitudes and competencies. Human life is understood as the impulse to dwell in its own nature, a pre-reflexive relation of immanence. The idea that life comes about through the experience of living together, and that there is no skill in being who we are, applies to mothers and infants alike. Winnicott makes the same point about mothers and 'the essential nature of their task' as he does about infants and their creative potential: 'Mothers who do not have it in them to provide good-enough care cannot be made good enough by mere instruction' (1960a: 49). What mothers understand, simply by virtue of the fact that they are mothers, is seen in contrast to what they know by learning about their babies. The argument is that understanding comes to us naturally as an expression of our original faith in the world.[7]

Starting with the problem of inner security, Winnicott casts the theory of primitive development against an environmental background. His particular version of object-relations theory accords with the fundamental idea that dwelling grounds the life from which it emanates. He confirms that while living remains the source of dwelling, including the infant's 'psyche in-dwelling in the soma', the latter is in fact the personal existent reality of being in the world. The two necessarily go together in the sense that dwelling, or what Winnicott (1970a: 264) calls 'personalization', arises out of the experience of living; at the same time, living remains essentially meaningless without dwelling. It is only when life is realized as dwelling that the infant's sense of self is securely located inside its body and, according to Winnicott, the infant realizes itself in this way by being loved.

How does this actually work? What is it about love that makes it developmental? Winnicott (1963e: 229) traces a twofold movement from absolute dependence to growing independence and from the subjective object to the object objectively perceived: 'first there is the creativeness that belongs to being alive, and the world is only a subjective world. Then there is the objectively perceived world and absolute destruction of it and all its details.' The movement involves a primordial use of faith, a feeling that life is worth living. Where this basic sense of belief in the potentials of a life is met by loving responsiveness on the part of the mother, the undifferentiated unity of infantile experience is organized into ever more complex unities. Life itself becomes *this* life, a way of living sourced in vitality and love. Although Winnicott did not draw out the philosophical implications of these ideas about love, belief, and the maternal frame; nonetheless, there are clear links with the phenomenological tradition from Husserl to Marion and Henry. Primitive emotional development is seen in terms of the manifestation of love as tenderness and care coupled with a passive pre-constitution that is introjected as faith and love. The relation to an object, therefore, proceeds from the passive synthesis of receptive intuition in the preverbal communion between babies and mothers.[8]

Ideas concerning a two-person psychology are consistent with the general theory of object-relations from Fairbairn and Klein onwards. Winnicott, however, went further in positing modes of existence *before* object-relations. The 'environment mother' is a pre-object mother. Thus, for Winnicott (1945: 152) life begins not as an interpersonal experience, but rather, with the concrete intercorporeity of maternal and infant bodies: while 'the baby has instinctual urges and predatory ideas'; at the same time, the 'mother has a breast and the power to produce milk, and the idea that she would like to be attacked by a hungry baby'. There is pleasure and satisfaction on both sides, including 'ruthless love' on the part of the baby.

The phenomenological orientation of Winnicott's thinking depends on his account of 'body management' (1988: 123), the bodily nature of love, or the original incarnation of mental states as primordial modalities of life: 'The beginning of that part of the baby's development, which I am calling personalization, or which can be described as an in-dwelling of the psyche in the soma, is to be found in the mother or mother-figure's ability to join up her emotional involvement, which originally is physical and physiological' (1970a: 264). In-dwelling is not a given, but relies on the care the mother takes in being with her baby. The implication is that dwelling is the well-being that comes from the care of being, and Winnicott (1970a: 261) describes well-being in this sense as an 'achievement of health'. It is important to stress the idea of 'achievement'. The fact that we are 'home-seeking beings' (Symington 2007: 30) does not mean that being at home is a given. On the contrary, it is the undifferentiated nature of maternal and infantile bodies at the beginning of life that allows for the world to gradually emerge as a place where we can live, starting with what Winnicott (1970a: 262) calls 'the inhabitation of the body'. We have to make of being a dwelling place such that it becomes a place of well-being, and as a psychoanalyst Winnicott was familiar with the many and diabolical ways in which life is troubled by hideaways, primordial enclosures, and psychic retreats.

Winnicott's idea of human nature, then, is based on the corporeal experience of human beings one with another, and this offers a spatial as well as a bodily perspective on experience. More explicitly than any of his contemporaries, Winnicott sets out the foundations for a general theory of dwelling, in which the phenomenology of primitive development is coupled with a spatial understanding of experience. Thus, looked at from the point of view of primitive psychosomatic life, the maternal frame provides the infant with a series of intimate experiences ranging in value from good (facilitative) to bad (impingement). The fundamental distinction that Winnicott makes between 'reliability' and 'unreliability' is organized around the mother's capacity (or not) to meet the infant's innate potential and developing needs. His account of the 'facilitating environment' is presented largely in terms of what bodies can and cannot do together as they begin to get to know one another. The experience of being together – what Suttie (1935: 33) described in advance of Winnicott as 'a sense of companionship' – develops in this way as a corporeal sense of well-being, a sense of being in one's own skin, but yet in the company of someone. As Winnicott (1962b: 56–7) put it, the self is integrated into a 'unit' that develops as the 'core of the personality'.

The infant's *dependence* on the maternal frame for its development is the central premise of the argument, the idea that growth depends on 'the actual mother' being in a position to meet the absolute dependence of 'the actual infant' at the beginning; in which case a sense of inner security arises based on the reliability of 'holding' (Winnicott 1968b: 97). The emphasis on 'holding' extends the bodily perspective of love. What the mother provides in 'the form of actual milk' is coupled with what is available in 'the way of management' (Winnicott 1964a: 32). The latter refers to the tender ministrations of the mother, in whose care the infant is seen to live, move and have its being. Management enables the infant to experience its feelings for what they are prior to the instinctual gratification that Winnicott clearly believed love also provides. In answer to our question, love is developmental as both *agape* and *Eros*, in the care it provides as well as the pleasures and excitement it occasions.

The dual aspect of Winnicottian love extends the reach of the maternal frame from the 'management of the first feed' (1988: 103) through the 'management of the skin in infant care' (1988: 122) to the role of the mother's face as 'mirroring' forms for infant experience. Based on the mutuality of looking, Winnicott describes a developmental process that depends on recognition: 'When I look I am seen, so I exist' (1967d: 134). Facial recognition is presented as paradigmatic of intuitive management, where the infant's 'striving towards being seen' constitutes the basis of 'creative looking'. Primordial recognition may be seen therefore as a manifestation of the *conatus essendi*, the aspiration to persevere in being at the beginning.

Wright (2009) offers a perceptive reading of this aspect of Winnicott's thinking, drawing out the phenomenological implications of the developmental argument. While gratification and recognition may be seen as complementary processes, Wright points out that for Winnicott love is not simply a matter of sublimation. As the account of primordial recognition demonstrates, Winnicott identifies the primacy of love as an experiential form. Thus, Wright notes that while 'our first experience of relatedness is sensual and bodily' (2009: 173), Winnicott's emphasis on recognition means that love is more than simply aim-inhibited sexuality.[9] The emotional tie between mother and baby is formed in the context of a giving environment; in being found through the experience of touching and looking, the breast, the face, and mother's open-handedness thus appear for the baby. In short, we love what we have been given to find.

Together with the phenomenology of love, Wright (2009: 172) also draws attention to the religious aspects of Winnicott's thinking, particularly the extent to which Winnicott identifies 'the deepest roots of religion ... in the preverbal core of the self'. The relationship between inner security and truths of faith will be a central theme of our argument, set out at length in Chapter 2 and elaborated further in Chapter 7. Suffice it to say here that Winnicott identifies the gift of love not with the maternal object, but rather, with types of emotional contact between mother and baby: infant feeding; intuitive bodily management; and face-to-face interaction. The time-frame of maternal love is more important for Winnicott than the maternal object, which allows for the fact that *commūnicāre* proceeds from *commūniō* in the human situation. Thus, in addressing the Winnicottian frame, Wright, Bollas and Meissner comment on the underlying work of 'spiritual communion' (Bollas 2009: 73).

Wright (1991: 11–14) extrapolates a theory of forms from Winnicott's account of 'the mirror-role of mother'. These should be understood as intuitive forms of contact prior to language.[10] The maternal frame consists of tangible forms (breasts, hands, face) rather than internal objects. Winnicott's description of the face-to-face contact between mothers and babies reminds us that contact is made before sense; that the mirroring response emanates from a pre-object mother; and that no sense can be made of anything, including internal as well as external objects, without the primordial recognition of what is there to be seen. The primordial apperception of forms may be grasped in terms of the 'pre-personal I' that, as Merleau-Ponty (1945: 276n1) suggests, provides the basis for 'the phenomenon of the real'. The suggestion is that, rather than the Kantian idea of synthesis, a primordial experience of recognition gathers and holds things together for the infant prior to the differentiation of 'me' and 'not-me'. If we accept this argument, then the primal frame may be understood as an intimate somatic synopsis of the pre-object world, a 'psyche-body bond' (Winnicott 1988: 124) that provides a subjective way of looking at the world and, in turn, enables the infant to make contact with reality.

Bollas (1987: 39) also draws out what he calls the 'sacred' dimension of primitive experiential forms, while at the same time emphasizing the 'transformational' nature of the maternal frame: 'Our earliest experience is prior to our knowing of the mother as an object in her own right ... the sacred precedes the maternal'. Bollas's (1987: 16) phrase may appear surprising at first, but becomes less so when the manifestation of the 'sacred' is identified with 'aesthetic moments'. Bollas defines the latter as occasions that evoke our earliest sensations and feelings. In turn, Wright (2009: 161; emphasis in the original) identifies these occasions, which he describes as 'significant moments', with *an intuition of the sacred*'. Whether we describe them as 'aesthetic' or 'significant', what appears in these moments is meaningful along the lines of primordial recognition, pre-reflective intuition, or pre-object experience.[11]

Looked at in terms of the pre-representational presence of the mother, the developmental process of recognition is based on Winnicott's fundamental idea that the infant's innate capacity to love flourishes in a lovable world. The religious provenance of the idea is hardly incidental: 'We love him, because he first loved us' (1 John 4:19). The logic of Christ's salvation is an implicit but strong reading of the logic of the created–found world, where the infant finds what is given in the tangible, experiential forms of love, as distinct from an internal object or part-object. Winnicott's created–found world amounts to the discovery of experience itself, which is essentially what I mean by the original act of faith: the wherewithal to find what is given. As Meissner (1984: 183) points out in his discussion of Winnicott, faith contains a 'transcendent element' insofar as it 'returns to the rudiments of trust in order to go beyond them'. What Meissner (1984: 184) describes as 'the creative moment in the illusion of faith' imbues Winnicott's notion of love with an intuition of transcendence. It is important to emphasize, however, that the 'transcendent element' is immanent in the experience of entrusting oneself to a life. The singular essence of the latter, what we call the sacred, is grounded in human experience through the transcendent meaning of material worldly forms. As his descriptions of intuitive management demonstrate repeatedly, Winnicott conceived of human existence as empirically transcendental.[12]

Catastrophic disillusionment

The link between intuitive management and inner security is the essential link in Winnicott's theory of human nature; on the basis of which he constructed his psychopathology around the early failure of management. Unlike Freud, Winnicott (1988: 100) derived his clinical arguments from the norm, and derived his understanding of the norm from life; arguing from health to ill-health, he proposed that, 'if the first feeds are mishandled, then a great deal of trouble may be caused and, in fact, a lasting pattern of insecurity of relationships may be found to have started'. Following what Winnicott (1952: 99) calls 'a good-enough technique', life appears to come into its own; 'the centre of gravity of being in the environment-individual set-up can afford to lodge in the centre, in the kernel rather than in the shell'. Conversely, '[a]ll failures (that could produce unthinkable anxiety) bring about a reaction of the infant, and this cuts across the going-on-being. If reacting that is disruptive of going-on-being recurs persistently it sets going a pattern of fragmentation of being' (1962b: 60).

It cannot be taken for granted that babies will feel at home in their own skin or enjoy being in the company of others. Life does not necessarily become living, but may fail to realize itself in the world. Winnicott (1970a: 264) described a situation in which the actual mother, as opposed to a 'good internal object' in the Kleinian sense, does the best she can for her baby, precisely by providing a framing structure for the baby's early emotional development: 'Being loved at the beginning means being accepted ... at the beginning the child has a blueprint for normality which is largely a matter of the shape and functioning of his or her own body ... these are matters of the very earliest days of the child's life'. It is hardly surprising that, following the upsurge of life from at least the moment of birth, being loved and accepted are seen as essential for the infant. For Winnicott, love provides a background of security by welcoming spontaneity. However, Winnicott (1956a: 303) also identified 'deficiencies' in the primary maternal frame where the mother is unable to provide adequate support at the beginning, or cannot provide 'a setting for the infant's constitution to begin to make itself evident'.

Winnicott (1956a: 304–5) described how infants who have not been loved or cared for at the beginning fail to come together in themselves; do not feel at home in their own bodies; and have no real sense of the outside world: 'The feeling of real is absent and if there is not too much chaos the ultimate feeling is of futility'. These conclusions are based not on the direct observation of infants so much as 'the treatment of the more psychotic type of adult patient', which Winnicott (1988: 2) claimed taught him more than any other kind of work. Where the 'true self' remains, as it were, no more than a rumour in the psyche, the patient is faced with only the semblance of a life, with affects that may be felt but cannot be appropriated or experienced. Environmental deficiency thus precipitates a failure of life, a state in which patients put themselves together as best they can out of the encapsulated impressions of something having gone disastrously wrong in the past.

Patients struggle to verify events they have not experienced, going to extraordinary lengths in some cases to put the record straight. Memories, however, are not integrated and remain no more than concrete references, a list of past events, without any real personal meaning. The flat and lifeless way in which patients attempt to convey their experience is symptomatic of what Winnicott saw as the failure of life, the profound difficulties patients have in laying claim to experience of any kind. Narrative gives way to a kind of tedious reportage; feelings are cut off and dissociated; and the self fails to cohere. While it can be monotonous and draining listening to patients in this state, the unconscious call on the analyst's attention reaches the primitive level of the frame. Although interpretation is not necessarily required, a live responsiveness to the patient's unconscious communication, what Parsons (2000: 25) calls 'a steady, unthreatening receptivity', remains essential. As such, listening itself provides a frame in the form of therapeutic management, the analytic version of an open-handed gesture, and a sign to the patient of 'live company' (Alvarez 1992). Listening is already a reconstruction of traumatic experience, even before anything is said.

When things break down in this way, love itself becomes an object of concern, giving rise to a series of therapeutic questions. Who is at risk? Where does the problem lie? What is to be done? These are not exceptional concerns. Winnicott describes an infant constantly on the threshold of 'unthinkable anxiety', managed in loving and reliable ways by its mother, or else in ways that do not facilitate life. He describes how the 'good-enough mother' is able to meet the baby's needs by putting herself in his or her place; whereas mothers who cannot manage the demands of 'ordinary' maternal care intrude upon the spontaneous aspiration to persevere in being and, consequently, leave the baby 'cluttered up with persecutory elements of which he has no means of ridding himself' (1967b: 121). The place of being is at issue on both counts, whether the mother takes the infant's anxieties into herself or else thrusts herself into the infant's emergent world as an unwelcome, traumatic presence, unable for reasons of her own to allow the baby to become whoever he or she is capable of being.

How did Winnicott make sense of these failures? Let us take a closer look at his diagnostic argument, particularly with reference to the management implications of 'disillusionment'.[13] The idea of catastrophic disillusionment, or negative illusion, indicates a crucial distinction between disaster and grief, with respect to an 'unthinkable' loss that occurs prior to the infant's capacity to mourn. The distinction continues to play out across the entire post-Freudian field with profound consequences for the interpretation of being in time. Following the classical definitions in Freud (1917) and Abraham (1924), together with the subsequent elaborations on the loss of the 'internal object' in Klein (1940), Winnicott (1958: 132–3) described mourning as a complex process by means of which the individual works through feelings of loss and grief. Freud's central insight that memory is a form of *work* is retained in Winnicott's account, and while indicating the feelings of hate and the 'internal persecutory elements' (1954a: 275) involved in the process, Winnicott emphasized the fact that mourning presupposes a degree of ego development.

Winnicott saw mourning as a 'mature reaction' to loss, and it is important to emphasize that maturity decides the matter. Winnicott (1958: 133) argued that it is not possible for the complex emotional processes of working through 'to be followed by an infant who has not reached a certain stage of maturity'. He saw mourning as an achievement of a relatively independent state of mind, an internal situation that is not available at the beginning of life. The capacity to mourn, therefore, cannot be taken for granted; nor is the infant concerned for the mother in this way to begin with, but is ruthlessly alive seemingly in a world of his own making. On this reckoning, we mourn as we learn to live, in the movement towards independence combined with a growing concern for others. We mourn only what we have found lovable, the loss of which mourning allows us to make use of in mature ways. Winnicott (1963d) equated moral concern with maturity; where the maternal frame fails, however, he argued that loss is experienced beyond the capacity of the ego to make things feel tolerable, and that the infant finds himself instead in a disastrous situation.

We find patients who, deprived of normal affective lives, attempt to fortify themselves in one way or another against life, for fear they might suffer any further loss. The stronger they appear to be, the less alive they really are. Thus, the disasters that Winnicott described in terms of 'impingement' and 'deprivation' involve fundamental forms of loss, although neither is amendable to the work of mourning. Instead of working-through, Winnicott described different kinds of 'reaction', namely, psychotic illness in the case of impingement, and antisocial action in the case of deprivation. Disaster is therefore not only incommensurable with the work of mourning, but is also internally differentiated, according to different levels of dependence or degrees of maturity.

Winnicott postulated three levels of dependency: 'absolute dependence' (from birth to about three or four months); 'relative dependence' (up to about two years of age); and 'towards independence'.[14] At the level of 'absolute dependence' the infant has no control whatsoever over the environment, but can only enjoy what comes his way, or else suffer the absence of what cannot be found. Nor can the infant do without actual care at the level of 'relative dependence'. But while he cannot look after himself or manage on his own at this level of development, he has a better sense of what he needs. Learning to live with what comes and goes, with what cannot always be removed or found, there is an increasing awareness that satisfaction and frustration occur in relation to the same person. The infant now feels he has a claim on his mother's person coupled with a right to his needs. Further to which, Winnicott described what lies beyond the beginning as the maturity of independence that one is capable of in becoming oneself.

Based on an account of the infant's dependence on the mother for his own inner security, Winnicott maintained that the earlier the failure of the environment, the more disastrous things will be for the infant. For instance, he saw failure at the level of absolute dependence resulting in 'mental defect non-organic; childhood schizophrenia; liability to mental-hospital disorder at a late date' (1962a: 66). The original calamity of environmental failure is seen as inimical to becoming a person, but also to the very movement of life itself. Winnicott described a failure of life at the origin rather than a breakdown of being, a disaster prior to the invention–discovery of the world. By contrast, he linked failure at the level of relative dependence with a 'liability to affective disorders; antisocial tendency' (1962a: 66). In this case, having once got going, the sense of being is somehow interrupted; there is a break in continuity rather than an original failure of life. As a result, the world becomes more or less meaningless rather than failing the infant altogether as an incomprehensible chaos.

For Winnicott, where the mature reaction to loss as mourning is not available, disaster cuts across life in the form of psychotic anxiety or severely disruptive behaviour. And insofar as dependence leaves babies vulnerable to trauma, Winnicott (1967e: 575) proposed that many 'babies start off ill' and many 'become ill early'. The classical Freudian model does not account for this finding. Winnicott made an important distinction, however, between infinite anguish and upheaval, a distinction that amounts to the difference between 'privation' in infancy and 'deprivation' in childhood. The former involves the fragmentation of experience; as Winnicott (1960a: 47) put it, the trauma of failure at the beginning 'interrupts being and annihilates'. This requires nothing less from therapeutic treatment than the reclamation of life.

In the case of deprivation, Winnicott (1962a: 66) held that the 'central core' of the ego is not at stake, insofar as there is someone there to be traumatized. In contrast to more primitive mechanisms of defence, antisocial action is understood as a sign that 'there has been a loss of something good that has been positive in the child's experience up to a certain date, and that has been withdrawn' (1956b: 124). Now even if it means ransacking people to see what they are worth, the child's unconscious search for lost love is judged worthwhile in turn. The decisive move here involves separating the child from his action and, thereby, making it possible to organize therapeutic management on the basis of forgiveness. This includes the child being able to forgive himself. It is immediately apparent that Winnicott's 'difficult child' is not culpable of envious attacks born of an irreducible hatred of life and the good object. Sanctioned by life, the affirmative argument is more profound than anything derived from the hypothesis of the death drive, namely, that the child is worth more than the evident consequences of his action. When parents are blamed for the behavioural problems of their children, and antisocial behaviour itself becomes a target of Draconian policies and moral panic, matters have gone beyond rehabilitation let alone redemption. It is possible to construe the logic of catastrophes in line with extremely severe forms of social control. However, much of what was radical in Winnicott's revision of Freud comes down to the idea that action does not exhaust potential, anymore than the most disastrous failure annuls hope. There is always hope of being more alive because there is always more life than one can possibly live.

Social management

Winnicott's diagnostic classification of disaster is based on a phenomenology of love. The latter represents the first of two oscillating poles in our reading of the Winnicottian revision of psychoanalysis. For Winnicott, management is originally a form of love; the applications of which, however, are not confined to the earliest relationship or to the therapeutic equivalent in clinical practice. Psychological distinctions and discriminations are invariably anchored in moral and political subjects, and while the question of our well-being is a fundamental question about human nature, it is also an historical question concerning the administrative arrangements of personal life and the related techniques of intimacy. Winnicott's argument straddled these different meanings of management: intuitive, therapeutic, and administrative. While he made a major contribution to clinical thinking with the notions of intuitive and therapeutic management; at the same time, his ideas were employed during and after World War II in the interests of social management.

The war proved decisive for the administrative application of Winnicott's ideas. Together with John Bowlby and Emanuel Miller, Winnicott (1939a: 14) wrote to the *British Medical Journal* setting out an argument against government plans to evacuate young children during war:

> It is quite possible for a child of any age to feel sad or upset at having to leave home, but the point we wish to make is that such an experience in the case of a little child can mean far more than the actual experience of sadness.

While the tragic and deleterious aspects of homelessness are noted in the case of orphans, the letter draws attention more specifically to the plight of children separated from their mothers, particularly between the ages of two and five. The letter thus spells out the 'dangers' involved in the evacuation of small children: 'Apart from such gross abnormality as chronic delinquency, mild behaviour disorders, anxiety, and a tendency to vague physical illness can often be traced to such disturbances of the little child's environment' (1939a: 13). Serious 'psychological disorders' were identified as 'social problems', most importantly, with respect to the link between separation (deprivation) and delinquency.

The damage it may have caused notwithstanding, the fact that the evacuation of children eventually went ahead proved decisive not only for Winnicott, but for the development of the health and social services in general. Notably, for Susan Isaacs (1941: 3) the evacuation of children provided 'an opportunity to learn priceless lessons for future social service'. The situation presented social workers with a new population to observe and manage, while the risks of prolonged separation of young children from their homes were brought increasingly to the fore. For example, the category of so-called 'unbilletable' children, some 15,000 to 20,000 during the war, focused attention on difficulties of behaviour or temperament.[15] Bowlby (1940; 1951) argued that many of the unaccompanied evacuated children 'may be expected to become prone to chronic anxiety or depression or to vague pains and illness of an apparently physical nature'.[16]

As Phillips (1988: 62) points out, the emotional and developmental problems of evacuation, for both children and mothers, 'marked a turning point in the work of Bowlby and Winnicott' and, at the same time, 'changed psychoanalytic thinking about childhood'. Bowlby played an important part alongside Winnicott during the war, with respect to the application of psychoanalytic thinking to social problems. Moreover, they both went on in the aftermath of the war to report on the mental health aspects of children who needed care either in foster homes or in state institutions. Alongside their otherwise incompatible contributions to clinical psychoanalysis, Winnicott shared with Bowlby a deeply felt concern with how best to contain anxiety in state institutions.

Winnicott was appointed consultant psychiatrist to a government-sponsored evacuation scheme in 1940, and was responsible for a number of local authority hostels set up in Oxfordshire for 'difficult children', or children for whom evacuation to foster families proved difficult to cope with.[17] This afforded him the opportunity to observe at close quarters the way in which both children and mothers reacted to abnormal separation from home. His findings formed part of a wider discourse in which the 'absent mother' and the 'deprived child' emerged as new objects of concern during the war, concerns that were taken up subsequently and no less urgently in the post-war disciplines of child psychotherapy and psychiatric social work.

A therapeutically informed approach to social problems was evident in the immediate post-war developments of British object-relations theory, an approach which predates the sociology of emotions by two or three decades.[18] Winnicott made a seminal contribution to this new way of thinking about individuals and society based on his ideas of inner security and the maternal frame. His ideas along these lines were made available, not least of all through his lecturing and radio broadcasts, to the general public; but also, more importantly, to a wide range of practitioners: child psychotherapists, psychiatric social workers, criminologists, probation officers, nursery nurses and teachers. In particular, anxieties arising out of separation and loss were taken up during this period as technical and governmental issues, instituting an administrative process with which Winnicott was directly involved. For example, in giving evidence to the Curtis Committee (which led to the passing of the Children Act in 1948) Winnicott identified specific themes relating to mother–infant relations; but more importantly, he provided new ways of thinking about social–emotional life in general. Outside of the clinic, the thematic content of specific concepts is less important than the reformation of the prevailing norms of truth governing the understanding and management of ourselves. In Winnicott's case, it is the application of the criterion of maturity to the wider process of normalization that keys into the governmental appropriation of psychoanalysis.

Worked out against the background of the war, the link between security and social provision opens up new possibilities for the rationality of government. Starting, then, with the idea of intuitive management as the basis of inner security, Winnicott introduced a new problematic of space into the discourse of administration. Subject to ongoing and extensive investigation, the spatial dimension of Winnicott's work has been dealt with in important ways by some of his most astute commentators, including Green (1975), Ogden (1986), and Parsons (2000). The frame of reference for these commentaries is the analytic situation itself, which is appropriate for the purposes of clinical investigation. However, we are primarily interested here in the political and moral extension of Winnicottian management beyond the context of the clinic.

There are various options available to us for taking the argument beyond the clinic, starting with Winnicott's (1986) own 'reflections on society'. Here, we have opted for a Foucauldian frame of reference. This will tell us nothing of any great interest about the clinical aspects of Winnicott's work. Foucault was not in a position to comment on such matters. On the other hand, Foucault's (1991) analysis of the relationship between power and space provides useful ways of thinking about the social aspect of Winnicott's work. For instance, by emphasizing the generalization of 'the power to punish', including the disciplinary distribution of individuals in space, Foucault (1975: 141–9) constituted the problem of security as a new field of inquiry.[19] The 'cellular' function of disciplinary power is presented as part of an administrative network of techniques which underpins juridical norms, while the rationality of modern government is described as a twofold process of 'social contracts' and 'micro-physics' (1975: 222). This is an important model for contextualizing the Winnicottian conception of social provision, but also for grasping the political uses of psychoanalysis in general. While Foucault's argument allows for the fact that universal juridical principles constitute the formal basis of the modern administrative state, at the same time, the technical basis of everyday life is presented as a series of 'corporal disciplines' and 'apparatuses of security'. Governmental arrangements so described include exactly the sorts of intimate techniques that we are discussing in relation to Winnicottian forms of social management.

How, then, does Winnicott's work contribute to these techniques of intimacy? The Winnicottian frame keys in with the post-war configuration of administrative–therapeutic thinking in at least three important respects. First, Winnicott's account privileges the relation between the mother and the infant; maternal love is seen as the original matrix of the self; and the mother is identified as the privileged anchorage point for administrative intervention. This has subsequently become such a widespread practice of social governance that it is easy to lose sight of its historical specificity. Mothers and motherhood have become routine targets of government intervention.[20] Second, Winnicott (1971b: 122) generalizes the spatial problematic of the maternal frame as an account of 'where we most of the time are when we are experiencing life'. Starting with infant feeding and management, Winnicott traces the thread of lived experience at the level of culture, extending the psychological matrix to the *locus* of everyday life. In which case the anxiety of separation is contained, according to Winnicott (1971b: 128), 'by the filling in of the potential space with creative playing, with the use of symbols, and with all that eventually adds up to a cultural life'. Everyday life therefore becomes a contested terrain of regulation and self-control. Third, Winnicott focuses on the consequence of environmental failure, where the child turns (for instance) to bed-wetting, lying, stealing, addiction, fetishism, and so on. This introduces new ways of thinking about rehabilitation, insofar as it is considered reasonable to institute an administrative–therapeutic intervention to make good the damage done by environmental deficiencies.

In what sense can this be seen as a new initiative? The Freudian legacy, in many ways, is continuous with modern developments in social life and, clearly, the underlying link between administration and space predates the contribution of psychoanalysis to problems of management. This is evident once again in Foucault's (2004) analysis of the general economy of power under conditions of modernity, which encompasses the emergence of new technologies of security in the eighteenth century as well as the history of government in the first centuries of the Christian era. We are not discussing entirely new initiatives, then, so much as realignments; new objects of concern; and the reorganization of existing problems on a new basis. These arguments are set out initially in Chapter 3 and elaborated in the following chapters on psychiatry and supervision (Part II), and sociology and regulation (Part III). What we are proposing with reference to

Winnicott's work is, first, that the link between intuitive management and inner security makes a decisive contribution to the historical–political field in the aftermath of the war. Second, that the preoccupation with environmental deficiency gives rise to new objects and activities of government. Third, that the relationship between therapy and rehabilitation is entirely reorganized from the standpoint of innate potential and its failure. These developments are not confined to clinical practice but, taken together, authorize the contemporary theme of government, and open up new possibilities for managing the permanent task of social defence along post-Freudian lines.

Notes

1 Following Winnicott, Rizzuto (1979: 209) argues that 'reality and illusion are not contradictory terms'; that psychic reality itself presupposes a 'transitional space for play and illusion'; and that God is 'a potentially suitable object' for post-Oedipal maturation. Similarly, Meissner (1984: 183) acknowledges Winnicott's influence on the changing attitudes towards religion in psychoanalysis, where illusion is no longer seen merely as wish-fulfilment, but as 'the repository of human creativity and the realm in which man's potentiality may find its greatest expression'.
2 See Ogden (1986: 195) for the use of the object as an act of faith, the idea that 'the infant's renunciation of the omnipotence of the internal [subjective] object entails a crucial act of faith'.
3 While the hypothesis of the death drive was not taken up in British psychoanalysis until Klein, whose followers turned it into an organizing *doxa*; the Freudian paradigm of war, that is as an articulation of the sexual life, was nonetheless elaborated contemporaneously in the English novel, most importantly by Ford Madox Ford in his *Parade's End* tetralogy.
4 Winnicott acknowledged the reality of hatred; but while giving it due weight as a clinical phenomenon (1947), he did not depend on hate for his view of human nature. For Winnicott (1968a), it is the loved object that is aggressively and ruthlessly attacked; indeed, *the* defining argument of his late work is that the infant is able to make use of the object only insofar as it survives these destructive attacks.
5 Lear (1992: 154–5) points to the prevalence in Winnicott of the idea that 'love is in fact an internalization of the loving world'.
6 Benjamin (1995) acknowledges the advance brought about by Winnicott's contribution, but questions the privileged association of the maternal with 'holding'. She addresses this problem from a clinical point of view in terms of the association of the maternal transference with 'object usage'. Instead, Benjamin (1995: 158) suggests that 'the paternal erotic transference may often be less oedipal than was previously thought [and] may well refer more to the dyadic preoedipal father of identificatory love and the ego ideal'.
7 Although Winnicott (1987a: 15) refers to 'two types of knowledge', I think it would be more accurate to describe 'knowing' and 'learning' as understanding and knowledge, respectively. I assume that Winnicott meant understanding is required in order to have knowledge; that he shared Heidegger's view in *Being and Time* of understanding (*verstehen*) as a primordial experience which comes before language. In practical terms a mother who cannot understand her baby has no way of knowing what to do.
8 Compare Husserl's (1913) account of 'the expressive act-strata' in *Ideas 1*, § 124, including the distinction between *a priori* passive beliefs and the active synthesis of cognitive representation. Further to the 'different modes of genuine givenness [*Gegebenheit*]'set out in *The Idea of Phenomenology* (1907: 54), where the fundamental

claim is that givenness is *'givenness in the phenomenon of knowing [Gegebenheit im Erkenntnisphänomen]'*, Husserl went on to include 'passive syntheses' in 'givenness'. For the reduction of phenomena to givenness beyond the transcendental ego, see Marion (1998).

9   In fact, Wright (2009: 166) goes further in seeing the breast and the face as opposing paradigms of the maternal frame; but as this is not how Winnicott viewed the matter, the argument need not detain us here. From the perspective of intersubjectivity, Benjamin (1995: 87) presents an alternative view of early development, in which she privileges the process of recognition but questions the appropriateness of 'the metaphor of the mirror', as well as the 'trope of oneness', to early mothering. While these arguments merit attention, Benjamin (1988; 1995) and Honneth (1995) extend the paradigm of primordial recognition beyond our more immediate concerns with the phenomenology of the Winnicottian frame. For a further elaboration of the recognition-theoretical revision of psychoanalysis, see Honneth (2012: Part IV, Chapters 11 through 14).

10 The claim that early management consists of intuitions prior to language raises complex philosophical questions. For instance, there is an ongoing philosophical tension in the post-Kantian context between truth as givenness (the disclosure of phenomenal givenness) and logically analyzed truth. See Marion (2011) for the confrontation between phenomenology, which posits non-conceptual contents of experience, and the likes of Wilfrid Sellars and John McDowell, who claim that discourse and discursive thought are integral to perceptual knowledge, and that all awareness is essentially a linguistic matter.

11 See Heidegger (1919: 61) on 'the meaningful' (*das Bedeutsame*) as 'primary and immediately given to me without any mental detours across thing-oriented apprehension ... a moment of signification [*ein bedeutungshaftes Moment*]'.

12 For the 'transcendental field' of pre-reflexive life, see Deleuze (2001). Deleuze (2001: 25) differentiates the 'transcendental' from the 'transcendent', the potential from the actual: 'we will speak of a transcendental empiricism in contrast to everything that makes up the [transcendent] world of the subject and the object'. For Deleuze, the transcendental field is a pure plane of immanence; at least, he would define it as such were it not for the presence of consciousness, which is seen as coextensive with, but irreducible to, the field of pre-reflexive life.

13 Milner (1977: 284) comments along similar lines to Winnicott on 'the intensity of the shock of disillusionment, the sheer incredulity and abysmal depth of dread that can come at the discovery that one is not omnipotent, if it comes, through environmental failure, at a moment when the ego is not strong enough to bear it'. Rycroft (1955) elaborates on the idea of 'catastrophic disillusion'; more recently, Roussillon (2010) has introduced the idea of 'negative illusion', as the opposite of the illusion of omnipotence. For Roussillon, negative illusion comes about due to a failure on the part of the environment to manage feelings of destructiveness and impotent rage at the level of primary narcissism.

14 See Winnicott (1960a; 1962a; 1963c) for the different levels of the infant's dependence on the mother.

15 For behavioural difficulties, see Titmuss (1950: 383); for the evacuee experience in wartime Britain, see Welshman (2010); and for the opportunities evacuation afforded in terms of the social administration of personal life, see Rose (1989: 159–63).

16 Together with Susan Isaacs, Melanie Klein, Margery Fry, Sybil Clement Brown and Lucy Fildes, Bowlby contributed to the Cambridge Evacuation Survey, which was established in October 1939. By the time he came to compile the report on the needs of homeless children in 1951, Bowlby was director of the Child Guidance Department of the Tavistock Clinic. See Winnicott's (1941) review of the Cambridge Evacuation Survey.

17 See Winnicott's (1984) collection of wartime and post-war writings; Winnicott and Britton's (1944) evacuation hostel findings; and Clare Winnicott's (1980) own account of the Oxfordshire evacuation scheme. The deprivation–delinquency couple emerges in these writings as symptomatic of 'the destructive potential' within the social. As we shall see in Chapter 3, the disasters of war are seen as so many social problems at the intersection of behaviour and management, calling for a twofold defence of ourselves and society.
18 See Barbalet (1998) for the sociological acknowledgement of 'emotion' as a category of explanation. We compare the Winnicottian frame with the sociology of emotions in Part III. For the common origins of Beveridge and British object-relations theory in the interwar years, see Zaretsky (2004); compare this to Donzelot's (1979) more broadly conceived analysis of the 'social sector', the modern history of which he brings to a close at the intersection of Keynesian economics and Freudian psychoanalysis. Donzelot's argument, which seems entirely correct to me, is that while Keynes secured the principle of private initiative in social organizations; at the same time, Freud furnished possessive individualism with functional status in the context of family life. Although not disagreeing with Donzelot, we are more interested in the uses generated by the inherent tensions *within* the post-Freudian development.
19 It was not until 1978, in his lecture course at the Collège de France (2004; English translation: *Security, Territory, Population*, 2007), that Foucault finally linked the problem of security to the notion of 'governmentality'. The link is crucial for our critique of psychoanalytic reason.
20 See J. Lewis (1980) and Wilson (1980) for the politics of motherhood in the early 1900s and the role of women in post-war Britain, respectively.

2
RECLAMATION AND THE UNTHINKABLE

Following our overview, in the previous chapter, of intuitive, therapeutic, and social types of management, in this chapter we present a detailed account of the management of regression as a coherent post-Freudian model of analytic practice. Considerable scepticism has been expressed about the idea of regression as an analytic technique, the technical details of which concern us only insofar as they relate to Winnicott's notion of management.[1] To avoid any unnecessary misunderstanding, I should make it clear that the chapter is not intended as a clinical discussion so much as a broadly defined theoretical study of therapeutic management. As such, the study of therapeutic reclamation represents the positive centre of the book: our basic argument is that Winnicott reworked the cultural themes of meaning and value, including the moral values of health and happiness, as technical problems of management. For Winnicott, as for Freud, it was necessary to find alternative therapeutic options for the problems posed by the impasses of 'interminable' analysis.[2] Thus the repetition of reactions to early environmental trauma, as distinct from later neurotic, Oedipal conflicts, tested the therapeutic resources of classical psychoanalysis. Winnicott responded to this situation in creative and imaginative ways, drawing on the deepest sources of the culture in wide-ranging reflections on time and experience.

Time is a central factor in Winnicottian management, the ethical as well as the clinical import of which, I propose, is based on a reworking of the Freudian concept of 'deferred action' (*Nachträglichkeit*) as reclamation. The importance of *Nachträglichkeit* was underlined initially by Lacan, who summarized Freud's view of psychical temporality as follows:

> To Freud's mind, it is not a question of biological memory ... in psychoanalytic *anamnesis* [recollection], what is at stake is not reality, but truth, because the effect of full speech is to reorder past contingencies by conferring on them the sense of necessities to come ... at each turning point at which the subject restructures himself – that is, as many restructurings of the event as take place, as he [Freud] puts it, *nachträglich*, after the fact.
>
> (Lacan 1953: 213)

Time is not just one more theme among others in psychoanalysis. The temporal frame of reference constitutes the very groundwork of psychoanalytic practice. For his part, Winnicott reworked the temporal dimension of classical theory from the clinical perspective of non-neurotic structures in children and adults. As we have seen, the failure of life as a consequence of environmental deficiency was central to Winnicott's clinical thinking, in response to which he conceived of therapeutic management as a process of reclamation.

The aim of the present chapter is to address the failure of life and its reclamation, the dialectic of disaster and hope, against the literary and spiritual background of Winnicott's clinical thought. Besides Freud and Klein, Winnicott's major intellectual influences came from outside psychoanalysis and included the King James Bible, English Romanticism, and the poetry of T. S. Eliot. The inconsistencies between these different sources notwithstanding, we aim to demonstrate Winnicott's primary indebtedness to Eliot. The depth of Christian feeling in Eliot's late poetry, especially *Four Quartets*, remains indispensable for our understanding of the Christian idiom of Winnicott's own thought. And while the claims of Eliot's criticism, together with Leavis's support for these claims, are relevant to our concerns, I am more interested in the pattern of meaning in the poems themselves.

I will argue that *The Waste Land* provides the underlying pattern of desolation and restoration, reworked by Winnicott along the lines of disaster and hope, where individuals and the world 'stand in common need of regeneration' (Matthiessen 1947: 61). And the point I wish to emphasize is that, from the perspective of reclamation, the augmentation of life takes precedence over the reparation of a damaged world. Moreover, with the shift in Eliot's intentions after 'Ash Wednesday' from *Inferno* to *Purgatorio*, as it were, I suggest the poems make available an *exemplar* for the redemption of time through the work of the imagination. Although Winnicott may not have been explicitly concerned with the 'waste land' of contemporary existence, like Eliot he sought new forms for our human ethical predicament and, thereby, elaborated radically new ways of thinking about time and experience. Reclamation may be seen in this case as part of the imaginative sense of reality afford by illusion. And once again, based on our critical reading of therapeutic forms of imagining, I focus in this chapter on truths of faith as expressions of recovered spontaneity, but also as available means of readjustment to life under conditions of profound disillusionment.

The failure–dissociation model

Winnicott demonstrated the extent to which traumatizing infant care results in a break in the continuity of being at the beginning of life. More like a 'basic fault' than a constitutive split, Winnicott described how ontological discontinuity comes about as a consequence of the trauma inflicted by a deficient developmental environment.[3] Anxiety is understood, in this situation, as a 'reaction' to an early failure of the environment that is tantamount to a failure of life. What Winnicott

(1988: 127–9) called 'impingement' leaves the baby with deficiencies for life. Crucially, Winnicott (1954b: 281; emphasis in the original) described how the baby defends 'against specific environmental failure by a *freezing of the failure situation*'. The result is a 'queer kind of truth' where one fails to experience what has already happened. The metaphor of 'freezing' conveys a sense of wintertime in the mind, a bleak and inhospitable internal world, coupled with an attempted anaesthetic manoeuvre against the 'unthinkable experience' of early failure. This suggests two contrasting forms of regression, one 'going back to an early failure situation and the other to an early success situation' (1954b: 282). The former denotes a type of catastrophic reaction, the latter, a normal form of experience. In both cases meaning and cause are inextricably linked: while the phenomenon of regression, depending on its cause, is sometimes symptomatic, sometimes normal; the process of living itself generates qualitatively different effects.

Winnicott (1988: 128) treated 'early failure' as traumatic, by which he meant 'a movement from the environment [that] has nothing to do with the life process of the individual', and that 'detracts from the sense of real living'. As such, the environment is both *deficient* and *anomalous*; it is incompatible with life not as 'a statistical fact' but as 'a normative type of life'.[4] Insofar as this kind of trauma is 'governed by the compulsion to repeat' (Roussillon 2011: 2), the infant defends himself against a repetition of the original experience of mental disaster by means of splitting or dissociation.[5] Life puts up a fight for itself by closing down, where trauma as failure runs counter to the normative activity of living. Winnicott conceived the failure–dissociation model of psychopathology in contrast to the model of repression and secondary trauma in classical theory. Primary trauma indicates an end *before* the beginning; a disturbance of life the severity of which causes a reaction that forecloses the experience of being in time.

Normal and catastrophic types of regression may be traced back to 'being' and 'reaction', respectively. This is the obvious meaning of 'reaction' in Winnicott's theory of trauma. However, if we start from the assumption that life *is* reaction, then another reading of 'the complexity of infantile mental life within a prevailing environmental set-up' (Williams *et al.* 2012: xiii) suggests itself. On this alternative reading, spontaneity generates what Canguilhem (1966: 262) describes as 'the vitality of an adaptive solution'. In *New Reflections* (1966: 282–4) Canguilhem distances himself from the importation of the biological concept of adaptation into psychology and sociology, thereby avoiding the reductive implications of determinism. This more nuanced reading of the concept of adaptation allows for a constitutive reaction, whereby the 'spontaneous gesture' itself elicits something developmental from the environment (Groarke 2010a). As a living being, the infant is equal to the tasks arising from a fallible world; this is true up to a point, beyond which the spontaneous struggle for life is liable to break down. On this reading, adaptation may be seen as innovative and constitutive; conversely, accommodation is pathological to the extent that it is compliant and restrictive.

In approaching Winnicott's account from the standpoint of normativity, we can differentiate more clearly between 'normal' and 'catastrophic' forms of reaction, and between different logics of 'catastrophe'. Normal reaction presupposes 'a margin of tolerance for the inconstancies of the environment' (Canguilhem 1966: 197). On the other hand, catastrophic reactions turn up in the baby only in traumatic situations and, as such, may be seen as both unprecedented and pathological. Thus, besides the normal and the catastrophic, catastrophe itself is subject to a further, albeit fluctuating distinction in relation to hope. There are grounds for arguing that catastrophic reaction is a *hopeful* mode of psychic functioning. For instance, Goldstein's (1933: 437; emphasis in the original) definition of illness as survived destruction is based on the idea of unprecedented reactions: 'The attitudes which have survived in the sick person *never arise in that form in the normal person*'. In this case, illness itself affords grounds for hope, with respect to the symptomatic expression of utopian longing in the unprecedented nature of catastrophic reaction. However, catastrophic reactions may be considered pathological where there is a 'narrowing' of the individual–environment set-up. In this case, the individual becomes adhesively identified with failure, frozen in a faulty situation, and thereby incapable of generating new psychosomatic norms. We would describe the patient in this 'extreme situation' as living a withdrawn life, where survival depends on not taking part in one's own life.[6]

The therapeutic action of reclamation is directed towards the inherent fluctuations between unprecedented reactions and pathological retreats. Nothing that a human being creates, however disastrous it might be, is wholly pathological; there is always a sign of life. Thus, even where it interrupts the continuity of being in the form of 'primitive agony', the catastrophic reaction of dissociation nonetheless anticipates being. While repression may conceal a dissociative split (Roussillon 2011: 15); at the same time, seen from *the point of view of life* the norm remains hidden beneath a basic fault (Canguilhem 1966: 184). This gives grounds for hope: the idea of 'freezing' suggests not only the loss of feeling in fending off the anxiety of annihilation; but also, a hibernal state of being in the world. Where reaction to failure results in identification with internal disintegration, Winnicott (1954b: 281; emphasis added) argued that there is nonetheless 'an unconscious *assumption* (which can become a conscious hope) that opportunity will occur at a later date for a renewed experience in which the failure situation will be able to be unfrozen and re-experienced'. Embodied in a complex intrasubjective 'network of assumed ideas' (Bollas 2012: 34), the dissociative erasure of disaster keeps alive the underlying sense of existential continuity, albeit in a non-symbolic 'solution' (Roussillon 2011: 25) or dormant state outside of historical time.

Paradoxically, this means that even the so-called 'annihilation of personal being' may be seen as a way of 'going on being'. Dissociation is a way of life, after all; the patient who may be described as 'annihilated psychically' does in fact 'survive bodily' (Little 1990: 62). Winnicott reminds us that life continues to anticipate living, that there are many ways of persevering in being. This includes the 'fear of breakdown' which, as Winnicott (1963a) described it, is not only symptomatic of the failure of life, but also exerts a negative claim on being.

Life 'shows up' in this case *as* the negative (Winnicott 1965a: 9). In terms of the mnemonic impressions encapsulated ('frozen') in unconscious assumptions about the future, the fear of breakdown constitutes a negative pre-figuration of the disclosure of being.[7] Fluctuating between unprecedented reaction and pathological retreat, the assumption acts like a kind of hibernaculum in the traumatized mind. A negative impression of life manifest as psychotic anxiety, at the same time the assumption may be seen as an unconscious anticipation of the reversal of foreclosure. That assumption runs to *exertion* is indicative of the tenacious hold of life, what Canguilhem (1966: 136) described as 'vital normativity', even where the world appears to have 'nothing to do with the life process of the individual' (Winnicott 1988: 128). A life insists beyond the failure of *this* life.

The description of hope as a combination of unconscious anticipation and utopian longing, including the exertion of the negative reaction in the transference, depends on the idea of *primary intuition*. The meaning of 'intuition' thus covers both the intuitive management of the maternal frame and the innate disposition in the infant. It is evident from his account of the fear of breakdown as a clinical phenomenon, that Winnicott assumed a proto-mental configuration of the 'environment mother', a type of pre-reflective belief originating in the psyche-soma. The latter precedes the constitution of good and bad objects. Primary intuition applies specifically to the '*environment* mother' and, as such, accounts for the subsequent feelings of fragmentation, but also for the possibility of hope against the background of encapsulated memory. The notion of pre-reflective belief also accounts for the paradoxical situation where psychological breakdown has taken place, but has not been experienced.

Therapy as an act of faith

Winnicott modelled the treatment of traumatized patients on the intuitive management of the maternal frame. This has given rise to some basic misunderstandings. André Green (2002: 89), for example, elaborates on Freud's fundamental insight that 'when traumas occur before language is acquired, remembering is impossible'. To this extent, Green's notion of 'amnesic memory' is comparable to the idea of encapsulated mnemonic traces in Winnicott.[8] Green (2005: 20), however, dismisses as naïve the therapeutic claims that Winnicott made for the reclamation of life. It would be naïve to think that it is sufficient for the patient to simply assume the analyst's instantiation of the maternal *imago* in the transference. Clearly, the analyst cannot become the mother whom the infant never had, but this is not what Winnicott proposed. Unlike Alexander (1950; Alexander and French 1946), Winnicott did not promote the idea of psychoanalysis as a 'corrective emotional experience', if by that one means an analyst deliberately presenting himself or herself as different from the patient's actual mother.

In the case of early trauma, the therapeutic task involves making the unthinkable thinkable, which requires more from the analyst than interpretation. To recover spontaneity and reclaim life in any meaningful sense the analyst has to make palpable contact with the patient. This means becoming an 'engaged witness to dissociated experience' (Goldman 2012: 355) as a condition of therapeutic interpretation. In applying himself to the problem of emotional contact in cases of severe disturbance, including the analysis of borderline states and narcissistic disturbances of self-identity, Winnicott acknowledged the methodological advances made by Margaret Little. He took over and developed the idea from Little (1986: 85) that, in analytic work with borderline patients and adults of psychotic type, the ego becomes accessible to transference interpretation only insofar as reality is 'presented undeniably and inescapably so that contact with it cannot be refused'.

What does this entail? While 'the infant's renunciation of the omnipotence of the internal [subjective] object entails a crucial act of faith' (Ogden 1986: 195), similarly, therapeutic contact requires faith in the analyst, but also in the transformative process of the analysis.[9] The act of faith is developmental on both counts and involves infants and patients, respectively, making contact with reality. Furthermore, together with the patient's faith in the analyst, the analyst's faith in both the patient and the process allows for Yeats's 'rough beast', or enables something unforeseen to come about through the collaborative work of reconstruction.[10] The latter comprises an imaginative reclamation rather than a reconstruction of historical reality, an elaboration of the unprecedented (the symptom) as the unforeseen.

As Gurevich (2008: 573) points out, 'if the analyst does not have faith in the absolute reality of the patient's dissociated part, analysis will be without impact'. And Gurevich (2008: 573) goes on to say that this does not involve 'a concrete historical reconstruction' so much as the *doubling* of 'an internal catastrophic psychic state' in the transference. Faith rests on a psychic fold rather than a semantic construct; on the dialectical overlap between past, present, and future rather than a chronological reconstruction. Winnicott extended the analytic framework of transference-countertransference, accordingly, in terms of the latent hope of encapsulated memory. The basic assumption, here, is that the figuration of hope renders us sensible to disaster on the model of *Nachträglichkeit*, but without recourse to historical time or actual historical events.

The act of faith presents the mother–baby relationship and the analytic encounter alike as forms of imagining, and in both cases knowledge is secondary to emotional contact. In the case of analysis, the primacy of imagination accounts for the way in which the patient makes use of the situation. Far from being a passive recipient of a retrospective solution to an original problem, the patient expresses a primitive, intuitive longing to meet the embodiment of the maternal environment in the analytic experience. These pre-reflective longings elicit something developmental from the analyst, making the analyst the kind of person the patient needs the analyst to be. There is no way of knowing, in this situation, what is needed ahead of the patient's intuitive demand. And so long as this is the case, it is hard to see how any kind of systematic approach could get a purchase on Winnicott's thinking: spontaneity continues to run ahead of rational planning of any kind; utopian longing remains irreducible to 'utopian realism' (see Chapter 8).

Following the thread of Winnicott's therapeutic argument, the primacy of imagination extends to the treatment of history itself, where 'historical thinking' no less than historical being may be understood as a 'psychic function' (Bollas 1995). Thus, instead of knowing what happened in the past in order to be free of it, analysis provides the patient with a way of imagining the past so that it might become a real experience in the present. As a figure of analytic narrative, the past is something that is jointly constructed in the session. Again, rather than simply conferring 'retrospective truth on the past' (Bollas 1995: 143), patients and analysts create–discover new meanings through a series of emotionally rooted collaborative reconstructions. The implication is that, through the 'revision' of the past, primary intuition becomes an object of consciousness in the form of a narrative construction and, as such, invests the patient's *sense* of the past with new meaning.

Narrative constructs in psychoanalysis are generated primarily by free association and, as such, represent what we might call the *analytic voice* of the unconscious, as distinct from the narrating voice of the patient or the analyst.[11] Based on unconscious assumptions, the reconstruction of the past depends on this narrative voice as a kind of third object. This is how I understand the figuration of hope in Winnicott: where life has failed it is down to the work of the imagination to amend the situation and to reclaim the capacity for aliveness. Winnicott was not interested in hidden phenomena so much as innate potential. And where dissociation itself is subject to further non-symbolic defences against the return of the earlier traumatic situation (Roussillon 2011: 14), therapeutic attention is directed towards expansive living. In this case, one can depend on memory neither as a defensive screen, nor as an evocative object. Psychic survival depends on the reclamation of experience itself through the psychic act of the 'historical' imaginary.

Far from being naïve, the subtlety here consists in rendering imagination as an act of faith, if not a spontaneous gesture of hope. The reach for meaning in the unconscious movement from pre-reflective intuition to narrative construct, is based upon a belief in the creative imagination. This is another way of saying that, starting with the patient's free associations, it is the unconscious assumptions of the narrative voice that do the real work in the dialectic of disaster and hope. Most importantly, the patient invents the analyst he needs to find, and it is the unconscious expectation expressed in the need that renders the invention true. No one has grasped the patient's urgent need to render the intuition of being as a gesture of being, to relive assumptions through exertions, more persistently than Winnicott. Neville Symington (2007: 44) seems to understand this better than Green, describing how a patient forced him 'with all the strength of her being to be the analyst she needed'.[12] For Symington, as for Winnicott, the force of the imagination should not be confused with consciousness or self-knowledge.

Green is not alone, however, in raising doubts about Winnicott's claims for the restorative potential of psychoanalysis. There is an ongoing debate about the significance of Freud's metapsychology in Winnicott, with recent contributions from both sides (Fulgencio 2007; Girard 2010). At the same time, Winnicott's adaptations and revisions of classical Freudian technique have been criticized by Hanna Segal for 'enacting and mobilizing primitive transferences rather than analyzing them' (qtd. in Rodman 2003: 262). As Elizabeth Bott Spillius (1988: 6) points out, Kleinian analysts in general 'strongly disagree with the idea of encouraging regression and reliving infantile experiences in the consulting room through non-interpretive activities. Analytic care, in [Klein's] view, should take the form of a stable analytic setting containing within it a correct interpretive process.'

There is little doubt that Winnicott held hands with some of his patients, provided them with blankets, tissues, tea, and biscuits, and extended the length of their analytic sessions. Are we meant to conclude from this that he actively encouraged patients to regress in the formal sense? Like many analysts (Ferenczi and Balint in particular), Winnicott seems to have accepted the fact that regression is inevitable in psychoanalysis, and that patients make use of regression to dependence within the analytic setting, where the acknowledgement of dependence, together with the return from regression, is managed by the analyst. It seems to me that Winnicott made the case against his critics on clinical grounds. Non-interpretive interventions are required as an essential part of the analytic task in many if not all cases, and the patient is able to regress to dependence where the analytic process itself provides for the safe management of regression.

Further to the classical regressive transference neurosis, Winnicott proposed a particular kind of analytic environment for making use of dissociated experience. Management and the regression to dependence describe how the treatment works; pre-reflective intuition and the pure immanence of life, what the treatment is based on. Where life has failed, analysis invests the imagined past with a redemptive promise and, as Green (2012: 1244) himself admits, the verification of this possibility according to 'positive criteria' is beside the point. Winnicott established the analytic process as an incomparable work of the aftermath, and I intend to make a strong argument for redemption and its therapeutic efficacy in this chapter.[13] Hopkins (1989) draws attention to the analogy between the resurrection doctrine and the account of destructiveness and survival in Winnicott's late work. Similarly, Kirschner (1996: 194) concludes that while psychoanalytic forms of redemption, including Winnicott's developmental narrative, are 'more modest, more truncated, certainly less enduring and absolute than the traditional religious forms'; nonetheless, the 'inherited spiritual code' survives in these 'forms of worldly redemption'. In my view, redemption lies at the heart of Winnicott's thought, not as deliverance from sin on the Christian model, but rather, as the reclamation of life and deliverance from failure.

The dissociation of experience presents itself as a clinical problem. In treating it as such, my argument is that Winnicott exalted hope not necessarily as a theological precept, but as a Christianized figuration. The hoped-for thus recalls life not as the end of failure through the secular coincidence of time and history, but on the grounds of redemptive possibility as a regulative idea (Williams 2012: 14–15).

Destructiveness, hatred, and fragmentation – indeed, disgust for life itself – are seen as redeemable through a principal commitment to maturity predicated on the primacy of creativity. Winnicott applied himself first and foremost to the therapeutic task, but in doing so articulated a Christian sensibility that balks at the idea of the void of empty space. This follows the central movement of Eliot's poetic vision, where a 'deepening sense of the horror of life, something more terrible than dreariness' (Gardner 1949: 185), compels the reach for meaning through the reclamation of experience. Assuming that the radical premises of psychoanalysis are continuous with literary modernism, my argument rests on the juxtaposition of Winnicott and Eliot. Furthermore (Eliot's *agon* with Romanticism notwithstanding), as disaster yields to the imagination's freedom, Winnicott drew on hope as a Romantic resource in the Wordsworthian tradition. And in the following discussion we see the extent to which, by managing the regressed situation and witnessing 'the parts that go to make the whole' (qtd. in Abram 2012: 312), Winnicott engaged with central aspects of the imaginative tradition of modern English literature.

The redress of psychoanalysis

The fear of breakdown indicates that something terrible has happened and, at the same time, communicates a negative claim on being. The fear itself fluctuates between claustration and redress. Seamus Heaney renders both sides of this anxiety in his poem 'Keeping going' (1966). Something continues to work its way through unthinkable experience, what Heaney calls 'stamina', as a manifestation of the perseverance of being: 'My dear brother, you have good stamina. / You stay on where it happens' (ll. 67–8). The poem affirms that our 'staying on' and 'keeping going' where it happened, is the best we can hope for in the aftermath of disaster, be it personal or historic. The point Heaney's poem makes is that living on in the aftermath gains ground against experiential loss, and therefore is not simply a repetition. The perseverance of being brings forth a world this side of the compulsion to repeat.

If this reading of the traumatic situation is in any way correct, it means that the analyst embodies not the object hoped for so much as the primordial grounds for hope. Where the framing structure of psychic life fails, analysis provides the patient with a facilitative rather than a substitutive environment. I take it as axiomatic that no re-creation of a past event can ever occur in the analytic situation. The redress of psychoanalysis does not involve uncovering the hidden contents of past traumas. More than a search for what lies hidden in the past, the Winnicottian process of therapeutic management involves gaining access to lived experience in the present. The aim of which is to help patients feel more alive. While this may be seen as a search for 'a picture of the patient's forgotten years' (Freud 1937: 258); to uncover by persevering, however, is not the same thing as the lifting of repression. Most importantly, that which is made present takes precedence over anything that is re-presented. Uncovering or discovering, in this sense, is a description of something being true as an expression of active living; something retrospectively and retroactively true to life.

The time of breakdown therefore remains paradoxical: on the one hand, there is a failure to experience something that has actually happened, resulting in a feeling of lost time. Patients who come to analysis in this state, irrespective of their chronological age, are convinced that they have come too late; the anxiety presents itself as a feeling of life having passed them by. The analyst is engaged in helping the patient acquire a sense of the future against an all-pervasive sense of ruin. Similarly, Eliot begins the final movement of 'East Coker' in a mood of despair over twenty wasted years. The despair is an expression of the unconscious thought that it was always too late, that life failed before it began. On the other hand, Winnicott described how the traumatic situation includes the unconscious assumption, if not the conscious hope, that one might re-experience what has not yet been experienced. On both counts there is a call to 'redeem the time' ('Ash Wednesday', IV, l. 26) in accordance with the inherited tradition that extends from the Metaphysical poets through Hopkins and Eliot to contemporary poets as different from one another as Geoffrey Hill and Seamus Heaney.

What does this mean for psychoanalysis? What does it mean for the patient to re-experience lost time? Under what conditions is this possible? For patients living in fear of a breakdown that has already happened, there is a fundamental derangement of memory and mourning alike. In disastrous situations, Winnicott (1963a: 92) maintained that therapeutic management works not as an objective memorial form, but rather, as 'the equivalent of remembering'. Green (2002: 89) concurs with Winnicott on the fundamental point that, in cases of early trauma, 'transference is a process of actualization more than one of remembering'. The therapeutic effects of redemption are felt and managed through this process of actualization. The analytic task involves uncovering something that lies beyond the reach of memory, an event that belongs to the immemorial past. This means that therapy provides grounds for hope without recourse to the experience of being in time. Management, in other words, does not fall entirely within time's dispensation, but holds out for another pattern on the order of redress and renewal.

How does one treat what falls outside the field of conscious *and* unconscious memory? Analysis cannot replace lost time. The failure of life at the beginning means that no one was there to experience what happened, and so there are no memories of the disaster. Being without memory is part and parcel of the traumatic situation. Memory itself becomes part of the paradox of disaster for the dissociated self. The work of the aftermath, therefore, is based on the idea of imagination as the equivalent of memory. In short, imagination becomes memory: 'The only way to "remember" in this case is for the patient to experience this past thing for the first time in the present' (Winnicott 1963a: 92). Winnicott's phrasing is taken from *Four Quartets*, while the idea of two different ways of relating to time is presented specifically in the first movement of 'The Dry Salvages': the lived time of the river, time 'with us,' or the temporality of historical being; and the time we experience only through our imagination, for instance, like the sea that 'is all about us'.

Winnicott posited a paradoxical situation in which memory is overlaid by an immemorial expectation, or pre-reflective intuition, without an experience of the past. The paradox takes the form of a utopian longing for what one has never had, a longing that allows instead for what is to come by providing a surface on which imagination emerges as an act of faith. There is, of course, any number of ways in which to approach Winnicott's view of psychical temporality and its philosophical import. Stolorow (2011), for instance, proposes a philosophical framework for the ontology of disaster along post-Cartesian lines.[14] Alternatively, it seems to me that Winnicott keeps faith with the *spiritual* promise of renewal, what Eigen (1993: 128) calls the 'foundational journey' of primary creativity, transitional experiencing, and object usage. This makes of faith an unconscious assumption in the context of pathological disillusion, where the promise of restored meaning is combined with the paradox of unthinkable experience.

Eliot provides a literary framework for the time-frame of reclamation. The failure of experience renewed, including the transformation of the defeated or unlived past, is rendered in poetic as well as religious language at the end of 'Little Gidding': 'We shall not cease from exploration / And the end of all our exploring / Will be to arrive where we started / And know the place for the first time' (ll. 242–5). Attitudes of disillusionment give way in Eliot's late poetry to a new reach for meaning in the present: 'We had the experience but missed the meaning, / And approach to the meaning restores the experience / In a different form' ('The Dry Salvages', ll. 95–8). This seems to me the single most important aspect of Eliot's poetry for Winnicott, the idea that the reach for meaning restores primary intuition or pre-reflective belief as a condition of experience. In their exploration of time and experience, *Four Quartets* continue to emphasize the present and, underlining the redemptive reading of the poem, Helen Gardner (1978: 157) quotes from Eliot's notes for the last of his *Quartets*:

> They vanish, the individuals, and our feeling for them sinks into the flame which refines. They emerge in another pattern & recreated & reconciled redeemed, having their meaning together not apart, in a union which is of beams from the central fire.[15]

There is a good deal of biographical as well as bibliographical evidence to support the view of Winnicott's indebtedness to Eliot. For example, in a letter to Bion dated 5 October 1967, he writes as follows:

> I am not quite settled in my mind about the idea of memory and desire or intention. When I got home Clare [Winnicott's wife] reminded me again that the phrase memory and desire, which you have used before, is a quotation from T. S. Eliot, and she was able to give me the whole poem, and for some reason or other I accept memory and desire as naturally interrelated in the poem.
>
> (Winnicott 1987b: 169)

Winnicott is of course referring to the opening lines of *The Waste Land*, which invoke 'mixing / Memory and desire' (ll. 2–3). More importantly, perhaps, Winnicott also gives us an insight into his positive evaluation of the 'interrelated' literary and biblical meanings in the poem, including, Eliot's 'Son of man' (l. 20) – after Ezekiel 2.1 – in a world where 'the dead tree gives no shelter' (l. 23), 'desire shall fail' (Ecclesiastes 12.5), and the question of hope is put to the very ground of things in accordance with 'the roots that clutch' (l. 19). To state our argument at its most basic, the Desert and the Garden provide an essential pattern for the dialectic of disaster and hope.

In his biography, Brett Kahr (1996: 106) also confirms Winnicott's debt to Eliot, noting the pleasure he took in hearing his wife recite poetry, particularly Eliot and Dylan Thomas. Marion Milner (1972: 250) suggests a reading of Winnicott's 'quietude linked with stillness' in consonance with Eliot's lines from 'Burnt Norton': 'still point of the turning world' (l. 64) and 'Words, after speech, reach / Into the silence' (ll. 142–3). The title of Winnicott's unfinished autobiography, *Not Less Than Everything*, is a quotation from the final movement of 'Little Gidding' (l. 257), from which he also took the epigraph for his book. Finally, a collection of his essays has also appeared under a title taken from the *Quartets*: 'Home is where one starts from' (l. 194), which is from the final section of 'East Coker' – providing once again the epigraph for the book.

There is no evidence to suggest that Winnicott possessed an original literary–critical intelligence. Nevertheless, he avoided the familiar pitfalls which tend to bedevil the psychoanalysis of art. There are two reasons for this: first, Winnicott did not assume an aesthetic perspective based on the extension of the model of dreams and the neuroses to cultural forms of experience; second, he did not use art and literature in order to illustrate his psychological theories. What distinguishes his contribution, rendering it meritorious relative to the majority of efforts in this area of applied psychoanalytic studies, is the idea of primary creativity as the groundwork of meaning and self-understanding. Winnicott did not confuse the theory of creativity with the theory of art. However, the use he made of literary patterns of meaning is confirmed by the culture of criticism; most notably, the way in which Leavis (1932) framed Eliot's achievement makes the poems particularly relevant for Winnicott.

Ahead of Winnicott, Leavis provides the central criteria of maturity, aliveness, and the true self. If Eliot is the authenticating spirit of Winnicottian reclamation, the basic terms of reference for the latter are consistent with Leavisite 'discriminations' on the moral life. The reorientation produced by Eliot, as Leavis defined it in *New Bearings in English Poetry*, is therefore an indispensable context for Winnicott's own revision of Freudian thought. Leavis (1932: 21) set out the criterion of maturity, what he saw as 'the interests of an adult sensitive mind', in his argument against enchantment, daydream, and the cultivation of withdrawal. The criticism applies from the Romantics through Tennyson and Swinburne to Rupert Brooke. Leavis argued that Arnold and Browning, and to varying degrees de la Mare, Hardy, and Yeats, can be counted as failures on this trajectory of contemplated withdrawal. Life falters for Leavis, as it did for Winnicott, on the matter of claustration and moral dearth. In particular, for Leavis (1932: 21) 'so interior a mind and spirit as Browning's could not provide the impulse needed to bring back into poetry the adult intelligence'. It would require another kind of inwardness, on this reading, to meet the criterion of maturity.

We are not concerned here with the merits of Leavis's argument as much as its general outline.[16] Again, following his pronouncements on the likes of Arnold and Browning, we find Leavis (1932: 167) repeating the same claims some twenty years later in his dismissal of Auden: in the 1950 'Retrospect' to *New Bearings*, Auden is judged to have 'made a rapid advance in sophistication' since the 1930s, but to have come no 'nearer to essential maturity'. Leavis's (1932: 168) appeal to the notion of 'sophistication' is supposed to account for Auden's 'failure to develop' in accordance with the criterion of maturity: 'Sophistication belongs to a climate in which the natural appetite for kudos is not chastened by contact with mature standards, and in which fixed immaturity can take itself for something else.'

The mark of an 'adult mind', according to Leavis's (1932: 15) set of principles, is evident above all in the poet's need to 'communicate something of his own'. For Leavis (1932: 24), maturity goes together with originality and independence, the expression of 'an intensely personal way of feeling'. This in turn confirms the idea of the important poet as someone 'who is more alive than other people, more alive in his own age' (1932: 16). Thus, maturity is coupled with the idea that the 'potentialities of human experience in any age are realized only by a tiny minority' (1932: 16). Eliot realized his potential for creativity to an incomparable degree, according to Leavis, who judged Eliot's 'modes of feeling, apprehension, and expression' as a 'new start' in English poetry. Based on an ideal of critical thinking, Leavis mediates the criterion of maturity in a way that makes Eliot even more important for Winnicott, giving weight to the central Winnicottian idea of creative apperception as the developmental basis of cultural experience.

In contrast to a programmatic conception of identity (see Parts II and III), there is an affinity here between the idea of English as a calling, which animates Leavis's thinking, and Winnicott's 'true self'.[17] The 'potentialities' in both cases are often the same: based on a common evaluation of vocation, Winnicott effectively elaborated on Leavis's (1932: 173) notion of the 'creative impulse' from the standpoint of experience and creative living. This is how Winnicott (1970b: 39) defined matters in a late work: 'Whatever definition we arrive at, it must include the idea that life is worth living or not, according to whether creativity is or is not a part of an individual person's living experience.' On this interpretation, necessity takes its bearings from maturity, an interpretation that proved decisive for Winnicott (1970b: 40):

> Creativity is the retention throughout life of something that belongs properly to infant experience: the ability to create the world ... The reality principle is the fact of the existence of the world whether the baby creates it or not ... The reality principle is just too bad, but by the time the little child is called upon to say 'ta,' big developments have taken place.

We shall come back to the sociological implications of maturity in the following chapter. Suffice it to note here that, by meeting the infant's creative impulse, the mother enables the development of mature experience, traces the contours of the moral life, and provides a model for therapeutic management and the redress of psychoanalysis.

The exigency of return

Alongside the debt to Eliot, the King James Bible remained essential for Winnicott, and a consciousness of biblical allusion runs throughout his work. Most notably, Winnicott's poem 'The Tree', written on 4 November 1963, exemplifies the depth of his Christian feeling.[18] Together with his analysis of the fear of breakdown, the poem – the title of which picks up Eliot's 'dead tree' as well as the True Cross in old English poetry – forms an important part of Winnicott's late works, in which his ongoing concern with anxieties about survival took a new and decisive turn. The late work, I shall argue here, makes use of what Habermas (2010: 18) calls 'the unexhausted force' (*das Unabgegoltene*) of religion and its traditions.

Winnicott's biographer describes how, through a 'series of junctures' in the 1960s, he 'moved into new and ever more profound territory' (Rodman 2003: 286).[19] The exemplary claim of the late works concerns the exigency of return, an emphasis on survival in the face of destructiveness, where exteriority is no longer confined to introjective–projective mechanisms. Winnicott was concerned with life as the groundwork of being prior to the constitution of objects through projective identification. He argued consistently throughout this period that the object survives destruction, precisely, 'outside the area of objects set up by the subject's projective mental mechanisms' (1968a: 227).

'The Tree' articulates Winnicott's central theme of psychological survival and, by the same token, exemplifies what he meant by the reclamation of life. To recall an earlier commentary of mine in light of the present discussion, the poem gives voice to the 'agonizing task' of bringing the dead mother back to life as the means of becoming a person oneself.[20] Winnicott, who was sixty-seven years old when he wrote the poem, had less than ten years left to live, and while his mother had been dead for almost forty years, it is her 'inward death' that weights the poem on the order of primary intuition: 'The sins of the whole world [cf. John 1.29] weigh less than this / woman's heaviness'. This is what the burden of living comes to in the poem: 'To enliven her was my living'.

As far as I know, there is no evidence of Winnicott's doctrinal commitment to the Incarnation. However, with the emphasis on experience in the present,

Winnicott seems to have found inspiration for the 'agonizing task' in the theme of resurrection. The redemptive work of 'The Tree' takes place in the intersection of the timeless with time. The poem adheres to the imperative of the immemorial past, even as the various annunciations of 'The Dry Salvages' assume 'validity through the one Annunciation' (Gardner 1949: 176). It is important here to emphasize the distinction between reclamation and mourning; the poem articulates the former in terms of the temporality of unthinkable experience: 'my father's business' intersects with the mother as 'I knew her // Once, stretched out on her lap / as now on a dead tree'. The latter is an allusion to the death of Christ (John 19.13–24); the former recalls Luke (2.49): 'How is it that ye sought me? wist ye not that I must be about my Father's business?'[21] Jesus takes the opportunity to instruct his parents on his task and its provenance: his work is God's work and, therefore, lies beyond historical time. His parents had good reason to know this and had no need to be so anxious. Where should a child be found, but in his father's house. Thus, the painful task attendant on the immemorial past is overdetermined by the allusion to concerns that are above the duty of obeying earthly parents. If we compare this to Eliot's treatment of the river and sea as symbols for time and timelessness, the poem becomes especially revealing of Winnicott's stance with respect to 'the difficult paradoxical Christian view of how man lives both "in and out of time"' (Matthiessen 1947: 183).

Winnicott confirms that the poet strives to say what matters, to uncover unthinkable suffering in the right way or as best he can, and that only the stricken voice of the poet may redeem the time. As 'The Tree' demonstrates, the work of the aftermath is necessarily a truthful way of speaking about inscrutable things. That having been said, Rodman's comments on Winnicott's identification with Christ are inappropriate and superficial, although he (2003: 411n8) does provide a useful footnote by Eric Korn that focuses on the Hebrew and Christian sources in the poem. Characteristically, Winnicott eschewed classical legend in favour of biblical language refracted through the traditions of English Romantic poetry and Celtic Christianity.

Here, as elsewhere, Winnicott's writing adheres consistently to a Christian idiom. His poem questions the work of its own making, and by implication the process of becoming a person, in the following terms: 'O Glastonbury // Must I bring even these thorns to flower? / even this dead tree to leaf?' Korn provides some of the relevant background. In Celtic legend, the Glastonbury thorn is part of the True Cross, brought to England by Joseph of Arimathea, who, it is believed, also buried Jesus in a tomb of his own making and later founded the first Christian Church of England at Glastonbury. Moreover, Winnicott states the essential relation to oneself as to one's death ('It is I who die') in the language of the canonical Gospels, left untranslated in the poem in the Aramaic idiom: 'And at the ninth hour Jesus cried with a loud voice, saying, Eloi, Eloi, lama sabachtani? which is, being interpreted, My God, my God, why hast thou forsaken me?' (Mark 15.34). The task of bringing the dead (mother) back to life doubles Christ's unthinkable agony (Matthew 26.38–9) as it appears in the poem.

What inspired Winnicott's decision to couple 'the cruelty of the nail's hatred' with the mother's 'weeping'? Why accept this as the best arrangement to be found? For Rodman, this is essentially an autobiographical question concerning Winnicott's early contact with a depressed mother. But it is also an historical question concerning the conditions of figuration and imagination in an English mode of thought. It may be that Winnicott had one of the most original analytic minds since Freud, but he was nonetheless of his time and place. However one views the biographical reading, the poem is redemptive according to different and conflicting traditions of English poetry, including, not only the vocabulary of spiritual life from the Metaphysical poets onwards, but also the tradition of English Romantic poetry. To redeem 'inward death' in this case would require the transformation of religion back into poetry after the Fall from Eternity. The failure to do so, however, which is inevitable from the Romantic perspective of our modernity, is what turns the poem into an allegory of illusion–disillusionment. It also renders the poem as a doubling of the reclamation of life on historical as well as personal grounds.

The references to God's promise and to Eliot's rendering of the time of meaning and value – *his* summoning of the dead – are implicit in Winnicott's own version of the redemption of time as reclamation. To the extent that the latter presupposes a mode of imagining modelled on the Incarnation, once again this puts Winnicott directly at odds with Freud, who remained critical of any kind of redemptive reading of time. Winnicott conceived of time and experience in a way that does not allow for Freud's (1927) critique of illusion as the negative value of reality; and as with illusion, Freud and Winnicott held alternative views about the use we make of time. Notwithstanding Winnicott's indebtedness to Freud's ideas about construction in the context of *Nachträglichkeit*; instead of the Freudian idea of working through, Winnicott envisaged another pattern for unthinkable experience that accords more with Heaney's (1995) idea of the 'redress of poetry'.

For Winnicott, as for Heaney (1995: 159), the creative imperative is first and foremost an imagined response, a promise to respond, and we make use of poetry in this way 'to be forwarded within ourselves'. The poem puts experience *there* as a work of figuration. There is ample evidence to suggest that Winnicott assumed hope along these lines as a Christian figuration. Nevertheless, Wordsworth remains the exemplary instance for the reclamation of experience in English poetry. For instance, in the English Romantic tradition, Wordsworth's 'light that never was' ('Elegiac Stanzas Suggested by a Picture of Peele Castle', l. 15) is paradigmatic of the transformation of experience into words. Accordingly, the idea of spontaneity as a virtue is set out in the preface to the second edition of the *Lyrical Ballads*, that is to say, in direct opposition to the poetical conventions derived from Pope and Dryden; an idea that Winnicott certainly made full use of in concordance with the consolation that the poetic imagination achieves over experiential loss. This applies, at once, to 'The Tree' and to the way in which Winnicott managed the regressed situation, where the emptiness of lost time is restored by the power of the imagination on the model of Wordsworthian solace.

Eliot (1933: 30) underlines the critical import of what we are describing as the work of figuration: 'We have to communicate ... an experience which is not an experience in the ordinary sense, for it may only exist ... in the expression of it'. It is not the case, then, that language represents something that pre-exists it, nor is Eliot referring to repressed experience. The fact that he is moving towards meaning and not starting from it, as Gardner (1949: 57–8) points out, is evident if we compare the obscurity of 'Burnt Norton' to the clarity of 'Little Gidding'. The reach for meaning is discernable in the work of poetry, understood as a sensible presentation of a non-existence rendered in words.[22] Leavis in turn makes the point that in the movement towards communication, 'the thing said' is indistinguishable from 'the way of saying', the poet's perfect command of experience and technique go hand in hand. Leavis (1932: 56) singled out Edward Thomas as an original poet on these grounds, attributing his 'habit of sensibility' to a 'delicate touch' that is a method of 'exploration' and, at the same time, one of 'expression'.

The distinction between reclamation and mourning becomes clear in the case of early trauma, where the imagined response to inner failure is an imaginative work of the aftermath. In accordance with an immemorial or ahistorical expectation that reaches back prior to remembering and before the existential experience of loss (cf. Botella 2010), the work of mourning is displaced by the work of the aftermath, understood as the enactment of imaginary restoration. Again, this is not a matter of finding words for something that has already been experienced. To conjure a sense of the world out of the fragments of being requires a particular work of the imagination, including receptivity to states of mind without representation. The imaginative work of psychic figurability amounts to an act of faith on the part of the analytic pair, a work of therapeutic reclamation that takes place within what Eigen (1993) calls 'the area of faith'.

Eliot provided Winnicott with a pattern of meaning for the failure of life, but also with a positive model for grasping the point at which words inevitably fail, the point where 'Words, after speech, reach / Into the silence' ('Burnt Norton', ll. 142–3) – silence pushed to extremes in 'East Coker', where each 'new start' is counted as 'a different kind of failure'. Translated into clinical terms this means that, alongside the patient's verbal communications, traces of hope may also be found in what *cannot* be said.[23] The problem is how to sound out not just the meaning of words, but also the silence and rhythms of the unthinkable.[24] Winnicott envisaged this as an essential part of the therapeutic task: how to allow for what lies beyond language even in words themselves and, at the same time, how to keep the silence within emotional reach. Evasions, enactments, elliptical manoeuvres, elisions and resistant energies of all kinds are the stuff of clinical psychoanalysis, and in the traumatic transference there is often no more to go on.

It is evident that Winnicott did not limit analytic therapy to verbal associations, but credited the associative possibilities of regressive enactment itself. In terms of the rhythmic sense of somatic communion, an experience of mutual contact prior to form, he modelled the reclamation of life on the tactile intimacies as well as the promise of maternal care. As the following description from the analysis of a forty-year-old woman demonstrates, Winnicott made use of the body and its rhythms as well as words:

> [S]he and I were together with her hand in my hands ... Without deliberate action on the part of either of us there developed a rocking rhythm. The rhythm was rather a rapid one, about 70 per minute (cf. heartbeat), and I had to do some work to adapt to this rate. Nevertheless, there we were with *mutuality* expressed in terms of a slight but persistent rocking movement. We were *communicating* with each other without words. This was taking place at a level of development that did not require the patient to have maturity in advance of that which she found herself possessing in the regression to dependence of the phase of her analysis.
>
> (1969: 258; emphasis in the original)

As Winnicott (1969: 258) points out, the essential thing here is the communion between the patient and the analyst, the emotional contact between them, based on the intimacies of the mother–infant relationship, particularly the recourse to 'the anatomy and physiology of live bodies'. Winnicott contrasts this corporeal experience of mutuality, the living of an experience together, to the Freudian model of transference and interpretation. To the extent that communicating in this way without words enables the patient to experience 'this past thing' here and now 'for the first time', regression to dependence is an alternative way of achieving something comparable to 'the lifting of repression that occurs in the analysis of the psycho-neurotic patient (1963a: 92). As Ogden (2004: 1352) puts it, to communicate in this way means 'uninterruptedly to be that human place in which the patient is becoming whole'. The frame takes precedence over the object; construction, over interpretation; and sensible presentation, over form.

The idea that the reclamation of life ('reliving') is equivalent to remembering represents an important and original contribution to our understanding of time and experience. It also marks a radical revision of the Freudian interpretation where the emphasis is on freedom through remembering. Psychologically speaking, the time of breakdown occurs prior to the formation of the world. In this sense, Winnicott deepens the fundamental Freudian discovery of archaic mental functioning. The primitive unconscious assumption, if not the hope, of persevering in being places the patient at the very beginning of the past, in the immemorial traces of the beginning, prior to the distinction between remembering and forgetting. Patients cannot remember what they have failed to experience. And for patients who find themselves in this state, to relive the past for the first time in the present and to know the place for the first time is itself a beginning, a psychological birth, rather than a return in the ordinary sense of the word. The analytic process, therefore, creates its own experience, enabling patients to think hitherto unthinkable thoughts, or to imagine what they have no way of remembering.

The paradox of reclamation

The idea that psychoanalysis actually generates new forms of experience was fundamental to Winnicott's clinical thinking. The irreducible dialectic of repetition and creation in the traumatic transference, the dialectic of disaster and hope, is predicated on a generative conception of the frame. Technically, the question is whether patients create or discover meaning in the transference. Green (1975: 293) questions whether the analytic process constitutes forms of experience *as such* for the first time.[25] This relates directly to the paradox under discussion. Winnicott (1963a: 92) insisted that through the process of reclamation the patient actually experiences the 'past thing for the first time in the present'. At the same time, however, he assumed that the frame facilitates the realization of *potential* meanings and forms of experience. It seems important to me, therefore, to make a distinction between analytic narrative as a movement towards figurability (Botella and Botella 2005) on the one hand and, on the other, the reflexive ordering of self-narratives (see Chapter 8).

The paradox is inevitable insofar as the analytic frame derives its form and function from the primary maternal frame. In this case, the analyst's role is considered analogous to the mother's capacity to frame the baby's potential to frame his own experience. For infants and patients alike, it is not a matter of complying with the frame, but rather, engaging in an ongoing framing process. It is important we keep the specificity of the clinical context in mind when considering these formulations. It is the failure of life manifest as a failure of memory that necessitates a revision of analytic technique, a revision which amounts to a realignment of the Freudian validation of remembering. In circumstances where agony outweighs grief and is more primitive than the feeling of sadness, Winnicott came to the conclusion that the exigency of return is experienced as a form of imagining. This is essentially what he meant by management in the case of trauma, where reliving requires imagination as an act of faith in a particular setting.

Let us try to draw the therapeutic argument together along temporal lines. Blurring boundaries between real and imagined memories, which is a matter of course in psychoanalytical treatment, assumes a particular form in the case of early trauma where the emphasis falls on the link between regression and reliving. By mapping types of breakdown in relation to levels of dependence, Winnicott (1954b) set out the management of psychotic anxieties at the limits of memory. He envisaged a new type of therapeutic understanding, distinct from the Freudian objective where the patient 'must be brought to recollect certain experiences and the affective impulses called up by them which he has for the time being forgotten' (Freud 1937: 257–8). For Freud, enhancing consciousness, so as to augment its cognitive and affective reach, produces something that actually turns out to be strangely familiar. Winnicott effectively redefined the Freudian 'uncanny' (*Unheimliche*) from the perspective of unthinkable experience. Intuition and creativity are accorded primacy over the recollection of experience. Again, the resultant preoccupation with 'unknown modes of being' owes more to

Wordsworth than it does to Freud: 'In my thoughts / There was a darkness – call it solitude / Or blank desertion' (*The Prelude*, Book I, ll. 420–2). The failure of memory proceeds from these 'blank misgivings' where, following the passage in which Wordsworth evokes the sublime object as it looms up in the night, he describes 'forms that do not live' and are altogether unfamiliar.

Winnicott, without conflating clinical and poetic thinking, sought to manage the sublime itself by way of imaginative forms. In attempting to meet the therapeutic needs of traumatized patients, Winnicott (1954b: 286) argued that the 'setting of analysis reproduces the early and earliest mothering techniques. It invites regression by reason of its reliability'. The 'invitation' to patients to act out regressed states issues from the 'analytic object' (Green 2005) understood as a triadic arrangement of setting-transference-countertransference. This includes above all the use the patient makes of the analyst, a process in which analyst and patient go back to the earliest relationship, but yet without recourse to the representation of the past effected by memory. It is not a case of uncovering repressed memories. There are no experiences available for the patient to recover or call to mind. Nor is memory a source of consolation. The regression to states of dependence relies on what comes about through the 'reliving' of a kind of latent birth. The intuition of being becomes a lived experience in the analytic situation, as Winnicott (1954b: 286) put it, through a 'specialized environmental provision interlocked with the patient's regression'. To restate the paradox at its most basic, *something comes back in the present for the first time*.

Margaret Little (1990) gives a detailed account of the technique of management in her treatment with Winnicott. She describes how she agreed to go into hospital as a voluntary patient during the summer break, allowing for an extension of the analytic setting:

> In my sessions with D. W. there had been 'token' infant care; he always opened the door to me himself, each session wound up with coffee and biscuits, he saw to it that I was warm and comfortable, and provided tissues, etc. But here was the full 'regression to dependence', an extension of what he had given me; and he kept in constant touch with the hospital and sent me postcards letting me know where he was.
>
> (Little 1990: 60)

Winnicott (1965b: 127) made it quite clear that regression in the analytic situation is not a technique of remembrance, a way of lifting repressed memories, any more than it is a work of mourning: 'It is not really true to say that the patient is trying to remember madness which has been and around which defences were organized'. In reacting to impingement by way of dissociation rather than repression, patients are left with what feels like nothing so much as an imminent sense of collapse. The question of course is what becomes of a human life in such devastating circumstances. What remains when experience fails? This is the basic question in response to which Winnicott came up with the technique of therapeutic reclamation. Although he did not propose a work of reparation along Kleinian lines, there is nonetheless amendment in survived extremity. The same holds for Winnicott as for Balint (1952; 1968): the work of the aftermath involves recovery from a 'basic fault'; it is a way of beginning again as far as the patient can imagine.

What does one begin with for imagination itself to remain a possibility? What is a life that it may appear out of the failure of *this* life? Regression is presented as a therapeutic technique capable of holding the patient on the assumption of a pre-reflective intuition of being. For Winnicott, the fact that hope is present at all under traumatic conditions, confirms the extent to which life precedes objects, ego and the world. This is how Little (1990: 62; emphasis in the original) describes her experience:'[Winnicott] told me that such fear of annihilation as I felt belonged to "annihilation" that had already happened: I *had been* annihilated psychically, but had in fact survived bodily, and was now emotionally reliving the past experience.'

It takes the paradox of living both 'in and out of time' to revive the continuity of being when life has failed; to transform unthinkable anxiety into imagined truth; and to reclaim through truths of faith the primary intuition of maternal love, if not the certainty of ultimate security in God. Winnicott held to this paradox, lest the patient be left without grounds for hope. We may recall the question that animates Shelley's 'Ode to the West Wind' – 'If Winter comes, can Spring be far behind?' It seems Winnicott had enough of the right kind of imagination to turn hope towards the past in the name of the future, to render psychic truth retrospectively and retroactively. If we think of this as a kind of purgatorial hope against despair after Eliot; clinically, Winnicott also anticipated the work (for instance) of André Green (2001), Pierre Marty (1976), and César and Sára Botella (2005). He shared with these French analysts a basic concern with the non-represented experience of early trauma, the negative of the trauma, alongside an emphasis on the analyst's 'work of figurability' in amending and restoring the associative field.

Holding

Disaster takes place beyond the reach of memory, but also as a spatial phenomenon on the periphery of life. And yet while space takes precedence over the object in Winnicott; nevertheless, by emphasizing the 'potential' and 'transitional' nature of space, Winnicott demonstrated no less consistently than Freud the extent to which temporality renders spatial phenomena intelligible. The fact that space itself is conceived from a temporal perspective is evident, for instance, in Winnicott's account of the environment, holding, and the analytic setting. We have indicated that Winnicott introduced a new problematic of space into the discourse of social administration (see Chapter 1), which we discuss in more detail in the following chapter. In this section, we elaborate on the spatiotemporal phenomenon of holding as a form of intuitive management, a concept that Winnicott began using from the mid-1950s onwards. For Winnicott (1969: 259), a 'wide extension of "holding" allows this one term to describe all that a mother does in the physical care of her baby'. Thus holding allows for a rudimentary experience of interiority together with the sense of a permeable psychic skin. In other words, for Winnicott (1952: 99) holding involves the kind of care that allows the baby to feel at home in the world: 'The human being now developing an entity from the centre can become localized in the baby's body and so begin to create an external world at the same time as acquiring a limiting membrane and an inside'. In spite of the precariousness of things (both internally and externally), basic management of the kind Winnicott described in the case of holding constitutes the indwelling of ourselves.

Winnicott consistently rejected accounts of emotional development that start with the ego or the subject, in whatever rudimentary form this is supposed to take, and then posit relations to others and the world. Instead, Winnicott (1966: 6) described how the mother, at the very beginning of the infant's life, becomes preoccupied to the extent that 'she is the baby and baby is her'. For Winnicott, experience is possible only insofar as the infant has internalized this primary maternal setting as the basic framework of meaning; indeed, it is the breakdown of 'primary maternal preoccupation' that constitutes the failure of life. A failure which is evident in the subsequent fear of breakdown as a series of encrypted mnemonic impressions lodged in the shell rather than the core of being. The shell retains these impressions on the surface of experience, so to speak, while at the same time experience is flattened to nothing on the inside.

Didier Anzieu (1985: 214) elaborates on this disastrous situation from a topographical point of view: 'Encircled and sealed off by a permanent counter-cathexis, the pain of the traumatic breach subsists in the form of unconscious psychical suffering, localized and encysted at the periphery of the self.' Together with Bick's (1968) notion of a 'second skin' and Tustin's (1986) accounts of 'autistic barriers', Anzieu (1985: 196) adds to our understanding of the sorts of defensive formations that Winnicott identified, where the primal skin, or *le moi-peau*, is not sufficiently developed 'to fulfil its functions of establishing contacts, filtering exchanges and registering communications'.

The failure of life leaves the infant between times, in the parentheses of being, but also – as these topographical descriptions indicate – exposed to the unthinkable anxiety of a boundless, gaping hole *in place of* the world. Winnicott described a traumatized infant who has nowhere to turn, nor any sense at all of being oriented that might give some respite or relief. Where the ontological centre of gravity is dislocated due to environmental failure, the infant becomes a stranger even to himself and in his own mind. Thus, in Winnicott's account of inner fragmentation, being becomes a kind of boundless sensation for an infant that finds itself without a world. Patients in this situation complain of feeling disorientated in the most profound sense, they cannot place themselves. Winnicott (1962b: 58) described these feelings of falling apart and being psychically broken up alongside the loss of orientation and the lack of 'relationship to the body'.

Where things turn out for the worse, one is left feeling 'homeless at home' (John Clare qtd. in Bate 2003: 4); at the 'primitive edge of experience' (Ogden

1989); and continually exposed to the madness of being without dwelling. It may be that as adults we are never quite at home again, but to begin with the infant needs to come into his or her own skin in order to feel really and truly alive. The maternal frame is primarily corporeal, rooted in the *corps-à-corps* of maternity. Where this framework is in some way deficient, Winnicott demonstrated the extent to which the resultant anxieties of estrangement give rise to particular defence mechanisms, namely, disintegration, self-holding and depersonalization, the recourse to secondary narcissism, and autistic manoeuvres. In each case, the aspiration to persevere in being is thwarted; it is important to note, however, that Winnicott (1963a: 90) maintained psychotic illness is not a breakdown, but 'a defence organization relative to a primitive agony'.

Looked at from the perspective of therapeutic reclamation, the aim once again is not to treat the psychic phenomena of trauma on the model of psychiatric breakdown, but to manage illness as a sign of hope. Unlike Freud (1911b), who saw psychotic symptoms (delusions and hallucinations) as restitutive, Winnicott (1963a: 90) maintained that psychosis itself is a defence: 'What we see clinically is always a defence organization, even in the autism of childhood schizophrenia'. The idea that psychosis is a defence makes sense of the central paradox of early trauma, namely, 'that what is not yet experienced did nevertheless happen in the past' (1963a: 91). The strangeness of the world *as* world appears, precisely, where experience remains unthinkable as a defence against disaster.

There is an absolute loss in the wake of early trauma that can never be recouped. In this case, as we have seen, hope relies on what the imagination can make of the past as well as the future. This is not how Freud saw things, insofar as he continued to speak of repression in relation to psychosis. Generally speaking, for Freud (1905) infantile amnesia explains the element of oblivion on the order of forgetfulness, but without recourse to the destruction or absence of memory. Freud (1937: 260) continued to doubt whether any psychical structure could be subject to total destruction. Following the experiences of childhood, especially the sexual impulses of early experience, Freud (1905: 175) proposed that 'a store of memory-traces' remain 'withdrawn from conscious disposal'. There is no question, however, of 'any real abolition of the impressions of childhood'. The notion of withdrawal short of erasure accounts for infantile and hysterical amnesia alike, and for essentially the same reasons; indeed, infantile amnesia is considered a condition for subsequent repressions on account of 'the part played in sexuality by the infantile factor' (1905: 176).

For Freud, the unintelligible and fragmentary recollections of our earliest beginnings may yet return as more coherent memories. The history of the analytic endeavour, by which I mean the institution of psychoanalysis itself, is inextricably bound up with this presupposition. No doubt it complicates matters that Freud sometimes held it was possible that primal experiences might not actually have taken place. But this does not call into question the 'return of the repressed' (*Wiederkehr*) as a phenomenon of experience. Winnicott took things in a new direction. As with the memory-traces described by Freud, the encrypted mnemonic impressions characteristic of early trauma may also cohere subsequently as encountered experience. In this case, however, there has been a foreclosure at the origin rather than a withdrawal from consciousness. The traumatic situation calls for a thoroughgoing construction of the past on the model of renewed experience and the work of figuration. In Winnicott's account of disaster, the past is more than long lost (as we would say of a friend); it is frozen over, sealed, and blanked out *before* entering the field of conscious or unconscious memory. There is at bottom a black hole of psychotic depression for patients living in this situation, a deep blankness beyond the reach of memory. Analysis works at depth in these cases, as Wordsworth described with perfect accuracy in the 'Immortality Ode', with the 'Blank misgivings of a Creature / Moving about in worlds not realized' (ll. 146–7). Again, paradoxically, the work involves experiencing unthinkable experience.

Winnicott's account of traumatic impressions sealed off or dissociated in this way compares, to some extent, with Lacan's (1954; 1959) rendering of 'repudiation' (*Verwerfung*) as 'foreclosure' (*forclusion*). In this case, what imagination makes of memory depends on encapsulated impressions that are neither integrated into the patient's unconscious, nor subject to return on the order of the repressed. Lacan proposes the notion of *forclusion* as an elaboration of Freud's thinking on the specificity of psychotic defence. The way in which Lacan sets out the fundamental distinction between neurotic repression and the disavowal of reality (*Verleugnung*) helps to clarify matters. It is evident on this reading that the traumatic nature of the event causes an abolition or deep blankness in the psyche, a refusal to admit an intolerable, excruciating perception. Consistent with Winnicott's account of disaster, Lacan describes a situation in which it appears as if the event had never taken place.

It is not clear that Winnicott and Lacan would agree about what is being repudiated (*verworfen*) or disavowed (*verleugnet*). However, leaving that question aside, for Winnicott it is the dissociated encapsulation of original failure, rather than the return of the repressed, that provides a surface of emergence for reliving and the subsequent reclamation of experience. We question after intuition as we reach to make sense of all that is fallen and would otherwise disappear. To the extent that patients are able to make contact with this state of primal depression, they find themselves re-encountering experience for the first time in the present. Fundamentally dependent as his thinking is on the redress of imagination, Winnicott does not succumb to nihilism in the face of the unthinkable, any more than Eliot (1929: 255) does in his thought of hell after Dante – namely, as the 'torment' that 'issues from the very nature of the damned themselves'. Compelled as we are by primitive agonies, Winnicott confirms that our imagination is nonetheless subject to the creative imperative of life, that it proceeds inexorably toward non-forgetfulness as the essence of truth, even as Eliot's 'dry concrete, brown edged' pool is filled with 'water out of sunlight' and raised up 'out of heart of light' ('Burnt Norton', ll. 36–7).[26]

In his central recognition of creative living, Winnicott held to the work of the aftermath in line with the poet's urgent task of making poetry in the space between event and utterance. In contrast to the Kleinian development, Winnicott emphasized the reclamation of experience over the reparation of an already existing damaged object. He allowed without further argument that the closeness of intuition, the contact it affords us with being, cannot be substantiated outside of the reach for meaning itself as an original, pre-reflective gesture.

Once again, Winnicott modelled the estrangement that looms up amid the empty semblance of being after Eliot. First, and most important perhaps, Winnicott followed Eliot – as Eliot followed Pascal from his 1931 introduction to the *Pensées* through the meditation on time in 'Burnt Norton' – in keeping faith with hope not as a doctrinal precept so much as a lived experience. The use of faith in both cases renders hope as a form of experience. Second, as doubt and uncertainty for Eliot 'are merely a variety of belief' (1927: 15); similarly, Winnicott construed the relationship between disaster and hope in dialectical terms, so that hope proceeds from the place of disaster, well-being from the fragmentation and disintegration of being. Third, although they do not necessarily agree about the translation of guilt into the category of original sin, Winnicott shared Eliot's faith in a purgatorial process that bestows meaning even on the most unthinkable suffering or primitive agonies.

However, Winnicott did not share the view, attributed accurately by Harding (1963) to Eliot early and late, that we have only ourselves and our illusions to blame for the failure of experience. Disillusionment is not primarily a projection for Winnicott. Nevertheless, he goes to Eliot before going to Freud for the grounds of hope, which in Eliot (1929: 256; emphasis in the original) is afforded by the theology of Purgatory:

> The souls in [Dante's] purgatory suffer because they *wish to suffer*, for purgation. And observe that they suffer more actively and keenly, being souls preparing for blessedness, than Virgil suffers in eternal limbo. In their suffering is hope, in the anaesthesia of Virgil is hopelessness; that is the difference.

The sentiments expressed here temper the darker pronouncements one comes across in 'East Coker', where Eliot would have us 'wait without hope (l. 126).

Winnicott would have found nothing comparable in Freud to the form of experience that Eliot made available in traversing the 'waste land' towards the maturity of his late work. Eliot reads Dante against the finality of oblivion in the Virgilian underworld, against the fate of forgetfulness that, as Anchises informs his son, awaits the souls summoned to drink the waters of Lethe (*Aeneid* VI, 956–9). At the interface of the Latin *letum* ('death') and Greek *lethe* ('forgetfulness'), Eliot pits hope against Virgil's version of Plato's 'River of Indifference', turning Virgil's 'without memory' (*immemores*) into the transcendent truth of 'non-forgetfulness' (*aletheia*). The latter is the essence of truth in Eliot, where the 'wish to suffer', rather than simply being in pain or remaining oblivious forever, is the means by which the soul may be restored, for instance, in 'Little Gidding' – 'The only hope, or else despair / Lies in the choice of pyre or pyre / To be redeemed from fire to fire' (ll. 207–9). Compare Canto 26 of *Purgatorio*: 'Then, maybe giving place to one behind, / He vanished through flames now he had done, / As fish dive to the mud and leave us blind' (ll. 133–5).

Whether we can assume a Promethean element that places Eliot closer than he would have us believe to Blake, Shelley, and Yeats, is not entirely clear. But this much is certain: laying claim to the ground of necessity *contra* infantile illusion, Freud believed in nothing save a future without illusion; whereas Eliot, in keeping faith with the Pentecostal fire, would have us keep helplessness on this side of hopelessness. Winnicott made of this purgatorial process a calling back to life, a claim issued out of the failure of experience. No less an act of faith than Eliot's poetry, there is nonetheless another side to Winnicottian reclamation, wherein the intuition of transcendence is aimed at its vocation of therapeutic care. The psychoanalytic task, in the last instance, is not confined to the 'surface glittered out of heart of light' ('Burnt Norton', l. 39) on the model of Eliot's reconciliation of essence and existence.

For Winnicott, the figuration of hope is a therapeutic as well as a phenomenological phenomenon. His singular account of the fragmentation of being augments the therapeutic aspects of regression as part of the care of the self. He continued to privilege the developmental model of transformation over the uncovering of hidden thoughts on the classical Freudian model of disclosure. The therapeutic achievement of the former, as Lear (1992: 68) has persuasively argued, involves an emotional transformation: 'it is not just that a distinctly existing emotion can finally be understood; the understanding helps to constitute the emotion'. In this case, Winnicott applied the technique of reliving, understood as the equivalent of remembering, to the unthinkable experience of encapsulated or encrypted trauma. The transformation of unthinkable anxiety into renewed experience presupposes that the disaster 'has already been'. And the idea that a sense of what happened is manifest as a fear of breakdown appears as a source of hope, but also as a continuing rationale for psychoanalysis as a collaborative work of creativity between the patient and the analyst.

Notes

1 Laurence Spurling (2008), for instance, questions the meaning and usefulness of therapeutic regression as a clinical concept. In the course of his critical overview he identifies different ways in which the idea of regression is employed in the clinical situation: first, as a way of eliciting primitive modes of experience; second, as an indication of the value of non-interpretive intervention in analytic treatment; and, third, as a description of the active fostering of regression on the part of the analyst. Together with these clinical distinctions, the concept of regression may be differentiated theoretically in metapsychological terms: 'topographical regression' refers to a retracing of pathways that have already been established, namely, from thought to images, dreaming and hallucination; 'temporal regression' consists of a return to an earlier stage of development (fixation); and 'formal regression' indicates a backward move to a less developed psychic structure. The metapsychological discriminations are derived from Freud.

2 See Green (2012) for a discussion of Freud's 'Constructions in Analysis' (December 1937) as a technical postscript to 'Analysis Terminable and Interminable' (June 1937); Green concludes that Winnicott 'enriches' the questions of temporality explored by Freud.
3 See Balint's (1968) description of an 'area of basic fault' where the failure of life leaves the patient feeling hopeless. Green (1975: 291; emphasis in the original) clarifies things by differentiating between the classical concept of trauma in which something occurs (sexual seduction) and trauma as failure, that is, something '*which did not occur, owing to an absence of response on the part of the mother/object*'. The identification of traumatizing infant care as the main pathogenic factor in psychopathology is a basic assumption in a wide range of intersubjective approaches to psychoanalysis. Thus, viewed from an intersubjective perspective, the 'freezing' of original failure may be seen as a 'pathological accommodation' (Brandchaft *et al*. 2010) to the disturbance of life itself. As a regressive phenomenon, it amounts not to a fixation so much as the placing aside of life in a 'dead end' (Canguilhem 1966: 264).
4 See Canguilhem (1966: 137) for the distinction between 'norm' and 'average'. We may extrapolate from Canguilhem's notion of 'vital normativity' a definition of the environment as normal (or not) relative to a functional norm.
5 The link between 'trauma' and 'dissociation' has subsequently been developed by Bromberg (1979; 1995; 1998; 2006), Goldberg (1995), Howell (2005), Mitchell (1993), Slochower (1996; 2006), and Stern (1997) as an essential argument of relational psychoanalysis.
6 See Roussillon (2011) for a clinical elaboration of primary traumatic experience after Winnicott.
7 Compare the idea of negative pre-figuration with Green's (1966–7) concept of 'negative hallucination' and Roussillon's (2010) notion of 'negative illusion'. Notwithstanding LaFarge's (2012) attempt to re-read the form and function of 'screen memory' in terms of its traumatic origin, the work of the negative seems to me more suggestive of the dissociated state in the fear of breakdown. In my experience, it is not the case that disturbed, traumatized patients are able to make reliable use of screen memory either as an organization of unconscious contents or as a form of experience.
8 Supported by Botella's (2010) idea of '*la mémoire du ça*' ('the memory of the id'), Green (2012: 1239) describes the analytic task of 'construction' with reference to 'the traces of what has been forgotten ... prior to remembering'.
9 See Bollas (2012: 83–5) for the analyst as 'the object of faith' in the 'spiritual matrix' of psychoanalysis. Based on the incorporation of 'the structural relation to God' into the analytic process, Bollas defines the religious aspect of psychoanalysis in *atheistic* terms. Finite existence 'moves into the infinite', as Bollas puts it, in relation to the 'presence' of the analyst, who 'is not visible but who would seem to hear and see all'. The analytic encounter thus links truths of faith to intimations of presence as well as facilitating symbolization in relation to absence.
10 'And what rough beast, its hour come round at last, / Slouches towards Bethlehem to be born?' (W. B. Yeats, 'The second coming', 1921, ll. 21–2). See Nina Coltart (1986) for the canonical and unsurpassed psychoanalytical reading of the Yeats text.
11 For the narrative voice as the endless murmur of *le dehors* ('the outside'), see Blanchot (1993); by contrast, see Chapter 6 for acts of disclosure in therapeutic supervision, and Chapter 8 for the narrative dimension of regulatory action.
12 Symington and Winnicott share a common preoccupation with what we call the creative imperative; thus Symington's (2012a) 'creative principle', understood in relation to 'totality', is comparable to Winnicott's notion of 'primary creativity'.
13 In presenting the case for psychoanalytic ethics *contra* the traditional 'ratiocentric' conception of philosophical understanding, Cottingham (1998: 149) credits psychoanalysis with the idea of 'a systematic redemption, or reclamation of the past'.

14 In light of Marion's (1999) interpretation of Descartes, however, there is scope for exploring links between the ontology of disaster and the Cartesian *cogito*. Cottingham (1998) also invites a re-reading of Cartesian ethics with reference to the 'psychotherapy' of the passions.
15 Matthiessen (1947: 189) focuses on the different symbolic uses of fire in examining 'the texture of the poetry [Eliot] has developed through the structure' of the *Quartets*.
16 For a history of Leavis and the *Scrutiny* tradition of cultural criticism, see Hilliard (2012).
17 Parsons (2000: 10 *et passim*) addresses identity in similar terms as an inherent tension in the analytic vocation.
18 Cited in Rodman (2003: 289–91). See Hoffman (2004) for a critical exegesis of the poem in which she identifies more than two dozen scriptural illusions, particularly to the Gospels.
19 See Abram (2008) for a descriptive chronology of Winnicott's writings.
20 See Groarke (2003) for a further elaboration on the poem.
21 See also Cordelia's protestation in *King Lear* (4.4.24–5): 'O dear father! / It is thy business that I go about'.
22 To note the Hegelian thematic in this perspective on poetic language, 'figurability' in 'the work of psychic figurability' (Botella and Botella 2005) is a matter of *Darstellung* more than *Vorstellung*.
23 See Parts II and III for a critique of the coincidence of speech and identity in mourning and everyday life, respectively.
24 Ogden (2001: 219) identifies the stylistic importance of rhythm at the level of the Winnicottian sentence, while Milner (1977: 283) writes in positive terms about 'inner silence', which she links to 'the basic formlessness from which all form comes'. The same holds for Milner as for Winnicott: there is a rhythmic coexistence of psychosomatic sensations, a primordial wholeness of life, anterior to form. Similarly, Tustin (1985) drew on Winnicott, as well as Klein and Bion, for her phenomenological description of the 'rhythm of safety'. In contrast to the total emptiness (formlessness as chaos) that babies face as a result of the intrusive rhythms of catastrophic disillusionment; Tustin described a wordless, empathic sense of communion between mother and baby, a deeply felt experience of 'rhythmical, adaptive interaction'.
25 Following the Congress for French-speaking Psychoanalysis in 2007, Green (2012) comes back to the question of construction in Freud and, *contra* Viderman, Schafer, Spencer and others, concludes that Freudian metapsychology is not a narrative genre. My view is rather different and amounts to a more comprehensive definition of narrative, which informs my reading of Winnicottian reclamation.
26 See Gardner (1949: 48–51) for an instructive gloss on Eliot's 'shaft of sunlight'.

3

SOCIETY'S PERMANENT TASK

In her novel *The Children's Book*, A. S. Byatt (2009) narrates the diverse and complex ways in which the spiritual values and social ideals of a modern liberal family run aground on the eve of the Great War. All the main characters, none of whom turn out to be who they imagined they were, are affected to a greater or lesser extent by a sense of immaturity and moral failure that runs like a basic fault through the culture and threatens to fracture their lives. Although not the cause of their turmoil, the war finally exhausts the possibility of an inner life, which is already teetering between purposeful illusion and mere pretence at the end of an imagined Golden Age. Not everyone survives, and most of those who do are variously damaged. Preoccupied with the question of their personal and social identity, what choices did the characters have? What was available to this generation of late Victorians looking to secure the emotional ties or identifications of communal life? Alongside children's literature, art nouveau, the English pastoral, the Fabians and the suffragettes, Bloomsbury makes a few inroads into the margins of the novel. The Freudian interpretation, however, is not yet part of the deep structure or moral landscape of these lives; psychoanalysis appears here, not least of all in the reported antics of Otto Gross, as an idea rather than a resource.

The Freudian interpretation, having since worked its way into the fabric of the culture, articulates many of the preoccupations of Byatt's novel. We have inherited a complex attitude towards catastrophe from Freud, which extends to our feelings about war; indeed, war acts as a catalyst at various points in Freud's work. For instance, in the context of the Great War, Freud (1915b) sought to give death its due in the interests of truth, while at the same time emphasizing the conflict between civilization and our unconscious wishful impulses. Later, Freud (1933b) singled out the strengthening of intellectual life, on the one hand, and an internalization of the aggressive instinctual impulses, on the other, as the defining characteristics of the civilizing process. Most importantly, the sociological themes in *The Future of an Illusion* (1927) and *Civilization and Its Discontents* (1930) come to the fore in the context of war and, as such, prove decisive in the elaboration of Freud's notion of the death drive.

War and death, then, are interwoven repeatedly in Freud's thinking. In privileging the hypothesis of the death drive, however, psychoanalytical ideas about war have had a limited range. A preoccupation with the 'psychotic factors' affecting war and social violence oversimplifies matters. Nevertheless, there are ways of addressing war from a psychoanalytic perspective without necessarily lapsing into a psychological caricature of war as innate sadism. Winnicott's account of primitive emotional development provides an alternative way of thinking about war. We shall take his discussion of war aims, then, as the starting point in this chapter for a more detailed examination of the concept of social management and its relation to maturity. Here, as elsewhere, our argument is based on the distinction between maturity and necessity. Although an advance to maturity is implicit in the Freudian interpretation, the discipline of necessity (*Ananke*) explicitly underwrites the 'reality principle' in Freud's late works. The Freudian critique of culture, as we have seen, is aimed largely at the phenomena of consolation and renunciation, concerned to do away with illusion on both counts. By contrast, Winnicott formulated a psychoanalytic conception of culture grounded in maturity and creativity. The use of maturity as a criterion of social management is the main theme of the present chapter. We aim to demonstrate, first, that Winnicott revised the sociological thematic of the Freudian argument as a permanent task of social defence. Second, that he retained the destructive element in his account of the infant's psychic experience, while at the same time revising the Freudian conjunction of culture and civilization.

Revaluation of the value of war

Concentrating on military aims and objectives, Winnicott (1940) sought to identify the war effort in strategic terms, distinct from any moral justification. The basic distinction between strategic and non-strategic arguments, between political calculations and moral values, proved decisive for Winnicott. On the grounds that war is about fighting to win, he endorsed Churchill's decision at the time not to discuss war aims beyond the fact that 'we fight to exist' (1940: 210).[1] Although it does have moral implications, particularly with respect to how we perceive those we describe as 'the enemy', this is not a moral argument. Winnicott (1940: 210) claimed that he was not 'ashamed' in assuming a strategic attitude towards the war, namely, the idea of fighting to win: 'We are doing no very extraordinary thing to fight simply because we do not wish to be exterminated or enslaved'. This extends the vital normativity of the individual–environment set-up, the basic idea of life as activity, to a social frame of reference. In particular, victory in this sense is tantamount to saving one's own skin. The political argument is valuable for Winnicott, precisely because it is *not* a moral argument. If we fight as a matter of survival, as Winnicott (1940: 210) put it, 'we do not thereby claim to be better than our enemies'. Far from relying on ethical judgements of good and evil, the strategic argument is valuable only insofar as it comprises a negative good. As long as we fight to exist, we do not make any moral claims over and above the actions of our enemy; we do not 'assert that we have some quality that our enemies lack'

(1940: 210). The basic assumption is that everybody in a state of health fights to exist, and that we are no better or worse than anybody else in this respect.

The legitimacy of the strategic argument does not issue from a position of moral authority. But does it accord with the norms of moral conduct? Winnicott supplemented the negative good of the political argument with a positive good, allowing for the possibility that we do, indeed, 'stand for something valuable' over and above the tactical manoeuvre of 'fighting just to win'. The idea that there is more to survival than pugnacious combat raises the issue not only of what we stand for, but also of whether or not our standing for this or that presupposes a moral argument. Winnicott maintained that we stand for something that is valuable in standing for 'democracy' and 'freedom'. He counted these as moral values, things that matter, and considered the freedom of the individual as permanently valuable.

Winnicott's views about moral values are not inconsistent with his political argument as the sound basis for a discussion of war aims. Defending the idea of democracy as a moral good is not the same as presenting the defence of democracy as a good reason for war. Winnicott (1950b: 242) remained resolutely opposed to the idea of a 'just war' in the name of democracy: 'It would be possible to take a community and to impose on it the machinery that belongs to democracy, but this would not be to create a democracy'. The imposition of democratic freedom, which is clearly a contradiction in terms, is not something Winnicott tried to pass off as a positive good under the guise of a political argument. The principles of freedom and democracy, for which Winnicott believed the war was being fought, were not used to invest the war itself with a just meaning. Winnicott continued in the belief that war is unjustifiable. Further to which he argued for an absolute distinction between strategy and value. Thus, Winnicott (1940: 213; emphasis added) continued to subscribe to the idea of a strategic imperative, while claiming that we are in fact better than the enemy insofar as 'we aim at a more *mature* stage of emotional development than our enemies do'.

The distinction between strategic and non-strategic arguments underscores the use of maturity as an evaluative principle. The criterion of maturity proves decisive in allowing for an initial distinction between political aims and moral values. In particular, it permits the idea that, while we stand for things that have moral value and that matter, including the freedom of the individual and the concomitant sense of inner security, we do not necessarily stand for these things on moral grounds. This is an important distinction in the context of war. Standing for something that matters is not seen as inimical to the use of violence, but neither does it legitimate the use of violence on moral grounds. Indeed, further to the substantive question of what we stand for or what matters, Winnicott (1940: 213) made a case for war on psychological as well as political grounds: he argued that if 'we could show that the Nazis are behaving like adolescents or pre-adolescents, whereas we are behaving like adults, we should have a good case'.

Whether or not one agrees with the substance of Winnicott's claim, the criterion of maturity nonetheless presupposes a further distinction between psychological motives (conscious and unconscious) and moral values. Winnicott's discussion of war aims is not contradictory but complex, comprising a threefold distinction with respect to political calculations, psychological motives, and moral values. There is nothing comparable to this set of distinctions in Freud's (1930) critique of morality as the cause of torment and the related insistence on the discipline of necessity. For Winnicott, although we may stand for democracy and freedom as moral goods, the morality of these values is not the issue when it comes to understanding why we wage war. Psychologically speaking, it is consistent that we fight for our lives and behave like mature adults. This is not a moral justification of war, but a defence of oneself and society along political and psychological lines. Conversely, social defence is not essentially part of Winnicottian ethics so much as a supplementary argument.

Winnicott derived a complex notion of survival, then, not only from clinical practice but also from his reflections on war. Rather than making a case for the use of violence on moral grounds, he presented a coherent statement of war aims by combining the political argument with a psychological model of maturation. Far from offering a comfortable solution to the problem of violence, Winnicott credits the 'value of war' as well as its horrors; by which he means psychological value, not moral value. In particular, Winnicott (1940: 220) argued that fighting itself may be a condition of our maturity: 'On mutual respect between maturing men who have fought each other, a new period of peace could be reached, perhaps lasting another couple of decades, till a new generation grows up and again seeks to solve or obtain relief from its own problems in its own way.' This stance affords genuine grounds for hope, but not for a final end to war. The optimism is burdened with the claim that it is not for others to sacrifice themselves for our freedom.

There is no reason to believe that Winnicott revised these views in the light of subsequent historical events, views that certainly belie the image of a sentimental thinker. Predicated on the criterion of maturity, the argument Winnicott set out in 1940 makes an uncompromising case for war on strategic grounds, but also as a psychological *rite de passage*. The idea of war as unavoidable is coupled with the idea of individual freedom as permanently valuable. Winnicott (1940: 220) envisaged maturity as a psychological process, but also as an historical encounter along the lines of survival and security: 'Allocation of war guilt has no part in this scheme, since all share it, for peace spells impotence except it be won through fighting and the personal risk of death.' Winnicott reckoned on war as a natural phenomenon, something immanent to the life of society. The implication is that we enjoy freedom from war, just as we enjoy periods of stillness and quiet in general, only insofar as we have fought our way through to these states. Winnicott revised the Freudian ethic of reality-testing on the grounds that we do not get something for nothing. According to this view, there is no peace that comes about without a real fight – no maturity without defiance and the ruthlessness it presupposes.

The way in which Winnicott differentiates politics and morality has direct implications for the meaning of aggression and destructiveness in human nature. The contrast with the Freudian-Kleinian argument is immediately evident. Winnicott does not address the phenomenon of destructiveness by way of general pronouncements on war as a collective expression of individual psychopathology. He thereby avoids the superficial implications of psychological reductionism. The 'actual fighting' provides for a violent overthrow that remains indispensable for Winnicott, particularly with respect to the relationship between destructiveness and creativity. Destructive defiance leading to a capacity for concern delimits the essential process of maturation in Winnicott. This is how Winnicott (1964a: 109) described the experience of infancy and early childhood: 'There is a natural sequence of ruthless love, aggressive attack, guilt feeling, sense of concern, sadness, desire to mend and build and give.' Crucially, destructiveness is seen here as a concomitant of living and growing, a form of destructive aliveness, rather than an expression of the death drive.

More immediately, the criterion of maturity is used in the discussion of war aims as a way of linking political and psychological arguments: 'If we think we stand more than our enemies do for maturity of development, we have a strong claim to the world's sympathy, but we do not thereby avoid having to fight, or being willing to die if need be' (1940: 219). The aim is first and foremost to win the war. Moreover, 'sympathy' is not a moral claim, but is included here as a psychological corollary to the strategic proposition of military 'superiority' and 'satisfaction'. For Winnicott (1940: 220), '[w]e aim at reaching a saturation point when there is military satisfaction, and mutual respect between combatants'. As a revaluation of the value of war, Winnicott's argument lends weight neither to those who object on grounds of conscience to military service, nor to those who, for reasons of personal or political gain, encourage us to war. Winnicott (1940: 214), unlike either conscientious objectors or warmongers, proposed that '[w]e are trying to feel free as well as to be free, and to be willing to fight without being pugnacious, to be potential fighters interested in the arts of peace'.

The calculus of security

By the 'arts of peace' Winnicott means all those activities that comprise the 'social provision', activities through which maturity enters into the calculations of the state. Winnicott did not conflate war and politics, and there is no suggestion that the defence of society amounts to anything like an ongoing *coup d'état*. Rather, he identified the continuity between war and peace in accordance with 'society's permanent task', a task underwritten by the freedom of the individual as a combined expression of inner security and social maturity. For Winnicott (1940: 219), the underlying aim of security involves making 'a personal advance to maturity', and he claimed that it is only insofar as elements of the enemy are 'mature' that we can 'usefully give them the idea of freedom'. War is understood as a way out of our immaturity, in the aftermath of which we are faced with the task, first, of re-establishing our democratic way of life among ourselves, and second, of welcoming 'the mature elements in the enemy countries' (1940: 219).

On this reckoning, the 'difficult task' becomes a 'permanent task' through the obligation to maintain peace as maturity.

Some ten years after his discussion of war aims, Winnicott (1950b) set out his thoughts on democracy as a form of 'social maturity'. While his ideas about how to manage life remained essentially the same, there was nonetheless a different object of concern under conditions of peace. The disequilibrium in relations of maturity shifted from the field of military action to the administration of the social bond. By 1950 the focus was on 'antisocial groupings' within society rather than the immaturity of hostile nations or enemy forces. Although Winnicott applied the criterion of maturity to the problem of internal danger, it would be misleading to suggest that he viewed the exercise of government as a more or less covert form of continuous warfare. For Winnicott, as long as the moral values of democracy and freedom pertain, the administrative task is not decided by means of military superiority. Further to his innovations in clinical practice, Winnicott (1950b: 241) adopted a more subtle approach to the post-war problem of social management in attempting to work out what he described as 'the emotional development of society'.

The comparison with T. S. Eliot once again is instructive: we have seen the degree to which Winnicott found in Eliot a critical authority for his concern with the maturity of feeling. Furthermore, in his social criticism and later literary essays, Eliot reflected on the relevance of traditional spiritual values to the contemporary problems of mass democracy.[2] Similarly, Winnicott (1950b: 254) attempted to extend the meaning of 'primary creativity' to 'the mature democratic way of political life'. But the conjunction of creative and political activity is problematic, and we shall focus here on the tensions as well as the subtleties in Winnicott's argument.

Like Eliot, Winnicott attempted to reconcile spontaneous living and mature reflection at the individual level, but also at the level of culture and society. The technique of management is therefore available for the purposes of defence and social control; indeed, Winnicott equated immaturity with 'internal danger'. These arguments were presented in the context of the Cold War, and the problem was the same for individuals and society: how to make what comes about naturally consistent with the best that can be done. The solution that Winnicott came up with reveals *the* underlying tension in managed lives between freedom and regulation. For Eliot (1948), Christian ideals and spiritual values could be realized in a common culture nurtured by an educated minority. Eliot's social criticism is consistent with his critique of Romanticism as well as his post-conversion poetry. Unlike Eliot, Winnicott continued to conceive of hope as a Romantic ideal as well as a Christian figuration; nevertheless, he concurs with Eliot in assuming that democratic society 'has a quality that is allied to the quality of individual maturity which characterizes its healthy members' (1950b: 240). Winnicott and Eliot agree that while the achievement of health is good for society and the individual, it is no less 'favourable to culture'.

Eliot employed 'classicism' in some of his later criticism, as Menand (2007: 172) points out, as 'a name for the reaction against liberalism and its culture'. Winnicott's arguments tend to run along similar lines. In making the case for democracy and freedom in terms of degrees of maturity, Winnicott (1950b: 243–5) classified the population as follows: 'healthy individuals capable of social contribution ... individuals who show their lack of sense of society by developing an antisocial tendency ... individuals reacting to inner insecurity by identification with authority ... [and individuals who are in] an indeterminate position'. Used as a calculus of security, the classification of social maturity reveals the *political* investments inherent in moral sentiments and the religious life. Intimations of sedition are evident in the views of Winnicott and Eliot alike. But what is the nature of the offence? What, exactly, is at stake in these calculations? For Eliot (1948: 82), it is only 'in the conflict with heresy that orthodoxy is developed to meet the needs of the time'. Eliot (1934) levelled the rational order of criticism at religion-making, particularly in Thomas Hardy and D. H. Lawrence. Winnicott (1950b: 245), in what amounts to a similar claim along psychological and statistical lines, calculated the risk to society as the percentage of 'individuals who are maturing as individuals, and who are gradually becoming able to add a social sense to their well-grounded personal development'.

In contrast to Freud's 'sense of guilt', Winnicott postulated a 'social sense' based on the infant's capacity to feel concern for its mother. Winnicott (1963d: 73) understood concern as a sign of maturity, and described how the idea of 'concern is used to cover in a positive way a phenomenon that is covered in a negative way by the word "guilt"'. Looked at from the point of view of 'social maturity', the 'capacity for concern' has political as well as psychological implications. In particular, Winnicott (1950b) claimed that only in a society where there is sufficient emotional maturity in a sufficient proportion of individuals can the 'innate democratic tendency' be brought to fruition. It seems there is an onus on the few to safeguard the many: 'only a proportion of individuals in a small group will have had the luck to develop to maturity, and therefore it is only through them that the innate (inherited) tendency of the group towards social maturity can be implemented' (1950b: 243*n*3). Eliot (1948: 108) came to a similar conclusion, namely, that 'we can will the means which are favourable to culture'. This represents a coherent revision of his earlier poetics along the lines of monarchy and Catholicism as set out, for instance, in *The Sacred Wood* and his essays from the early 1920s on seventeenth-century poetry.

Winnicott, however, took the argument further in the direction of governmental thinking by introducing a calculation of maturity. If, as Winnicott (1950b: 243) argued, the 'whole democratic burden' falls on the mature minority, then it is important to know, first, 'what proportion of mature individuals is necessary if there is to be an innate democratic tendency', and second, 'what proportion of antisocial individuals a society can contain without submergence of the innate tendency towards democracy'. Along with degrees of maturity, being reasonably well informed about the numbers of antisocial, if not disaffected individuals is an essential part of the arts of peace. This seems to me at odds with Winnicott's therapeutic concerns. Rather than a focus on the moral contours of inner security, the argument shifts to a measurement of social maturity. Winnicott worked out the calculation for 1950s Britain on the basic assumption that the number of mature individuals is probably 'quite small'; the more consequential point, however, is that management is coupled with calculations of risk.

The calculus of security translates the criterion of maturity into a risk assessment, the political implications of which are by no means confined to the clinic or the immediate post-war period. Indeed, our central argument with regards to the management of oneself is based on the extension of the permanent task through the reflexive norm to the regulated life (see Parts II and III for the supervised and regulated life, respectively). For his part, Winnicott (1950b) defined antisocial behaviour as a type of 'social immaturity' and, at the same time, linked the 'antisocial tendency' to the 'antidemocratic tendency'. The comparison with Eliot remains essential: for Eliot (1948), the community of belief is grounded in a common Anglo-Catholic culture, a constitutional monarchy, and a traditional way of life; whereas the community of feeling assumes a psychological form in Winnicott. Nevertheless, they share a common preoccupation with the social problem of maturity, a preoccupation that reveals a fundamental tension between the achievements of culture and the defence of society, between freedom and security. In Winnicott's estimation, a good outcome for society 'all depends' on the contribution of healthy and mature individuals, which means that encouraging or cultivating emotional development becomes a priority. For Winnicott, as for Eliot, society has to defend itself against the threat posed by the twin spectres of social immaturity, namely, futility and disorder. Further to Eliot's (1964: 157) response to the 'destructibility of everything', Winnicott extrapolated an historical definition of the permanent task from a clinical understanding of meaninglessness and disorientation leavened, in the late works, by a notion of destructiveness as a concomitant of living and growing.

How does society manage this task? The question brings us to the family as the *locus* of tension in the Winnicottian conception of security. Winnicott did not broach the issue of equality of opportunity or egalitarian access, nor is there any mention of social class in his essay on democracy. The social bond takes precedence over social structure and systemic contradictions. Alongside the management of antisocial groupings, the defence of society is defined in terms of the upbringing of the healthy minority. Anything that derives from the individual's relationship to the environment, that nourishes and enables the individual to flourish, including the original cathexis of the 'environment mother', is counted as an object of government. The basic discrimination between antisocial elements and the healthy minority is derived from the family as the underlying object of concern and intervention. Winnicott's (1950b: 258) main conclusion is that the 'innate democratic factor in a community derives from the workings of the ordinary good home'. The psychological distinction between 'immature identification with society' and 'individuals capable of social contribution' stems from a central preoccupation with the mother and the home. It is easy to see how this argument could be used to blame parents, especially mothers, for the behavioural problems and disruptive behaviour of their children, and to target socially and economically disadvantaged working-class families as part of a strategy of normalization.

In sum, social maturity is defined as a governmental problem on two counts, with respect to disruptive elements and the population as a whole. First, the environment emerges as a definite object of management in the case of 'individuals who show their lack of sense of society by developing an antisocial tendency' (1950b: 243–4). Second, if things are to work out for the best, there must be adroitness in managing the link between the healthy family and the good society. Tact is an essential aspect of Winnicott's image of government. The good social worker, for instance, is the tactful social worker insofar as he or she recognizes 'that at any one time we can do nothing to increase the quantity of [the] innate democratic factor comparable in importance to what has already been done (or not done) by the parents and homes of these individuals when they were infants and children and adolescents' (1950b: 246). Winnicott allowed that 'ordinary good parents do need help', including good medical treatment, instruction in childcare, and access to social services and psychiatric support. But he insisted that in asking for and receiving help, parents should not have their parental responsibilities taken away from them. Only that which enables us to help ourselves is counted as worth having, just as the sacrifice of others will not do when it comes to our freedom. Managing ourselves remains *the* mark of maturity in times of war and peace alike. As regards the kind of professional help and support he envisaged, Winnicott (1950b: 259) himself clearly came down in favour of freedom over regulation and supervision, advocating the 'avoidance of interference with the ordinary good home'. But of course the problematic of social maturity is open to other uses.

The antisocial imagination

Winnicott conceived of 'the difficult task' of war and 'the permanent task' of peace as comparable activities of government. This was exemplified, for instance, in his work with evacuated children; in the advice he offered to parents in his wartime radio broadcasts; and, subsequently, in his therapeutic approach to the care of young people in need. Children and families are what mattered most to Winnicott in these various concerns, and public recognition of the value of his work is evident in the fact that, alongside John Bowlby, Susan Isaacs and Clare Britton, he was called on to give evidence before the Curtis Committee. The Committee was convened to advise the post-war Labour government on legislation for the provision of a comprehensive service for the care of children deprived of the benefits of normal family life. A strategic alliance between psychoanalysis and social welfare was inherent in the 1948 Children Act, an alliance that remained available in support of a diverse range of post-war initiatives in social policy across the political spectrum.

We have seen that, as with early trauma, Winnicott defined deprivation in terms of a break in the continuity of being; in the case of deprivation, however, the break is identified at the level of 'relative' rather than 'absolute' dependence. This accounts for a shift of emphasis, on clinical grounds, from the primary maternal setting to family life, the household, and the wider community; and, second, from management of the regressed situation to the institutional containment of 'difficult children' and behavioural problems. In the case of deprivation, then, Winnicott focused on 'the wholesale break-up of family life' (1963b: 104); and, in terms of making amends for the 'loss of family life' (1950a), he emphasized the wider picture: how to contain the disaffected, antisocial elements in society. Managing hope and the defence of society were seen as two sides of the same problem, which resulted in an acknowledgement of unconscious communication combined with new techniques of rehabilitation, as distinct from more punitive measures of social control.

As well as a therapeutic strategy, managed hope emerged as a particular historical form of experience in post-war Britain. For example, the 1944 governmental report on special hostels for 'difficult children' highlights the significance of wartime experience for future developments in state provision and environmental health. Winnicott (1956b: 123; emphasis in the original) made a decisive contribution to these developments with the idea that the 'antisocial tendency is characterized by an *element in it which compels the environment to be important*'. The child is seen as inextricably linked to the environment *rather than* his actions; beyond an expression of hope, which is seen as crucial, the act itself is judged inessential. Deficiency invariably takes precedence over culpability in Winnicottian space; and, as the other side of therapeutic reclamation, rehabilitation is set out as a strategic alternative to coercive legislation and moral pedagogy. Winnicott was not particularly interested in the link between the law and the antisocial act. Instead, he proposed a schema of administrative valuation in which government arises out of the corruptibility of the environment itself. There is no question that 'difficult children' are out of control and in need of containment. Winnicott argued, however, that the child's behaviour neither merits nor deserves blame. More than a fatuous plea for leniency, Winnicott advanced the notion of managed hope as a form of social inclusion. As such, the administration of deprivation lies beyond the juridical formation of juvenile justice; but it also tests the limits of psychoanalysis and its clinical resources.

What does it mean to constitute hope as a form social inclusion? And why is it considered the most appropriate form of treatment for the antisocial elements or groups in society? Some thirty or forty years before it became a slogan for New Labour, the category of 'social inclusion' was implicit in Winnicott's argument for social management. He proposed a therapeutic–managerial strategy for the treatment of deprived children on two grounds. First, he argued that the deprived child (unlike the psychotic patient) is sufficiently mature to perceive that '*the cause of the disaster lies in an environmental failure*' (1956b: 129; emphasis in the original). Second, he came to the conclusion that the stability of environmental provision, rather than psychoanalysis, delimits the form and function of care for these children. In which case, the provision of child care links the reliability of the environment to the continuity of management at the level of social and personal life: 'what these children need is *environmental stability*, *personal* management, and *continuity* of management' (1948: 74; emphasis in the original). The therapeutic–managerial strategy is a defensive manoeuvre on two counts: the task of government consists in the alignment of reliability and continuity as conditions of inner security, but also as prerequisites of social and moral order.

The technique of 'cure by environmental provision' (1956b: 129) was not confined to the immediate circumstances of the war. The treatment of antisocial children provides an opportunity for the generalization of this particular practice of institutional management. Thus, based on his experience of evacuation, Winnicott went on to recommend the strategy of environmental provision for children in peacetime. He singled out two categories of deprivation for special attention: on the one hand, 'children whose homes do not exist or whose parents cannot form a stable background in which a child can develop' (1948: 74); and, on the other hand, 'children with an existing home which, nevertheless, contains a mentally ill parent' (1948: 74). The generalization of hope as a strategy of social inclusion proceeds from the category of deprivation itself. The antisocial tendency is not a diagnosis so much as a general descriptive term, which applies equally to normal and pathological populations. Indeed, the Winnicottian category of deprivation has an administrative scope such that managing the problem applies not only to normal children, but also to the parents, the households, and the communities of deprived children: 'When we are able to help parents to help their children we do in fact help them about themselves' (1956b: 122). The practice of child psychotherapy proceeds from this basic assumption.

Given that the generalization of social management is a function of its categories of concern, what does Winnicott mean by 'help'? He continued to present the problem of management in terms of hope. Managed hope is understood as the essential task in cases of deprivation and privation alike, where the work of mourning is invariably replaced by techniques of management. We have seen how regression to dependence in the analysis of early trauma is predicated on the latent hope of encapsulated memory. Similarly, in the case of antisocial children management goes beyond conventional analytic treatment; but in this case the problem of management focuses on the *manifest* moment of hope: first, '[*t*]*he antisocial tendency implies hope*' (1956b: 123; emphasis in the original); and second, 'the treatment of the antisocial tendency is not psychoanalysis but management, a going to meet and match the moment of hope' (1956b: 123–4).

We have seen that in the case of early trauma it is the unconscious that upholds the therapeutic work of reclamation; the same applies in the case of antisocial behaviour: it is the 'unconscious communication' of the child which 'compels someone to attend to management' (1956b: 123). To this extent, the social management of manifest hope presupposes an entirely new way of thinking about society. The problem of order becomes inseparable from what is expected of a mature individual. Winnicott was clearly not alone in making this connection (as our comparison with Eliot demonstrates); nonetheless, his work was instrumental in articulating both the utopian and the technological aspects of the problem of order. Our sense of maturity stands at the intersection of the art of living and proper conduct, and may be understood therefore as both a personal expression of who we are and a representation of our social identity. In light of these two distinct but related meanings, antisocial behaviour gives rise to a new question in the discourse of social governance: What is the best way to manage hope? The question takes us beyond the juridical model of disobedience as well as the admonitory tone of moral pedagogy. The conduct of life is invariably in question for Winnicott. He did not envisage conduct, however, in terms of the rectitude of morality or the censoriousness of the law; but rather, believed that individuals are always worth more than their actions.

As with intuitive and therapeutic management, Winnicott's theory of social management is inextricably linked to the idea of potentiality. The most important thing for Winnicott (1963b: 103–5) was not to 'waste' the hope expressed in otherwise intolerable and disruptive behaviour. He found legalism and moralizing equally wanting on these grounds. In Winnicott's view the law cannot be relied upon to stand up long-term to the moment of hope; repressive measures may satisfy the short-term needs of society in the policing of antisocial elements, but this clearly fails to address the underlying question of environmental provision. Control society was not seen as the answer. Nor is moral counsel reckoned to fair any better, insofar as 'moral educators' stand on 'the wrong side' of a fundamental division that separates the deprived child from the good object. Managed hope is presented as a counterpart to juridical and moral rationalities of government and, as in the case of early trauma, is arranged along temporal as well as spatial lines. The focus on time in the case of deprivation encompasses a break in continuity alongside the moment of hope. The former produces a gap; the latter, an act that promises to reconnect the child with his unconscious awareness of what is missing. For Winnicott, to manage the manifest hope of antisocial behaviour is to manage the moment when the child reaches across the gap that, under adverse environmental conditions, has opened up in the continuity of being.

As far as the gap itself is concerned, Winnicott (1963b: 104) argued that the child actually experiences 'a break in the continuity of the environmental provision'; there is an awareness of what is missing, albeit in the form of 'a painful confusional clinical state'. Unlike the original calamity of environmental failure, which is considered inimical to the very continuity of psychic life, Winnicott described a child for whom the experience of having been dispossessed causes a certain degree of emotional upheaval. The disturbance or disruption in this case is not seen as devastating, insofar as a good relationship with the mother is somewhere in the child's mind. The deprived child is not deprived of a basic framework for living. Rather, Winnicott described a break that takes place at a certain level of maturity, where the world itself is already in place, being has been realized as dwelling, and the child has some sense of himself inside his own body.

Antisocial behaviour, then, is seen as indicative of an interruption in the experience of original possession, including the sense of pre-natal possession. The deprived child is not necessarily freighted with a 'dead mother' (Green 1983); instead, for Winnicott (1962a: 71) emotional development is brought to a standstill ('held up') on account of a break in 'the continuity of the child's object relationships'. The discontinuity does not amount to a fundamental dissociation, but constitutes a blockage in an already constituted world; an exclusion or retreat *within* the formation of dwelling. There is no movement in or through discontinuity itself, only a feeling of being stuck between 'something good', on the one hand, and the hope that is 'locked up' in the antisocial act, on the other. The link to the maternal frame is not altogether broken, but remains confused in the child's mind. Winnicott described children in this situation who find themselves caught in a moral quandary, but also suffering from painful and confused states of mind. Of course, there is no guarantee that the child's unconscious communication will be recognized and understood, which accounts for the tragic element that pervades Winnicott's reflections on the conduct of life, where the maturity of character appears as an emotional as well as a moral phenomenon routinely assailed and perplexed by disappointment and further endangered by failure.

How are deprived children supposed to find their way out of the muddle? How might they reclaim their place in the world? In this case, hope is no longer seen as a question of renewed experience ('reliving') on the model of regression to dependence; nor is moral education seen as adequate to the task of accommodating the moment of hope. The antisocial state of mind is understood rather as a search for a lost 'good relationship with mother'. Notwithstanding the inevitable setbacks, Winnicott (1963b: 103–4) cast this searching for mother in a hopeful light: 'a manifestation of the antisocial tendency in a child means that there has developed in the child some hopefulness, hope that a way may be found across a gap'. For Winnicott, the moment of hope represents neither a reliving of the cleavage at the origin, nor a work of mourning on the Freudian model of working-through. With respect to the latter, the child's 'capacity to keep alive a memory' is still in question (1956b: 124). Here, as elsewhere, the deprived are not counted among the bereaved. An entire historical evaluation of the inner life turns on this distinction: instead of either regression or remembrance, Winnicott described how the child turns back in the hope of rediscovering the good that has been lost. Between the interruption of well-being and the moment of hope, deprivation itself becomes an event in the child's psychological imagination along the related axes of object-seeking and destruction.

Let us consider these two formations of hope in turn. Winnicott (1956b: 125) depicted a child engaged in an unconscious search for the mother's body: 'looking for something, somewhere, and failing to find it [the child] seeks it elsewhere, when hopeful'. Attempting to reach back in this way over the gap in the maternal frame, Winnicott explained how the child resorts to theft and general deceitfulness. Stealing and lying do not give rise to feelings of guilt (nor would it help to treat the deprived as guilty), precisely because the child is searching for something more than this or that object: 'The child who steals an object is not looking for *the object stolen but seeks the mother over whom he or she has rights*' (1956b: 125; emphasis in the original). Stealing is the equivalent of remembering in the child's search for lost things.

Winnicott differentiates the antisocial state of mind manifest in the moment of hope from the 'organized antisocial defence' of delinquency proper. In attempting to reach across the gap that separates him from his good object, the child does not express a delinquent intent so much as a right to what he needs. In this respect, at least, Winnicott's concept of antisocial action is essentially different from Bowlby's notion of delinquent character. Winnicott addressed the plight of homeless and deprived children from the point of view of social provision, but also in terms of the imaginative life of the antisocial mind. To reclaim the world is at once a reaction to deprivation and an affirmation of primary creativity. In the case of deprived children, Winnicott's account of object-seeking presupposes an underlying creative imperative, if not an imagination educated into virtue by the real. For Winnicott, listening to one's conscience presupposes a spontaneous gesture that enlivens the imagination, which applies even when stealing is all that the child can come up with for the moment.

More than the object stolen, Winnicott proposed that the antisocial child is engaged in a search for his or her sense of self. The child is not looking for the lost object, according to Winnicott (1956b: 125), so much as the wherewithal by means of which objects may yet be found: 'the child is seeking that amount of environmental stability which will stand the strain resulting from impulsive behaviour'. More fundamental than object-seeking, this state of mind is closer to the anxieties of survival pertaining to the original failure of experience. Something essential is at issue for the child, where the real is at stake as a condition of object-relations. In short, the child is trying to find its capacity to find things. The antisocial child thus 'provokes total environmental reactions, as if seeking an ever-widening frame, a circle which has as its first example the mother's arms or the mother's body' (1956b: 125).

At its most fundamental, the antisocial imagination turns on this articulation of sense and incarnation, and is primarily concerned with the problem of the maternal frame. It comprises a reclamation life along two lines, including, a search for the lost good object, and an expression of the want to be. On both counts, the child attempts to claim back his natural right to a place in the world, and there is enough here to warrant a return rather than an imagined restoration. The fate of the deprived child is seen as less disastrous than that of the psychotic patient. Instead of the unthinkable experience of disaster, the manifestation of hope is coupled with the recollection of failure. The child retains the knowledge that at some point in his life something went wrong. The experience of being comes back to someone who experienced the world in the first place. But while the moment of hope contains the thought that the world *has been* a good place; at the same time, a break in the continuity of environmental provision at this level, means that the child is not yet in a position to mourn the lost object, nor all the good with which it is associated in his memory. Winnicott described how the deprived child is unable to keep alive the sense of maternal presence when the mother is actually not there. We might say that the imagination is deprived of spectres, even as loss fails to become an object of mourning.

If the work of mourning is not available, and regression to dependence is considered inappropriate, then how do 'good things' come back? For Winnicott, the return of the good object together with a reanimated sense of self is predicated on the technique of managed hope. The argument is that so long as the child perceives environmental failure as the root of his troubles, it is therefore necessary to provide forms of institutional care the reliability of which may be 'rediscovered by the child'. Winnicott (1956b: 130) recommended the provision of residential management rather than psychoanalysis as the best way of handling the moment of hope: he argued that this is the most effective way of allowing the deprived child 'to experience despair in a relationship'. While the argument is clearly informed by his experience of the evacuation hostels during World War II, he was nonetheless keen 'to relate such problems as were specifically related to the war situation to the corresponding problems of peacetime experience' (Winnicott and Britton 1947: 54).

The hostel was presented as a 'substitute home' that makes good things available for the child, including, 'a building, food, clothing, human love and understanding; a timetable, schooling; apparatus and ideas leading to rich play and constructive work' (Winnicott and Britton 1947: 70). In the case of deprived children, at least, social management was seen primarily as a way of providing an institutional alternative to inadequate family homes. The essential presupposition here is that the 'substitute home' has to stand up to the test of the child's destructiveness; for Winnicott, this requires reliability as the basis of trust.

Consider Winnicott's description of the typical pattern following the placement of a child in a hostel that is considered adequate to the task of management. He described how the child initially is well-behaved and idealizes the setting and the staff. This is seen as a short-lived, honeymoon period when the real sense of 'goodness' is yet to come. The child quickly becomes disillusioned with his ideal placement and begins to test whether the environment can withstand his destructiveness. In describing the way in which the child takes it out on the world, Winnicott included both physical and emotional acts of aggression directed towards the building, the staff, and other children. These destructive attacks are understood as unconscious manifestations of hope. And Winnicott argued that if this antisocial behaviour is physically and emotionally managed, then the child 'settles down with a sigh of relief, and joins in the life of the group as an ordinary member' (Winnicott and Britton 1947: 71). Faced with the consequences of their own destructiveness, children are able to re-experience the goodness of good things in a stable and reliable environment. The hostel enables the child to 'experience despair in a relationship', according to Winnicott (1956b: 130), as a condition of ongoing emotional development.

But while the hostel exemplifies the kind of institutional setting in which hope becomes a valid technique for secure management, the technique itself was not confined to the evacuation hostels but recommended as a type of residential care for categories of deprived children in peacetime. Winnicott (1948: 77) consolidated the administrative value of his therapeutic argument in concluding that 'wartime provision' offered a solution to 'the peacetime problem of management of the early antisocial case'. Management is seen to invigorate the deprived child even as it fortifies the spirit against deeper desolations of experience. From the latent hope of primary intuition in traumatic situations to the manifest hope of the antisocial imagination, Winnicott described a world without ghosts, or at least, a world where the exigency of return is more disastrous than haunting. Psychoanalysis meets this disaster only halfway, leaving a decisive opening between being and well-being where the permanent task of government finds its footing.

Leave-taking

Winnicott's view of the managed life was complex and conflicted; he belonged to a generation for whom the link between inner security and the social order was consolidated under conditions of post-war uncertainty. In managing the antisocial tendency as a combined problem of psychological confusion and social danger, Winnicott's efforts were directed explicitly at a better emotional world. But although the criterion of maturity underwrites the claim that society must be continuously and permanently defended, the administration of life was not Winnicott's main concern. He was not in any thoroughgoing or lasting sense a political thinker. Psychology runs deeper than politics in his thought and, in the last instance, he represented no one but himself. He neither cultivated nor achieved a faithful following comparable to other luminaries in the British Psycho-Analytical Society and other schools. Comparable to Eliot's (1928: 27) type of ideal critic, Winnicott was 'simply and solely himself'. That there are no Winnicottian acolytes is consistent with the fact that, at its most incisive, the use of maturity as an evaluative principle proceeds from the freedom that characterizes Winnicott's own thought.

The tensions and inconsistencies in the argument notwithstanding, Winnicott's independence of mind is evident in his trenchant revaluation of the value of war coupled with an affirmation of the freedom of the individual. An emphasis on 'the acquisition of freedom of thought' (Widlöcher 2012) goes hand in hand with a comprehensive and coherent statement on security and the defence of society. Unlike Freud, however, Winnicott did not articulate freedom and security from the standpoint of paternal authority; he did not follow Freud's line of thought on authority as the crucible for identification with society. Instead, Winnicott (1950b: 252) pointed to a fear of women at the centre of emotional life, which he saw as 'related to the fact that in the early history of every individual who develops well, and who is sane, and who has been able to find himself, there is a debt to a woman'. The fear of women is seen as symptomatic of this debt, an indebtedness that confirms the irreducible significance of the maternal frame as a profoundly important addition to classical Freudian theory.[3]

Winnicott (1957) elaborated on devotion and debt as the basis of maturity in the postscript to his first published collection of radio talks in the 1950s. The debt that becomes manifest as a fear of women is owed to the mother, on whose devotion the infant is absolutely dependent at the beginning. The infant is seen as 'doubly dependent' to the extent that, as Winnicott (1950b: 252) put it, he remains 'totally unaware of dependence'. Winnicott (1957: 125) maintained that 'every man or woman who is sane, every man or woman who has the feeling of being a person in the world, and for whom the world means something, every happy person, is in infinite debt to a woman'. In its infinitude, the debt is understood to go back as far as the mother's devotion to her baby before it comes into the world. These are extreme claims, the idea that the mother is absolutely responsible for the baby before she 'knows' who it is, and the complementary assumption that the debt one goes on to accept without reserve exists before one is born, and certainly before any awareness of the debt.

For Winnicott, acceptance goes deeper than resolution and, as such, reveals an inscrutable dimension in human experience. This presupposes a level of self-experience that extends from devotion and the mother's desire to the mature acceptance of dependency, something that ultimately cannot be searched into or communicated.[4] Moreover, maturity is described in such a way that self-sufficiency, the primary illusion of narcissism, is obviously not enough to ensure happiness in social life. That our happiness depends on what comes from the outside (*le dehors*) applies both ways in the earliest relationship. On one hand, the mother does not wait for reciprocity but is simply devoted to her baby. The mother–infant relationship is essentially an asymmetrical relation in which the mother feels herself bound to respond *before* the mutual recognition of attachment. Maternity is a subject position in which the mother, so to speak, is ordained before she becomes attuned. On the other hand, the fear of women manifests as a result of not knowing how to assume the debt in its infinite and absolute dimensions, the debt goes 'unrecognized precisely because it is immense'. The paradox of maturity itself is inscribed in what Ricoeur (2005) calls 'the course of recognition': acceptance precedes recognition as devotion and debt. At the same time, Winnicott (1957: 125) maintains that growth is possible only where there is 'a true recognition of the mother's part' and, moreover, where society itself makes a 'full acknowledgement of absolute dependence'.

There is an irreducible tension in Winnicott's argument between acceptance and recognition. In a singular thought that confirms the exigency of the real as the framework of human experience, Winnicott (1957) argued that recognition does not take the form of gratitude or thanksgiving. Instead, he proposed that the mature response to devotion is to accept the fact of dependence. For Winnicott, the mother-baby couple is present from the beginning as the inviolable figure of the life-world where, at the interface of devotion and acceptance, ruthless love becomes love and being becomes well-being. Nothing can stand in for acceptance, be it in the form of maternal devotion or the infinite debt. Care is incumbent on the mother exclusively, even as one's indebtedness cannot under any circumstances or in any way become someone else's responsibility.

The earliest relationship between mother and baby provides the model for this account of human happiness, where love is seen as part of the intuitive fabric of the psyche. But what role do fathers play? The question relates directly to the permanent task. Winnicott identified the paternal function with social management: how to manage the fantasy of violent overthrow and defiant conduct without reducing things to a juridical model of paternal authority. That society must be defended is not in question. But instead of recourse to the law, Winnicott assigned fathers the role of meeting the child's need for a constant and stable ('indestructible') framework by safeguarding the mother. The paternal function is set out at the intersection of security and need. Together with the mother's devotion and the child's growing acceptance of dependence, the criterion of maturity sanctions the father as 'the protecting agent who frees the mother to devote herself to her baby' (1950b: 248). The father is called upon to protect the mother from 'everyone and everything that gets between her baby and herself' (1957: 127).

Winnicott described how the process of maturity begins in the home and extends to a widening field of social interaction and responsibility. In this case the father embodies the task of protection as a 'collective task', shielding the nursing couple from danger and guaranteeing it against interference or impingement, even as he defends society as a whole. His task is our task, insofar as we are committed to the freedom of the individual in conjunction with the moral welfare of society. Winnicott (1960b: 93) came to the fundamental conclusion that maturity is possible only where 'the family has provided the bridge leading out of parental care (or maternal care) right across into the social provision'. The permanent task is open to several meanings. For Winnicott, it comes down to meeting the individual's needs, by which he meant: the libidinal and emotional satisfaction of need; the acknowledgement of the child as an individual with a creative contribution of its own; the acceptance of defiant destruction; and the management of routine regression to dependence. Note that satisfaction alone is not enough, but can result in a feeling of being 'fobbed off' (1945: 154n1) if it is not coupled with recognition and an opportunity for the expression of primitive as well as imaginative love. It is the emphasis on management as an irreducible combination of satisfaction, recognition, and tolerance that proves decisive for the Winnicottian definition of maturity.

The Freudian model of psychosexual development does not cover all of what Winnicott meant by the satisfaction of need, nor does satisfaction exhaust Winnicott's description of managed lives. During the final phase of his work in the late 1960s, Winnicott (1968c: 240) linked the 'parental task' and 'society's task' not only in terms of permanence, but more specifically, with respect to the 'survival' of the object, including 'the quality of non-retaliation, that is, a containment of what the individual adolescent brings without becoming provoked even under provocation'. Parents thus provide an opportunity for dependence (starting with the infant's absolute dependence on the mother's body), but also for the older child's need to break away from and return to the family. It is the possibility of regaining the relationship with the actual parents, according to Winnicott (1960b: 91), that renders the inevitable unconscious destruction involved in breaking away from the home a condition of maturity rather than 'a disruption of the individual's personality'.

This is not primarily an argument about the symbolic representation of internal objects, but concerns the part the parents play in the actual experience of the child. Winnicott (1960b: 91) insisted that management allows for 'the individual's ability actually to get back to the parents and to the mother, back to the centre or back to the beginning, at any appropriate moment'. The parents need to be there in order for the child to leave, a leave-taking that comes to nothing short of failure in their physical and emotional absence. At the same time, Winnicott effectively restated the self-evident truth that one cannot return to a place one has not left. He made this last point on two counts: first, we are able to return only as long as the inevitable ambivalence and destructiveness of our leave-taking has been tolerated and survived without retaliation. Leaving tests the limits of survivability. Second, we return dependent and acceptant to the contested ground of our primordial dissociations and disaffections. The allusion to Eliot is clear enough, but the thought is quintessentially Winnicottian. That we return by way of our original need to defiantly leave, and thereby discover for the first time that which was the beginning, is yet one more paradox Winnicott has left us to consider, a paradox that lies at the heart of what he meant by maturity.

Notes

1 It is interesting to note that Eliot, in his 'A Note on War Poetry' in *London Calling* from 1942, emphasized the strategic nature of war as a 'situation' rather than a 'life': 'One which may neither be ignored nor accepted, / A problem to be met with ambush and stratagem' (ll. 18–19).
2 Menand (2007: 152–63) provides a useful gloss on the 'turn' in Eliot's thinking, with respect to the notion of culture. He addresses the basic shift in Eliot's habit of mind after the early 1920s; drawing on the arguments of Raymond Williams, Menand differentiates culture as a criterion of literary value, on the one hand, from the use of culture in defence of society, on the other.
3 It would be a mistake to dismiss Winnicott's account of family life and the role of women as simply reactionary and outdated. Alongside ongoing clinical and governmental applications, his work also continues to inform important developments in philosophy and social theory. For example, see Benjamin (1995) and Honneth (1995; 2012) for Winnicott's influence on the theory of intersubjective relations of recognition.
4 Winnicott's (1963f: 187; emphasis in the original) clearest statement on the inscrutability of self-experience can be found in the late paper on communication, where he proposes that '*each individual is an isolate, permanently non-communicating, permanently unknown, in fact unfound*'. Again, I think this paper, which seems to me one of the most profound things Winnicott wrote, supports the view that, in the human situation, *commūnicāre* invariably proceeds from *commūniō*.

Part II

THE REFLEXIVE NORM

Despite the inherent tensions and ambiguities in Winnicott's thinking, clinical contact with patients remained his basic point of reference; psychoanalysis provided him with both a situation of practice and a frame of meaning. The clinical setting, however, was not a privileged anchorage point for mainstream developments in mental health in post-war Britain. In this respect, the comparison between Britain and America is particularly instructive. Although the tide has now turned with the rise of neuroscience and psycho-pharmacology, psychoanalysis dominated academic psychiatry in America throughout the 1950s and 1960s. Departments of psychiatry-based psychoanalytic institutes were established on a firm academic footing in several prestigious universities during this period.[1] By contrast, in Britain psychoanalysis was far less visible or esteemed, excluded from the mainstream by alternative models and techniques. But this in itself is part of Freud's contested legacy: the history of psychoanalysis, in Britain at least, is inextricably linked to the resistance it incurred.

To demonstrate how post-war developments in community psychiatry overshadowed the contribution of psychoanalysis, we shall turn to the example of bereavement studies. How we mourn, particularly the way we have come to recognize ourselves as subjects of grief, confirms the central place that memory occupies in the contested domain of administered intimacy. Psychoanalysis and bereavement studies, in many respects, cover the same ground, particularly with respect to the experience of time. Conflicting interpretations of temporality cut across the entire field of post-Freudian thought and, against the background of this contested terrain, we explore the extent to which bereavement has been rendered amenable to management along the related axes of self-identity and community.

From a social as well as a personal point of view, the question is not whether, but how we remain preoccupied with death and dying. Far from the repression of mortality, human culture depends on finding ways of inscribing death in the collective imagination. Facing our own death as well as the death of others is a profoundly personal matter, but it is also an historical question concerning the changing relationship between mortality, individuals, and society. Traumatic loss and related forms of grief informed the public concern over death throughout the twentieth century, particularly with respect to institutionalized forms of mass death, epidemic disease, and natural disasters. Moreover, in terms of our ordinary day-to-day lives, it would be misleading to see death as something hidden or set apart by so many cultural taboos. It will be evident in the following discussion of grief that death is neither an entirely private matter nor a taboo subject; that the sequestration of death is no more prevalent in contemporary European society than in any other society.

That having been said, this still leaves the question of whether traditional ways of mourning are simply disappearing. It seems to me that, rather than a breakdown in the institution of mourning, there has been a selective appropriation and reformation of traditional practices of community mourning in contemporary society. The current preoccupation with death is evident, for example, in an emphasis throughout the caring professions on ways of coping with loss, where the bereaved no less than the dying are subject to a whole series of calculations, interventions, and conflicting interpretations. The problematic nature of grief is thus part of the wider confrontation between the theories and techniques of psychoanalysis, on the one hand, and the post-war developments in psychiatry and community healthcare, on the other. A confrontation which is largely about the way we manage ourselves as active subjects with regards to our own feelings, taking responsibility for our vulnerabilities as well as managing the risks we face in our lives.

To say that people are no less mournful today than they were in the past, is obviously not the same as saying that mourning continues unchanged. In fact, as we mean to demonstrate, there have been significant changes over the last fifty years or so in the process of mourning. These changes reflect and consolidate wider developments in management practices and the supervision of conduct. Bereavement therefore marks an important point of entry for the administration of life in the domain of death, including the institutionalization of an active, self-conscious mode of government coupled with a particular formation of treatment and expert counsel. Basically, my argument is that bereavement has become part of a more comprehensive governmental programme of therapeutic supervision and community care. I aim to demonstrate this in the following chapters, with respect to the regulation of mourning as a normative process. Although the question of faith and therapy is not an explicit theme in the following chapters (as it was in the first part of the book), the question is nonetheless relevant insofar as the psychiatric supervision of grief may be seen as a replacement for religious ways of attending to the dying and the dead.

Focusing, then, on the work of Colin Murray Parkes, we examine the epistemological and technical differences between social psychiatry and psychoanalysis. Parkes is an important figure in the institutional context of mourning; having worked closely with Cicely Saunders as consultant psychiatrist to St Christopher's Hospice since its inception in 1966, he has played a key role in the hospice movement in Britain. At St Christopher's, Parkes established the first hospice-based bereavement service, as well as conducting research and initiating evidence-based practice in hospice care. Formerly Chair and subsequently Life President of Cruse Bereavement Care, Parkes also served as consultant psychiatrist to St Joseph's Hospice in Hackney and as a scientific editor of *Bereavement Care*, the international journal for bereavement care. He was a senior lecturer in psychiatry at the Royal London Hospital Medical College and, over a period of thirty years, worked with John Bowlby as a member of the research staff at the Tavistock Institute of Human Relations.

Further to his clinical and research work, Parkes extended his range of expertise in acting as consultant and adviser following the disasters in Aberfan, the Cheddar/Axbridge air crash, the Bradford Football Club fire, the capsize of the *Herald of Free Enterprise*, and the Pan American aircraft explosion over Lockerbie. Already evident in this series of local interventions, the strategic interface of disaster and security is consolidated in Parkes's work in the global context of military violence. At the invitation of UNICEF, Parkes acted as consultant in setting up the Trauma Recovery Programme in Rwanda in April 1995; and, at the invitation of the British government, he helped to set up a governmental programme of support in New York to assist families from the United Kingdom following the terrorist attacks on 11 September 2001. More recently, in April 2005 Parkes was sent by Help the Hospices to India to assess the psychological needs of people bereaved by the tsunami.

As this brief summary indicates, traumatic bereavement is the central preoccupation of Parkes's work. He combines this with a concern for those who, following the loss of attachment in adult life, are deemed most at risk of psychiatric illness. How does this combination of trauma and risk compare with the work of mourning in Freud? Parkes inherited a model of social psychiatry initially developed by Lewis (1951; 1957; 1962) and, in terms of the problem of security, what he has done with this model has proved decisive. Basically, Parkes assimilates the work of mourning to a self-reflective project, institutionalizing therapeutic management along supervisory lines as a form of community care. As we shall see in the final part of the book, self-reflection proves no less decisive for the sociological appropriation of psychoanalysis. Indeed, although the sociology of death and dying is not our topic here, Parkes's psychiatric model shares some of the basic assumptions of sociology and anthropology.[2]

For Parkes, as for Winnicott, personal life emerges as a composite problem of mental health and social well-being. As far as bereavement is concerned, the interface of self-reflection and community care provides for a 'mapping in advance of the mourning process as something through which people should be taken' (Craib 1998: 157). The point is not that individuals pass through stages *in seriatim*. According to Parkes, at least, the bereaved work their way through a series of overlapping 'phases' in an effort to reflect on what has happened; to cope with the anxieties of separation and loss; and, in the process, to arrive at some kind of reconciliation and self-understanding. The process may be understood in terms of our capacity to establish new psychosocial norms, where consolation itself becomes a technical problem concerning the formation of a 'new identity'.

As such, the work involved in mourning becomes yet one more occasion for managing oneself, a way for the bereaved to take charge of themselves and their conduct under supervisory conditions. As we intend to demonstrate, while Parkes approaches private feelings and emotional needs as psychosocial categories of value; at the same time, he subjects the bereaved to a normative ideal of social behaviour, rendering the work of mourning itself as a process of normalization.

The fact that Parkes does not approach mourning through the category of 'depression' reveals an important chapter in the recent history of mental illness and its treatment. Parkes formulated his model initially in the 1960s, whereas the use of 'depression' as a descriptive category for various kinds of behaviour represents a later development in twentieth-century mental health. Parkes's work pre-dates the rise of biological psychiatry during this period, coupled with the overwhelming predominance of pharmacological forms of treatment for mental illness. Indeed, our argument depends on the fact that Parkes does *not* reduce bereavement to depression, but rather, remains focused on the experience of grief as an emotional reaction to loss, together with the process of mourning as a way of reflecting on one's life and future plans.

Parkes's studies stand at a crossroads with regards to the assimilation of Freudian psychoanalysis. In our study, his work is placed midway between Winnicottian management and the sociology of self-regulation. Initially, Parkes was not in a position to judge psychoanalysis wholly redundant from the vantage point of genetics and neurobiology. Nor would it necessarily have served his purpose to have done so. Nevertheless, the radical import of psychoanalysis, including Winnicott's innovative conception of management, is necessarily compromised in a context where the treatment of individuals relies increasingly on the assertion of therapeutic supervision and psychosocial norms of conduct. The primacy of reflection in bereavement studies is a double-edged sword; it privileges individual experience over genetic and biological explanations of mental illness. At the same time, the emphasis on the self-understanding of the reflective subject, whose conduct is therefore amenable to self-government, undermines the fundamental proposition of unconscious structures and processes.

Arguing along these lines in the following chapters, we propose that post-war bereavement studies represent a transitional phase in the dismantling of the Freudian argument. The chapters are organized as follows: we begin with a general discussion of Parkes's concept of mourning, together with an outline of some important post-war developments in social psychiatry. This will allow us to situate psychiatry in a governmental context. It will also indicate the way in which the study of grief contributes to a restructuring of medicine on the model of self-identity and communities of care. Focusing on theoretical and institutional obstacles to medical reform in the post-war period, we look at the way in which Parkes has sought to overcome these obstructions, before turning to a more detailed consideration of his alternative model of medical rationality and therapeutic action. The implications of this model are examined with respect to therapeutic management and the supervised life.

Notes

1 For the prominence of Freudian psychoanalysis in American psychiatry, as well as the culture as a whole, see Burnham (2012). *After Freud Left* presents a critical evaluation of the lectures Freud delivered at Clark University, in September 1909, on the origin and future development of psychoanalysis. The volume also provides useful commentaries on Freud's legacy in America after World War II and the subsequent 'Americanization of Freud', for instance, in the work of Heinz Kohut.
2 For classic studies in the sociology of death and dying see, for example, Feifel (1959), Fulton (1963), Mitford (1963), Glaser and Strauss (1965), Gorer (1965), and Sudnow (1967). For more recent accounts, see Ariès (1976; 1983), Elias (1985), Kearl (1989), Prior (1989), Walter (1991), Mellor (1993), Mellor and Shilling (1993), Seale (1998), and Willmott (2000).

4

NORMS AND FACTS

In order to appreciate what Parkes has achieved in the field of social psychiatry it is necessary to detail the obstacles he faced. We shall approach Parkes as we approached Winnicott, focusing on his innovative conception of management against a background of epistemological and technical obstacles.[1] Parkes has been primarily concerned with developing reflexive models of grief, the obstacles to which are derived from inside as well as outside medicine. Chief among the internal obstacles, medicine hinders the progress of reflexive models with its reliance on diagnostic signs, while epidemiology presents further obstacles in terms of statistically defined norms. We shall consider how far the medicine of symptoms is inimical to Parkes's reflexive project, particularly with reference to the methodological precepts of the health survey in social medicine. Further to the limits imposed by the 'social point of view' within psychiatric medicine, Parkes also faces difficulties outside the field of psychiatry. Sociology is an indispensable frame of reference for Parkes's studies, but as a science of 'social facts' it presents him with additional problems. Parkes does not engage explicitly with the work of Durkheim; nonetheless, the social science of hygiene represents a major obstacle to the development of reflexive models of health and illness. In effect, Parkes reworks the Durkheimian classification of the normal and the pathological from the perspective of reflexivity. We need to take a close and detailed look at Durkheim in order to establish the distinction between hygienic and reflexive norms. But before turning to this distinction, we shall begin with an initial overview of Parkes's research methods and his basic epistemological assumptions.

Communities of care

Bereavement studies emerged in post-war Britain as part of a wider institutional reorganization of medical policy and practice. Questions concerning the future of hospital medicine were combined with a restructuring of the classificatory system of psychiatric knowledge.[2] Accordingly, the widow became a new object of concern in a governmental context where the policy of community care was coupled with the idea that the death of a husband is 'the commonest type of relationship loss to give rise to psychological difficulties' (Parkes 1996: 121).

The work of Bowlby and Parkes in the 1960s represents the beginning of a new phase in the understanding of the relationship between mourning, the individual, and society. The idea that health is in some degree commensurate with illness lies at the heart of this new perspective.[3] As psychiatry lays claim to the phenomenon of mourning, it is seen increasingly as a type of mental illness; at the same time the notion of mental illness itself is subject to important modifications and revisions. Essentially, psychiatric categories of health and illness are reclassified under the more comprehensive category of 'mental health'. Bereavement studies make a significant contribution to this development in the public health sector by forging links between the development of community care and a more reflexive concept of medicine.

The care of the insane throughout the modern period is not a straightforward history of progress, but remains a complex arrangement of poor law, charitable, private, and community provision (Bartlett and Wright 1999). Moreover, the concept of 'care in the community' is not confined to medicine or mental health, let alone the problem of bereavement. We are not suggesting that bereavement is necessarily a privileged object of concern in the field of mental health. Nevertheless, the attempt to organize the process of mourning on the model of self-identity, including new ways of thinking about the relationship between individuals and communities, consolidates the changes taking place in medicine and elsewhere throughout this period. Craib (1998: 160–1) dates the beginning of the contemporary discourse on mourning from the early 1960s, and it is the 'dramatic changes' in the understanding and treatment of the bereaved during this period that we focus on in our study.

Historically, Parkes may be considered alongside Winnicott in terms of the wider formation of therapeutic management in post-war Britain. This raises an important methodological point: while systems of thought and modes of action are tied to specific domains, there is nonetheless significant cross-fertilization of concepts and techniques throughout the governmental field. Far from an isolated event, the attempt to manage grief in the community forms part of an overall shift in the concerns and activity of government.[4] The question of 'advanced' liberal governance, therefore, forms the background to our main themes: the reclassification of health and illness; the integration of medicine in the community; the reconstruction of psychiatry along reflexive lines; and the delivery of public health care and social services in accordance with the choices of autonomous individuals and their capacity for self-mastery.

Parkes's studies of grief exemplify these developments in twentieth-century medicine by emphasizing the importance of self-reflection in conjunction with the model of community medicine. His work demonstrates the extent to which, as Rose (1994: 63) puts it, 'the ideal territory of the community serves as the basis for innumerable utopian projects for the reintegration of the practice of medicine'. In particular, together with the work of Bowlby (1961; 1963), Parkes's studies on grief establish a link between the psychology of loss and the government of emotion. For Parkes, grief is less a symptom than a phenomenon of subjectivity amenable to certain types of supervision. Rather than a psychopathology founded on localisable symptoms, Parkes sets out a general psychosocial model of grief in which personal experience plays a central role.

While the immediate historical–political context is defined by the advanced liberal community–family couple, more broadly conceived, the reformulation of normative capacity in bereavement studies is consistent with the distinction Canguilhem (1966) draws between Comte and Bernard, on the one hand, and René Leriche, on the other, in Part I of the *Essay*. This places our comparative reading of Parkes and Durkheim in the wider debate about positivism and the social sciences. Epistemologically, Parkes's studies belong to a tradition of modern thought in which the patient's point of view constitutes the criterion of health. Thus, one sees in Parkes's studies – including his study of the case records of forty-four widows (1964), the Bethlem Study (1965), and the London Study (1970) – two related sets of problems concerning *modes of reaction* and *forms of regulation*.[5]

First, Parkes draws attention to the problem of process rather than symptoms, emphasizing individuals' reactions to bereavement rather than the vicissitudes of grief.[6] For Parkes, the study of grief is first and foremost a study of modes of reaction; his *theoretical* argument rests on an analysis of modes rather than a classification of types. Second, 'community' becomes a governmental problem through the use that Parkes makes of the patient's family, neighbours, and other social networks as a therapeutic resource. The *therapeutic* argument is set out along these lines in favour of non-hospital based treatment. Vulnerable groups of people who are seen as presenting special risks, including 'grief-prone' individuals as well as those who suffer unusually traumatic forms of bereavement, are subject to preventive modes of treatment. The latter comprise communities of care under psychiatric supervision. Clearly, while this argument is consistent with the general policy of 'de-institutionalization', community-based forms of action provide psychiatry with specific rather than diminished powers.[7] Indeed, in some respects the use of non-hospital community resources allows for far greater regulation than hospital medicine. This is due to the fact that communities of care are located at the interface of self-management and therapeutic expertise in an augmented field of regulation that includes prevention and supervision.

The complexity of this model begs the question as regards the 'institution' of mourning. Where, exactly, does the process of mourning take place? What does government amount to in the case of self-management and community supervision? Instead of either the hospital or society providing the institutional *locus* of mourning, Parkes posits the ideal of family life as the model of community care. Notwithstanding the wide range of contemporary research that Parkes draws on in *Bereavement*, his central argument is already set out by the end of the 1960s in two seminal essays: 'Bereavement and mental illness, part I: A clinical study of the grief of bereaved psychiatric patients; part II: A classification of bereavement reactions' (1965); and 'The first year of bereavement: a longitudinal study of the reaction of London widows to the death of their husbands' (1970). Together with his 1964 study, these two essays identify the widow as a particular object of concern; and they focus on modes of reaction as the central issue in the study and treatment of grief. Presented in the first edition of *Bereavement* in 1972, subsequent editions of Parkes's principal work confirm his basic assumptions. Thus, Parkes elaborates first on the alleviation of misery as a problem amenable to management, and second, on the classification of the normal and the pathological as modes of behaviour rather than types of morbidity. The promulgation of a consolatory therapeutics and the description of modes of health and illness are two sides of the same development.

It will be argued that Parkes's findings posed a fundamental challenge to clinical thinking in the 1960s. But this is not to say that his studies are any more or less reliable than social science research in general; the fact that bias is built-in to the social and human sciences is evident in Parkes's sample. The 1964 study, for instance, focuses on widows whose husbands had been under the age of 65 when they died; and the other main studies focus on widows and widowers under the age of 45. The studies are therefore not 'a good sample for generalizing about grief in a modern society', where most deaths are of the elderly (Walter 1991: 301). The same criticism applies to Parkes's reliance on bereavement counselling, hospices, and befriending organizations as the general evidence base for his research work. Clearly, these institutions are disproportionately concerned with 'difficult bereavement' and do not count as representative. The same argument, of course, can be levelled at Winnicott's treatment of difficult children and antisocial behaviour.

However, we are not concerned here with 'the actual truth-content' of Parkes's findings so much as 'their relation towards a truth' (Gordon 1980: 241). More than the 'truth-content', it is the 'truth-effects' or veridical normativity of his propositions and assumptions that render Parkes's studies operational as rationalities of government. Like Winnicott, Parkes may have truthful things to say about human suffering and the need for solace; he may get at something irreducibly real in human beings through his descriptions of loss and the deeply felt need for consolation. None of this is in dispute. Nevertheless, his work is authoritative primarily in accordance with the 'relations of reciprocity' (Rose and Miller 1992: 63) that pertain between the social sciences and social governance, a relationship that is concerned above all with the normalization of social conduct.

The institution of mourning thus becomes a programmatic question with respect to the distinction between normal and pathological grief. How do Parkes's studies contribute to this distinction? Set against the background of the 1954 Parliamentary debate on mental health, and following immediately after the publication of the report of the Royal Commission on Mental Health in 1957 and the 1959 Mental Health Act, the Bethlem Study is an investigation of 'atypical grief' carried out at the Bethlem Royal and Maudsley Hospitals during 1958–60.[8] Parkes's sample consisted of twenty-one patients undergoing psychiatric treatment, eighteen in-patients and three out-patients (seventeen women and four men), all of whom had developed a 'mental illness' within six months of the death of a spouse, child, parent, or sibling.

At the interview 'the patient was encouraged to talk freely about the dead person and the bereavement, and questions were asked, when necessary, to supplement the information given' (Parkes 1996: 222). The patient's point of view is placed centre stage.[9] The encouragement to engage in a dialogue with the interviewer, to give voice to one's feelings, and to provide 'information' about oneself plays a decisive role in the management of mourning. Technically speaking, this is the litmus test of Parkes's relation to the Freudian legacy. The interview itself may be seen as a technique of intimacy, linking the therapeutic expertise of the psychiatrist, clinical psychologist, or counsellor with the active self-management of the patient or client. Bereavement counselling, however, operates only so far along these lines as a psychotherapeutic encounter. In this case, the therapist is 'expert' not in handling the transference of melancholic grievance or in translating the mechanisms of unconscious identification; but rather, in facilitating the self-regulating skills and capacities of the bereaved. The unconscious refusal to let the object go is not the main problem for Parkes (1996: 222–3), who is more concerned with using the interview to construct a 'checklist' in order to assess the 'presence or absence of some common features of grief'. Modes of reaction are privileged over the irreducible singularity of analytic patients. We shall come back to the distinction between the therapeutic interview and the analytic encounter in a moment.

While information and assessment remain the most important technical issues in the 1970 London Study, Parkes set out subsequently to establish a picture of 'normal' mourning. His account is based on an assessment of an unselected group of twenty-two young and middle-aged widows. Referred through their general practitioners, the women were interviewed individually at least five times, starting at the end of the first month of bereavement, and again at the third, sixth, ninth, and thirteenth months. On each occasion the women were encouraged to use their own words in describing their manifest reactions to bereavement. The technical investment of Parkes's clinical research rests on this systematic investigation of the self-conscious processes at work in normal and pathological mourning alike. By 'self-conscious processes' I mean the self-understanding of the bereaved that Parkes renders amenable to classification, assessment, and treatment. It is through this type of research that the widow comes increasingly to the fore as a particular object of concern: 'Among 171 people who have been referred to me in recent years for the treatment of psychiatric problems following bereavement, 45% had lost a spouse (35% a husband, 10% a wife)' (1996: 121). As we shall see, Parkes extends the notion of 'psychiatric problems' to a broadly defined category of 'special needs', which means that the problem of widowhood is not confined to 'atypical grief' but cuts across the classification of the normal and the pathological.

To summarize, Parkes draws on these two studies (the Bethlem and London Studies) as the principal sources of information for *Bereavement*. While the therapeutic authority of its argument is limited in ways that I shall try to demonstrate, the book nonetheless determines new directions in social psychiatry at the intersection of illness, identity, and community. Critically, Parkes's work represents a break with the symptomological rationale of clinical medicine. Concentrating on the personal experience of the bereaved rather than the observation of signs and symptoms, Parkes establishes grief as a problem of special needs. These are in fact two sides of the same argument. The critique of clinical reason extends the possibility of individuality internal to the logic of biomedicine (Osborne 1994). Thus bereavement studies exploit the considerable degree of ambivalence under which psychiatry itself applies the norm: 'Aetiologies are usually missing or weakly specified in psychiatric medicine, and diagnosis therefore lacks an analytical base in physiological mechanisms and tests for their presence independent of observation' (Hirst and Woolley 1982: 103). The scientific limitations of psychiatric medicine allow Parkes to combine the critical aspect of his argument with a positive application focused on the subjectivity of death and dying. Based on his use of the therapeutic interview as a way of helping patients to manage their grief, Parkes draws out the reflective possibilities of psychiatric medicine in accordance with practical techniques of intimacy. Furthermore, in conjunction with technologies for establishing and maintaining self-management, the phenomenological emphasis implicit in medical perception consolidates the link between patients' individual needs, the individual clinical judgements of psychiatrists, and the therapeutic possibilities of the community.[10]

Rules of method

The self-management of the bereaved within the context of communities of care represents a new development in medical practice. The institutionalization of the British hospice movement in the 1960s may be seen as an important part of this development. However, the emphasis in bereavement studies on individuality and special needs is not confined to hospice care. To appreciate the wider implications of the argument for self-management in the community we need to say more about Parkes's clinical research background, including his methodological rules and epistemological assumptions. Parkes joined John Bowlby's research staff at the Tavistock Institute of Human Relations in 1962, and their collaboration over a period of some thirty years was based on a shared preoccupation with modes of behaviour as well as types of personal expression. Notably, they shared a common interest in the expression of 'sorrow' in human infants and adults, as well as other primates (Bowlby and Parkes 1970).

Parkes acknowledges that his approach to the problem of bereavement is indebted to Bowlby in a number of respects. First, Parkes (1996: 30) explains how Bowlby's work provided the possibility for 'a biological theory of grief'. It is important not to lose sight of the biological aspect of Parkes's model, including the idea of biological normativity, when considering its interdisciplinary applications.[11] Like Bowlby, Parkes remained considerably less impressed by speculative psychoanalytic theories of infantile states of mind than by the scientific observation of embodied human responses to instinctual experience. Drawing explicitly on Bowlby's ideas about the evolution of 'attachment behaviour' and 'instinctual needs', Parkes (1996: 10) points out that while

> there is no longer any good reason for a widow to fear attack by hyenas, it is no surprise to find that the lack of a close attachment to another person is often associated with a subjective feeling of insecurity and danger.

Parkes takes these 'subjective feelings' seriously as an expression of the need for attachment.

Second, Parkes emphasizes the importance of the intimate 'social networks' surrounding the bereaved self, including above all the obligations that family members have in helping to care for bereaved relatives. Together with the criterion of need, he extends the schema of security through the family to the community. For Parkes, inner security is invariably a social problem; similarly, Bowlby's stress on the family as a therapeutic agent was singled out by Titmuss as a key factor in the provision of community care for the mentally ill (Welshman 1999: 222). Together, Bowlby and Parkes consolidate the link between inner security and the social order on the basis of family-community attachments.

Third, Parkes *et al.* (1997) underline the importance of wider social and cultural factors in the scientific analysis and treatment of grief. For example, Parkes's work includes cross-cultural references to funeral and mourning customs after Rosenblatt *et al.* (1976), Burgoine (1988), and Lovell *et al.* (1993). The problem is essentially the same from modes of attachment in individuals through social networks to the general level of 'cultural evolution'. Parkes (1996: 10) remains concerned with what he sees as the breakdown in formal structures of community mourning, where 'bereaved individuals get little support from society at large and from their own families in particular'.

By drawing on his research work with Bowlby, making links between the individual, the family and the community, Parkes outlines a general psychosocial model of grief with biological underpinnings. The basic strategic aim here is to connect the governmental problems of family, neighbourhood, and community with the psychiatric problems of 'disturbance' and 'readjustment'.[12] The connection presupposes the importance of 'secure attachment' in the mourning process: for Parkes, as for Bowlby, managing grief in the community is about managing attachment. For example, in the London Study, which includes an assessment of 'social withdrawal' alongside a range of psychological measures, Parkes (1996: 154) argues that the widows 'who saw the smallest number of friends and relatives during the thirteenth month of their bereavement had significantly more psychological disturbance than those who saw more friends and relatives'. This modest finding has far-reaching implications. The psychosocial model of grief contributes to a general reorganization of the concept of human behaviour on the model of 'attachment', which in turn provides a general criterion for personal and collective well-being.

By engaging the established disciplines of biology, psychiatry, and sociology in an attempt to construct an interdisciplinary model of grief, Parkes anticipates the emergence of psychosocial studies as a new disciplinary field towards the end of the twentieth century. The originality of his contribution is evident, for example, when we compare the concepts of 'attachment' and 'withdrawal' with the sociological concepts that Durkheim formulated in his analysis of variation in suicide rates. It is important to note that we are not making a general distinction here between psychiatry and sociology. Rather, the focus is on the different epistemological projects and contrasting perspectives of governance in Durkheim and Parkes. Most notably, in *Le Suicide* (1897) Durkheim set out to explain the social causes of suicide without recourse to individual differences in personality, motivation, or states of mind. He identified two independent variables as the basis of his sociological explanation: 'integration' and 'regulation'. Too much or too little of either, according to Durkheim, results in social situations where suicide occurs. Briefly, suicide is classified according to high levels of integration ('altruism'); low levels of integration ('egoism'); high levels of regulation ('fatalism'); and low levels of regulation ('anomie'). Furthermore, Durkheim advanced a sociological diagnosis by identifying 'egoism' and 'anomie' as the main causes of suicide in modern society.

The accuracy or otherwise of Durkheim's schema is not the issue here. Again, we are more concerned with what Donzelot (1991) calls 'the mobilization of society' in and through the sociological argument. So long as the sovereignty of the individual afforded insufficient grounds for the institutions of social welfare, an alternative perspective had to be formulated. Thus, the problem of welfare came increasingly to the fore in the early 1900s as a political problem, notable solutions to which were provided by the social sciences. Far more than a theory of suicide, Durkheim made a defining contribution to what was perhaps the most efficacious solution to the problem of liberal democratic government for much of the twentieth century, namely, the problem of 'social solidarity'.[13] This is evident above all in the emphasis Durkheim placed on integration and regulation. He argued consistently that 'solidarity' was proportional to rates of social interaction and, at the same time, dependent on both regulatory state intervention and the moral rules that integrate society. From the combined perspective of regulation and integration, and distinct from the notion of sovereignty, the social logic of solidarity was thereby instrumental in the formation of the modern welfare state. It served as an effective criterion of government, defining 'not only the framework but also the specific mode of state intervention, one which affects the forms of the social bond rather than the structure of society itself' (Donzelot 1991: 173).

It would appear that Durkheim and Parkes are preoccupied with similar problems concerning collective as well as individual well-being. For example, Durkheim (see *Le Suicide*, Book Two, Chapters 2 and 3) concluded that 'egoistic' groups of people interact less and are more withdrawn; they have less of a sense of community; and they are generally less connected to one another. This appears to chime in with the themes of attachment theory. More particularly, Durkheim

(1897: 259) also included widowhood as a type of acute anomie: 'The suicides occurring at the crisis of widowhood are really due to domestic anomie resulting from the death of husband or wife.' He argued that suicide became an increased risk for this group due to the fact that old habits of life had given way suddenly and new rules of conduct were yet to emerge. Durkheim thus established an important causal connection between personal loss and the breakdown of rules of conduct. These and other similarities notwithstanding, Parkes construes the problem of social withdrawal, the loss of self-identity, and feelings of hopelessness in an entirely different way to Durkheim. Once again it would be misleading to see this as no more than a conflict of interpretation between sociology and psychiatry; indeed, Parkes includes sociology as an essential part of his comprehensive study of grief. The fundamental difference between Durkheim and Parkes lies elsewhere and concerns the conditions under which their views on 'solidarity' and 'attachment', respectively, are deployed.

The problem of attachment, a problem which is conceived as distinct from that of social solidarity, represents a new rationality of government. The fact is that Parkes's contribution to the management of attachment in the late 1960s and 1970s came at a time when the social criterion of government was entering a period of crisis; when the mobilization of society through the notion of solidarity stood at a crossroads; and when the welfare state itself was coming increasingly under attack. These are the conditions under which government through community operates. In place of social welfare and solidarity a new rationality of government promulgates 'the self-governing properties of the subjects of government themselves in a whole variety of locales and localities – enterprises, associations, neighbourhoods, interest groups and, of course, communities' (Rose 1996a: 111). The governmental problematic of community care is formulated in this context.

Of course this new rationality is not set out in Parkes as a political theory, but remains imbedded in his psychiatric studies of bereavement. Parkes turns consolation itself into a technical problem. He invests reassurance with psychiatric significance, while at the same time proposing that mental health and mental illness alike are characterized by a particular set of norms. The distinction between the normal and the pathological remains central for Parkes, but only insofar as illness is construed as a type of normality.[14] The relationship between health and illness is constructed in relation to the problems of attachment and individual needs, solutions to which are presented in the form of new management practices and new types of therapeutic expertise. Community care thus provides a framework for the integration of reflexivity and supervision, a framework in which the exercise of therapeutic authority is combined with individualizing forms of governance.

The shift from 'society' to 'community', which is discernable throughout in the details of Parkes's argument, is framed by his epistemological as well as his substantive claims. Again, the comparison with Durkheim is instructive. Together with his studies of social solidarity, in *Les Règles de la méthode sociologique*

(1895) Durkheim attempted to provide a consistent epistemological foundation for sociology. Parkes attempts something similar for bereavement studies in the 1960s, but comes to entirely different conclusions. It is the inclusive nature of Parkes's classification of the normal and the pathological that is particularly important, his attempt to provide a general psychosocial theory of individuals in communities.

As well as Bowlby's 'phases of mourning' (1980), the phenomenological descriptions of grief in Kübler-Ross's 'phases of dying' (1973) form an important part of Parkes's perspective on grief. On the other hand, while he does not confine the definition of the norm to a quantitative variation in modes of reaction; nonetheless, Parkes continues to address bereavement as a problem of measurement. At once descriptive and quantitative, Parkes's methodology is designed to account not only for the patient's subjectivity, but also for the objective nature of cognitive, behavioural, and social experience. The self-understanding of the bereaved subject is coupled with a statistical measure of behavioural pathology: the phenomenology of mental suffering (*pathos*), with scientific techniques of monitoring and assessment (*logos*). That Giddens comes up with a similar perspective some twenty years later, including an emotive–cognitive approach to the problem of self-identity (see Part III), supports our argument concerning the alliance between psychiatric and sociological thinking. Indeed, the similarities between the perspectives of Giddens and Parkes reinforce the idea of psychiatry as a branch of social medicine (Lewis 1945a: 492). We shall come back to Parkes's relation to Lewis in our discussion of health surveys.

Further to his general research orientation, how does Parkes actually go about doing his research? What methods does he use? And how does he substantiate his claims to knowledge? The following statement illustrates the interdisciplinary nature of Parkes's approach:

> In the London Study the twenty-two young and middle-aged widows were assessed at each of the five interviews on a number of psychological measures. Assessments were based on information from the widow combined with my own direct observation at the interview, and each feature was rated on a five-point scale as "very marked", "marked", "moderate", "mild", or "absent" ... The mean year scores (the mean of each measure over the whole year) were inter-correlated and the significance of all correlations was tested.
>
> (Parkes 1996: 220)

The combination of observation and assessment is indicative of Parkes's methodological approach, an approach in which 'direct observation' is situated in a composite system of modes and ratios. We address the question of ratio in our discussion of risk management. As for the idea of modes, this is perhaps the single most important aspect of Parkes's interdisciplinary model. It provides the field of psychosocial research with the indispensable notion of *modes of life*. Again, placing Parkes in the context of modern clinical medicine, he does not collate individual reactions to bereavement in accordance with 'the field of signs and symptoms' (Foucault 1963: 91); nor does he rely on norms as either statistical averages or ideal types (Canguilhem 1966: 151–79). Instead, Parkes (1996: 220) delineates medical observations in terms of 'certain clusters of associated variables'.

In the London Study, for example, the data collected at each interview included the following information: first, 'a subjective assessment by the widow of her "general health" (scored as "good", "indifferent" or "bad")'. Second, 'a count of the number of physical symptoms she had experienced since the previous interview'. Third, 'a count of the number of consultations she had had with her GP since the last interview'. Finally, 'an assessment of irritability or anger as observed at the current interview (scored as "very marked", "marked", "moderate", "mild" or "absent")'. Through the therapeutic interview, then, psychiatry provides a model for mourning as a form of mental illness on two counts: first, as a mode of reaction rather than a type of symptom; and second, as a cluster of associated variables rather than a formation of pathological spaces or states of mind. Bereavement studies is confined neither to the medicine of species nor to the spatial problematic of modern medicine.

Parkes aims at an entirely new arrangement of clinical cases without recourse to the diagnostic sign. In particular, he formulates two contrasting modes of reaction to loss: a 'passive' mode 'oriented towards the dead husband'; and an 'active', self-reflective mode turned towards life and the future. The distinction, which is directly analogous to Canguilhem's (1966: 183–2) differentiation of 'rigid' and 'flexible' normative capacity, pertains above all to the *identity* of the bereaved. Parkes emphasizes the capacity of individuals to play an active role in the work of mourning. Moreover, the distinction itself renders grief amenable to techniques of self-management, that is, in accordance with the 'active response' of the patient. And active self-management is not confined to this or that section of the population. Unlike normal and pathological types, active and passive modes operate throughout the entire population. Parkes (1996: 222) anchors management to the population on two grounds: first, he argues that passive and active modes of reaction 'are found in most bereaved people'; and second, he claims that these reactions 'represent tendencies rather than discrete types of response'.

The basic assumption is that we suffer as a matter of course according to the kinds of beings we are; that our mental suffering is not a state of morbidity, but a normal mode of being; and that it is only through suffering the pains of illness, the acute and episodic 'pangs of grief' (1996: 43), that we are able to access a new dimension of life. In order to sustain this argument, the relation between the normal and the pathological needs to be redefined. Thus, instead of a typology of different categories, Parkes comes up with a diagrammatic model of associations and modes that redefines the meaning of social normalization. Starting with the idea that bereavement is 'a major psychological trauma' (1993: 91), Parkes argues that it 'leaves behind a gap' (1996: 13) such that our trust in others and in the world, our basic sense of inner security, may be called into question. Trauma becomes the *locus* for the redefinition of the normal and the pathological.

Parkes's attempt to treat the 'traumatic event' of grief as a phenomenon of psychosocial normativity stands in direct contrast to the Winnicottian model of therapeutic reclamation and the inherent fluctuations between unprecedented reactions and pathological phenomena. Parkes describes 'styles' of grief, the associations of which he plots on a continuous surface of normal and atypical reaction. Starting with the therapeutic interview, assessment is coupled with an interpretive understanding of grief. The resultant cartography includes self-knowledge alongside an objective measure of behaviour. At the same time, Parkes eschews the Freudian technique of interpretation. As Craib (1998: 162) points out, Parkes is not interested in the 'internal psychological process of conflicts' brought about by the work of mourning, including the subsequent 'reorganization in the internal world'. Instead, Parkes maps observable modes of reaction in the form of passive and active behaviour. Bereavement studies are presented as a kind of social psychology, including a causal model based on modes of behaviour rather than mental symptoms, combined with a descriptive account of the subjective experience of traumatic events.

The differentiation of modes is already invested with technical implications in terms of the conduct of the bereaved. Mourning is subject to a diagrammatic delineation that explains the meaning of bereavement as a positive experience. Set out along these lines as a demarcation of individual capacities, the differentiation of active and passive modes is based on a problematic of psychological adjustment. Modes of behaviour are mapped against a background of psychiatric disorders and treatment programmes. The self-knowledge of the bereaved is counted as part of the underlying objective, namely, to 'reduce pathology and encourage psychological growth' (Parkes 1996: 27). Far from ignoring subjective experience, Parkes concentrates on the differences between individuals in their response to loss. Bereavement emerges along these lines as a twofold question of psychosocial disturbance and readjustment. First, why do some people come through the event of bereavement without breaking down, while others require some form of psychiatric or professional help? Second, insofar as the event has detrimental effects upon physical and mental health, what can be done to prevent these effects from becoming unnecessarily deleterious and by whom should this care be administered? The skills and capacities of patients are thus linked with the therapeutic expertise of the psychiatrist or counsellor.

The governmental aspect of bereavement studies becomes immediately apparent when the focus of concern shifts to the 'failure' on the part of the family to provide help for the bereaved.[15] The family and the community do not represent separate lines of intervention in the contemporary management of grief. On the contrary, families are construed as exemplary communities of care in the face of loss. This is not a 'natural' arrangement, but an historical development that Parkes was instrumental in bringing about in the case of psychiatric medicine. As we have seen, Parkes emphasizes problems of identity and self-expression, encouraging patients to 'talk freely about the dead person and the bereavement', to organize their feelings in the work of self-reflective narratives. But this is more than a personal matter, more than a therapeutic encounter between patient and therapist, and quite different from the Freudian paradigm of free association. The attempt to organize the mourning process along reflexive lines requires both a familial strategy and a wider approach to risk management.

Theoretically, the contemporary field of bereavement studies includes not only clinical description; but also, psychometric measurement (Parkes and Weiss 1983), sociological analyses (Rosenblatt 1993), and the physiology of bereavement (Bartrop *et al.* 1977). The theoretical model itself constitutes a complex domain of problems in which the policy of community care is able to operate as a familial strategy, giving rise to an underlying preoccupation with the 'unsupportive family' as one of the strongest predictors of poor outcome after bereavement.[16] The conversion of the medical model of illness into a series of individual responses has direct technical implications: the statements that the bereaved are encouraged to make about themselves articulate a field of intimacy in which all manner of problems come to the surface and, therefore, are amenable to intervention. Indeed, it requires the bereaved to say that something is wrong with them for psychiatry to gain a purchase on modes of life.

The psychiatric model of behavioural modes is therefore a corollary of government through community, which results in two lines of critical engagement in Parkes. First, the emphasis on modes of behaviour is inimical to psychoanalysis and Freud's alternative model of unconscious processes. Notwithstanding Walter's (1991: 304) claims to the contrary, the study of bereavement relies only to a limited extent on a psychotherapeutic framework. If Parkes makes a contribution to so-called 'therapy culture' (Furedi 2004), he does so in opposition to psychoanalysis. As we shall see, Parkes remains essentially at odds with Freud on the fundamental question of symptoms and their interpretation. Second, Parkes's studies are no less incompatible with developments in post-war psychiatry that continue to rely on the problematic of solidarity. Government through community is neither a psychoanalytical initiative nor a technique of insurance and social security; but represents a new direction in community mental health.

In sum, Parkes approaches grief essentially as a problem of social normalization. Rather than a negative classification in which grief is seen merely as a deviation from the norm, Parkes addresses the source and the necessity of pathology at the intersection of emotional experience and communal relations. He treats illness as a form of normality. Concentrating on modes of reaction and forms of attachment, Parkes approaches health and illness alike as phenomena of everyday life. Accordingly, the institutional practice of mourning is matched to the observable behaviour of grief. Addressing the determinants of grief from the point of view of the health care system, Parkes (1996: 194) argues that since there are 'several types of pathological grief' these require 'quite different methods of treatment'. This is not a commitment to pluralism so much as an argument for a wide-ranging mechanism of regulation. For Parkes, the problem of understanding is already one of regulation, namely, how to manage bodies of people as part of the whole. Technically, the problem for Parkes is how to include even the most traumatic events, or the most extreme modes of psychiatric reaction, within a comprehensive psychosocial norm. In trying to come up with viable solutions to this problem bereavement studies furthers the development of reflexive medicine as an inclusive social practice.

The Durkheimian norm

One might think of psychiatry as a cumulative discipline, a practical body of knowledge whose adherents attempt to advance understanding and modes of treatment based on the ideas and findings of influential predecessors. This presupposes an underlying narrative of progress with gains in proficiency and greater insight over the course of time, a view that tends to predominate. Alternatively, looked at from an administrative perspective, the history of psychiatric knowledge seems beset by continual dissatisfaction, internal disagreement, and intrinsic failure. As Miller and Rose (1990: 35) point out, this situation is characteristic of rationalities of government: an 'eternally optimistic' endeavour, in practice psychiatry turns out to be 'a congenitally failing operation'. In adopting this view with respect to bereavement studies, we need to identify the obstacles that Parkes faced as well as the controversial discussions that form the essential background to his contribution to social medicine.

As we have seen, Parkes combines an implicit critique of medical signs with a more positive emphasis on the needs of individuals. However, in attempting to reconstruct the practice of social psychiatry on the model of self-identity, he immediately runs up against two obstacles. In making a case for community care from the comprehensive perspective of individual needs and social norms, Parkes is supported by neither the statistical methods of epidemiology nor the sociological explanation of 'facts as things' in the Durkheimian sense. Formulating his model in the 1960s, he had to contend with the diagnostic sign and the interpretation of symptoms, on the one hand, and the legacy of social hygiene, on the other. We are not suggesting that Parkes set about the task of studying grief in adult life with this epistemological agenda in mind. But in order to become a viable therapeutic option, Parkes's model of bereavement had to overcome these obstacles to reflexive medicine. In order for the conjunction of needs and norms to render health and illness intelligible, norms had to be redefined not as statistical averages or ideal types but as modes of reaction.

To illustrate the underlying controversies, we shall consider in turn the rules of Durkheimian sociology and the methodological precepts of the health survey. Although we are discussing them in turn, public hygiene (*hygiène publique*) and health surveys are complementary aspects of social medicine.[17] Furthermore, in singling out these two aspects, it is important to repeat that Parkes does not address Durkheim explicitly, any more than he engages in a detailed discussion of health surveys. The controversy is implicit in the alternative perspectives on how to manage ourselves and others. In Parkes, the theory of health and illness is predicated on the idea of continuity at the level of agency, together with the idea of inherent complexity at the level of norms. It will be argued that this particular combination of reflexivity and norms is impeded by the social logic of hygiene and, in equal measure, by the symptomological rationale of health surveys. Social facts and the survey of sickness, therefore, will be discussed as distinct but related obstacles to reflexive medicine and the reflexive norm.

The obstructions apply to different aspects of everyday life: the sociological obstacle concerns the relationship between the individual and society; the medical obstacle, the relationship between physiology and pathology. From the perspective of reflexive medicine, these obstacles intersect along two related axes. The Durkheimian norm opens up a gap in knowledge, a kind of moral lacuna, between the individual and society; whereas ultimately the medico-administrative survey maintains a categorical distinction between health and sickness. There is no possibility of linking the norm to the purposive character of human behaviour on either count. More specifically, so long as sociology divides individuals and society, and medicine maintains an essential distinction between health and illness, it is impossible to organize the study of grief in terms of a functional analysis of agency. So long as these divisions and distinctions pertain, the reflexive model of grief is not viable.

Starting with sociology, apropos the contrasting perspectives of solidarity and attachment, there are certain fundamental differences we can see between Durkheim and Parkes.[18] Most notably, while Durkheim plots the frequency or range of occurrence of types of pathology in the normal population (see *Le Suicide*), Parkes describes the reactions of healthy individuals with special needs as a continuous series. Social life is thus construed on the basis of two contrasting models of human relations. It is evident that Durkheim was no less interested than Parkes in establishing the conditions of health on scientific grounds. However, common perspectives of social physiology notwithstanding, Durkheim and Parkes present different conceptions of the normal and the pathological. Starting from the objective totality of society, Durkheim (1895: 47) conceives the normal and the pathological as 'two different types of facts'. By contrast, Parkes maintains the coincidence of illness and self-identity in terms of a comprehensive norm, where pathology itself constitutes another form of normal. Moreover, Parkes does not assume that the meaning of either the 'physiological normal' or the 'pathological normal' is exhausted by objective measurement.

The contrast brings us to a decisive question. In what sense is the Durkheimian tradition inimical to the comprehensive nature of the reflexive norm? What is the error that Durkheim appears to have made from Parkes's perspective? The argument is over the rules of method. For Durkheim, the theory of cognition presupposes the theory of social facts. In Durkheimian sociology, as with the clinical gaze, 'observation is logic at the level of perceptual contents' (Foucault 1963: 108). The same applies from physiology to sociology; hence the perspective of social physiology: 'The gaze of observation and the things it perceives communicate through the same *Logos*' (Foucault 1963: 109). In setting out rules for the consideration of 'facts as things' in their generality, objectivity, and externality, Durkheim defines the 'social' as that which is given to the observing gaze through the analysis of signs. This is another way of saying that sociology is exempt from doubts arising on the basis of value judgements; that things are given inasmuch as and because they are subject to observation: 'All that is given, all that is subject to observation, has thereby the character of a thing' (Durkheim 1895: 27).

The social is set out as a fact rather than a value on the organic analogy. Durkheim views society as an organic whole with each of its constituent parts, or elementary units, operating as an expression of the underlying foundation. Norms are seen therefore as organic phenomena of society. For Durkheim, the parts maintain and reproduce the whole, the essence of which is given as a matter of fact. As such, sociology concerns itself with the normal and the pathological as two different varieties of social facts. The latter are differentiated in terms of things 'which conform to given standards', on the one hand, and things 'which "ought" to be different' on the other (1895: 47). Thus, Durkheim follows in the positivist tradition of Comte and Bernard, for whom pathology is derived from the science of physiology.[19] At the same time, Durkheim (1895: 49) insisted that the criteria for distinguishing between the normal and the pathological are inseparable from matters of practical concern: 'for societies as for individuals, health is good and desirable; disease, on the contrary, is bad and to be avoided'.

The organic analogy underpins the logic as well as the substance of Durkheimian sociology. As far as Durkheim (1895: 74) is concerned, the principal objective of the social sciences 'is to define and explain the normal state and to distinguish it from its opposite'. The discrimination of the normal and the pathological is made first and foremost at the level of social order. Whereas physiology is valued above all as a form of scientific knowledge; similarly, sociology is seen as a science of administration. And in both cases, science is already conceived as a question of government: 'Why strive for knowledge of reality if this knowledge cannot serve us in life?' (1895: 48). Sociological thinking is the answer to its own question. In particular, for Durkheim (1895: 75) sociology assumes its governmental task in managing solidarity as a technical problem: the 'desirable' is determined on the same grounds as 'health' and 'normality', namely, on the assumption that they are 'inherent in the nature of things'. As a permanent imperative, the sociological task is simultaneously given and constructed; like the physician, the sociologist has either to 'prevent the outbreak of illnesses by good hygiene', or else 'seek to cure them when they have appeared'. Scientific explanation and social normalization, therefore, are one and the same problem, the task is at once to know and to make good: 'In order that sociology may be a true science of things, the generality of phenomena must be taken as the criterion of their normality' (1895: 74–5).[20]

This still leaves the question of classification and its value. In the *Rules*, the normal and the pathological are classified in terms of social hygiene. Durkheim presents the theory of social types as a continuation of his social physiology, where the unconditional nature of society is set out along the lines of normality, health, and objectivity. More precisely, the social is construed as a *functional* object of scientific analysis along three related axes: first, the normal exists as a given through the combination of generality and externality: 'We shall call "normal" [those] social conditions that are the most generally distributed' (1895: 55). Second, the essential constitution of society is given in the coincidence of normality and health: 'The healthy constitutes the norm *par excellence* and can consequently be in no way abnormal' (1895: 58). Third, the coincidence of normality and health is given as an objective social fact rather than an individual phenomenon; the average, in other words, 'expresses a certain state of the group mind [*l'âme collective*]' (1895: 8). Durkheim concludes that health and normality apply to the whole of the population not only as categories; but also, more important, as social facts. They are seen as objective expressions of the *conscience collective*, the statistical codification of which identifies 'currents of opinion' as irreducible to individual consciousness. For Durkheim, at least, the sociology of health and normality is based on the assumption that value judgements are derived from social facts.

The idea of norms as statistical averages leaves the content of pathological states to be determined, a consequence that is played out in terms of the unconditional nature of society as compared to the problematic nature of the self. A contrast that proves decisive when it comes to managing our lives. For Durkheim (1895: 69), '[i]t is impossible for all to be alike, if only because each one has his own organism and that these organisms occupy different areas in space'. However, he goes on to say that '[w]here crime exists, collective sentiments are sufficiently flexible to take on a new form, and crime sometimes helps to determine the form they will take' (1895: 71). Sociology itself becomes a permanent task in terms of the problems individuals present to society. Thus, in accordance with the science of society, Durkheim identifies the existence of problems the jurisdiction of which he assigns to moral institutions. Most notably, in his analysis of education he combines individual differences with the possibility of new social formations along moral lines. For Durkheim, the classification of the normal and the pathological as two distinct categories opens up a space in the social for the constitution of new moral types. This is what social physiology amounts to in the Durkheimian tradition: the moral consciousness of society is linked to the immediate physical milieu in which the individual exists, which means that society administers to itself, according to a single universally valid hierarchy of ends, at the point where the individual demarcates the limits of the social. Sociology is conspicuously well placed from this perspective to manage antisocial and disruptive elements.

Social medicine and health surveys

So long as the normal and the pathological are constructed as types of facts rather than modes of reaction – to this extent, sociology impedes any attempt to understand health and illness along reflexive lines. Indeed, Durkheim was concerned neither with modes of behaviour nor with the meaning individuals assign to their actions. He envisaged the administration of solidarity without recourse to techniques of self-conscious governance. While this frustrates the prospect of a comprehensive psychosocial perspective, the obstacles Parkes is faced with are not confined to sociology. Bereavement studies run up against a similar preoccupation with rates and types of morbidity in health surveys.

The Survey of Sickness, which was introduced in the 1940s as a national Survey of health and illness covering England and Wales, will serve as an example of what Parkes was up against within medicine. This study goes beyond standardized mortality ratios as a measure of health status, and includes information about use of services and incapacity. Introduced during World War II, the Survey of Sickness can be seen as a response to the more or less widespread anxieties about the nation's health.[21] It was carried out by the Wartime (later the Government) Social Survey, later the Social Survey division of the Office of Population Censuses and Surveys, under the heading of the Health Index. In use until 1952, Cartwright (1983: 5) describes some of the variations in the methods of assessment and classification used in the Survey. For instance, categories varied over time with respect to age: 16–64 years in 1943–4, 16 and over for December 1944–51, and 21 and over during 1951–2. The number interviewed each month also varied: 2,500 initially, it was between 3,000 and 4,000 at later stages. The period asked about changed from the previous three months in 1943–9 to the previous two months during July 1949–52. Finally, the classification of illness itself used the Medical Research Council Provisional Classification in 1943–8, and the International Statistical Classification in 1949–52.

As for the types of questions asked, the Survey included a general question on health: 'How was your general health during ... (Study month)?' And also an equally broad question on illness: 'Did you have any illness, ailment, poisoning or injury of any kind or trouble with long standing complaints during ...?' There was a more specific question about ill-health consisting of a number of symptomological categories:

> Have you had anything wrong in the way of colds, catarrh, or nose and throat trouble or anything wrong with your eyes, ears, teeth, head pains, chest, heart, stomach or indigestion, liver, kidneys, bowels or constipation, legs, feet, hands, arms or rheumatism, skin complaints, infectious diseases or [added to the checklist of symptoms relating to September, October, November, 1945 onwards] anything wrong with your nerves?

Women were asked an additional question: 'Have you had anything wrong in the way of women's complaints?'

While the emphasis on symptoms is clearly evident from this list of questions, it is important to note that the problem of morbidity is not confined to the so-called 'medical model'. As we have just mentioned, while data from the Survey of Sickness was categorized according to the Medical Research Council's classification of diseases and injuries (later the International Classification of Diseases); the diagnoses of symptoms and conditions were nonetheless based on a random sample of the population. In other words, the Survey of Sickness employed detailed medical coding, but was based on non-medical statements. The rationale of the Survey is consistent in this respect with the Durkheimian combination of pathological categories and the normal population. Indeed, a similar criticism applies in both cases: medical records are not necessarily a reliable source for national morbidity statistics. As Stocks (1949) pointed out at the time, only about a quarter of those who recorded an illness or injury for a given month had consulted a doctor during the same period. In addition to which the Survey of Sickness was susceptible to the inaccuracies of memory.[22]

These criticisms notwithstanding, the *British Medical Journal*, in a leader titled 'Are the people more healthy?' (1946), identified the essential link between 'the health of the people' and the investigation of 'larger samples of the population'. The summons for 'less propaganda' and 'more information' extends beyond the confines of medicine, not least of all, in terms of the sociological significance of the survey method. This is not to say that social science necessarily turned to the studies of health and illness, or morbidity statistics, as sources of data; for instance, there is no mention of the Survey of Sickness in the important works of Morris (1957) or Titmuss (1968). Intrinsically, however, the health survey maps the normal and the pathological onto the social body, as distinct from the 'spaces' of clinical medicine. More than a mere methodological expedient, the medical survey is first of all a model of health and illness; it emerges not as a means of support for medical sociology so much as an integral part of the new hygiene of social medicine. With a combined emphasis on empirical research and public health, the survey complements rather than facilitates the social logic of hygiene.

To take a notable example, the wartime practice of social medicine under the guidance of John A. Ryle relied on the use of the health survey method. Ryle advanced a mode of investigation, particularly with respect to the spatial distribution of community morbidity, based on the survey as distinct from clinical medicine. As such, Ryle's contribution marks an important threshold in the history of twentieth-century medicine. For example, the survey Ryle (1948) conducted at the Institute of Social Medicine at Oxford during the war, which involved observing the health of children registered in the town at birth through to the age of five, makes social medicine an altogether 'realizable goal'.[23] As Armstrong (1983) points out, through the apparatus of the sample survey, both the ephemeral and chronic health problems arising within the normal population emerge as quantifiable objects of concern. In this respect, the health survey maps an increasingly detailed domain of social pathology, namely, from child health to mental health, geriatrics, and general practice. Deployed by a range of specialists through the system of the dispensary (Foucault 1980: 178), survey techniques thus involve a general reorganization of medical perception.

On the basis of these methodological developments in epidemiology, it is possible for social medicine to operate not only as a separate discipline from clinical medicine, but also beyond the jurisdiction of the hospital; hence the specific objectives of social medicine: first, to measure and classify the natural course of a disease in the population; second, to subject the normal population itself to an ongoing and detailed investigation. While the systematic and comprehensive treatment of normality is now a distinct possibility, social medicine does not amount simply to a break with the medicine of diseases. It is important here not to conflate the symptomological and the clinical. While the health survey operates independently from the practice of clinical medicine; nonetheless, it continues to generalize the medicine of symptoms at the level of the social. The subject of clinical medicine is replaced by the 'epidemiological clinic'; the individual medical consultation, by the multiplication of systems of health checks.[24] The organization of medical knowledge thus advances only so far in the socialization of health care. Based on the Survey of Sickness, social medicine continues to forge an alliance between health and normality, while at the same time it persists in the classification of populations in terms of two types of facts. To this extent, at least, the symptomological rationale of health surveys and the social science of hygiene are part of the same administrative discourse.

The promotion of preventive measures at the level of everyday life is coupled with the analysis of the disturbance of function, which does not amount to a contradiction in medical knowledge so much as a strategic arrangement. For Ryle, as for Durkheim, the category of pathology is given as an object of valid knowledge in the form of a symptomological sign. But as Durkheim (1895: 71) points out, nothing is seen as 'good indefinitely and to an unlimited extent'; hence the permanent task of social defence. Canguilhem draws attention to this point in *New Reflections* (Section Two, Chapter II), with regards to the differences between the organism and society: whereas organic norms are immanent; social norms are necessarily constructed. That to which we can attribute the quality of being a fact is nonetheless subject to constant regulation.

However, neither Durkheim nor Ryle augments the definition of statistically defined norms or types of morbidity, respectively, along self-reflexive lines. To take another prominent figure in the field whose work is more immediately related to Parkes's studies, Aubrey Lewis represents a further advance in social medicine. Lewis joined the staff at the Maudsley Hospital in 1929, and in 1946 was appointed to the chair of psychiatry at the hospital. In addition to this appointment within a post-graduate school of the University of London, Lewis was also director of the Occupational Psychiatry Research Unit (Medical Research Council) from 1948. The unit was twice renamed under Lewis's directorship, becoming the Unit for Research in Occupational Adaptation in 1951, and the Social Psychiatry Research Unit in 1958. Lewis used the survey in this research context as a method for collecting and analyzing statistical data, enabling him 'to chart the neurotic topography of the population' (Rose 1989: 25).

Lewis was instrumental, then, in extending the survey method to the practice of social psychiatry in the post-war period. Following his appointment as honorary secretary to the Neurosis Sub-Committee of the Royal Medico-Psychological Association established in 1942, Lewis was one of three psychiatrists invited to appear before Goodenough's Inter-departmental Committee on Medical Schools.

In his role as governmental advisor, Lewis focused attention on the social issues affecting mental health. For example, a series of memoranda produced by the Sub-Committee under Lewis's guidance underline the governmental alliance between psychiatry and social policy, including a statement on the implications for social psychiatry of the Beveridge Report.[25] Furthermore, in his wartime paper 'Psychiatric Investigations in Britain' (1945a: 491), Lewis compares the 'gross survey' and the 'refined experiment' in social medicine, on the one hand, with the use of 'bedside observation' and 'laboratory studies' in clinical research on the other. The comparison is not confined to rules of method. Here, as elsewhere, Lewis couples an account of officially sponsored surveys with a policy-oriented discussion of rehabilitation. The conclusion he comes to is that, more than a hospital or clinic based practice, psychiatry should be seen as 'an integral part of medicine, especially of social medicine'.

These conclusions confirm the findings of Lewis's (1935) earlier investigation into the problem of unemployment. Carried out in 1931, the unemployment study represents Lewis's initial contribution to social psychiatry and, as such, it lays the foundations for his ongoing argument in favour of a comprehensive methodology designed to collect the 'social information' necessary for the treatment and understanding of individual patients. As Shepherd (1979: 194) points out, in the 1931 study Lewis 'supplemented the standard clinical information with a social history obtained from a relative by a psychiatric social worker and also by a further interview conducted in the patients' homes by a research social worker at a later date'. The study draws important conclusions concerning the previous history and present state of the group of unemployed men under investigation: 'In their present circumstances may be seen a continuation of the external factors which for the greater part of their lives have interacted with inherited predispositions to make them in various ways unsatisfactory' (Lewis 1935: 297).

Lewis's contribution is particularly instructive for us, demonstrating the extent to which a strategic distance was worked out between social and clinical psychiatry that allowed new ways of thinking about the 'social' to emerge. In contrast to the Winnicottian concept of environmental deficiency, Lewis emphasized the significance of 'inherent deficiencies' with respect to the problem of adaptation. Lewis (1957) viewed the patient as 'disabled' in relation to the environment, and defined his proposed programme of rehabilitation as treatment from what he called 'the social point of view'. Indeed, it is 'the social point of view' that renders the mental state of the population, understood as a phenomenon of solidarity, amendable to government. This remains an important trajectory of post-war government. In the immediate aftermath of the war, and modelled on the Wartime Social Survey, the scientific distinction between the normal and the abnormal rests on the generalization of methods of sampling, interviewing, and sociological analysis. As Rose (1989: 30) points out, the medico-social survey 'had made itself so much a part of the thinking of government that it was incorporated after the war into the Office of Population Census and Surveys'. Together with Seebohm Rowntree, Cyril Burt, and others, Lewis formed a scientific advisory panel responsible for the redeployment of the survey after the war. Rose (1989: 30) makes the further point that, albeit with a more limited range, surveys of health and illness were employed in the post-war context with a 'precisely targeted set of enquiries'.

Notes

1 See Bachelard (1984) for the idea of 'epistemological obstacles' as well as 'epistemological breaks'. We can profit from the use of these terms, in our discussion of innovations in the history of psychoanalysis and the social sciences, so long as we allow for the generative nature of obstacles and, at the same time, for continuities through breaks.
2 Our discussion in Part II is informed by Foucault's (1963; English translation: *The Birth of the Clinic*, 1976) history of the modern conception of disease, including his account of the shift from the classical medicine of species to a new, non-essentialist view of disease, and the concomitant shift from a medicine of health to a medicine of normality. Further to Foucault's account, we shall trace the course of bereavement studies in Parkes's thinking beyond abstract classificatory structures, but also beyond the linguistic structure of the diagnostic sign.
3 Compare Canguilhem's (1966: 200) central argument in the *Essay* that health may be defined in terms of our 'capacity to overcome organic crises in order to establish a new order'.
4 For the revaluation of 'community' from the perspective of government, see Rose (1996a). Rose points to a fundamental shift in collective and personal relations in the post-war period, namely, from the problematic of 'society' to 'post-social' governmental strategies. He defines the latter in terms of a 'new territory' of political thought and action characteristic of 'advanced' liberal democracies. Our analysis of bereavement studies relies on the notion of 'government through community', as distinct from the social point of view. On the other hand, it seems to me that 'government through community', as Rose outlines it, is entirely consistent with the detailed analysis of 'government through the family' (Donzelot 1979). Rather than two distinct rationalities of government, my argument is that family life itself is presented as the model of community. While accepting the historical distinction with regard to 'society' and 'community,' I propose that bereavement studies are based on a combined community-family strategy.
5 First published in 1972, we cite the third edition of *Bereavement* (1996) throughout as a convenient reference for these studies.
6 See Chapter 2 for the distinction between normal and catastrophic forms of reaction.
7 See Castel *et al.* (1979) for an account of the exercise of psychiatric power in advanced liberal society. Notwithstanding the differences between Britain and America that we have already mentioned, the authors provide a useful historical framework for thinking about the emergence of communities of care in the treatment of mental illness. They propose two fundamental shifts that are particularly instructive for our discussion of bereavement studies: first, a shift from the binary opposition of the normal and the pathological, starting in the early years of the twentieth century with the rise of a psychoanalytic model of treatment; and second, a 'post-psychoanalytic' phase of psychiatric practice which, in the aftermath of World War II, extends things yet further beyond the discrimination of the normal and the pathological towards a 'therapy for normalcy'. The historical antecedents of the latter are set out in Foucault's (1963: 34) account of medicine's 'normative posture'.
8 The 1959 Mental Health Act made admission to psychiatric hospital treatment possible on the same voluntary basis as for general hospitals; as such, it represents a 'liberalization' of the legal framework of committal.

9. Canguilhem (1966: 93–4) traces through the work of Leriche the coincidence of illness and the person in physiology, but also more generally in the modern context of self-consciousness and self-identity.
10. For the therapeutic link between the bereaved, the immediate family, and the wider collective networks of the community, see Thornicroft and Tansella (1999: 61–2).
11. See Part One, Chapter II of Canguilhem's *Essay* (1966) for the concept of 'biological normativity'.
12. See Ablon (1973) and Raphael (1977) on community support for the bereaved.
13. The problematic of solidarity is evident, for instance, in the application of psychiatry to poverty, unemployment and workers' compensation along the lines of social insurance (Ewald 1991; Defert 1991). It is also operative in the extension of the therapeutic principles of groups from military settings to post-war collective state provision in hospitals and other medical and welfare institutions (Shepherd 1979: 196). For a revaluation of the value of 'solidarity' in the contemporary context of European unification, the solidarity 'we need today' and for the future of the European Constitution, see Michalski (2006a; 2006b).
14. See Canguilhem (1966: 203–26) for the distinction between the physiological normal (constants with propulsive value) and the pathological normal (constants with repulsive value).
15. See Rosenblatt *et al.* (1991) on the therapeutic role of the family in bereavement.
16. See Raphael (1977) on outcome predictors and the 'unsupportive' family.
17. The institutional basis of public hygiene is discussed by Armstrong (1983) and by Foucault (2000a).
18. A clear definition of the Durkheimian norm is important not only for our discussion of Parkes and bereavement studies; it may also be read alongside the critique of self-regulation in the third and final part of the book (see Chapter 7, 'Social facts and reflexive norms'). The theoretical and historical obstacles which stand in the way of reflexive medicine are also, and for the same reason, a hindrance to the sociological schema of managed lives.
19. See Canguilhem's *Essay* (Part One, Chapters II and III) for the idea of pathology as a quantitative variation of the normal in Comte and Bernard; and Hirst (1975) for a comparative study of Durkheim and Bernard.
20. Canguilhem (1966: 177–8) posits, *contra* Durkheim, the logical independence of the concepts of 'norm' and 'average'.
21. See Box and Thomas (1944) and Logan and Brooke (1957) for a discussion of health surveys.
22. For the influence of 'memory error', see Slater (1947).
23. Following his discussion of 'norm' and 'average' in the *Essay* (Part Two, Chapter III), Canguilhem (1966: 267–9) considers Ryle's attempt to make the concept of the statistical normal more 'flexible' apropos the variability of functions in physiology. For a general discussion of Ryle and the viability of social medicine, including the use of the survey, see Armstrong (1983). Shepherd (1979) discusses the historical formation of social psychiatry along similar lines; for the administrative background to psychiatry as a form of social medicine, see 'Training of Doctor's: the Goodenough Committee's Report', *British Medical Journal*, 1944, vol. 2 (4359): 121–3. Drafted alongside the White Paper on 'A National Health Service', the Report argued for a system of health care based on medical teaching and research initiatives with a broadly defined set of aims and objectives. See also Lewis's war-time research programme (1942; 1943a; 1943b; 1945b; 1945c); Lewis and Slater (1942); Lewis and Goldschmidt (1943); and Lewis and Goodyear (1944).
24. See Castel (1991: 282) for the displacement of the doctor–patient relation by 'a system of multifarious but exactly localized expertise'.
25. See Council of the Royal Medico-Psychological Association (1944).

5

ILLNESS AND IDENTITY

We can now pose the question of bereavement in an appropriate historical context by asking whether Parkes studies grief from 'the social point of view'. In other words, does he treat grief as a problem of solidarity? Clearly, there is a marked degree of continuity between the work of Lewis and Parkes: compared to the sociological problematic of hygiene, the disciplinary field supported by the use of health surveys is more closely connected to bereavement studies. Applied in the aftermath of World War II, health survey methods and the psychiatric study of grief represent new developments in the history of social medicine. Most importantly, Lewis and Parkes (the same applies to Winnicott) share a preoccupation with the health and well-being of individuals and populations *traumatized* by illness and loss. This is not simply a case of contemporaneous fields of investigation; a common concern with the socialization of medical rationality puts social psychiatry and bereavement studies, in many ways, at variance with the prevailing medical culture.

A closer examination of Parkes's model, however, will reveal the extent to which government through community displaces the 'social point of view'. Parkes is able to advance the study of grief only so far along the lines set out by the likes of Ryle and Lewis. While he follows their lead in seeing social psychiatry as a distinct formation of medicine; on the other hand, the combined problematic of adaptation and rehabilitation proves too restrictive for the purposes of reflexive medicine and its psychosocial norms. The health survey is not an adequate methodological basis for the type of intervention that Parkes envisages. As with the discriminations of hygiene in Durkheim, the health survey falls short of the subjective experience of the bereaved, failing to provide the practical techniques of intimacy that active self-management requires. Parkes thus comes up with an alternative model in an attempt to articulate the *experience* of grief, an alternative that is motivated, to a large extent, by the supposed inadequacies of psychoanalysis. In this chapter, we consider in turn the epistemological, strategic, and therapeutic aspects of Parkes's alternative psychiatric model.

Needs and norms

Parkes is actually struggling with a new set of problems based on the idea that the bereaved have special needs. It becomes possible to speak of special needs only once the idea of mental incapacity and its residual hold on social psychiatry has given way to a more direct focus on the skills and competencies of individuals. Thus Parkes goes further than Ryle and Lewis, and anticipates later developments in the sociology of identity, in attempting to integrate needs and norms. The formulation of psychosocial norms presupposes a break not only with the sociology of hygiene, but also with the medical model of pathological spaces. At odds with the orthodoxy of clinical reason, the problematic of special needs calls for a thorough overhaul of welfare provision, including the symptomological rationale of health surveys. In order to allow for individual experience, Parkes has to come up with a different way of managing life, an innovative use of administrative techniques and resources, as well as a new logic of human relations.

For Parkes, collating samples of sufficient size, or classifying combinations of social types, is relevant but, ultimately, not equal to the task of reflexive medicine. The statistically defined norm is not adequate to the concrete problem of attachment and its disorders. Psychosocial norms, as Parkes's studies demonstrate, are derived neither from the Durkheimian tradition of sociological thought, in which concepts are based on a standard of functioning and organic structure; nor from the tradition of the wartime social survey, where the supervision and management of normal populations is based on the quantification of observational knowledge. Parkes eschews the 'social point of view' on both counts: he reconstitutes the framework of social medicine in a discursive manoeuvre that goes beyond the medical opposition of health and morbidity, on the one hand, and the statistical distribution of the normal and the pathological on the other.

Once the question of health has been posed in terms of special needs, a gap opens up between clinical medicine and bereavement studies. It is no longer possible to treat grief simply as a phenomenon of clinical observation. The problem of special needs thus concerns the rationale of clinical thinking itself. Broadly speaking, following the integration of pathological anatomy into clinical medicine, which Foucault (1963) describes with reference to Bichat and Broussais's work on fevers, the body remains the privileged site of observational data. In this arrangement, the body constitutes a concrete space of perception for the distribution of the normal and the pathological.[1] By contrast, the complex configuration of mental suffering and somatic complaints that Parkes proposes to manage announces and inaugurates a new category of need. Knowledge of the latter derives from neither a semiotics of pathology nor a statistical calculation of populations (rates and types of morbidity). Grief is treated instead on a comprehensive model of health and illness, consisting of behavioural systems and modes of reaction.

How does Parkes propose to link needs and norms? The question highlights the technical as well as the epistemological implications of his model. Parkes is concerned with neither the abstract space of classification nor the clinical determination of bodies. Instead of locating individual differences within a science of diseases, Parkes turns to the general problem of continuity, a reorientation that paves the way for a thoroughly comprehensive theory of self-identity in the human and social sciences. For Parkes, the problem is how to construct a surface of consistency along social, psychological, and physiological lines. As such, bereavement studies become preoccupied with modes rather than types, and with reflexive norms rather than quantitative variation. It requires a move in the order of an 'epistemological act'[2] to free the science of mourning from the limits imposed by a combination of clinical medicine and *l'âme collective*. This is not to say that Parkes simply discards the spatial problematic. On the contrary, by extending the continuum of the normal and the pathological beyond segregative modes of treatment, Parkes allows for an alternative 'geographical' consciousness of health and illness based on self-regulating communities of care.[3]

To be clear, there are continuities as well as breaks between bereavement studies and the general field of social psychiatry. The medico-social survey itself marks an important break with respect to the distribution of diseases within the patient's body. As we saw in the previous chapter, health surveys do not operate on the model of pathological medicine. The distribution of bodies is already displaced by the relative position of bodies in the medical examination of large, randomly selected populations. From the perspective of the health survey, there are no inherent distinctions between bodies at alternative ends of the continuum; significance is assigned only to the spaces separating bodies (Armstrong 1983: 51). This means that while *types* of pathology persist in epidemiological discourse, the relationship between the normal and the pathological is nonetheless defined as a general phenomenon of the population. In short, position takes precedence over distribution.

Nevertheless, in spite of the advances made by Ryle, Lewis and others towards the socialization of medicine, the development of a comprehensive normative perspective remains wanting. This is evident, for instance, in the coincidence of norms and morals at the level of social regulation. The priority assigned to the spaces between bodies establishes the moral significance of relations in accordance with a normative conception of the collective consciousness. The space in question is described in any number of ways by Durkheim: the 'moral conscience of nations'; the 'psychic life of society'; 'popular consciousness'; and the 'mentality of groups'. These descriptions suggest certain possibilities for a sociology of intimacy and everyday life, but only insofar as the social is confined to a quantitative measure of the normal and the pathological. Sociology becomes caught up in the moralization of its own categories. Although Durkheim, in *Le Suicide* and elsewhere, maintains pathology exists to the extent that the moral conscience becomes too rigid and restrictive, at the same time, the proposal to limit the authority of the *conscience collective* is itself a moral argument. Pathology is ultimately defined in terms of deviations from a fixed norm.

However, Durkheim's arguments to the contrary notwithstanding, the 'good' that must be done in the name of society does not arise spontaneously from the structure of society. And so long as society has no intrinsic norm, the organic analogy does not stand up to scrutiny. The decisive break between the Comte–Durkheim tradition of classical sociology, on the one hand, and modern reflexive social science, on the other, occurs at the point where the constitutive nature of social norms forms part of a fully integrated theory of regulation.[4] Bereavement studies operate along this discursive fault line from the 1960s onwards; contemporaneously, special needs emerge as an object of concern throughout the public sphere: from education and employment to mental health, social welfare, and the law. Bereavement studies articulate this historic conjuncture of special needs and constitutive norms. It is now possible to think of the bereaved in governmental terms. Thus Parkes relies on the norm neither as a measurement of objectivity at the level of social facts, nor as a condition of individual perception. The norm is anything but an abstraction in Parkes's studies. The principle of need articulates the normative structure, where norms proceed from needs and are knowable only in the psychosocial context of normalization.

It stand to reason for Parkes (1996: 208) that, 'after it has occurred', a given life-event can be classified only in accordance with the meaning assigned to the event by the individual. This requires a fundamental change in clinical thinking, if not in the very organization of truth and its practice across the social sciences. For whereas the sample survey, for example, displaces the norm as the referent external to the population under examination (Armstrong 1983); the problematic of special needs no longer relies on the norm as the spatial principle of classificatory knowledge. In this respect, bereavement studies operate according to a more pervasive transformation of veridical discourse. This has technical as well as theoretical implications: therapeutic supervision and social regulation operate in tandem, where the norm is free to function in the service of needs along the lines of normalization. As far as the study of grief is concerned, the manner in which the norm is defined occasions a shift in the structure of psychiatric medicine, namely, from pathological spaces and states of mind to continua and processes. The symptomatic surface gives way to a more comprehensive image of mental health; the generality of the collective mind is displaced by active modes of self-reflection; and illness itself is seen as a form of situated action on the model of self-identity. It is within this normative context that the community itself becomes a problem of care.

Family-centred model of treatment

Together with the coincidence of norms and needs, bereavement studies offer a coherent framework of therapeutic intervention. As such, the treatment of grief is indicative of a wider development in post-war health care. The meaning we give to the pains we feel is inevitably subjective and subject to change, which is why any attempt at universality risks superficiality. However, given this proviso, how we suffer pain, the *pathos* of our pain, depends not only on what we as individuals make of our feelings, but also on the collective representations of painful experience. We name even our most private feelings, our most intimate pains, based on the available repertoire of meanings in the movement from perception to experience. This is an historical phenomenon where, in modern societies, it is largely through diagnostic systems of classification that the psychological dispositions of individuals are rendered knowable as forms of experience. From the modern perspective of secular reason, we know who we are on the basis of the scientific categories applied to our experience. In this respect, at least, communities of care have replaced religious communities.

The self-knowledge of modernity, however, is not a settled enlightenment, but requires ongoing revision. Accordingly, bereavement studies represent a historic revision which is evident, for example, in the technical problem of categorization. Parkes came up against the problem of categorization insofar as the available diagnostic systems made no reference to the *experience* of grief. In mainstream psychiatry, during the immediate post-war period, bereavement appeared neither as a specific nosological category nor as an identifiable object of treatment. A recent controversy concerning the categorization of bereavement demonstrates the persistent nature of the problem. In a draft proposal for the American Psychiatric Association's new edition of the *Diagnostic and Statistical Manual of Mental Disorders* (DSM-V), subsequently published in May 2013, the Mood Disorder Work Group made certain recommendations with regard to bereavement.[5]

First, the DSM-V's Work Group proposed to remove the bereavement exclusion criterion that had previously been in place, when determining the diagnostic symptoms of Major Depressive Disorder. Hitherto a person who had experienced a recent bereavement was not eligible for a diagnosis of major depression. The thinking in the DSM-V's Work Group, however, was that the exclusion criterion amounted to under-diagnosis, resulting in a possible failure to treat a debilitating depressive disorder. Second, then, Prolonged Grief Disorder was proposed as a new diagnostic category, which allowed for a classification of pathological bereavement where the psychological and physiological sequelae of loss persisted for longer than two weeks. Earlier editions of DSM proposed that a psychiatrist should wait 1 year (DSM-III) or 2 months (DSM-IV) before categorizing an abnormal grief reaction as depression and treating the bereaved person with anti-depressants and psychotherapy. The new proposal was subsequently amended, following a vociferous debate within the profession.[6] Prolonged Grief Disorder was replaced by Persistent Complex Bereavement Related Disorder. The amended category comprises an unresolved, debilitating form of grief that is nonetheless diagnostically distinct from Major Depressive Disorder.

Since DSM-III in 1980, the psychiatric debate on bereavement has shifted from a discourse of psychosocial norms to 'a research-led medical model based on descriptive psychopathology' (McGinley 2012: 2). Nevertheless, presented with a comparable lack of precision in psychiatric diagnosis during the 1960s, Parkes was faced with the task of having to construct a concept of grief within psychiatric discourse. It is what he did with the problem that proved decisive from the point of view of reflexive medicine. Basically, Parkes generalizes the diagnosis of grief not as a universal category, but rather, in terms of individual and collective experience. As far as individuals are concerned, Parkes identifies the process of grief as a normal reaction to a traumatic situation. He argues that while grief appears to be a form of extreme behaviour, it is in fact a normal response to a major psychological upheaval. We shall come back to the specific problem of traumatic bereavement, or catastrophic reaction, in our discussion of the management of 'special risk'. For the moment, the important point is that Parkes's diagnostic argument is based on a comparison between normal grief and the dying patient.[7] Parkes maintains that the phases of dying bear a close resemblance to the phases of grief; in both cases, modes of reaction are described specifically in sequential terms. Thus, Parkes (1996: 165) describes dying as 'a process of psychosocial transition', including feelings of isolation, denial, anger, bargaining, depression, and acceptance. Similarly, he argues that, with the stress of grief, the bereaved are subject to a process of numbness, yearning and searching; disorganization and despair; and, finally, a greater or lesser degree of reorganization.

The normative conception of 'transition' underpins Parkes's account of the experience of grief. As such, it confirms the basic assumptions underlying his earlier work on modes of reactive behaviour: 'These kinds of phenomena are also commonly found in amputees and other disabled people, and they are best viewed as typical components of a psychosocial transition' (1993: 97). The continuum of dying, grief, and disability is important for at least two reasons: first, it identifies bereavement more broadly as a category of special needs. This has direct implications with respect to the social inclusion of what we might call transitional forms of conduct. The grief-stricken widow falls between the normal and the traumatic, in the same way as the antisocial child falls between ordinary mischievousness and the law. The widow is identified on the threshold of illness; the child, on the threshold of criminality. The difference in perspective notwithstanding, DSM-V inherits and consolidates the logic of psychosocial transition in the category of Persistent Complex Bereavement Related Disorder. In this case, bereavement may be seen as a form of abnormal conduct, but not as a major depressive disorder. As we shall see, Parkes introduces the practice of therapeutic supervision on this diagnostic basis, making adequate provision for the bereaved to be systematically monitored and assessed for appropriate interventions.

Second, the link between dying and grief presupposes a normal course of mourning based on the ideal of reintegration or reorganization. As a consequence mourning becomes yet one more problem of regulation at the level of need. This is a political as well as an historical argument, the bereaved find common cause with the sick and the disabled in a culture of human rights. Supervised communities of care are in all fundamental respects dependent on the political reason of the liberal state, where the sick have recourse to the law as social justice. Two incommensurable formations of therapeutic experience may be identified here as alternative negotiations of justice: on the one hand, clinical rationality as 'a style of totalization'; on the other hand, the psychosocial problematic of social inclusion.[8] Taking Parkes's argument to its logical conclusion, the positivism of modern medical practice is displaced by a psychosocial model of disturbance and adjustment, with an emphasis on chronic debilitating forms of conduct rather than mental illness as such.

The psychosocial norm is obviously not confined to individuals, but extends to the population as a whole. Parkes combines the inclusive category of grief with a diffuse diagnostic field. This calls into question the form and function of clinical diagnosis. Whereas the medical model of illness is confined to a clinic of symptoms, the inclusive category of grief presupposes a generalized diagnostics. Based on our foregoing discussion, we can see how the incommensurability of clinical and reflexive medicine becomes evident at the level of the diagnostic sign. While clinical medicine is based on a symptomatic surface of types; by contrast, reflexive medicine is arranged in the form of modes, sequential processes, and clusters of variables. The prevailing medical model classifies the normal and the pathological as two types of facts; the psychosocial model maps a series of special needs at the level of a comprehensive norm. This represents a new development in the institutional process of normalization, where a community with special needs emerges as an object of psychiatric and administrative knowledge without recourse to discrimination. The deliberations of the Mood Disorder Work Group of DSM-V, and the amended category of Persistent Complex Bereavement Related Disorder, may be seen as a legacy of Parkes's efforts to locate the process of grief between the normal and the pathological.

To underline the importance of the political context, juridical and ethical claims about the rights of individuals with special needs are inextricably linked to the diagnostic argument pertaining to communities of care. As Parkes (1996: 193) puts it: 'The treatment of pathological reactions to bereavement follows the same principles as those that have been indicated for the support of bereaved people in general'. Again, this is not to say that Parkes simply disregards the categories of the normal and the pathological, any more than he dispenses with the problematic of clinical medicine. Indeed, Parkes (1996: 194) continues to argue that there are several modes of 'pathological grief', each of which requires a different method of treatment. Nevertheless, the principle of classification is the same as that of treatment, where the transformation of pathological grief into normal grief takes place on an unbroken continuum that describes the usual course towards resolution. The detailed investigation of normality, which is already set out in the apparatus of the survey, is no longer distinct from the line of pathology traced across the whole of the population. As such, the field of reflexive medicine incorporates and reworks the spatial conception of disease and the distribution of illness, allowing for a new strategic alliance between pathological medicine and community medicine. Most importantly, illness and identity are mapped together along the lines of self-management at the level of community care.

The framework of community care and the generalization of diagnosis are mutually dependent developments in the case of bereavement. The manner in which the norm is defined is not confined to the identification and description of the phenomenon, but is also linked to modes of intervention and the problem of treatment. Essentially, the *locus* of intervention shifts from the established domain of clinical observation to communities of care; from the combined clinical and pedagogic domain of the teaching hospital to the continuum of care between the hospice and the home. We are not suggesting that things simply revert to a situation that pertained before the institutionalization of hospital medicine.[9] Nor are we proposing that the administration of grief takes place in some kind of authentic familial setting. Rather, what we can see is that a functional amalgamation emerges within the domain of personal and collective relations, pertaining not only to the home and the community, but also to the medical and the domestic sphere. This is another way of saying that the process of mourning takes place in an open-ended arrangement, a complex setting in which individual well-being continues to assume a community form through the mediation of a broadly defined medical expertise.[10] Again, this is not something altogether new. As Foucault (1980: 178) points out, the replacement of the hospital by a domestic form of health care, a medical staffing of the population, and the use of dispensaries in a supervisory function, are already present throughout the eighteenth century. Indeed, the care of insanity outside formal institutions dates from the same period.[11] It would be more accurate to say that bereavement studies reconstructs rather than invents the concept of care in the community. As such, the treatment of grief represents a development in a wider history of social medicine, where family and friends are reckoned to provide a 'natural' setting for an event the special needs of which turn on problems of integration, regulation, and supervision.

The treatment of grief indicates the extent to which psychiatric medicine is not best served by an enclosed form. Institutional support is seen only as a 'temporary retreat', where things are routinely open from the first to the environment, to the family, and to the wider community of friends and neighbours. The restriction on institutional care applies to various types of provision, including, day centres, night hostels, or in-patient psychiatric units. The strategic emphasis of the argument, in this case, is clear: 'the care of the bereaved is a communal responsibility, and family members and others should not withdraw their support simply because a person has been referred to a psychiatrist' (Parkes 1996: 197). In cases where the National Health Service or local authorities are involved in the treatment of bereavement, that is, through the work of community psychiatric nurses and psychiatric social workers, Parkes argues that the service is nonetheless 'family-centred'. Here, as elsewhere, the family underpins the argument for a community-based form of action.

The familial strategy of government through community represents the institutional corollary of the reflexive norm. Parkes invests the family itself with a kind of therapeutic expertise through the programme of community care. At once innovative and prescient, Parkes exemplifies the immediate post-war developments in social psychiatry and, at the same time, anticipates the consolidation of community care throughout the subsequent decades of the twentieth century. In the field of mental health and elsewhere, throughout this period the policy of reintegration prevails increasingly on families, neighbours, and friends. For instance, with the advent of AIDS the reflexive model of care relies on the extension of the familial strategy to an even wider community of intimates. Parkes (1996: xii) himself is receptive to this situation in referring to 'a new population of people of whom many suffer multiple bereavements'. Together, strategies of self-management and psychosocial norms apply from one population to the next, be it vulnerable widows in the immediate aftermath of the war or AIDS-related bereavement.

To place the treatment of bereavement along these lines in a governmental context, the deployment of needs and norms in the form of a familiar strategy keys in with some of the main trends in healthcare policy from the 1950s through the 1980s. For example, the mixed economy of care recommended in the 1957 report of the Royal Commission on Mental Health, and reflected in the 1959 Mental Health Act, identified the family as an important partner in the care of the mentally ill. Contemporaneous with Parkes's initial studies, these statements marked the beginning of a trend in post-war mental health policy that became yet more explicit in the 1970s. For example, in both the 1971 White Paper *Better Services for the Mentally Handicapped* and the 1975 White Paper *Better Services for the Mentally Ill*, there was a consistent emphasis on non-medical, non-hospital support. The notion of a family-centred mental health service was consolidated subsequently in the 1979 report of the Royal Commission on the National Health Service, which placed the onus for care primarily on 'families or neighbours' (1979: 58).

The 1989 White Paper *Caring for People* represented a further development along these lines, where the emphasis was now on 'care by the community' rather than 'care in the community'. While the local health authority and the local authority social services department continued to farm out their responsibilities for routine care and social welfare, there was nonetheless a more systematic alliance operating between family-centred care and the private sector. Finally, bringing things more or less up to date with the third edition of *Bereavement*, the report of the Commission on Social Justice, published in 1994, represented a whole-hearted endorsement of the underlying strategy of decentralization and market regulation: 'it is not feasible to extend the founding principle of the NHS – that treatment should be free at the point of use – to the *comprehensive provision* of care and help with everyday activities' (1994: 299; emphasis added). The Social Justice Commission posed the problem of community care explicitly in terms of private long-term insurance schemes. While the bereaved were not identified as such, there was nonetheless a particular focus on the elderly and those with chronic illnesses of one kind or another. The emphasis on solidarity gives way in these recommendations to government through supervised communities of care. As Donzelot (1991: 178) puts it, 'legalized state protection of the individual' is replaced by 'an apparatus for the collective mediation of fulfilment and satisfaction'.

The line adopted in this series of policy statements marks a threshold in the way we think about ourselves and our intimate relations with one another; it represents a new image of social justice. As Rose and Miller (1992: 79) point out, the strategy of government through community indicates the emergence of 'active entrepreneurship' in place of 'the passivity and dependency of responsible solidarity'. From the 1960s onwards, the 'social' itself is in question as a principle of government as well as a criterion of well-being. While individuals are encouraged to fulfil and satisfy themselves, at the same time they are increasingly thrown back on their families as sources of care. The family therefore remains 'the most constant agent' of medical intervention and supervision (Foucault 1980: 173), while at the same time assumptions about personal and social management are reconstituted along new 'entrepreneurial' lines. And this new economy of care requires a complementary norm. Thus, throughout the mental health sector, the familial strategy is pushed increasingly in the direction of broadly-defined networks and arrangements of care. This strategy presupposes supervision and professional intervention, without which it would not be viable. As far as bereavement is concerned, families function as nodal points for management practices only to the extent that the self-regulating capacities of the bereaved are contained by means of a therapeutic investment in the family. In this respect, Parkes's studies exemplify the extent to which the community is constituted as an object as well as a mechanism of care through the psychiatric supervision of families.

There are various ways in which mental-health professionals aim to harness the patient's family as an economic and emotional resource. For example, new techniques of measuring family involvement and the impact of care are advanced in order to enhance the effective collaboration of professionals and families in caring for the mentally ill (Kuipers and Bebbington 1991; Schene *et al.* 1994). On the assumption that relatives may be incorporated within communities of care only on an 'informed' basis, it requires mechanisms to convey knowledge, skills, and agreed information to family members (Szmukler and Bloch 1997). And without holding relatives to blame for patients' problems, there is nonetheless a clear research agenda on the mental health problems of carers themselves (Thornicroft and Tansella 1999). These examples illustrate ways in which, underpinned by a reflexive norm, the apparatus of self-management may be applied to the problem of mourning. Together with the hospice–home couple as a template for domestic 'hospitalization', these research initiatives indicate the importance of the familial strategy in the institutionalization of mourning. Making the most of the family, including its economic resources, emotional assets and moral values; at the same time, the strategy of governing through communities of care breaks new ground in attempting to locate the bereaved self within a general 'mental health matrix' under the supervision of psychiatric expertise.

Awareness that something is wrong

We have argued that bereavement studies forms part of a wider development in post-war social psychiatry, the reflexive nature of which runs up against some fundamental obstacles. These obstacles include the articulation of the normal and the pathological on the model of social hygiene, and the symptomological format of health surveys. Parkes advances an alternative model of reflexive medicine on at least three counts: first, through the study of modes rather than types of grief; second, in determining the normative dimension of life by means of the criterion of need; and, third, by extending the familial strategy to the management of grief in communities of care. As such, Parkes's studies constitute a decisive break, first, with pathological medicine and epidemiology, and second, with the spatial conception of disease and the distributive schema of health and illness. Having discussed the epistemological and strategic aspects of this break, we shall now turn more directly to the therapeutic argument.

The widow is at the centre of Parkes's therapeutic argument. As well as a scientific understanding of bereavement, Parkes's studies present ways of managing grief based on the experience of widows. Keeping in mind our discussion of his epistemological project and strategic objectives, Parkes privileges the widow as an object of concern at the intersection of modes of behaviour, special needs, and the familial strategy. The experience of widows thus brings us to the central therapeutic objective that Parkes sets himself in linking the process of mourning with the management of risk. It also demonstrates explicitly Parkes's engagement with Freud and psychoanalysis.

What does Parkes mean by the process of mourning? How, more broadly, does a profoundly personal experience of this kind become a problem amenable to government? What does it mean to manage ourselves in the face of loss? Bereavement emerges in Parkes's studies as a new form of mental illness, but also as an ordinary everyday phenomenon. This sets up an ambiguity rather than an inconsistency in his therapeutic argument, an ambiguity which proves decisive if individuals are going to manage their own problems with professional help. Parkes includes a pathological mode of grief in terms of 'a subgroup of the anxiety states', but without reducing the patient's experience to the symptomatic form of clinical medicine. Thus, Parkes (1996: 23) concludes that 'most of the complaints which take [widows] to their doctors are reflections of anxiety and tension rather than of organic disease'.[12] The most important role for the family doctor, according to Parkes, is to reassure widows that they are not sick rather than to label them as sick.

This is a decisive intervention. The doctor does what is most needed by telling the patient that she is well when she feels unwell. There are two reasons why this is important in the broader context that we are describing under the heading of managed lives. First, the doctor's reassurance of well-being requires the patient's initial expression of ill-health. The experience of grief becomes manageable under psychiatric supervision insofar as it is treated from the patient's point of view, but according to the ultimate authority of the doctor. Parkes describes various ways in which the bereaved feel unwell, including, feelings of anger, guilt, anxiety and stress.[13] The expression of these feelings is significant in the context of the doctor's response. The patient is encouraged to confer meaning in consulting her doctor, but within a form of experience that is strictly delimited by supervisory authority and scientific knowledge. Through this arrangement ill-health is reformulated as anxiety or tension; the category of illness itself is continuous with normal reactions to stressful situations.

Second, Parkes makes a fundamental point about labelling. The reflexive norm covers the stressful feelings and anxieties to which bereavement gives rise, and in doing so incorporates a 'realm of pathology' entirely free of stigmatization. The inclusive definition of bereavement operates now in the direction of social normalization ('they are not sick'), now in the direction of mental illness. Parkes (1996: 5) retains the definition of illness on physiological as well as psychological grounds: 'The assertion that because grief will be experienced by most of us sooner or later it cannot be said to be an illness is not valid. There are many illnesses that most of us experience.' This amounts to an ambiguous state of affairs that cannot be settled by a typology of grief based on normative measurements and standard deviations. The fixed duality of the normal and the pathological no longer pertains to the extent that the bereaved are seen as both ill and normal. In effect, the category of illness is subsumed under the more inclusive notion of mental health.

Reassuring widows that they are not sick, telling the patient that she is well when she feels ill, defines the task of therapeutic supervision in the case of bereavement. There is no contradiction in this argument. Grief is posited as a problem of special needs on a continuum of normalization within a common range of pathology. Parkes treats grief like chicken pox or measles. But while grief is seen in this way as an ordinary experience, it is nonetheless acknowledged as an interruption or irregularity of sorts. Grief is something that affects people's mental health without becoming a distinct category or symptom of psychopathology. Parkes allows for the fact that grief throws things out of order to a greater or lesser extent, that it 'disturbs function', while at the same time causing people to suffer. The *pathos* of bereavement is central to Parkes's therapeutic argument, and his (1996: 32 *et passim*) insistence on anxiety makes the point that grief is at once a 'distressing' and 'distressed' condition. Feelings of panic, as Parkes (1996: 44) points out, are combined in the bereaved with

> restless but aimless hyperactivity, difficulty in concentrating on anything but thoughts of loss, ruminations around the events leading up to the loss as well as loss of interest in any of the people or things that normally give pleasure or claim attention.

In making us anxious and causing us to suffer in this way, grief keeps us from the life we normally lead.

According to Parkes, however, the profound stress that grief may cause does not warrant a label of sickness. What does this tell us about the place assigned to mourning in a so-called normal life? Loss is seen after all as a kind of 'wound'. That Parkes relies explicitly on the notions of 'disturbance' and 'injury', describing the subjective experience of grief in these terms, indicates the underlying and unavoidable engagement with psychoanalysis. Freud (1887–1904: 103–4) is the source for the idea of an 'internal haemorrhage', operating as a hole in the psychic sphere on the model of physical pain. The 'wound' in this case is manifest in the very midst of normality, even as it is discernable on the threshold of psyche and soma. Parkes (1996: 6) applies these ideas about psychic pain to the experience of grief on two counts: first, he proposes that, '[o]n the whole, grief resembles a physical injury more closely than any other type of illness. The loss may be spoken of as a "blow"'. Second, Parkes concludes that, as with a physical injury, the wound which the blow of loss inflicts usually heals over time.[14]

The therapeutic interview does not allow Parkes to pursue Freud's (1917) central proposition on pathological mourning, namely, that the internal conflict due to 'ambivalence' towards the object is reconstituted in the relationship with oneself. This marks a parting of the ways: whereas Winnicott reworked the Freudian coincidence of melancholia and narcissistic impasse as unthinkable anxiety (Roussillon 2010); Parkes decouples anxiety, guilt, and stress from the model of unconscious motivation. But while he deliberately avoids any reference to the unconscious, Parkes nonetheless takes up Freud's idea that the self-reproaches of pathological grief reflect 'a dim awareness' of the feelings of hostility towards an ambivalently loved object. Thus, Parkes (1996: 86) recalls that 'at least one woman in the London Study, and a large proportion of those in the Bethlem Study, expressed intense feelings of guilt which could be explained in this way'. And he concludes that 'it was the frequency and intensity of guilt that most clearly distinguished the bereaved psychiatric patients of the Bethlem Study from the unselected widows of the London Study' (1996: 86).

By extending the argument from the organic analogy of pain to subjective feelings of guilt, Parkes places the anxieties and stresses of pathological mourning within the reach of therapeutic practice. Should we take this as an argument for Freudian therapy? Parkes seems to approve of Freud's therapeutic efforts in making connections between traumatic events and particular symptoms. He concludes that 'where major stresses are concerned (and loss of a close relative is normally a major stressor), [the Freudian] approach fully justifies its results' (1996: 3). But his approval is qualified on the grounds that the aetiology of grief is invariably complex. That there are very few 'mental illnesses' whose causes are straightforward is not something many people would dispute. Further to which, however, Parkes makes no mention of the function of unconscious motives in what he sees as the causal connection between events and symptoms. Instead, he anticipates an advanced stage in *scientific* knowledge when we can expect a psychiatric understanding of grief replete with reliable theories of causation. In the meantime, causal explanations are found wanting to the extent that 'few of them are yet amenable to testing by scientific means' (1996: 4). His ultimate dismissal of psychoanalysis, therefore, is presented on similar grounds to his implicit critique of medical signs.

This is clearly not an argument for psychoanalysis. 'What Freud did', as Rycroft (1966: 44) points out, 'was not to explain the patient's choice causally but to understand it and give it meaning, and the procedure he engaged in was not the scientific one of elucidating causes but the semantic one of making sense of it.' Parkes does not pursue the fundamental Freudian insight that unconscious symptoms are meaningful. He presents an alternative argument along two lines from the perspective of scientific reason: on the one hand, he maintains the principle of causation alongside his critical comments on the perception of clinical observation in its current state. On the other hand, he identifies the semantic nature of therapeutic knowledge with the reflexive norm. The image that Parkes gives us of the bereaved self is derived neither from the Freudian interpretation of unconscious phenomena nor from the clinical gaze. Parkes advances a third option based on the patient's awareness that something is wrong. Freud, from the 1895 *Project* onwards, emphasized the complicated links between traumatic events and symptoms as part of the therapeutic task, identifying the psychological conditions of pathological mourning in terms of the semantic connection between signs and states. Parkes (1996: 7) focuses instead on the reaction to loss as a normal part of human experience: 'the process of grieving' is described along these lines as 'a succession of clinical pictures which blend into and replace one another', distinct from a 'set of symptoms' or 'states of mind'. As a condition of therapy, the doctor is encouraged to take up the patient's feeling that something is wrong as a transitional mode of consciousness.

A duty to the dead

Parkes privileges the 'succession of clinical pictures' as the basis of his therapeutic argument. He defines mourning in this way as a self-reflexive project, which he compares not only to the recovery from physical injury, but also to the phases of dying. We have already indicated the link he makes between dying and mourning. As such, his account of the process of mourning is similar to Kübler-Ross's (1973) description of the act of dying. For Parkes (1996: 43), the reaction to loss is not typically one of prolonged breakdown or depression, but of 'acute and episodic "pangs"'. The latter denote 'an episode of severe anxiety and psychological pain', but within an ongoing process of recovery and restitution. However acute or severe, these painful feelings of anxiety and stress are considered part of the process; as such, they provide a reconstituted psychiatric medicine with an inclusive and comprehensive concept of grief.

It is possible on this reading to identify someone as suffering from mental illness without recourse to clear and distinct symptomatic indications. In fact, it is enough in principle that the survivors sob or cry aloud. Following an initial feeling of numbness, Parkes (1996: 43) describes how the process of mourning proceeds through this second phase of anxious pining:

Pangs of grief begin within a few hours or days of bereavement and usually reach a peak of severity within five to fourteen days. At first they are very frequent and seem to occur spontaneously, but as time passes they become less frequent and take place only when something occurs that brings the loss to mind.

This is what Robertson and Bowlby (1952) call the phase of yearning and protest, which they claim usually lasts for a period of months, but can sometimes continue for years.

The idea of acute and episodic anxiety underpins a narrative of ordinary mental anguish, the process of which amounts to a series of 'clinical pictures' rather than symptoms or unconscious states of mind. These pictures tend to blend together in Parkes's description of numbness, panic, pining, searching, anger, guilt, anxiety, and stress. The ambiguous nature of the bereaved self is evident throughout this process, an ambiguity that Parkes maintains by treating grief, at once, as a psychiatric disorder and a normal event of everyday life. And far from resolving the ambiguity, Parkes's notion of anxiety consolidates the idea that, unlike other psychiatric illnesses, grief does not cause people to 'lose control of their behaviour', or to 'become incapable of acting rationally' (1996: 4). The ambiguity at the heart of Parkes's concept of mourning rests on the coincidence of affect and cognition. The therapeutic argument, in other words, draws immediately on the epistemological perspective of reflexivity. The acknowledgement of 'ambivalence' and 'aggressiveness' towards the dead notwithstanding, Parkes treats the reaction to bereavement in terms of the cognitive capacity of the bereaved. He describes a process in which individuals are more or less capable of using the resources available for managing themselves. The clinical picture is calculated in terms of the magnitude of the reaction to the loss of a loved object as a 'major stressor'. But no matter how bad people react, the assumption is that the process of recovery depends on the individual as an active and rational agent.

The therapeutic argument, then, is based on the assumption of self-control. The idea that modes of reaction constitute an active relation to the process of mourning presupposes a capacity to manage ourselves and maintain control. It may not be immediately obvious how this argument is at odds with the Freudian interpretation. Parkes and Freud seem to be preoccupied with the same problem. Typically, a woman bereft, consumed by her own vulnerability and painful memories, poring over her emotional life and its intimate realities, is made sick by her response to love's loss. But for all the apparent similarities, the differences between Freud and Parkes are more fundamental.

To summarize Freud's (1917) argument in 'Mourning and melancholia': first, Freud presents an analysis of psychic structure rather than a description of empirical behaviour; second, the temporality of grief is complicated by the nature of identification, which Freud traces back to the oral or cannibalistic phase of libidinal development; and, third, Freud reconstructs pathological mourning as the work of the negative. The basic insight in this seminal essay concerns the way in which the bereaved, at once, withdraw their emotional investments into themselves and identify with the abandoned object. 'In this way', Freud (1917: 249) concludes, 'an object-loss was transformed into an ego-loss and the conflict between the ego and the loved person into a cleavage between the critical activity of the ego [later the superego] and the ego as altered by identification.' It is the ego rather than the world that loses its meaning in Freud's account of pathological mourning, where the bereaved are subject to delusions of inferiority and expectations of punishment; hence the narcissistic impasse of melancholia. One finds life itself repeatedly devalued in working with patients in this state of mind.

Parkes simply ignores the intrapsychic conflict that drives Freud's melancholic mad in the form of self-reproaches. Far from a catastrophic loss of self-regard, for Parkes the bereaved are invariably seen as capable of managing *on their own terms*, albeit in some cases with psychiatric supervision. We should not be misled by references to 'ambivalence' and 'guilt'. Parkes uses these terms, without the technical underpinning of the transference, as descriptions of emotional behaviour. In the case of Anna O., for example, Parkes (1996: 3) argues that her 'father's illness and death can be regarded as the precipitating circumstances without which [her] illness would probably not have arisen'. That having been said, the essential link between symptoms and structure is immediately obscured by an emphasis on the self-identity of the bereaved. Again, notwithstanding the degree of disturbance, for Parkes identity remains an accessible psychosocial ideal throughout the process of mourning.

The emphasis on rational reflection is most apparent in the way that Parkes describes what he sees as the final stage of mourning. That the bereaved should 'give up their withdrawal from life' and 'start building a new life' seems straightforward enough. Taken at face value, the aim is not inconsistent with the Winnicottian idea of reclamation. But there are various ways of achieving this objective. The technical differences between Parkes and Freud once again come to the fore. Freud (1911c: 94) credits 'the guidance of the unconscious', the steer given by the patient's free association in conjunction with the analyst's evenly suspended attention, over and above the recourse to 'conscious purposive aims during the treatment'. Finding out what they are doing and how they come to be there is a central task for each analytic couple. The matter cannot be settled in advance, even as it continues to elude a definitive answer. The Freudian patient does not have 'issues' and cannot expect 'solutions'.

By contrast, Parkes situates the therapeutic objective within a definite configuration of normative conduct and mutual responsibility:

> In a situation in which well-established norms are absent, the expectations of those around are potent determinants of behaviour. Thus friends or relatives can indicate, implicitly or explicitly, that grief is expected and permitted, but they can also indicate that it has gone on long enough. To some extent grieving is seen as a duty to the dead and it may take an outsider to point out that the duty is now done, or at least that the mourner can be permitted to let up a little.
>
> (Parkes 1996: 177)

The break with psychoanalysis is unequivocal when our duty to the dead is reckoned in terms of the capacity to exercise responsible self-control. This is not how Freud understood the problem of mourning. Unlike Parkes, Freud continued to emphasize the disturbance of self-regard in melancholia, the self-destructiveness of melancholic grievance, where the bereaved are seen to eat away at themselves through unconscious hostility and a deep sense of guilt. It is important here to differentiate between accepting responsibility in the Freudian sense and taking charge (Lear 1992: 65–6). The latter involves reinstating ourselves, including our personal attachments no less than our social roles and obligations, within the very community of family, friends, and others that enables us to do so. And at this stage in the process, Parkes (1996: 177) argues that the community exercises its duty of care by helping the bereaved to 'establish their own autonomy'. For Parkes, the link between autonomy and responsibility applies throughout the grieving process, where responsibility is assumed initially in honouring the dead, and maintained thereafter in the abiding attachment to community. The mutual responsibility around which communities of care are organized constitutes mourning itself as an opportunity for the bereaved to retain self-control and to behave in a more or less reasonable way. Parkes allows for the fact that the reaction to bereavement may take a pathological course, but he does not see this as a separate 'type' of experience at odds with the rationally ordered life.

In contrast to the work of mourning (*Trauerarbeit*), Parkes refers to a process of 'psychosocial transitions' based on the reformation of identity through illness. For Parkes, experience does not become unthinkable in traumatic situations. To the contrary, he assumes that we know what has been lost, what causes us to suffer, and what prevents us from living. There is actually nothing to interpret here. The process of mourning consists largely in making good these recognizable pains and inhibitions. We cope with what we recognize, and the psychiatrist supports the patient in the task of coping with what has evidently happened on account of having lost a loved one. This leaves no room for any gaps or discontinuities in consciousness: while 'atypical' expressions of grief 'differ in intensity and duration from the more usual reactions to bereavement, certain aspects of which may be exaggerated or distorted, *they do not differ in kind*' (1996: 116; emphasis added). Thus the ambiguity of mourning cuts across the discriminations of the normal and the pathological. The implication being that when it comes to grief, we cannot rely on the symptom as the meaning of *pathos*. This applies to observations within the perceptual field of clinical medicine, but also to the Freudian symptom. Parkes (1996: 116) remains equally sceptical of clinical medicine and psychoanalysis: 'there are no symptoms that are peculiar to pathological grief'.

What Parkes makes of his disagreement with Freud is more important than the disagreement itself. Even at its most traumatic, grief is not normally considered as a breakdown. Illness and identity merge on a continuous and comprehensive surface that comprises a series of 'psychosocial transitions' and 'turning-points'.

In this case, symptomatic complaints are more broadly defined as a set of transitional events. Although the notion of 'illness' still applies, it is no longer a question of the relative position of bodies on the model of the medical survey. At the same time, the practical task of managing grief takes place outside the clinic in supervised domestic space. Through the study of processes rather than symptoms, pathological space itself becomes transitional; the 'facts' of sickness and health are replaced by an irreducible combination of illness and identity; and, in principle at least, the treatment of individuals is conducted openly in supervised communities of care that the bereaved are free to use as their needs dictate.

The idea that grief is a process of psychosocial transition not only generalizes the meaning of anxiety, but also removes the disgrace or stigma of mental illness. Grief may be seen as a normal part of responsible living. In an effort to manage the prevalence of painful emotions as transitional as well as traumatic events, Parkes proposes a mode of intervention in which the shame and disgrace of disability and disease are displaced by an alternative line of action. Derived from the psychosocial norm of special needs, the proposal is based on the assumption that the management of mental health passes by way of grief from pathological spaces to a continuous surface, from the disreputable to the everyday. The epistemological shift of the former combined with the moral revaluation of the latter delimits the basic form and function of reflexive medicine.

To repeat our main conclusion, Parkes's therapeutic argument is based on the idea of the bereaved actively attempting to manage themselves. Typically, the widow completes the task of mourning only when 'she gives up her view of herself as being a "partnerless half" and becomes an autonomous individual' (1996: 106). In this way, the process of mourning itself provides the conditions of responsible self-management: the bereaved woman ceases to be a wife and becomes instead a widow and, eventually, a 'new person'.[15] To the extent that grief is considered from the point of view of the self-governing capacities of individuals, the loss of identity remains neither total nor catastrophic so much as episodic and reparative. There is a positive narrative of recovery and self-control built-in to the process of mourning, where the widow regains an identity for herself as an autonomous subject. Thus grief plays out across the surface of a human subject centred in the experience of self-consciousness. For Parkes, we are always more or less self-reliant, even as self-reliance includes re-establishing the grounds for ourselves on the authority of therapeutic expertise.

Parkes concludes that while we experience the pain of grief as so much damage to ourselves and our sense of identity; bereavement is nonetheless a mode of illness in which we characteristically retain our powers of agency throughout.[16] This allows for the fact that it takes time for things to heal. At the same time, Parkes proposes that the process of recovery depends to a greater or lesser extent on professionals operating within communities of care. Psychiatric supervision is the basis of Parkes's therapeutic argument. From this perspective there is nothing other than self-conscious understanding that facilitates the process of grieving and the restoration of personal identity. Consider Parkes's remarks above on

Anna O. For Parkes, we are free to mourn, even as we actively construct a new identity, 'a fresh set of assumptions', in place of our previous sense of self. Our freedom to mourn, to reflect on what loss has made of us, is seen as the essential opportunity that mourning affords us. In accordance with its modes of behaviour, grief is depicted as a transitional event mapped onto a comprehensive surface of continuous variation. The bereaved self is affected by stressful experiences and episodes of acute anxiety, but only as a responsible citizen whose conscious actions are credited with holding back the fundamental threat of worthlessness in grief's lamentations.

Notes

1 See Canguilhem's *Essay*, Part One, Chapter I, for the origins of theories of general pathology in Bichat, John Brown and Broussais, theories that 'were influential only to the extent that Comte found them advantageous' (1966: 63).
2 The 'notion of epistemological acts corresponds to the leaps [*saccades*] of scientific genius that introduce unexpected impulses into the course of scientific development' (Bachelard 1951: 25).
3 For the distinction between segregation and self-regulatory techniques, see Foucault (1982: 208).
4 For the neo-Kantian paradigm of the Comte–Durkheim tradition, see Rose (1981).
5 See McGinley (2012) for a comment on the background to the controversy surrounding DSM-V's categorizations for mourning, prolonged grief, and depression.
6 See Kleinman's (2012) comment in *The Lancet*.
7 Parkes is indebted here to the work of Aldritch (1963).
8 For the organization of medicine as a centralized structure at the end of the eighteenth century, see Foucault (1963: Chapter 2).
9 See Ariès (1983) for an account of the earlier arrangement where intimate family members and other relatives maintained a dialogue with the dying in a wholly visible domestic space.
10 See Rose (1994: 66) for the nineteenth-century campaigns to medicalize the family.
11 See Bartlett and Wright (1999) for the history of non-hospital based treatment of the insane.
12 Cf. Clayton's (1979: 1532) view that 'bereavement need not be regarded as an illness'.
13 Canguilhem (1966: 208) elaborates on the implications that it is the 'sick man' who draws the doctor's attention to 'certain surprising or painful changes in his morphological structure or behaviour'. See Selye (1954) for the study of non-specific pathological syndromes in terms of the patient's feelings of ill-health; in this context, the physiology of 'stress', as set out by Selye (1955; 1956) and Selye and Horava (1950), plays an important part in the contemporary management of well-being. While Parkes (1996: 31) expresses doubts about the research on the physiology of stress, he nonetheless includes the general, non-specific reaction to stress as an important part of his perspective on grief, applying the concept of 'stressor' in physics to physiology and psychology.
14 See Engel (1961) on the comparison between mourning and the physiological healing process.
15 Golan (1975) describes the process of grief in similar terms.
16 Cf. the findings of Grinberg (1964).

6

VULNERABILITY AND TRAUMA

A new figure has emerged over the last fifty years or so the essential characteristics of which are discernable, for example, in Joan Didion's *The Year of Magical Thinking* (2005) or Joyce Carol Oates's *A Widow's Story* (2011). Preoccupied with the widow's vulnerability to trauma, these eloquent accounts of grief parallel some of the main concerns in the professional psychiatric literature. In their loquaciousness as much as their mythology, these memoirs typify a historical response to grief that gives voice to deep feelings of responsibility, guilt, and remorse. The figure of the bereft widow, seeking her lost husband more or less in despair, brings the conscience of mourning, the sufferings of Freud's melancholic, into the light of day. In turn, the Freudian interpretation is displaced by a new genre of *écrire la vie*, a different kind of autobiographical frame of meaning that is exemplified by popular literary memoirs.

A similar figure may be found in the psychiatric image of the widow supplemented by her own words.[1] Consider the following description:

> The woman who will not handle bereavement well tends to be young, with children living at home and no close relatives living nearby to help form a support network. She is timid and clinging and was overly dependent on her husband, or had ambivalent feelings about their relationship, and her cultural and familial background prevents her from expressing her feelings. In the past she reacted badly to separation and she may have a previous history of depressive illness. Her husband's death causes additional stress in her life – loss of income, a possible move, and difficulties with the children, who are also trying to adjust to the loss. At first she seems to be coping well, but that slowly gives way to intensive pining and feelings of self-reproach and/or anger. Instead of declining, these feelings persist as time goes on.
>
> (Worden 1991: 40)

The basic assumptions in this description originate in Parkes's studies, where the high-risk widow, including war widows, emerged as a privileged object of concern for post-war British psychiatry. The preoccupation with risk brings the bereaved self more sharply into focus, and in this chapter we explore vulnerability and trauma as the major determinants of pathological grief. In the context of managed lives, the identification of vulnerability forms part of a wide-ranging predictive project. Alongside which the facilitation of traumatic feelings involves giving vent to oneself under the tutelage of some kind of therapeutic expertise, more often than not outside the clinic, and usually in domestic settings of one kind or another. As we shall see, Parkes aims at a strategic combination of predictive hypotheses and acts of disclosure, at once scientific and autobiographical in its focus, as the groundwork of therapeutic intervention.

The predictive–preventive strategy

Parkes set the agenda in the 1960s for what was to become the paradigmatic at-risk category in bereavement studies: the vulnerable widow. In an innovative move that linked pathology to the normative continuum of opportunity and risk, Parkes rendered pathological mourning as one of the inevitable hazards of everyday life. His contribution to the identification of 'at-risk' groups singles him out as one of the architects of post-war risk management. Parkes is not a theoretician and nor are we treating him as such. He approximates more closely to the model of the physician–researcher: on the one hand, managing problems posed by patients aware that something is wrong; and, on the other, articulating the norm from the perspective of reason. We are not debating the compatibility of these objectives here. Parkes assumes they are congruous and, drawing on data from detailed ethnographic studies as well as statistical studies of larger samples, he combines therapeutics and social science, essentially, by identifying the factors most likely to affect the outcome of bereavement.[2] His studies cover a range of variables from the quality of attachment to the mode of death; from demographic variables to psychological, sociological, and economic factors. Sets of predictors derived from a comprehensive psychosocial field, are arranged in terms of antecedent, concurrent, and subsequent factors. And elaborating in more detail in this chapter on therapeutic practice, we discuss Parkes's predictive hypotheses and preventive strategies. In particular, we are interested in the recourse to probability and the concomitant rationale for prevention as a therapeutic perspective.

Parkes (1996: 119–20) sets out a list of antecedent factors affecting the outcome of bereavement, with a clear emphasis on security. First, he identifies four components of intimate relations based on the findings of attachment theory, including, strength of attachment, security of attachment, degree of reliance, and involvement. Second, he includes insecure parenting and losses of significant persons in childhood. Third, there is a similar emphasis on the loss of significant others and the problem of emotional insecurity in later experiences. Fourth, a previous history of mental illness is highlighted as well as critical life events prior to bereavement; mode of death (violent, disenfranchised, or culpable deaths); and previous warnings and preparation for bereavement. These elements are combined with concurrent factors comprising a wide range of psychosocial categories: age and gender; aspects of personality such as the inhibition of feelings; social class, nationality, and religious background; and cultural and familial factors influencing the expression of grief. Finally, a list of subsequent factors completes the predictive schema, namely, support networks or social isolation, secondary stresses, and emergent life opportunities. The latter include the 'turning-points' that prove decisive for administrative supervision as the basis of community care.

Extrapolating from this broadly defined group of psychosocial predictors, Parkes identifies vulnerability and trauma as the major determinants of pathological grief. Starting with the calculation of vulnerability, for Parkes risk is at once a statistical and a therapeutic problem; he combines scientific knowledge of the determinants of grief with a revaluation of the emotional reaction to loss. This combined approach is evident throughout his work, most notably in the way that he links patterns of behaviour with statements of subjective feelings. In contrast to the Winnicottian typology of management, the criterion of maturity plays no part in these calculations of security and insecurity. In wanting to avoid what he sees as the implicit reproach in notions of emotional immaturity and impairment, Parkes foregrounds the widow's vulnerability to suffering in her own words. This does not override the psychiatrist's judgement concerning the nature of bereavement. The coincidence of illness and identity remains a psychiatric construct. Nevertheless, in conjunction with his reliance on systematic and quantitative methods of prediction, Parkes credits the meaning the women give to their grief. This has direct practical implications. When it comes to the identification of high-risk categories, in many respects predictive measures and screening methods, coupled with questionnaires and therapeutic interviewing techniques, are more useful than notions of incapacity, lack of resilience, mental deficiency, and immaturity.

The methods on which Parkes's studies are based facilitate access to a wide range of factors in the psychosocial history of individuals that would otherwise remain invisible. Set out along these lines, quantification and assessment allow for the application of predictors to bereaved groups in a way that stigmatization clearly does not. This is particularly important in the case of mourning, where the governmental task is one of inclusion rather than segregation. The therapeutic emphasis on techniques of intimacy is consistent with the aim of supporting the bereaved as active participants in their own communities of care, rather than subjecting them to disciplinary apparatuses.[3] Far from singling out and hiving off individuals with a predisposition to atypical or pathological mourning, Parkes integrates them by means of a more subtle therapeutic–administrative approach.

Once again, the contrast with Winnicottian management is telling: whereas Winnicott aims to combine social management with the creative imperative in the treatment of disaffected children; Parkes extends the form and function of social provision as a self-conscious mode of action under supervision. Further to Winnicott's efforts at managing the antisocial tendency, Parkes is altogether more explicit, his aim is to include the entire population as part of a predictive–preventive strategy of health care. The idea is that everyone recognizes themselves even in the most vulnerable image of the widow. The permanent task shifts, accordingly, from the defence of society in the face of immature elements to the management of oneself as a vulnerable but responsible member of the community. What strikes us in the image of the bereaved is not only how 'fragile' and 'unstable' they appear (Didion 2005: 169), but how familiar this seems. We recognize our own insecurity in the exposure of grief. Parkes exploits this recognition on the grounds that risk becomes endemic where, rather than immaturity, fragility is judged the more salient feature of our human ethical predicament.

How does this shift occur? How do we come to recognize ourselves as subjects of grief? The supervisory principle of inclusion operates in two ways. First, bereavement itself is seen as a normal process, and the difficulty that individuals routinely experience in this process means that ordinary daily life becomes the proper domain of psychiatry. Second, atypical grief is rendered continuous with the normal process of mourning in terms of several relatively predictable modes of behaviour. These behaviours in turn are seen as amenable to different methods of psychiatric treatment. From the point of view of prediction, the risk that loss presents opens up the possibility of managing ourselves through a comprehensive and inclusive framework of preventive strategies. Therapeutically supervised communities of care may be established on a 'sound scientific basis', according to Parkes, with respect to the predictors of later distress. Thus prediction presupposes an emphasis on individuals as active agents in their own psychological and social management.

The predictive–preventive strategy of risk management consolidates the reformation of identity through illness by augmenting its field of operation. Based on entirely different methods of treatment, Winnicott and Parkes are nonetheless contesting the same ground: 'We should not be concerned solely with attempting to reduce the prevalence of mental illness but should be seeking to improve the quality of living' (Parkes 1996: 209). I take this objective to be the common denominator of managed lives in post-war Britain, where rational plans for the good life are subject to a heterogeneous range of criteria. In Parkes's studies, identifying the at-risk bereaved effectively opens up a comprehensive psychiatric discourse on the well-being of the population as a whole. The problem of grief, therefore, bridges the phenomena of illness and identity at the level of everyday life. This makes caring for the bereaved not only a specialized psychiatric task, but also a general concern about the welfare of families as well as the community at large. The coincidence of illness and identity thus becomes operational as a therapeutic strategy adequate to the inherent risks and uncertainties of life. Once again, the therapeutic argument is couched in terms of special needs. Parkes identifies a minority of individuals in need of special help from general practitioners, the clergy, bereavement counselling services, and so on. For the vast majority of the population this kind of professional support or guidance is not seen as appropriate or necessary. The important point, however, is that the distinction is not rigidly laid down or adhered to in practice. On the contrary, need remains an open-ended problem under the general auspices of therapeutic authority.

While the more troublesome aspects of mourning are seen as amendable to intensive psychiatric treatment, the therapeutic emphasis continues to fall explicitly and primarily on the individual's capacity to manage. This is evident, for instance, in the way that Parkes promotes the role of the family doctor. First, Parkes (1996: 192) argues that

> family doctors, because they are likely to have cared for the dead person during the last illness and to have helped the relatives to prepare for bereavement, are in a very advantageous position to give psychological support after this event has occurred.

In particular, Parkes (1996: 181) emphasizes that general practitioners are 'able to provide reassurance about the normality of many of the physical symptoms that can worry bereaved people'. General practitioners, in other words, are well placed to co-ordinate needs and norms, to facilitate normative capacity, on the threshold of mental health inside the family. Second, Parkes (1996: 181) points out that the family doctor is 'in a good position to decide when or if the help of a psychiatrist is needed'. Once again, from inside the domestic or intimate space of the family, the general practitioner operates the open-endedness of needs in local communities of care. Third, so long as it becomes necessary, the doctor is seen to play an important part in facilitating a 'close collaboration' between the family and the psychiatrist, thereby averting any further danger. Finally, Parkes (1996: 192; emphasis added) proposes that the general practitioner 'who can recognize grief as the painful process through which a family must pass *in becoming another kind of family* is aware that the symptoms to which it gives rise must be seen in perspective'. Moderation is seen as the most effective means of transformation.

The family doctor, then, is assigned a decisive role at the interface of family life, therapeutic authority, and risk management. The doctor, operating as a technician in what we might call normative communities of care, maintains strategic links between the family and the community, on the one hand, and between psychiatric medicine and social welfare on the other. The family doctor, however, is not alone in supporting the practice of active self-management. Similarly, community nurses, health visitors, and psychiatric social workers treat the bereaved on the basis of psychosocial norms within the domestic setting; while at the same time operating with an open-ended category of need. The psychiatric grounds for the treatment offered by these personnel are clearly stipulated, notwithstanding the fact that the norms of conduct they promote pass into domestic life without the stigma of mental illness.

The emphasis on therapeutic supervision in the community does not imply that the risks associated with bereavement are less serious than the risks presented by other forms of psychiatric disorder. Parkes (1996: 181) acknowledges that there is always a risk of suicide in the case of pathological mourning and that one should not ignore 'the plea for help' expressed in every case of attempted suicide; moreover, he advises that 'caregivers should never be afraid to ask direct questions about suicide'. Nevertheless, these are matters requiring attention at the limits of a mental health strategy that is expressly designed to be inclusive, to predict problems, and therefore to prevent disasters. The emphasis on the individual's capacity to manage is maintained, even where the more so-called sophisticated forms of bereavement counselling are employed for the minority. None of us are considered exempt from the techniques used even in desperate circumstances. For Parkes, it is the job of mental health professionals as well as trained volunteer counsellors to endorse the self-reflective work of mourning across the board, to apply the lessons learnt *in extremis* without reserve, if not in all cases.

The calculation of risk

What makes therapeutic supervision an especially useful strategy from a governmental perspective, is the continuum it establishes not only between the normal and the pathological, but also between risk and opportunity. While assimilating the realm of pathology into a comprehensive psychosocial norm, at the same time Parkes extends the scope of risk management to a familial strategy of community supervision. We have illustrated this strategy with reference to the family doctor. To take another example, let us consider the Bereavement Risk Index formulated by Parkes and his colleagues at St Christopher's Hospice, which identifies family members in special need of support (see Parkes 1981; Parkes and Weiss 1983). Parkes (1996: 235–6) reports his findings in the case of widows and widowers of 164 patients who died in St Christopher's Hospice, where the bereaved were identified according to three categories of risk: a 'low risk group' of 85 patients; a 'high risk intervention group' of 28; and a 'high risk control group' of 29. The remaining 22 bereaved subjects were identified by the hospice staff as being in 'urgent need' and were not included in the findings.

The two 'high risk' groups were treated as follows: 'The intervention group were visited in their homes by volunteer counsellors under [psychiatric] supervision. The help given varied from case to case but seldom involved more than three to four visits. These visits, though few in number, were often very lengthy. It was not unusual for them to last for one or two hours … The control group were not offered help and in fact none of them asked for help from the Hospice' (1996: 235). Some twenty months after bereavement, Parkes reports that all three groups were followed up by a research interviewer who conducted a shortened version of the Health Questionnaire which he and others had used in the Harvard Bereavement Study in the early 1970s.[4] The two main findings in this case amount to an endorsement of the predictive–preventive strategy of risk management. Figures for the overall outcome of the three groups show, first, 'that the predictive questionnaire did, in fact, predict outcome, since the high risk control group did have a poorer outcome than the low risk group' (1996: 235), and second, 'that the intervention was successful in that the intervention group had a better outcome than the control group' (1996: 235).

We are not concerned with the accuracy of these findings, but with the extent to which the Bereavement Risk Index illustrates Parkes's predictive–preventive approach to psychosocial management. The set of predictors included in the questionnaire range from socio-demographic variables (employment, social class, the number of young children living at home) to personality factors (ratings for anger, pining, and self-reproach). The inclusion of social support variables, as well as a coping assessment for rating individuals in terms of their need for help, is further evidence of the underlying rationale of the Risk Index. The critical implications of Parkes's perspective, regarding the structure and application of the diagnostic sign, come to the fore in this example. In effect, the Risk Index exposes the sign as an inadequate measure of modes and levels of functioning. More clearly and directly than an official statement of health policy, the Bereavement Risk Index represents a particular rationality of government. The codification of pathological symptoms and states of mind is displaced by a predictive–preventive schema based on the notion of causal probability and risk. Most importantly, risk is set out in this model as a permanent and manageable phenomenon, the strategic aim being to extend the scope of the norm as a function of probability. 'Where danger becomes normalcy', as Beck (1992: 78) point outs, 'it assumes permanent institutional form'. The Risk Index exemplifies this line of thinking in the case of bereavement, with respect to the treatment of inevitable risk.

It is clear, then, that bereavement studies provides an evidence-based supervisory programme replete with predictive questionnaires, risk factors, and statistics on behavioural outcome. But there is still any number of questions outstanding. To what extent does the predictive questionnaire postulate a provident individual? Are techniques of intimacy commensurate with the technology of social insurance? How does the shift from the social point of view to government through community, from solidarity to attachment, affect strategies of risk management? Without attempting to give definitive answers to these questions, it will be helpful to say more about the relationship between risk and vulnerability. Staying with the St Christopher's Hospice evaluation study, in presenting his findings Parkes adds an important qualification. The identification of the at-risk bereaved, conducted in the study with reference to levels of emotional disturbance and modes of behaviour, is consistent with the basic psychosocial model of grief. However, Parkes (1996: 160) notes that 'we are speaking only in terms of probabilities'.

What makes this caveat so consequential? The emphasis on probability, which means that the predictive statement itself is open to variation, locates bereavement studies at a particular vantage point in medical discourse. Foucault (1963: 107–23) discusses the probabilistic structure of clinical cases, together with the linguistic structure of clinical signs, as the basis of modern medical modes of perception. The complex relationship between bereavement studies and medicine is apparent on both counts, with respect to signs and probability. Thus, together with his critique of the diagnostic sign, Parkes reworks the inevitable uncertainty of medical knowledge, the unpredictable variations among patients' case histories, as a positive phenomenon of psychiatric supervision. To this extent, at least, the mathematical and philosophical concepts of probability and statistics developed by Laplace and others lend weight to the psychosocial perspective.[5] As Foucault (1963: 97) points out, in the period of Laplace 'medicine discovered that uncertainty may be treated, analytically, as the sum of a certain number of isolated degrees of certainty that were capable of rigorous calculation'. For his part, Parkes aims to confer probability on propositions or statements about modes of behaviour and, thereby, to quantify risk.

It is important to note, here, that Parkes does not assume that one set of predictors applies to all at-risk groups.[6] Calculable at the level of the population as a whole, the basic assumption is that normal outcomes are established by the local community itself. This tells us something important not only about Parkes's notion of risk, but also about the way in which he conceives the problem of management. Risks do not arise simply from individuals or groups as such, but from statistical correlations between various phenomena in a particular milieu. As Castel (1991: 287) puts it, risk 'is the effect of a combination of abstract *factors* which render more or less probable the occurrence of undesirable modes of behaviour'. Accordingly, the permanent task is seen as one of comprehensive and systematic 'pre-detection' attuned to the specificity of risk factors in a given population or environment.[7] For example, a family may match all the predictors of pathological mourning, as Parkes (1996: 160) explains, 'and still not break down after bereavement, or they may have none of them and yet break down'. Expressed as a ratio of positive cases to total potential cases, the probabilistic structure of psychiatric knowledge is open to 'unpredictable events and circumstances', if not in principle to infinite variation.

It is a salutary reminder that this is what 'evidence' amounts to in the social and life sciences. Thus, correct predictions do not follow as a matter of course in psychiatric medicine, least of all when the observation of signs and symptoms has been replaced by a theory of modes and relations modelled on a continuous surface. As Parkes (1996: 160) concludes, in 'an infinitely variable world' there is 'infinite room for variation'. This is not to say that the outcome of bereavement is indeterminable. Rather, uncertainty itself becomes the condition of management, the fact of being manageable proceeds from the unpredictability of the norm. This is another way of saying that the concept of probability is applied under conditions of uncertainty. And while probability furnishes the work of mourning with a principle of reason, at the same time, it is the irreducible complexity of risk that underwrites Parkes's model as a technique of intimacy.

The admission of infinite variation is indicative of a sceptical attitude towards diagnostic signs. Parkes accepts that, in attempting to make predictions about human vulnerability in an uncertain world, the predictive project itself is far from perfectible. This applies to all aspects of human social management. When it comes to predicting the needs of human beings, be it in physiology, psychology or sociology, one can never be certain. While this does not rule out the use of predictive hypotheses, calculations of probability in medicine and the social sciences may be considered adequate only at the level of individual meaning. Parkes does not necessarily draw the logical conclusions of his own argument, with respect to the narrative or biographical implications of the reflexive norm (see Chapter 8). Nevertheless, he relies on the personal life histories of bereaved individuals as a matter of course. Rendering a high index of at-risk probability intelligible as an experiential phenomenon is part of the therapeutic task for Parkes; hence the combination of statistical and observational data:

> Relevant data can be obtained from detailed studies of a few people or from statistical studies of larger samples. Ideally, the two types of study should complement each other, for it is only by studying large numbers of people that we can generalize, and only by intensively studying a few that we can evaluate the significance of the mathematics of many.
>
> (Parkes 1996: 118)

Risk is presented as both a fact and an abstraction, indicating the extent to which the scientific and technological aspects of risk management remain inextricably linked. On the one hand, risk remains calculable as a degree of certainty relative to observational and statistical evidence, including, 'the mathematics of many' cross-referenced with detailed studies of smaller samples and case histories. On the other hand, risk is managed through a series of strategic interventions institutionalized in different types of help. Parkes (1996: 180) includes, for instance, 'specialist or non-specialist help; individual or group help; help from professionals or volunteers; medical or non-medical help and religious or secular help'. These are not unrelated developments. The management of risk operates on both counts more or less outside the hospital. As well as an epistemological shift within clinical thinking, the psychosocial logic of probability provides a new rationale for administrative supervision.

The problem of vulnerability, then, gives rise to a co-ordinated framework of techniques ranging from predicative questionnaires and risk indices to supervised home visits and therapeutic interviews. Parkes approaches bereavement along these lines as an intelligible and quantifiable series of modes and relations, linking the treatment of the bereaved self with a complex formation of statistical probabilities and unpredictable events (variation in series) in domestic and communal life. As such, the calculation of risk, including above all the identification of at-risk groups, institutionalizes the process of mourning as a governmental problem. The implications for the social organization of mourning are clear: the treatment of grief is conducted on the medical model of social psychiatry, but as a diffuse practice rather than a discrete formation. The medicine of cases is integrated into techniques designed to manage the process of mourning in line with the well-being of families and local communities.

To summarize, first, the predictive–preventive model of risk management allows for emotional breakdown to a greater or lesser degree, but without the shameful attribution of mental illness. Parkes invariably describes reactions to loss in positive or optimistic terms, emphasizing the transformation of identity through mourning. Second, through the identification of at-risk groups, Parkes maps a thoroughly comprehensive domain of human vulnerability at the level of individuals, families, and communities. While widowhood remains the privileged target; nonetheless, a whole series of related objects of concern emerge: divorce, childlessness and unemployment; eviction, homelessness and forced migration; and, indeed, the loss of illness itself following the recovery from cancer.[8] Widowhood thus provides leverage into the wider territory of community life. Third, Parkes addresses behaviour as well as emotion from the perspective of self-reflection. The self-governing capacities of individuals are harnessed to the work of mourning at the level of self-identity. Parkes does not rely on the clinical gaze for evidence of vulnerability; instead, he links the idea of predictable dispositions, or typical modes of reaction, with the coincidence of identity and illness. Construed from the point of view of empirical events and individual agency, 'typical' and 'atypical' modes of grief are identified with intimate trajectories of human feeling. Intimacy itself is subject to prediction and regulation. Thus, in accordance with the calculations of intimacy, and at the critical juncture of personal vulnerability, mourning becomes a work of the managed self.

Traumatic grief

The identification of vulnerability goes only so far in addressing the risks associated with mourning. This is especially true in the case of Parkes's studies, where the aim is to consider risk from the standpoint of experience. Beyond the formulation of predictive hypotheses and preventive strategies, there is a further therapeutic problem concerning the expression of feeling. With reference to the social networks that surround the bereaved, especially the family and the community, Parkes (1996: 154) cites evidence in support of the view that cultures 'which encourage the expression of grief are likely to have fewer problems following bereavement'.[9] Parkes is keenly aware that giving voice to feelings of loss is a central part of the grieving process. We have argued that the coincidence of illness and identity constitutes individuals as active agents in the treatment of their own intimate needs. Let us now turn to the problem of expression in the case of traumatic bereavement.

A reliance on the personal life histories of bereaved individuals raises fundamental questions about the use of language in therapeutic practice.[10] It also brings Parkes up against the cornerstone of Freudian psychoanalysis as a form of treatment. Freud established new grounds for the idea that language is the sphere of action as well as the field of enquiry in psychoanalysis. Analysis provides a setting in which patients are able to experience an intimate conversation with themselves in the company of someone whose listening amounts to a singular act of attention.[11] Psychoanalytic therapy works when patients end up overhearing themselves in the presence of someone who is listening. But of course feelings, including feelings of loss, do not always go into words, and Parkes seems to share a concern with analysts about experiences that resist expression. We have looked at Winnicott's attempts to manage this problem in the case of borderline psychotic patients, and a similar problem arises for Parkes in the treatment of traumatic bereavement.

Alongside vulnerability, Parkes counts the mode and circumstances of death as the second major determinant of grief.[12] The addition of 'traumatic events' alongside the notion of ordinary grief extends the remit of risk management. Parkes (1996: 129) argues that whereas natural deaths are not necessarily traumatic; on the other hand, '[s]udden unexpected deaths, multiple deaths, violent deaths, and deaths involving human agency (murders, suicides, *et cetera*) represent a special risk to mental health even in the absence of other vulnerability'. Parkes (1996: 134) also includes 'disenfranchised grief' as a category of special risk, citing AIDS as the most obvious example where loss 'cannot be openly acknowledged, socially validated or publicly mourned'.[13]

While he is not especially concerned with AIDS-related bereavement, Parkes (1996: xii) acknowledges that '[t]he advent of AIDS has created a new population of people of whom many suffer multiple bereavements as well as threats to their own lives'. Indeed, the psychosocial perspective has played a significant role in the treatment of this 'new population'. For example, Worden (1991), who covers much the same ground as Parkes, addresses the problem of AIDS-related bereavement together with the emotional reaction of survivors in cases of suicide, sudden unexpected death, sudden infant death, miscarriages, still births and abortion. Indebted to Parkes's perspective, Worden (1991: 112) describes 'a population of mourners with few existing guidelines for care'. He also claims that a number of factors, which he associates with AIDS, present particular problems when it comes to mourning. The list includes contagion, protracted illness and disfigurement; the stigma of 'unspeakable loss'; lack of social support networks in the context of non-traditional intimate relations; untimely deaths, multiple losses and bereavement burnout.

The emphasis on acknowledgement is seen as particularly significant in the case of AIDS-related bereavement, but also in the general context of disenfranchised grief. The question of intimate disclosure, which is always on the psychiatric agenda for Parkes, becomes more urgent when he turns to traumatic forms of bereavement. The problem is how to render the 'special risks' associated with traumatic events amenable to therapeutic supervision. Parkes (1996: 106) describes how the bereaved grapple repeatedly with feelings of 'impending disaster'; how loss made one widow feel as if 'half of myself was missing'; and, in the London Study, how the widows 'seemed at last to find their new identity emerging from the altered life situation which they had to face'. These depictions of ordinary grief already open the way for a form of personal disclosure through the coincidence of disaster and identity. A further concern with those who have suffered 'unusually traumatic forms of bereavement' (1996: 129) is broadly conceived and goes beyond any one population of mourners. Again, we are dealing here with fluid, open-ended discriminations rather than strict oppositions.

Parkes points out in fact that all those who have sought psychiatric help from him after bereavement have suffered traumatic loss. As with the terms 'identity' and 'illness', there is an inherent tendency in the supervisory model to blur the distinction between 'ordinary' and 'unusual' circumstances. From vulnerability to trauma, the treatment of risk continues to cut across these distinctions.

Nevertheless, Parkes argues that, compared even to those who demonstrate prior vulnerability, people who are bereaved under traumatic circumstances are at far greater risk of mental health problems. The question, then, is how the problem of 'special risk' admits of the active attitude to risk management devised in the case of vulnerable widows. Parkes differentiates *external* trauma from *internal* vulnerability; the modes and circumstances of death, from the strengths and weaknesses of individuals. At the same time, he maintains the principal coincidence of illness and identity by treating trauma as a normal reaction to especially intense levels of stress. The technical challenge consists in rendering this reaction in line with an active relation to risk, enabling the bereaved to manage even the most traumatic aspects of loss. Parkes rises to the challenge. Bringing the self-regulating capacities of individuals to bear on trauma is among Parkes's most significant achievements. But unlike Freud, who forged a link between trauma, memory and fantasy at the level of the unconscious, Parkes persists in treating the problem of traumatic bereavement from the perspective of identity and self-conscious management.

While traumatic events present Parkes with a particular problem in the form of special risk, the link between trauma and grief is nonetheless at the very centre of his general therapeutic argument. Parkes (1996: 6) confirms this link with reference to the current state of psychiatric knowledge: 'I know of only two functional psychiatric disorders whose cause is known, whose features are distinctive, and whose course is usually predictable, and those are PTSD [post-traumatic stress disorder] and grief.'[14] The claim is presented with a number of contiguous propositions. To recapitulate briefly, Parkes proposes, first, that grief comprises a series of reactions rather than discrete symptoms; second, that the process of grieving is based on the coincidence of identity and illness; and, third, that it is possible to calculate the probability of grief and, thereby, to implement preventive measures which bring about a general improvement in the quality of living.

Trauma forms an integral part of this picture. While traumatic bereavement gives rise to a specific preoccupation with special risks; at the same time, grief is seen invariably as 'the consequence of a psychological trauma' (1996: 5). The ambiguity in this view runs throughout Parkes's entire argument with productive results. In fact, the therapeutic argument comes together around the problem of trauma, where the generalization of special needs through the coincidence of illness and identity, is coupled with the inscription of special risk within the normal process of mourning. It now seems indisputable that the bereaved have special needs, that is, so long as trauma is part of the normative calculation of psychiatric supervision. This has immediate implications for therapeutic practice; most importantly, trauma is the ground on which Parkes confronts Freud's legacy head-on, and the point at which their respective rationalities of therapeutic treatment diverge.

Freud arrived at the notion of psychological trauma early on, elaborating on the so-called seduction theory in the years leading up to and including the publication, with Josef Breuer, of *Studies on Hysteria* (Breuer and Freud 1893–5). The idea that psychological events in themselves can produce hysterical symptoms was already evident to Freud by the time he translated Charcot's lectures in 1892:

> The core of a hysterical attack, in whatever form it may appear, is a *memory*, the hallucinatory reliving of a scene which is significant for the onset of the illness. It is this event which manifests itself in a perceptible manner in the phase of *'attitudes passionelles'*; but it is also present when the attack appears to consist only of motor phenomena. The *content of the memory* is as a rule either a psychical *trauma* which is qualified by its intensity to provoke the outbreak of hysteria in the patient or is an event which, owing to its occurrence at a particular moment, has become a trauma.
> (Freud 1892–4: 137; emphasis in the original)

Obviously, the subsequent displacement of literal events by primal scene fantasies changed things radically, but the significant link between trauma and memory remains in place. Freud continued to argue, first, that past but forgotten psychological trauma is a cause of psychopathology, and second, that symptoms can be relieved through the recollection of lost memories. The inaugural presupposition that psychic events can produce neurosis, coupled with new ideas about memory and forgetting, continues to define the Freudian interpretation. Freud himself acknowledged that he was not the first to put forward the idea of psychological trauma.[15] Nevertheless, starting with Freud's studies on hysteria, traumatic events occasioned the invention of a new technology of memory based on the seminal notion of 'deferred action' (*Nachträglichkeit*). In what turns out to be a defining statement of his analytic technique, Freud (1914) described how patients arrive at therapy unable to become fully themselves; how events from the past that they cannot remember but repeatedly act out stand in their way; and how, through the technique of interpretation and the use of the setting, the analyst tries to help the patient find ways of speaking about the past rather than repeating what has been repressed. What interests Freud most of all, is the way in which the patient's 'compulsion to repeat' is played out in the course of analytic treatment, that is to say, in the configuration of transference and resistance.

Parkes appears to take up the problem of trauma where Freud left off. This is evident, for instance, in Parkes's (1996: 40) account of 'psychic traumata' as typically manifest in the form of nightmares and haunting memories: 'The horror may now be over but we remain haunted by its memory and we feel as if it could return at any time'. It would seem this allows not only for the importance of dreams in understanding traumatic events, but also for Freud's theory of repeating as an equivalent activity to remembering. The 'intrusive post-traumatic memories', as Parkes (1996: 166) describes them, appear to be repetitive reactions to the trauma of loss. But whereas Freud addresses the structural specificity of memory in trauma and dreams alike, and continues to approach the 'repetition compulsion' (*Wiederholungszwang*) as a symptom under the conditions of resistance; Parkes treats 'post-traumatic reminiscence' as both a mode of behaviour and a special kind of risk. The link between trauma and risk is more important for Parkes than the analysis of memory and forgetting. Parkes is not interested in delving into the patient's distant past, or in making transference interpretations based on the fantasies of childhood sexuality. To the contrary, in meeting patients' needs in the community, Parkes treats traumatic bereavement as a normal situation with which one has to learn to cope. Here, as elsewhere, mourning is treated not as a constitutive work of memory so much as a pragmatic exercise in dealing with distress.

The notion of 'abreaction' (*Abreagieren*) crystallizes the fundamental technical differences between Freud and Parkes. Freud used the term abreaction to refer to the emotional discharge whereby individuals free themselves from the affect attached to the memory of traumatic events. The way in which one reacts to a particular event, according to Freud, affects the extent to which the affect remains attached to a memory. The argument is that a sufficiently intense or uninhibited reaction, in the first instance, allows for a large quantity of the affect attached to the event to fall away; whereas a restrained or inhibited reaction causes the affect to remain tied to the memory. Once again, although it tends to be associated with Freud's early use of the cathartic method, the notion of abreaction is actually implicit in his therapeutic argument from beginning to end. The psychoanalytic treatment of traumatizing affects invariably involves emotional discharge. It is not simply a matter of putting things into words. The process whereby remembering takes the place of repeating, depends on the emotional consequences of what is said.

What prevents someone from abreacting? The answer that Freud gives to this question leaves us in no doubt about his emphases. In *Studies on Hysteria*, Breuer and Freud suggest various reasons why a person might not react initially to a psychological trauma:

> because the nature of the trauma excluded a reaction, as in the case of the apparently irreparable loss of a loved person or because social circumstances made a reaction impossible or because it was a question of things which the patient wished to forget, and therefore intentionally repressed from his conscious thought and inhibited and suppressed.
> (Breuer and Freud 1893–5: 10)

In deciding matters in favour of the sexual aetiology of the neuroses Freud established the groundwork of psychoanalysis, while at the same time positing the primacy of psychical reality over the impersonal modes and circumstances of trauma.

We are about as far away as one could possibly be from the idea of external trauma *contra* internal vulnerability. Indeed, by introducing this distinction Parkes adopts an entirely different therapeutic practice to Freud. Not only does he warn against taking the idea of abreaction too far, Parkes also reduces the entire topographic-economic argument to a reflexive model. As far as bereavement is concerned, the repeated recollection of traumatic events is treated primarily as an indication of one's failure to sufficiently reorganize oneself. Thus, Parkes (1996: 133) explains how families who consulted him, having been bereaved under traumatic circumstances, typically 'saw themselves as stuck in a rut from which they could not escape'. We shall come back to the idea of 'escape' in a moment.

In the meantime, the problem under consideration in the name of 'special risk' concerns a breakdown in the functional capacity of families as well as individuals. It is as if something has gone wrong with *the mechanisms of everyday life*, or with the model that ordinarily frames the world of relationships to which one is attached. Post-traumatic reminiscence is likened to the ruminations of an emotionally damaged and/or cognitively impaired subject. For Parkes, things begin to function imperfectly as a result of external circumstances beyond the individual's control. On the one hand, the 'traumatic grief reaction' includes severe anxiety and panic syndromes; on the other hand, the work of mourning is invoked as a normative standard by means of which individuals can measure their capacity to manage risk. For Parkes (1996: 106), the problem is how to establish a realistic appraisal of the 'external situation' and make 'appropriate plans to cope' with whatever the situation demands, including, 'a willingness to plan for a new future'. Notwithstanding a common concern in Freud and Parkes with the significance of trauma, Freudian states of mind are nonetheless displaced by psychosocial disorders of conduct and a preoccupation with rational life-plans.

Unlike Freud, Parkes is not concerned with the intrapsychic causes of traumatic grief; he does not trace traumatizing affects back to unconscious ideas. Far from relying on symptoms as signs of repressed material, he presents the process of grieving as a 'process of re-planning'. For Parkes (1996: 99), one completes the process of mourning with 'plans to do something'. The theory of psychosocial transitions explains psychic change, essentially, as a process of 'reviewing' and 'rebuilding' (1996: 133). This is not simply a matter of whether or not one credits external reality. Our study of Winnicott demonstrates the absolute centrality of the environmental factor in post-Freudian psychoanalysis. Indeed, Freud (1923) himself was forced to reconsider not only his instinct theory but his entire model of the mind, following the discovery of traumatic neuroses caused by external events. The important point, here, is how the interaction between internal and external reality is construed. Two contrasting ideas of human endeavour are evident in the way that Freud and Parkes, respectively, account for the relationship between social and psychological reality.

Freud set out our options in favour of freedom: either we attempt to eliminate the memory of a traumatic event, to dissociate or split off the traumatizing affect, or else work our way through to more or less uninhibited ways of living with the past. On this reading, becoming a person *is* freedom, which was never a convenient proposal. The way that Freud was apt to wield the hidden truth of psychic structure was always problematic, and has not proved expedient to the humanist project and its ideological pronouncements. To countenance no refusal on matters of interpretation makes freedom itself seem absolute.[16] But beyond the dilemma in which Freud tended to place himself, there is the further problem of bringing analytic therapy to bear as a practical endeavour. If programmes, objective, and evidence-based outcomes are required, then the shortcomings of Freudian psychoanalysis are clear enough. Freud's 1895 *Project for a Scientific Psychology* was not so much ill-fated as misnamed; there are no projects in psychoanalysis – scientific, political, or otherwise – short of capitulation.

The test for Parkes, as for Winnicott, consists in formulating efficacious techniques for managing ourselves; in other words, meeting the challenge where Freud's legacy can only disappoint our administrative ambitions. To this end, Parkes proposes that we should do what we can, not by searching after inner truths, but by taking stock and making a new start in the world. Winnicott and Parkes offer different solutions to the same problem. In Winnicott, the normative stance is emphatically and solely the experience of living itself, maintained without compromise at the point where imagination and memory make one thing. By contrast, for Parkes (1996: 96) '[m]aking a new start means learning new solutions and finding new ways to predict and control happenings within the life-space'. It is this far more modest proposal that proves expedient under the circumstances, the way in which Parkes (1996: 200) manages to link the idea of turning-points, or psychosocial transitions, to 'the adoption of a new model of the world' in the form of rationally articulated plans. There is no call for interpretation, nor any need for an affect to be abreacted. Instead, the exercise of management depends on the generative links between events and models; hence the reasonable conception of the supervised life.

How are these links supposed to produce the intended outcomes? Here, as elsewhere, Parkes is indebted to Bowlby and the cognitive framework of representational models. In place of Freud's theory of unconscious structures and processes, Parkes (1996: 91–2) uses the concept of 'internal models' to account for the intrusive memories associated with traumatic events. He explains the persistence of post-traumatic memories in terms of a failure to bring about appropriate changes in our internal working models. The therapeutic objective, according to Parkes (1996: 93), is to provide the conditions within which it 'becomes possible to modify our assumptions and with them our sense of identity'. Starting from the coincidence of illness and identity, Parkes models therapy on self-recognition. This raises yet more questions for us. Psychotherapeutic arguments rest to a large extent on what is meant by the 'internal world', which is why it is particularly important to be clear about the link in bereavement studies between traumatic events and internal models. In bringing the chapter and our study of Parkes to a close, it will be helpful to reiterate the technical implications of Parkes's emphasis on reactions, modifications, and transitions. This will also serve as a bridge to our critique of the cognitive bias of the sociological reduction in the third and final part of the book.

The case of Henry

Parkes allows that the past is not simply over and done with, that disasters 'already past' continue to haunt us in the form of unwanted memories and intrusive fantasies. But whereas memories and fantasies are treated as a combination of intrapsychic and intersubjective phenomena in psychoanalysis, Parkes privileges the 'external situation' from a psychosocial perspective. Traumatic bereavement is understood in relation to an identifiable external event, where modes and circumstances of death account for the 'horrors' that are manifest in our fantasies and symptomatic complaints. It is clear that Parkes's findings on trauma are taken from a wide range of contexts, including, unexpected deaths; multiple concurrent losses and natural disasters; bereavements by murder or manslaughter; and the families of suicides. The concept of 'traumatic grief', however, is applied as yet one more mode of reaction, predictable under certain circumstances and, therefore, amenable to therapeutic examination and modification.

While unusually traumatic forms of bereavement afford psychiatry a further point of entry into families and communities, it is the general application of the notion of 'traumatic grief reactions' that proves significant from the point of view of supervision and regulation. In this way, trauma becomes part of a broadly defined therapeutic concern, ranging from psychiatric medicine to the social sciences, where identity is managed as a self-reflexive project of transitions. As for the internal world, the psychosocial perspective evidently refuses to treat psychic reality as irreducible. The passage of events in the unconscious, including what Bollas (2012: 77) calls the 'grief barrier' of the intrapsychic core, is entirely absent from this account of trauma. Parkes (1996: 90) insists that, when somebody dies, 'a whole set of assumptions about the world that relied upon the other person for their validity are suddenly invalidated'. Internal reality, our 'internal model of the world' as Parkes describes it, is identified with the application of 'assumptions' not as a series of preconceptions and associative thoughts, but rather, as self-conscious mechanisms of everyday life. In place of the 'unconscious assumption' that forms the basis of 'conscious hope' in Winnicott (1954b: 281), Parkes anchors the opportunity for a new beginning in regularized modes of behaviour, habits, and routines.

The cognitive emphasis on modes of reaction and habits of thought works in ways that psychoanalytic treatment does not, bringing traumatic grief in line with the problem of basic security in attachment theory, and linking traumatic events with the internal model of the world at the level of self-identity:

> A widow will come down for breakfast in the morning and find that she has laid the table for two when there is now only one person to eat it. Faced with a problem she will catch herself thinking 'I must ask my husband about that'. In either case she has continued to operate a set of assumptions that are now obsolete ... The familiar world suddenly seems

to have become unfamiliar, habits of thought can let her down, she has lost confidence in her most essential possession, her internal model of the world, and because of this she may lose confidence in herself.

(Parkes 1996: 91–2)

What kind of practice does this perspective imply? In particular, what does Parkes make of the things patients say to their therapists? Typically, Parkes includes vignettes rather than detailed case histories as illustrative of his therapeutic practice. An example of which will give us an idea of the testimonial model of self-management that he uses in cases of traumatic bereavement. The case of Henry is a good example. Henry consulted Parkes two months after several members of his family were killed when the *Herald of Free Enterprise* capsized outside Zeebrugge in March 1987.[17] The circumstances in this case were certainly traumatic; a total of 193 people were killed in the disaster, and most of the victims were trapped inside the ship. Recoverable bodies were removed in the days immediately following the accident, although it was several weeks before all the bodies were recovered. Some 90 per cent of survivors and relatives of passengers were identified as suffering from post-traumatic stress disorder.

Parkes describes his patient feeling 'numb' and 'depressed' in the immediate aftermath of the disaster, and points out that his surviving daughters feared that their father might attempt to kill himself. Three months after the event, Parkes reports on the patient's reaction to a thunderstorm:

> Henry appeared haggard and exhausted. 'It was the thunder', he said. 'It was the same noise that the boat made as it turned over. I heard the children screaming'. He then related, in great detail and with the tears pouring down his cheeks, his memories of the disaster. The experience was so vivid that I too felt caught up in the situation. After a while I said, 'You're still waiting for them to come out aren't you?'
>
> (Parkes 1996: 41)

What does Parkes make of this consultation? The storm is described as a 'trigger', insofar as it precipitates a series of thoughts and feelings starting with a recollection of the traumatic event. From the material that Parkes presents, it is not possible to gauge this series in terms of the patient's associations and/or enactments in the therapeutic consultation. Nevertheless, the recollections that the storm sets in motion are seen as the start of the grieving process. But if, as Parkes indicates, the process of therapeutic recovery begins when the patient no longer succeeds in avoiding thoughts about the traumatic event, from what exactly is he recovering? What happened to Henry?

Far from contradicting Freud's findings, it would appear that Parkes's account in this case is consistent with the distinction Freud (1940: 184) makes between transference neurosis and traumatic neurosis:

In every case the later neurotic illness links up with the prelude in childhood. It is possible that what are known as traumatic neuroses (due to excessive fright or severe somatic shocks, such as railway collisions, burial under falls of earth, and so on) are an exception to this: their relations to determinates in childhood have hitherto eluded investigation.

As we have already pointed out, following the discovery in the aftermath of the 1914–18 war of a neurosis with an exclusively external aetiology, Freud admits a formation of psychopathology in which repressed infantile wishes play no part whatsoever. In which case, the emphasis is not on repressed memory, but on what Parkes describes in Henry's case as 'memories of the disaster', where hallucinatory repetition is identical to traumatic perception.

Freud leaves open the possibility of discovering common ground between the psychoneuroses and non-neurotic traumatic conditions. Some of the most important developments in post-Freudian therapy have taken place along this trajectory, developments that Parkes's work disputes. In assuming that Henry is traumatized by an accident that took place in the recent past, Parkes decides the matter in favour of natural disasters. This is a decisive and important development in the theory of mental health, and it is noteworthy that while Parkes (1996: 147) acknowledges Bowlby's work on the harmful influence of childhood losses, he takes this as further confirmation of the primacy of external events in the aetiology of traumatic reactions. The absence of infantile prototypes results in a coherent account of post-traumatic memory that owes nothing to the psychoanalytic account of neurotic symptoms. The therapeutic series of trauma, memory, and repetition is set out without any reference to infantile fixations, sexual trauma, or regression. In particular, whereas the notion of *Nachträglichkeit* constitutes a point of departure for Winnicottian reclamation (see Chapter 2), it is given no explanatory significance in Parkes.

In spite of a common preoccupation with the external aetiology of the traumatic neuroses, Freud and Parkes take the therapeutic argument in entirely different directions. To come back to Henry, the case illustrates the phenomenon of repetitive dreams following psychological trauma, where the patient continues to repeat painful experiences. It is not immediately obvious in such cases what lies behind the repetition. The question has spurred a vociferous debate in psychoanalysis. Claims about the origins and function of repetition range, for instance, from the abreaction of excessive tensions to a general tendency towards discharge in terms of the death drive. Winnicott's emphasis on environmental deficiency is a further alternative. In Parkes, the aetiological debate seems less important than the therapeutic emphasis on 'escape'. Parkes argues that so long as Henry avoids thinking about the disastrous event he cannot escape from the memories which continue to threaten him. Unlike Freud (1914), who brings the notion of 'working-through' (*Durcharbeitung*) to bear on what continues to offer resistance in the course of treatment, Parkes sets the patient the task of placing himself out of danger from a threat.[18] The aim is to get out of harm's way, to survive in the sense of making a safe place for oneself.

The aim of escape is consistent with the perspective of psychosocial transition. Instead of confronting inner truths, patients are left with the task of extricating themselves from a series of false assumptions and dysfunctional patterns of attachment. As an approach to trauma, escape works by directing the therapeutic effect of disclosure towards the self-regulating capacities of the patient. Essentially, what Parkes offers in place of Freudian therapy is a scene of intimate disclosure without symptoms; hence a clinical series of psychiatric cases. Healing by recollection takes a momentous turn in the context of bereavement studies, where the paradigm shifts from the hysteric and sexuality to the disasters as well as the frailties of everyday life. As the developments in attachment theory demonstrate, psychoanalysis is inevitably caught up in this historic shift, and yet is taken as corroborative only so far. Beyond a certain point the Freudian case history becomes yet another obstacle to innovative attempts at securing the positive content of grief and, thereby, initiating rational life-plans for human welfare.

For Parkes, patients like Henry are faced with the same task as vulnerable widows in having to re-establish their identity and, through the traumatic event of loss, renegotiate the moral meaning of their lives. The causal explanation hesitates once again between familiar and exceptional circumstances. The figure of traumatic grief, which proves useful in its very ambiguity, presupposes a traumatized subject who is nonetheless capable of integrating death into a reflective project of self-management. It is precisely at the point where mourning becomes a way of coping with loss, where the feeling that life has lost its meaning presents an opportunity as well as a risk, that the tragic dimension pertaining to 'the recollection of things [*Aufzählen der Dinge*]' (Sebald 1998: 3) gives way to the optimism of testimonials and lifeplans. These testimonial statements, exemplified by contemporary memoirs of grief, owe nothing to the medicine of symptoms. The failure of clinical medicine and psychoanalysis alike, a failure to measure up to the permanent task of psychological and social defence, is traced in an intimate trajectory from modes of attachment to the disclosure of internal working models. The 'Freudian moment' is occluded, if not subject to closure at the point where the logic of risk management coheres through the coincidence of illness and identity. As an alternative to psychoanalysis, psychosocial studies uphold the norms of conduct across an increasingly wide range of human experience: from vulnerability through everyday grief to some of the most traumatic events of our time. It is possible based on a new psychiatric discrimination of fragility to identify holocaust survivors as 'well-adjusted' or 'less adjusted', and to treat AIDS-related bereavement as a category of 'special needs'.[19]

Notes

1. To underline the comparative range of narratives under discussion throughout the book, while memoirs of grief remain essentially at odds with constructions in psychoanalysis (see Part I), they are nonetheless consistent with the narrative dimension of regulatory action in the sociology of managed lives (see Part III).
2. For comparable sets of predictors on the predisposition to pathological grief reaction, see Raphael (1977); Sheldon et al. (1981); Worden and Silverman (1989); and Worden (1991).
3. For the idea of disciplinary apparatuses as 'dividing practices', see Foucault (1975; 2000c).
4. The findings of the Harvard Bereavement Study, which comprises a study of sixty-eight young Boston widows and widowers under the age of 45, are reported in Glick et al. (1974) and Parkes and Weiss (1983).
5. See Hacking (1975; 1990) for the origins and development of probability and its impact on scientific reason.
6. Cf. Worden's (1991: 42) claim that '[w]hat predicts difficult bereavement in one population may differ from that which predicts difficulty in another group'.
7. See Castel (1984) for the articulation of risk indices and differential population profiles.
8. Parkes identifies reactions to other types of loss after Kitson (1982); Fagin and Little (1984); Munoz (1980); Houghton and Houghton (1977); and Maker (1982). In addition, Parkes (1972; 1973; 1976) elaborates in more detail on reactions to loss of a limb, and loss of a home. See also Chapter 14 of *Bereavement*.
9. See Burgoine (1988) for a comparative study of socio-cultural factors influencing the expression of grief. Burgoine applied the interview schedule used in Parkes's London Study to interview a comparison group of newly bereaved widows in New Providence, Grand Bahama.
10. See Foucault's (1961: 517) discussion of the problem of expression and madness in the concluding chapter of *History of Madness*: '*Le Neveu de Rameau* and the whole literary fashion that followed it indicated a reappearance of madness in the domain of language, a language where madness was permitted to speak in the first person.'
11. See Faimberg (1981) for an innovative theory of listening in the analytic context of transference and resistance.
12. See Worden (1991: 93–115) for a comprehensive summary of modes and circumstances of death, including their impact on the process of grieving.
13. For the notion of 'disenfranchised grief', see Doka (1989).
14. Studies of shell shock in Britain, and traumatic neurosis in Germany, date from World War I. Post-traumatic stress disorder (PTSD), however, was first identified as a diagnostic category in the third edition of the American Psychiatric Association's *Diagnostic Statistical Manual of Mental Disorder* (DSM-III) in 1987. Following diagnostic categorization, and the subsequent clinical and research interest in the condition, Parkes included a chapter on PTSD in the third edition of *Bereavement* (1996). The chapter is an important source for the inclusion of trauma in Parkes's statement on the determinants of grief.
15. See Breuer and Freud (1893–5: 12): 'we concur with Binet and the two Janets [Pierre and Jules]'. Cases of psychological trauma appear throughout Pierre Janet's work: ten cases in *Psychological Automatism* (1889); seventy-three cases in *Neuroses and Fixed Ideas* (1892); twenty-six cases in *The Mental State of Hystericals* (1893–4); and one hundred and forty-eight cases in *Obsessions and Psychasthenia* (1903).
16. See Rudnytsky (2011) for the view of Freud as an authoritarian character.

17 Parkes acted as consultant and government adviser following the *Herald of Free Enterprise* disaster. For a further elaboration on the concept of the 'aftermath', see Parkes (1991).
18 For a seminal account of working-through in the countertransference, see Brenman Pick (1985).
19 See Kaminer and Lavie (1993) for holocaust survivors, and Martin (1988) and Martin and Dean (1993) for AIDS-related bereavement.

Part III

THE MANAGED SOCIETY

The term and concept 'reflexivity' remains central in contemporary formations of managed lives and, following our consideration of the reflexive norm in therapeutic supervision and the management of grief, we concentrate in the final part of the book on the role of reflexivity in day-to-day conduct. The value of reflection *per se* as well as the specific reflexive values of agency and autonomy matter for any meaningful human life. It is what these values stand for in the context of administrative decentralization that is under discussion here, particularly with respect to what has been made of psychoanalysis in this context. As we have seen, psychoanalysis makes available specific forms of reflective self-understanding, including a range of applications from clinical regression to the collective task of social defence. In the following chapters we are primarily concerned with the link between rational reflection and orders of conduct in everyday life. Our aim is to demonstrate the extent to which reflexive norms, supported by a sociological revision of psychoanalysis, are mobilized as mechanisms of self-regulation.

We discuss the sociological appropriation of psychoanalysis in a series of studies by Anthony Giddens dating from the mid 1970s through the 1990s. Giddens (1991: 214) argues that new formations of 'life-politics', by which he means the politics of 'a reflexively mobilized order', have 'radically altered the existential parameters of social activity'. While the argument applies to the management of 'damaged identities' under the conditions of modern life, Giddens draws on psychoanalysis in support of the more general claim that self and society are integrated through the normative routines and mechanism of daily life. This emphasizes the sociological value of psychoanalysis as a theory of regulatory action. However, given the selective nature of Giddens's reading of psychoanalysis, we are not proposing a general discussion of the relationship between the disciplines of sociology and psychoanalysis. Unlike Parsons (1958), for example, who attempts a similar integration of post-war sociology with the psychoanalytic theory of personality, Giddens engages less with Freud than with various ideas in post-Freudian thought. His work includes references, for instance, to Lacanian psychoanalysis, American ego-psychology, and selected readings in British object-relations theory. Giddens shows no interest in the fundamental differences between these perspectives, but employs an eclectic frame of reference to account for our basic sense of security and its social implications.

As part of his comprehensive theory of 'structuration', Giddens addresses the problem of security along the axes of cognition, competence, and governance. We shall discuss the interconnections between these three basic areas of concern: first, the assimilation of affectivity to cognitive representation at the mundane level of practical consciousness; second, the identification of individuals as autonomous subjects characterized by a capacity for reflection, most notably in the form of self-narratives; and third, the reformation of political radicalism combined with moral individualism in the form of generative politics and positive welfare. My basic argument is that over a period of approximately twenty-five years, dating from the middle of the 1970s to the end of the 1990s, Giddens formulates *a general problematic of security* in which psychoanalysis plays a decisive role. Although Giddens does not have the advantage of clinical practice, his argument is nonetheless continuous, in many respects, with the perspective of psychosocial norms set out in Parkes. Thus, in addition to our discussion of his explicit use of psychoanalytic concepts, we shall also draw out the parallels as we see them between structuration theory and attachment theory. In particular, we focus on the analogous concepts of 'reflexive project' in Giddens and 'reflective function' in contemporary versions of attachment theory (Fonagy *et al.* 2002).

The aim in the final chapters is to draw out a series of problems that, I shall argue, constitute the sociological schema of managed society. To avoid misunderstanding, the problems as I have formulated them are based on my reading of Giddens; they are interpretative constructs of my own. My critique of the regulated life in the so-called 'late modern age' is based on an examination of these problems, starting with the cognitive bias of Giddens's schema in *New Rules of Sociological Method* (1976), *Central Problems in Social Theory* (1979), and *The Constitution of Society* (1984). Through a preoccupation with the realization of belief as knowledge, Giddens grounds subjectivity in the capacity for rational reflection. In particular, he outlines two problems along the axis of cognition: the problem of trust (how to believe in the world); and the problem of knowledge (how to appropriate our belief in the world). For Giddens, the articulation of trust and knowledge constitutes a secure sense of self that underpins social action.

Second, the focus of Giddens's work shifts in the early 1990s from an epistemological critique of constitution and realization to an historical analysis of intimacy and identity. The focus is now on integration and regulation; most notably, in *Modernity and Self-Identity* (1991) and *The Transformation of Intimacy* (1992), the principle of knowledgeability is supplemented by the principle of competency. Reflexive function operates along these lines as a particular kind of skill or mechanism of self-regulation. This involves two further problems: the problem of anxiety (how to defend our sense of the world); and the problem of autonomy (how to transform what we believe into what we are capable of doing). The combined operation of defence and autonomy consolidates the notion of security as the precondition for achievement. Most importantly for us, the human experience of believing remains central in this particular series of historical and theoretical problems, and here we shall compare the work of Giddens and Winnicott in some detail.

Third, Giddens presents a framework for democratic politics in *Beyond Left and Right* (1994b) and *The Third Way* (1998a), with respect to the related problems of attachment or solidarity (how to live in the world with one another) and happiness (how to thrive in the world). Giddens puts the traditional sociological question of solidarity back on the political agenda within a moral framework. What are good human social relations? How are we to flourish as persons? What are the conditions of our well-being? Giddens addresses the renewal of social solidarity and the pursuit of happiness as two sides of the same governmental question. The idea that globalization and a greater capacity for self-reflection have fundamentally changed the way we live becomes increasingly important for Giddens and, seeing these historical developments as an opportunity as well as a source of potential danger and harm to ourselves, he calls for a re-moralization of the social. It will be argued in the final chapter that the schema of security coheres through an emphasis on self-management as a form of democratic experience. Again, we draw parallels here between the sociological schema and the notion of moral emotions in contemporary attachment theory.

The problematic of security provides coherence for a seemingly disparate set of epistemological, existential, and political questions. It links the theoretical trajectory of the contemporary sociological argument, broadly speaking, from constitution through representation to mobilization. As part of his contribution to the reformation of centre-left politics, Giddens is inevitably faced with the problem of security; indeed, the norm of radical insecurity, together with the stringent measures of social defence, has become an established part of the political imaginary. Further to the traditional concern in political theory with the relationship between the state and civil society, we have become increasingly preoccupied over the last twenty or thirty years with security as a general experience of social life. The problematic of security may be viewed in this context with respect to the connections between terrorism, policing, and the state, on the one hand, and debates about national security and personal safety on the other. Moreover, with the fall of Communism in the late 1980s, Giddens contributes to the wider political debate about the deployment of liberal democracy as the global model of social order. The problematic of security thus provides a framework for debates about global capitalism.

Against the general background of increased political vigilance and social austerity, we are interested more specifically in the idea of security as a reflexive function of everyday life. In this respect, Giddens has made a decisive contribution to the understanding of basic security in contemporary society, combining a traditional sociological emphasis on social order with a more existentially oriented account of personal experience. We see this as consistent with the psychosocial perspective. Giddens construes trust, anxiety, and happiness as problems of self-management, and therefore extends the meaning of security to our most intimate aspirations. Thus for Giddens, as for Winnicott and Parkes, our vulnerability to trauma of one kind or another places the emphasis on inner security as the condition of personal and social well-being. In short, together with a sociological analysis of politics and the state, Giddens uses psychoanalysis to link security, first, with the capacity to believe; second, with the competent use of self-narratives as a defence against anxiety; and, third, with the entitlement to happiness and its pursuit in the name of the good life.

The fact that psychoanalysis allows for an altogether more subtle, diffuse approach to the government of ourselves brings us full circle. Giddens 'resolves' the tension in Winnicott's argument between the redemptive promise and the administrative task in favour of the latter. The primacy accorded by Giddens to the modern self-understanding of secular reason will be apparent, particularly in our ongoing discussion regarding the capacity for faith. And when we come to the proposal of positive welfare, we shall see that Giddens elaborates on the dynamic possibilities of individualism in conjunction with responsibility and prosperity once again from the perspective of political reason. In a further development of the reflexive norm, Giddens extends the potential of human agency to so-called constructive risk-taking in the context of a social investment state. On this reckoning hope requires security in order to sustain itself as a social phenomenon as well as a personal experience. It is possible to sustain this argument and, therefore, to ground the problematic of security in the logic of society, only insofar as the 'unconscious' is conceived as an intentional structure of the knowledgeable agent. In this respect, Giddens exemplifies the revisionist reading of Freudianism that is prevalent throughout the culture, privileging real-life events and conscious mechanisms of self-regulation over endopsychic entities or intrapsychic structures and functions.

Finally, it is important to indicate in these introductory comments the neo-Kantian paradigm of Durkheimian sociology that informs the principles of knowledgeability, competence, and self-governance. These are principles that Giddens maintains, as part of the contemporary sociological project, on theoretical as well as political grounds. In reworking the Durkheimian tradition along the lines of reflexive function and self-regulatory action, Giddens demonstrates the extent to which the sociological reduction operates beyond the phenomenological *epoché*. For Husserl, the phenomenological attitude is established by bracketing 'matters of fact' as well as everything that is posited by consciousness as 'real'. By means of the 'eidetic reduction' and the 'transcendental reduction', respectively, one is left with the essential structures of the pure phenomena. To recall Husserl's (1913: xx) basic proposition: 'Our phenomenology is to be an eidetic doctrine, not of phenomena that are real, but of phenomena that are transcendentally reduced'. By contrast, the Durkheimian tradition lays claim to a science of facts *contra* 'cognitions of essences'. This represents an irreconcilable conflict of interpretation in modern thought between the phenomenological *epoché* and an anthropological–sociological perspective on the constitution of phenomena. To posit the 'constitution of society' requires a sociological reduction by means of which it is possible to reconstruct the historical as well as the epistemological conditions of 'social facts'.

INTRODUCTION

We are primarily concerned in this book with the constitution of inner security and social order, a project that Durkheim (1895: 159) orients along sociological lines by presenting the principle of causality as an 'empirical postulate' rather than a 'rational necessity'. We begin, then, by considering the extent to which Giddens reworks the Durkheimian orientation specifically in terms of the 'duality of structure', drawing out the normative implications for the problematic of security. We then turn to a more detailed discussion of the psychoanalytic underpinning of this problematic in structuration theory, starting in Chapter 7 with Giddens's reading of Lacan, Erikson, and Winnicott. Giddens attempts to explain how social actors function in an orderly manner according to self-prescribed norms, an explanation which is based on a notion of basic trust derived from psychoanalysis. In this chapter, we explore the links between the so-called 'crisis of trust' and post-Freudian uses of faith through a comparative reading of Giddens and Winnicott. Alongside the basic problems of trust and knowledge, Giddens addresses a wider series of social and political concerns, some of the more important aspects of which are reconstructed in our final chapter along the lines of reflexive governance. Thus in Chapter 8 we discuss in turn: the post-Freudian concept of anxiety in structuration theory; the analogous concepts of 'reflective function' and 'reflexive project' in the context of the biographical frame; a new sociology of morals based on the idea of social welfare as a psychic concept; and, finally, the practical programme of moral individualism in the form of 'positive welfare'.

7

BASIC SECURITY

What sociology makes of psychoanalysis and what psychoanalysis enables sociology to do are the entwined themes in the following two chapters. To demonstrate the sociological revision of psychoanalysis, we shall concentrate on the use that Giddens makes of post-Freudian thinking in support of the 'reflexive project' of the self. Essentially, Giddens's appropriation of psychoanalysis is coupled with his post-Durkheimian stance towards the mobilization of society, and we begin by looking at the problematic of security in relation to the Durkheimian tradition of sociological thought. This will allow us to expand on the normative conception of management set out in Parts I and II. We have seen how Parkes redefines the norm itself in his attempt to overcome the obstacles of moral hygiene and the explanation of social facts as 'things'. Further to which Giddens derives a normative schema of the managed society from a revised notion of Durkheimian order, extending daily conduct in a reflexive direction through a cognitive model of self-knowledge. Psychoanalysis is used in order to conceptualize the reflexive norm as a mechanism of self-regulation and, I shall argue, Giddens's notion of 'reflexivity' is thus analogous to the concept of 'reflective function' in the work of Fonagy *et al.* (2002).

Giddens uses psychoanalysis in order to extend the sociological understanding of self-identity, which includes an understanding of the conditions of belief together with the realization of belief as knowledge. Through the general schema of security, Giddens addresses the central problems of 'basic security' and 'existential anxiety'; essentially, the aim is to place the problem of social order in a larger existential setting. A new figure emerges in this context beset by moral uncertainties as well as emotional discontent, a figure with an apparently unprecedented historical option of managing anxiety by reflexive styles of living. The onus falls on individuals to manage themselves through socially and culturally sponsored lifestyles, drawing on a seemingly inexhaustible variety of options, including therapeutic endeavours that are identified as part of 'a methodology of life-planning'. Therapy is promoted beyond the clinic; indeed, the break with clinical psychoanalysis in Giddens and Parkes takes place along the same fault line. Giddens (1991: 180) proposes that while psychoanalytic treatment 'developed as a means of combating pathologies of the personality ... the prime importance of therapy in circumstances of late modernity does not lie in this direction'. Psychoanalysis is seen instead as 'an expression of generalized reflexivity', a social formation as well as a technique of intimacy that, according to Giddens (1991: 180), 'exhibits in full the dislocations and uncertainties to which modernity gives rise'.

Giddens effectively historicizes Parkes's notion of special risk; at the same time, the reflexive project appropriates the vital normativity that characterizes Winnicott's living self. We shall concentrate on Giddens's concept of belief as an example of the sociological reconfiguration of living. Viewed in terms of modern dilemmas and practices, in the context of what Taylor (2007) describes as 'exclusive humanism', psychoanalysis is inextricably linked with the re-evaluation of belief. Under the conditions of modern secularism, the human experience of believing is itself an historical dilemma. And so while secularism as such is not our topic, the secular context of belief is nonetheless indispensable for an understanding of the Freudian interpretation and its revised uses.[1] As we mean to demonstrate, the sociological appropriation of psychoanalysis aims to place Freud's legacy on a firm footing not as a clinical method, but rather, as a formation of modern moral and social order. In particular, further to Winnicott's pronouncements on the 'social provision', new directions in attachment theory keep problems of conduct, disaffection, and the antisocial response on the agenda as pathological phenomena of reflection (Fonagy *et al.* 1996). A corresponding development in sociological theory, the reflexive project of the self exemplifies a post-Durkheimian dispensation (Taylor 2007: 512), wherein basic trust extends to self-sufficiency and the re-moralization of the social. Management remains an expansive phenomenon in this context as an ethical construction rather than an intuitive form modelled on maternal love, a construction that underpins the mobilization of society and the formation of sponsored lifestyles.

Social facts and reflexive norms

Sociology has been primarily concerned with the problems of order and meaning since it first emerged as a discipline in the late 1800s. Elias (2001: vii) has thus summarized the central issues of sociology in terms of the 'relation of the plurality of people to the single person we call the "individual", and of the single person to the plurality'. How is society possible? What sense do individuals make of themselves and their actions? These substantive preoccupations with the society of individuals are coupled with clearly defined rules of sociological method. Accordingly, Durkheim (1895: 45) identified the most fundamental phenomenon of sociology in the concreteness of 'social facts', the objective reality of which he posited as the basic principle of sociological thinking. 'Things' and 'facts' are thus inseparable aspects of the sociological imagination. Problems and methods operate in tandem to form an integrated understanding, wherein the idea of social phenomena as 'real things' grounds the analysis of social order and human meaning. As such, the sociological reduction results in a preoccupation with the maintenance of personal and social structures at the mundane level of daily life.

Giddens inherits these defining problems and procedures, while at the same time revising the Durkheimian tradition as a theory of structuration. For Giddens, sociology deals with the inherent complexity of the society of individuals manifest as the event of structure in action. In other words, Giddens (1979: 69) accounts for the intelligibility of social life in terms of the 'duality of structure', by which he means the 'mutual dependence of structure and agency' as well as the 'fundamentally recursive character of social life'. He turns to psychoanalysis therefore with a preconceived agenda, and the use he makes of it is circumscribed by the basic premises of structuration theory on the one hand and, on the other, by the methodological orientation of the sociological reduction. Arguing from the objectivity of social facts, Giddens advances two basic propositions: first, the individual is seen as a participant in the social world through the irreducible duality of self and society; second, the work of the self is characterized in this respect as the real- and this-worldly event of mundane order. These propositions recall the very groundwork of sociological thinking and its immanent frame of reference, namely, the idea that the generative nature of social forms is coupled with the internal coherence of self-identity. In short, the theory of structuration elaborates on the fundamental sociological problem of order in line with the constitutive function of rational reflection.

There are important ways in which this account differs from both functionalist and phenomenological models of social theory. Looked at from the point of view of the duality of structure, society comprises a composite of social facts and reflexive norms. As Giddens (1979: 69) puts it, 'the structural properties of social systems are both the medium and the outcome of the practices that constitute those systems'. The connections between self and society are seen in terms of 'the structural components of social institutions' and, at the same time, 'the contingently accomplished activities of situated actors'. The emphasis on the practical activities of individuals proves decisive for reflexive models of self-management. Giddens reworks Durkheim's insistence on the concreteness of social facts, emphasizing the extent to which sociology studies things that are real, recurrent, and accountable in self-conscious modes of conduct. Following Durkheim, Giddens renders the knowing subject identical with the subject of conduct; indeed, they express a common concern with what Durkheim calls 'collective *ways of being*' (1895: 57; emphasis in the original). The duality of structure is presented as an objective fact not only in relation to actors' accounts of their behaviour, but more importantly with respect to the 'accountability' of action itself at the level of practical reason. Society, in other words, is understood in terms of the enactment of the mundane phenomena of social order coupled with 'the rationalization of action' (Giddens 1979: 57). The basic assumption is that we regulate our lives, that it is incumbent on us to do so as competent social actors, even as society itself makes sense as a coherent entity.

The cognitive bias of the sociological reduction is apparent in the way that Giddens construes the 'knowledgeability' of social actors. Tacit and discursively available types of knowledge are viewed as part of the rules and resources of social action. As such, the accountability of action as a matter of fact is seen as coextensive with the giving of accounts by individuals themselves. In a continuous but contested line of sociological thought that originated in the nineteenth century with Comte, Giddens is indebted as much to Garfinkel as he is to Durkheim.[2] Most importantly, Garfinkel's account of the 'ethnomethods' involved in the mundane structuration of meaning and order affords Giddens an insight into 'the endless living midst of ordinary things' (Garfinkel 2002: 74). For Giddens, as for Garfinkel, the interminable and recursive nature of accountability is evident as a social fact, but also as a form of consciousness. The Durkheimian tradition to which ethnomethodology belongs, places an emphasis on sociological exercises in both social reproduction and the formation of individual identity. Social action itself is seen as a way of life for which actors are continually accountable, indeed, Giddens (1984: 375) is primarily concerned with 'knowledge of "how to go on" in forms of life'. Looked at from this perspective, reproduction becomes explicable only through the accounts that individuals give of their actions. Thus, in contrast to Winnicott's formulation of the 'continuity of being', for Giddens the capacity to 'go on' is predicated on the link between the rationalization of action and the constitution of society, between knowledge and conduct. In this sense, going on being presupposes the idea of reflexivity as both a skill and a mechanism of regulation.

Alongside the purposeful nature of social action, then, social order remains the central fact and the central problem for sociology. The problematic of security therefore may be seen as yet one more variation on a central theme; and 'ontological insecurity', as part of a sociological series that includes alienation, anomie, disaffection, disenchantment, and so on. This is not to say that sociologists share the same approach to these problems. Indeed, Canguilhem (1955: 70–1) differentiates the life of the organism and social life on the grounds that 'the purpose [*finalité*] of society is precisely one of the capital problems of human existence and one of the fundamental problems that reason poses itself ... by contrast, men agree much more easily on the nature of social ills than on the scope of the remedies to apply to them'. Where its purpose may be seen as immanent to the organism; on the other hand, the question of order inevitably divides sociologists.

As an example of this inherent conflict of interpretations, the alternative readings of Durkheim in Parsons and Giddens are particularly important for us, insofar as they presuppose two contrasting sociological applications of psychoanalysis. Thus, while Giddens addresses the constraining nature of social facts in relation to reflexive norms and the prevailing moral form; Parsons saw the Durkheimian problem of order as a problem of normative control. Parsons viewed the persistence of stable patterns of social activity as a consequence of the internalization of normative patterns of need-dispositions. The idea being that individuals are positively motivated to co-operate with one another, which makes them want essentially what is required of them at the societal level. The argument presupposes an integration of self and society along the following lines:

> It is through internalization of common patterns of value-orientation that a system of social interaction can be stabilized. Put in personality terms this means that there is an element of superego organization correlative with every role-orientation pattern of the individual in question. In every case, the internalization of a superego element means motivation to accept the priority of collective over personal interests, within the appropriate limits and on the appropriate occasions.
>
> (Parsons et al. 1951: 150)

Parsons placed the anxiety–defence couple of Freudian psychoanalysis at the centre of his sociological account of personal relations. At the same time, he dealt with the problem of order in terms of the internalization of norms combined with the motivational role of values. Norms and values are therefore seen as the causal factors in human social action.

Giddens is no less interested than Parsons was in the integrative mechanisms of social systems. He accepts the basic sociological assumption that mechanisms of integration and regulation are necessary for the maintenance of ordinary society's orderliness. The principle of regulation is a given for the sociology of managed lives. Unlike Parsons, however, Giddens does not address order as a problem of egoistic self-interest; he sees the problem as essentially Durkheimian rather than Hobbesian. For Giddens, social facts are not refractory to the human will; the autonomy of the individual is seen as consistent with the generative nature of social interaction. Moreover, Giddens maintains that Durkheim did not hold to the problematic of externality in the way that Parsons assumed. The implication is that Parsons made too much of the externality of social facts; by contrast, Giddens emphasizes the degree of agency in Durkheim's (1895: 40) claim that all social facts 'consist of ways of thinking and acting'. This is decisive when it comes to the articulation of rational reflection and ways of living. The idea that individuals are simply regulated by society, an idea that enters the sociological imagination with Comte, does not allow for the extension of the reflexive norm to daily life in the form of self-regulative systems.

The interchangeable use of the terms 'constraint' (*contrainte*) and 'coercion' (*coercition*) has been the cause of significant confusion in the critical literature on Durkheim. To establish the principle of regulation on reflexive grounds, it is necessary to clarify the Durkheimian concept of control. Managed lives presuppose a particular formation of control society, as distinct from Foucault's (1975) notion of 'disciplinary society'. For his part, Giddens (1977b: 283) draws two critical conclusions from the Durkheimian problematic of control: first, that Durkheim does not accord society objective reality at the expense of the autonomy of action; and second, that he does not posit an inherent antinomy between the individual and society. The basic assumption being that social life is at once constraining and spontaneous:

> If...we recognize with some authorities that social life presents itself to the individual under the form of constraint [*contrainte*], we admit with others that it is a spontaneous product of reality. What logically joins these two elements, in appearance contradictory, is that the reality from which social life emanates goes beyond the individual.
>
> (Durkheim 1895: 144)

The social reality of personal life, the fact that social life extends beyond the individual, is a methodological presupposition as well as a central theme in the neo-Kantian tradition of Durkheimian sociology. The passage we have just quoted, which may be read as a summary statement of the sociological reduction, is not tantamount to the idea that the exterior regulates the interior. Rather, the rejection of individualism as a methodological approach is consistent with Durkheim's commitment to liberal individualism as a form of moral authority. Durkheim saw the latter as the basis of solidarity in modern society. Similarly, following Durkheim's rejection of both the Hobbesian notion of order and utilitarian individualism, Giddens comes to the conclusion that the objective reality of social facts is consistent with the lived accomplishments of knowledgeable agents.

Unlike Parsons, then, who arrived at an external analysis of norms and values understood as constraining and determining, Giddens extends the reflexive norm as a mechanism of self-regulation. He postulates a state of basic ontological security in which, first, the rationalization of action is irreducible to the Parsonian problematic of internalization, and second, the moralization of the social is accountable as part of the real- and this-worldly work of human agency. At odds with Parsons on the fundamental question of order; nonetheless, Giddens attempts to combine Durkheim's basic assumption that social facts consist of ways of thinking and acting with an historical sociology of personal values. The attempt to derive an ethics from sociology in the form of reflective governance is examined in the final chapter.

Giddens aims to establish the problem of constitution through the sociological reduction. What does this mean in normative terms? The link between basic security and personal values, which proves decisive for the notion of self-management, rests neither on the externality of social facts nor on the functionalist conception of norms as purely motivational factors. The know-how of social actors is privileged over external regulation in structuration theory. In assigning rational reflection a central role in sociological analysis, Giddens (1984: 42) emphasizes the importance of 'the interpretative schemes and norms which actors utilize in the constitution of their conduct'. Constitution is not a one-way street for Giddens; the norm is seen at once as the condition and the outcome of conduct. In this respect, the configuration of norms and interpretative schemes operates as a sociological version of Bowlby's 'internal working model', where knowledge itself is counted as a reflexive form of life. For Giddens, what actors know about the conditions of their own actions, or are able to say about those conditions, reproduces the conditions under which knowledge itself is possible.

In what may be seen as a critical juncture in the history of sociology, Giddens's adoption of the reflexive norm sets his argument apart from the Parsonian model of internalization. But it also introduces an alternative to the philosophy of the subject in the phenomenological tradition, most notably, Husserl's constituting ego and the 'temporal particularity' (*Jeweiligkeit*) of Dasein in Heidegger's *Being and Time*. The sociological reduction runs counter not only to the eidetic and transcendental reductions, but also to Heidegger's existential reduction. We shall come back to Giddens's reading of Heidegger in the following chapter. What I want to propose here is that, distinct from the basic problems of phenomenology, through his reworking of the Durkheimian tradition in sociology Giddens aligns himself with a Kantian thematic in post-Freudian theory.

Freud's own relationship to the Kantian legacy remains complex (Tauber 2010). In a recent contribution to the debate Longuenesse (2012) notes the structural similarities between the views of Kant and Freud, particularly with respect to moral motivation. By contrast, Gardner (2012) identifies two opposing philosophical trajectories in Freudian thought, including, a post-Kantian conception of the unconscious associated with rational reflection and a conception of human motivation based on Spinoza's notion of affectivity. Looked at in the context of this debate, our proposal that Giddens upholds basic Durkheimian assumptions on Kantian grounds thus provides a philosophical framework for the sociological appropriation of psychoanalysis.[3] That society presupposes its own principle of reason, with respect to the coincidence of knowledge and conduct, sets out the parameters for the psychoanalysis of everyday life.[4]

The normative basis of Giddens's (1984: 26–7) argument is evident in his claim that the 'duality of structure is always the main grounding of continuities in social reproduction across time-space'. The claim is upheld on three counts: first, Giddens argues that the constitution of structures and agents is coterminous. Second, that structure is not external in the sense of normative imperatives, but internal to the cognitive intentionality of the subject. Third, that structure is simultaneously constraining and enabling in all aspects of daily life. This suggests a systematic reformulation of the basic question of sociology, concerning the manner in which, as Giddens (1984: 24) puts it, the conduct of individuals reproduces the structural elements of society. Giddens is not interested in discovering a foundation or groundwork beneath the 'ramified connections' of human society and its manifest associative forms. While the sociological nature of managed lives remains indisputable, the functionalist model of social reproduction appears to be redundant. But although he is largely critical of the methodological dogmas of functionalism and structuralism alike; nonetheless, Giddens (1984: xxiv) continues to focus on norms as mechanisms of integration and regulation, that is, as prerequisites for 'the flux of encounters involved in daily life'.

Giddens turns to psychoanalysis for the concept of reflexivity as a form of self-regulation. Closer to Parkes and attachment theory than to Winnicott and object-relations theory, he puts security into question from the perspective of self-identity. To what does our feeling of security attest? We remain focused on this question, it seems to me, at a definite cost to our understanding of emotional life, a cost which is borne above all by a preoccupation with adaptation and security. Starting from Durkheim's (1895: 45–6) insistence that 'social phenomena, although not material things, are nevertheless real', Giddens renders the experience of daily life meaningful in the psychoanalytical vocabulary of security and defence. And, critical misgivings about the social appropriation of psychoanalysis notwithstanding, it seems to me that Giddens's problematic of security represents his most original contribution to sociology, if not a major synthesis in post-war British sociological theory.

Giddens uses psychoanalysis, then, to underwrite our sense of security as an attribute of identity, but also as a constitutive social form. The habitual, taken-forgranted nature of daily life is understood in terms of familiar activities and forms of conduct, which, according to Giddens (1984: 376), are 'both supporting and supported by a sense of ontological security'. Again, while he draws more explicitly on the work of Erikson and Winnicott, Giddens's attempt to reformulate the sociological theory of order as a principle of regulation has clearer affinities with an attachment-theory framework. Presenting a combination of trust and knowledge as the basis of inner security, Giddens formulates a general schema that extends from emotional states of mind to types of sociality. The perspective is evidently comprehensive, ranging from a psychosocial conception of trust to a political sociology of anxiety, and from a programme of re-moralization to the government of happiness. Indeed, what may appear as a disparate set of arguments is actually a coherent account of the cognitively intentional structures of subjects living under modern conditions. In turning to psychoanalysis, Giddens extends the sociological frame of reference to the most intimate techniques and mechanisms of social order.

The crisis of trust

Richard Sennett (2012: 27–9) argues that a crisis of trust in contemporary neoliberal regimes has resulted in the emergence of 'a distinctive character type', with individuals under the yoke of inner anxieties and moral uncertainties in search of some form of existential relief. It is largely in response to this perceived crisis that Giddens attempts an integration of psychoanalysis with sociology. Giddens and Sennett are dealing with similar problems from different vantage points: whereas Sennett construes the problems of trust and anxiety with respect to the decline of co-operation in modern life; Giddens (1991: 137–9) addresses the same problems in terms of the deskilling of day-to-day life. Focusing on the capacity to co-operate and the capacity for self-reflection, respectively, they are both concerned with the breakdown of solidarity in everyday life. How, under post-industrial conditions, can we manage what Giddens calls 'damaged identities'? Of course solutions and problems are inextricably linked, and by turning to psychoanalysis Giddens constructs the problems of trust and anxiety in a way that delimits the options for managing feelings of insecurity. We have set about in the final part of the book to retrace the construction of these problems through the sociological appropriation of psychoanalysis.

Giddens begins his reading of psychoanalysis in the early 1970s with reference to the work of Lacan, who was summarily dismissed in *New Rules of Sociological Method* for his failure to conceptualize the 'active subject' (1976: 21–2). Giddens remains committed to the coincidence of reflection and action; however, in *Central Problems in Social Theory* he proposes a cautious application of Lacanian psychoanalysis, drawing 'critically and sparingly' on the structuralist problematic of the unconscious. He focuses particularly on the construction of identity in Lacan, the idea that the inscription of the infant in a subject/object relation is achieved through the identification of the 'mirror-stage'. While Giddens (1979: 120–1) comments approvingly on the deflection of the specular *I* into the social *I*, he remains no less critical of the fact that 'the reflexive, acting subject' is all but absent from Lacan's account of 'signifying structures'.

These critical comments reveal a fundamental incompatibility between sociology and psychoanalysis over the question of the sign. Lacan announced and initiated a new development in psychoanalysis with his Rapport de Rome (1953), placing psychoanalysis on an entirely new footing in terms of the relationship between language and the unconscious. Most importantly, Lacan's critique of the self-sufficiency of consciousness, as seen from the perspective of the signifier, is directly at odds with the traditional sociological bias towards self-identity. It is important to note that, as was evident in our discussion of psychiatry and bereavement studies, the problematic of self-identity is not confined to sociology, but represents a more pervasive resistance to the radical import of Freud's legacy. Lacan's uncompromising return to Freud undermines the idea of the self as a cohesive entity. That we provide reasons for our actions by reflecting on those actions, and that those actions alone count as meaningful for us, is not an adequate account of human experience for either Freud or Lacan. On the other hand, Giddens (1979: 39) laments the reduction of subjectivity to 'a series of moments brought about by the intersection of signifying structures'. As such, he is critical of Lacan's failure to view signification as 'an integral element of social practices in general'.

Giddens's critique of Lacan is important for two reasons. First, it reveals the extent to which Giddens presupposes the coexistence of identity and the unconscious. Giddens (1984: 376) identifies reflexivity with the purposive or intentional character of human behaviour. Clearly, Freud did not confine matters to the intentional structures of the knowing subject, but allowed for ways in which we continually run up against the apparent implausibility of things, including things we find either unacceptable or unknowable in ourselves. The theory of unconscious determinants is essentially irreconcilable with the concept of reflexive function, and coming to a better sense of external reality scarcely offsets the ignorance Freud counted as both ground and measure of our tolerance. For Freud, realism is not a guarantee against conflict, but a way of taking its measure, even if the veto of the 'reality principle' may be considered premature from a Winnicottian perspective. Lacan brought home the same message as Freud by exposing the ego's pretence to a relationship with reality. However, according to Giddens's (1979: 56) 'stratified' model of the self, 'unconscious motivation' is not in the least incompatible with the 'reflexive monitoring of action'. On this reckoning, there is no need for us to tolerate not knowing, or to suffer the extremes of internal conflict. Giddens (1982: 10) argues that while '[u]nconscious sources of cognition and motivation form [a] "boundary" to the knowledgeability/capability of agents', the identity of the subject is nonetheless intact. Giddens (1979: 40) accepts the 'bounded' nature of action as entirely consistent with the exercise of autonomy and agency, including the exercise of 'active trust' (1994b: 14) as a type of self-reflective commitment to oneself and others. In short, whereas Freud viewed things in terms of an irreducible internal conflict, Giddens sees the 'unconscious' itself as a co-ordinate of self-identity.

Second, Giddens parts company with Lacan on the decisive question of self-formation, dismissing Lacan's (1949) critical account of the formative effects of a *gestalt*, 'spatial captation', and the function of 'misrecognition' (*méconnaissance*). Far from acknowledging the fundamental disagreement between Lacan and Winnicott over the question of primordial recognition, it serves Giddens's (1991: 60) theoretical purposes to discern 'a close connection' between them in terms of 'the flow of day-to-day conduct' and its possible breakdown. Arguing from the standpoint of what he calls a 'basic security system', Giddens (1991: 45) proposes that the 'essential threshold in child development' derives from the association of agency and speech. However, unlike Lacan, Giddens views language primarily as a problem of competency and control. The constitutive function of language, together with the resultant heterogeneity of the psyche, is glossed over in favour of 'the syntactical mastery of language' (1984: 52). The criterion of coherence neutralizes the problem of the signifier at the level of 'generalized capacity'. For Giddens, the problem is essentially one of trust understood in terms of practical consciousness, if not self-awareness. Giddens (1979: 122; emphasis added) argues that the 'capacities of tension-management in relation to organic wants', which he describes as 'the first and most all-encompassing *accommodations* the child makes to the social and material worlds', form the basis for our subsequent mastery of the techniques and mechanisms of everyday life.

Giddens runs the order of basic competencies together with the compatibility of self-identity and the unconscious. The concept of self-regulation is formed by combining the problem of control with the logic of identity. While the social reality of mother–infant interaction continues to delimit the form and function of basic security, the notion of 'accommodation' extends the scope of regulation along the lines of adaptation. If we start from the basic assumption that there is no society without regulation, it is also the case that no society is self-regulating. Addressing himself to what he sees as a confusion in the confounding of 'organization' and 'organism', Canguilhem (1955: 76–7) concludes that inasmuch as and because society has no inherent 'purpose' (*finalité*) regulation is always supplementary and unstable. The reflexive norm is conceived in this context as a *political* concept. Thus Giddens uses psychoanalysis as the basis of a political argument, in which the concept of regulation is applied not to the problem of instinctual tension, but rather, to the problem of self-control and the management of everyday life. To put it simply, in the Freudian argument the ego regulates id-impulses in relation to the demands and constraints of external reality. Giddens extrapolates a socio-political argument from this account, shifting the focus from the regulation of inner tension by means of defence mechanisms to the self-regulation of a securely founded self. The point of this argument is that, in an inherently unstable world, a secure sense of self rests on mechanisms of self-regulation.

We discuss the politics of self-regulation in the final chapter. However, to set the scene for the governmental application of Giddens's theory of security, we shall add a brief word here on the key texts in his political argument. This will highlight the historical context in which Giddens elaborates a hypothesis of competency as the basis of his sociology of trust. The continuity of identity and polity is characteristic of Giddens's work from the beginning. The theory of social governance set out in his later works is not a new departure, but an elaboration of the general schema of security. As far as the more immediate problem of trust is concerned, the structuralist reading of psychoanalysis is found wanting not only in *New Rules of Sociological Method* and *Central Problems in Social Theory*, but also in *The Consequences of Modernity* and *Modernity and Self-Identity*. In these later works, Giddens raises the question of trust more specifically in relation to the 'transformations' of modernity, where his account of emotional security is set out explicitly along historical lines.

The historical import of Giddens's political argument turns on the problem of belief in 'post-traditional society'. Giddens (1994a: 57) describes 'two directly connected domains of transformation', namely, 'globalization' and 'detraditionalization'. These are seen as 'dialectically related' phenomena in the context of a general sociological theory of action, comprising 'action at distance' in the case of globalization, on the one hand, and 'the excavation of traditional contexts of action' on the other. Giddens (1990: 100–24) addresses the problem of belief at this point through a comparative analysis of environments of trust in pre-modern and modern societies. The so-called crisis of trust is treated as part of the 'transformation of intimacy' under conditions of late modernity. For Giddens (1994a: 95), the end of tradition in everyday life includes the transformation of intimacy, which in turn 'has been largely created by globalizing influences'. In short, Giddens (1990: 114) elaborates a political conception of security in response to the problems of trust and anxiety, based on the connection between 'the globalizing tendencies of modernity' and 'the transformation of intimacy in contexts of day-to-day life'.

The generalization of the problematic of security extends yet further in *Beyond Left and Right* and *The Third Way*. This indicates the extent to which the sociology of emotions forms an integral part of Giddens's critique of political morality. In particular, his analysis of modernity relies on the idea that the modern citizen is a type of emotionally secure subject. The good society presupposes a securely founded self. Thus, Giddens addresses the ethical problem of how to live after the end of tradition from the standpoint of 'reflexive modernization'. The argument concerns the democratizing of personal life and its emotional underpinnings. Viewed more specifically in terms of the crisis of trust, Giddens (1992: 188) sets himself the task of developing 'an ethical framework for a democratic personal order'. In the wider context of intimacy and its transformation, trust is presented as a problem of 'stable lifestyle habits' (Giddens and Pierson 1998: 134). At the same time, the sociology of trust informs the account of self-autonomy intrinsic to the order of democracy. The general schema of security, therefore, combines the sociology of emotions with a critique of political morality. Emotional states of mind are linked with social mechanisms of self-regulation; the sense of security, with apparatuses of security.

The social logic of identity

In linking the reflexive project of subjectivity with democratic rationalities of governance, Giddens effectively rejects a whole field of psychoanalytic thinking, not least of all the advances made in psychoanalysis through the use of structural linguistics. He opts instead for selective readings of ego-psychology and British object-relations theory, while advancing a reflexive model of the subject in tandem with the new directions in attachment theory. We draw out the parallels between structuration theory and attachment theory in the following chapter, while focusing in the present chapter on his readings of Erikson and Winnicott.

What does Erikson offer Giddens? In his most important work, *Childhood and Society* (1950), Erikson presents a post-Freudian model of the human life cycle alongside a cross-cultural analysis of character. An original, if somewhat unwieldy series of observations and insights, the book encompasses detailed clinical material of both children and adults, comparative sociological accounts of national character, and a normative developmental framework. This multifarious and complex arrangement is held together by the underlying theme of 'ego-identity', the developmental and socio-historical aspects of which are seen as two sides of the same phenomenon. It is Erikson's contribution to a developmental understanding of a secure sense of self that proves most important for Giddens.

From a developmental point of view, then, Erikson was primarily concerned with how we manage to get beyond ourselves and engage with others in social relations, while at the same time establishing and maintaining a mature sense of identity. The humanist problematic of self-identity cast the Freudian interpretation as well as the criterion of maturity in a new light. As he continued to address the problem of identity from the mid-1930s onwards, Erikson eventually replaced Freud's model of early psychosexual stages with a comprehensive psychosocial developmental schema that covered the entire life cycle. 'It is one of the purposes of this work', Erikson (1950: 243) proposed in the most important chapter of *Childhood and Society*, 'to facilitate the comparison of the stages first discerned by Freud as sexual to other schedules of development (physical, cognitive)'. The critique of identity, in Erikson's (1950: 256) estimation of the matter, 'becomes as strategic in our time as the study of sexuality was in Freud's time'.

The revisionist nature of Erikson's 'eight stages of man', which places him alongside the likes of Margaret Mead and Ruth Benedict, is already evident in his 1946 paper 'Ego development and historical change'. The paper, which marks a decisive turn towards sociology in the post-Freudian development, articulates this shift through the notions of agency and self-identity. First, Erikson confirms the ideational concept of mind in contrast to Freud's application of an energetic model of mental functioning. Meaning is privileged over the economic aspect of Freudian metapsychology. This becomes part of a more wide-ranging break with Freud's emphasis on the biological basis of affects, and is something which characterizes the sociological assimilation of psychoanalysis in general. Thus, for Erikson (1946: 363) the idea that 'instinctual energy is transferred, displaced, transformed in analogy to the preservation of energy in physics no longer suffices to help us manage the data which we have learned to observe'. The emphasis is on meaning as the 'mutual complementation of ethos and ego, of group identity and ego-identity' (1946: 364).

Second, instead of allowing for 'the Oedipus trinity as an irreducible schema for man's irrational conduct', Erikson (1946: 360) emphasizes the extent to which 'social organization predetermines the structure of the family'. Nor is he concerned only with the constraints and prohibitions of the superego as they arise in the context of family life. Erikson (1946: 360) extends the meaning of organization beyond 'the restrictions to which the ego must bow', focusing instead on 'the problem of the infantile ego's origin in organized social life'. For Erikson (1946: 360), the development of a secure sense of self is evident in what *society* grants initially 'to the infant, as it keeps him alive', administers to his needs, and invests him with a 'particular lifestyle'. In light of our discussion in Part I, it is clear that Erikson, unlike Winnicott, conflates intuitive and social management.

Erikson's (1946: 389) account of the ego's habits and modes of conduct is coupled with an emphasis on its 'relation to changing historical reality'. This proves crucial for the sociological assimilation of Freud on two counts. First, Erikson (1946: 367) describes how the historical conjuncture provides individuals with a finite range of 'socially meaningful models' of identification. History provides the framework for a sense of identity that Erikson (1950: 371n1) claims cannot 'develop outside of social processes which offer workable prototypes and roles'. It becomes increasingly clear that the central aim of Erikson's (1950: 187n1) work is to 'delineate a new conceptual area encompassing both the struggles of the ego and of social organization'. Erikson's contribution is indispensable, then, as part of the groundwork for the sociology of inner security and social order.

Second, Erikson not only describes the formation of identity in socio-historical terms, but also presents an historical *explanation* of the crisis of identity. In particular, he outlines the problem of 'social pathology' in the case of black Americans, adolescents, and the war neuroses. In *Childhood and Society*, Erikson

(1950: 256) attempts to give a comprehensive account of the loss of identity in contemporary industrial society; as he puts it, 'we begin to conceptualize matters of identity at the very time in history when they become a problem'. As to the question of managed lives, most importantly Erikson (1950: 330) believes that the problem of identity calls for a re-moralization of the social, namely, 'in the very widest sense – a "protestant" morality'. Thus, Erikson (1950: 362) would have us draw on the values of Protestantism – 'our Protestant revolution'– as a bulwark against the anxieties arising from the threat posed to our sense of security by bureaucratically managed societies.

The same holds for Erikson as for Giddens: the self is threatened from outside and, therefore, prone to feelings of anxiety and insecurity. It is the problem of self-identity and its anxieties that forms the background to Giddens's reading of Erikson, a reading in which Giddens draws out the sociological implications of the first three stages in Erikson's developmental schema. Let us take these stages in turn, the first of which, the first 12 months of life, is equivalent to Freud's (1905: 198) oral stage, but with an emphasis on 'social trust' rather than pre-Oedipal drives. Giddens finds this emphasis particularly conducive, combining the notion of 'social trust' with 'basic security' at the level of personal autonomy. The problem of regulation comes immediately to the fore. For Erikson (1950: 222), a sense of trust constitutes 'the infant's first social achievement' through the mutual regulation of the infant's 'receptive capacities' with the mother's 'techniques of provision'. While they are clearly covering much the same ground, the difference between Erikson's concept of 'social trust' and Winnicott's notion of 'belief in' is instructive, not least of all for the alternative routes it offers out of Freud. We come back to the capacity to believe in the following section.

For Freud (1940: 186) conflict exists from the beginning between instinctual gratification and social restraint, between desire and prohibition; subjectivity is invariably besieged by the excitations arising out of 'the component instincts of sexual life'. By contrast, for Erikson the tension which arises in the relationship between the mother and infant is routinely resolvable through socially learnt meaning. There is ample scope for turning Freud's model of conflict into one of adaptation, where our sense of self is seen as the result of routines and habits, techniques of self-regulation, and modes of conduct. 'Psychoanalysis today', Erikson announces (1950: 13), 'is implementing the study of the ego, a concept denoting man's capacity to unify his experience and his action in an adaptive manner.' Giddens assumes a developmental rather than an evolutionary notion of adaptation along similar lines and, given the task he has set himself concerning the historical crisis of trust, has every reason to opt for Erikson's thoroughly revised account of Freudian psychology as a theory of self-conscious social achievement.

The second stage in Erikson's developmental schema, the second and third years of life, consists of the polarity between 'autonomy' and 'shame'. Freud (1913: 321) described this as the anal stage, a pre-genital organization where anal–erotic and sadistic instincts predominate. Holding on and letting go are the 'behavioural correlates' of the underlying tension characteristic of this stage. As with basic trust, Erikson (1950: 226) argues that the tension in this case may be resolved in a 'relatively benign' or 'more disruptive' way. Furthermore, he describes two simultaneous sets of *social* modalities corresponding to these alternating psychological possibilities. While holding on may be seen as an expression either of care or of primitive greed; on the other hand, letting go may be a peaceful, relaxed feeling ('letting things pass') or, alternatively, the unleashing of aggressive, destructive impulses. When Giddens (1984: 55) notes that the second stage stands in 'a relation of generalized tension' to the first, he is simply repeating Erikson's (1950: 246) point that 'trust must have developed in its own right, before it becomes something more in the critical encounter in which autonomy develops'.

The further point is that basic trust must not be jeopardized by the infant's ability to hoard or spend without reserve. In learning to hold on or to let go with care, the infant has to be properly managed. For Erikson (1950: 226), it is only in this way that infants remain protected against 'meaningless and arbitrary experiences of shame and of early doubt'. Again, the conflation of intuitive and social management is implicit in Erikson's argument. Similarly, the ideal of competency underpins the management of anxiety in Giddens's social and historical account of the transformation of intimacy. Extrapolating from Erikson's analyses of the sense of meaninglessness as a result of pre-Oedipal disturbances, Giddens (1992: 175–6) identifies a link between rising propensities to 'the experience of shame' in our personal lives, on the one hand, and 'the spread of modernity's internally referential systems' on the other.

The third developmental stage, between about three and six years, adds the quality of 'initiative' to the pre-Oedipal formations of 'basic trust' and 'autonomy'. Erikson (1950: 229) describes how the child is now able to engage in the world in a more purposeful way, 'undertaking, planning and "attacking" a task for the sake of being active and on the move'. The child becomes more integrated at this stage, according to Erikson, insofar as the force of self-will is turned away from defiance and protest towards the power of action itself. For Erikson, the evident pleasure the child derives at this stage comes not from instinctual satisfaction so much as the realization of one's capacity to act on the world. The idea that young children enjoy their newfound sense of agency in the form of regulatory action is couched in terms of a developmental milestone as the equivalent to Freud's genital stage. Unlike Freud, however, Erikson does not concentrate solely on the sexual conflict in the phase of Oedipal transition. The Oedipal family situation is rendered as a general economy of social interaction, where Freud's formation of internalized parental prohibitions (the superego) is revised as an inclination to do things for oneself.

Following Erikson's emphasis on the transformative capacity of agency at this crucial stage in the child's development, Giddens assumes the dialectic of 'initiative' and 'guilt' as an elementary form of social life. Viewed from the perspective of interpersonal relations, the child is seen as routinely subject to an internal struggle not on the Lacanian model of *méconnaissance*, but rather, with respect to the different social formations of identity. What the child knows how to do and is capable of doing comes to the fore in this model of security. For Giddens, it is the realization of basic trust as practical consciousness that demonstrates the child's securely founded sense of self. This involves an existential rather than a linguistic model of difference in which the power of action is seen as 'logically prior to a subject/object differentiation' (Giddens 1979: 92). In sum, Giddens concludes, first, that doing is the groundwork of being; second, that the relationship between thought and language is essentially a matter of competence; and, third, that the 'duality of structure' accounts for the internal differentiation of the ego or the self.

These conclusions are consistent with Erikson's revision of Freud. Erikson followed Freud in mapping the formation of self-identity onto the oral–sensory, muscular–anal, and locomotor–genital stages of psychosexual development. He took things in a significantly different direction to Freud, however, by generalizing these stages and combining each libidinal zone with a corresponding mode of identity: mouth–reliability; anus–autonomy; and genitals–initiative. Moreover, Erikson (1950: 221) placed a greater emphasis than Freud on the social and environmental conditions of development, identifying the emergence of a secure sense of self in terms of 'the critical periods of development'. The social environment is seen as constitutive; the self, as a social construct. Erikson contributed in this way to the acculturation of the Freudian legacy, which has finally resulted in the entire Freudian drama of instinct and chance, including the biological analogies of instinctual energy and discharge, being irretrievably cast aside in many quarters in favour of the person as a self-regulative, cohesive phenomenon. As such, Erikson's (1950: 13) account of personal integrity and social integration, his description of 'man's capacity to unify his experience and his action', proves indispensable for the sociological appropriation of psychoanalysis.

Giddens views the break with classical drive theory as a positive development and welcomes the post-Freudian emphasis on the unitary construction of identity, together with the anthropological focus on variations within and between societies. As far as development is concerned, Giddens (1979: 123) comes to the conclusion early on that 'competencies' are more important than 'needs' or 'organic drives'. When we come to the moral dimensions of security, we shall see that Giddens replaces the criteria of maturity and need with those of cohesiveness and solidarity. And in rejecting a needs-based model along with the classical Freudian model of drive–defence, Giddens thereby rules out any real concern with the role of internal psychic organization. This goes hand in hand with his refusal to credit Lacan's close attention to language and its effects on psychic structure.

It seems rather anomalous, then, that we should find Giddens attempting to distance himself from Erikson's developmental thinking. Giddens (1984: 59) concludes: 'I consider the least interesting areas of Erikson's work to be those for which he is probably most famed – to do with the formation of "ego-identity" and with the importance of developmental stages in personality'. This claim seems untenable and misleading to me. Indeed, Giddens views the successive polarities of the first three stages of Erikson's life cycle as a progressive movement towards the autonomy of action; but also, and more importantly, as a condition of self-knowledge and the monitoring of self-conduct. In particular, Giddens's (1991: 244) account of self-identity as 'reflexively understood by the individual in terms of his or her biography' depends on the developmental concept of trust. His refusal to accept the idea that the psychological phenomena of trust, anxiety, and shame are directly related to types of social institutions does not stand up to scrutiny.

This is immediately apparent in his account of the 'routinized' character of everyday life. In supplementing his reading of Erikson with a contiguous reading of Goffman, Giddens argues that the 'substratum of trust' is both the condition and the outcome of day-to-day social activities. And with an eye to the normative implications of the argument, he pays particular attention to the routine nature of these activities. For Giddens (1991: 128) 'basic trust' is a condition of the 'viable *Umwelt* [environment]' that each of us supposedly 'takes around from situation to situation'. The precariousness of these daily routines, the idea that events may at any time 'puncture the protective mantle of ontological security' (1991: 131), will be clear enough when we come to the combined problem of anxiety and defence. The conception of society as a 'tool' (Canguilhem 1955: 77) arises on account of its inherent instability. It is precisely on these grounds that the psychology of trust proves decisive for the *political* problematic of security. This is evident above all in the way that Giddens conceptualizes the reflexive norms of modern life. Arguing in terms of 'the pervasive influence of habit', Giddens (1990: 98) concludes that the 'predictability of the (apparently) minor routines of day-to-day life is deeply involved with a sense of psychological security'.

To summarize, Giddens's reading of Erikson consolidates the cognitive bias of sociology, first, with respect to the compatibility of self-identity and the unconscious, and second, through the combination of basic security and competence. Giddens (1984: 41) renders 'the reflexive monitoring of encounters in circumstances of co-presence' (face-to-face interaction) continuous with 'unconscious components of personality'. The general proposition proceeds from Giddens's (1990: 97) assumption that basic trust is formed alongside 'emergent social capabilities' in the earliest relationship between mother and baby. Far from differentiating sociology and developmental psychology, the emphasis on primary and elementary forms of social interaction underpins the assimilation of the Freudian unconscious to the social logic of identity. Giddens shares Erikson's revisionist reading of the Freudian unconscious, emphasizing the habits of living and the routines of daily life rather than the vicissitudes of the drive. Together with his cross-cultural childhood studies, Erikson's model of the human life cycle effectively underwrites Giddens's evasion of the schism in the self in favour of a unitary construction of identity.

Faith and knowledge

There is an important distinction to be made in the case of inner security concerning what we believe, on the one hand, and our basic disposition to believe on the other. Whereas the former consists of what matters to us, the propensity of human beings to believe in anything at all is an expression of faith. In matters of faith the *conditions* of belief come to the fore, including, the historical conditions of belief in a secular age. We have discussed Freud's views on religious belief and the central role his critique of norms and values plays in the sociological assimilation of psychoanalysis. To elaborate further on the divergent uses of psychoanalysis, we shall continue looking at questions of faith, trust, and knowledge through a comparative reading of Giddens and Winnicott.

The challenge of faith remained central for Winnicott. As we have seen, Winnicott continued to invest in the therapeutic efficacy of faith as a means of recovered spontaneity, but also as a way of coming to terms with irreparable damage. And insofar as we remain positively inclined towards religion, dependent as we are on religion to keep alive in us, as Habermas (2010: 19) puts it, 'an awareness of what is missing, of what cries out to heaven' – to this extent, Winnicott contributed to our understanding of truths of faith through a revaluation of illusion. In short, whereas Freud reduced religion to wishful illusions; Winnicott credited the illusory substance of religious experience. Unlike Freud (1927: 31), who counted illusion *per se* at odds with reality and comparable in many respects to psychiatric delusions, Winnicott allowed for creative forms of illusion, if not religious feelings of transcendence. Giddens (1991: 38) proposes a third alternative in approaching the conditions of belief in terms of a 'combined emotive–cognitive orientation towards others, the object-world, and self-identity'.

What does the emotive–cognitive orientation mean for the relationship between passion and reason? What does the combination reveal about the sociological appropriation of psychoanalysis? Most importantly, what are the implications of this orientation for the question of security? On the face of it, Giddens appears to accept the idea that trust is a condition of reliable cognition rather than a cognitive phenomenon as such. The implication being not only that feeling comes before knowing, but also that a trusting orientation towards the world is distinguishable from the recognizable coherence of the world. There is an implicit distinction here between primary and secondary forms of awareness, which suggests that we render the world intelligible on the basis of an underlying sense of security. This is another way of saying that meaning proceeds from the capacity to believe and, as such, is rooted in affect. On this reckoning, trust may be understood as a form of inner awareness or intuitive understanding, the irreducible interiority of which precedes rational reflection and the acquisition of practical knowledge.[5] The different forms of awareness reflect the basic distinction between specific beliefs and the propensity to believe.

Winnicott viewed matters more or less in these terms, assuming that feeling secure in ourselves precedes whatever values we derive from our feeling this way.

This means that inner security is not reduced to a social construct. A securely founded self has a purpose in a way that society does not and cannot. Far from a reflexive norm, security is an expression of the vital normativity of the self. The infant's innate passion for *believing in* and *living on* is expressed in the ideal of a secure sense of self. At the same time, the argument that faith holds us to what matters assumes that the capacity to believe is prior to the coincidence of value and valuation. Winnicott accepts that the knowledgeable use of pre-reflective understanding is a condition of mature experience. This does not mean, however, that knowledge itself gives us a feeling of security, or that feeling is a type of reflective understanding. To the contrary, faith is considered irreducible to the value of knowledge. Tellingly, Winnicott (1961: 14) hesitates when considering the idea that science itself implies a faith. He concedes that 'if there must be faith *in something*', then science has faith in 'the inexorable laws that govern phenomenon'. But his point is that faith in anything at all is always an expression of a prior capacity to have faith. Again, faith is originally faith in nothing but its own spontaneous expression, an expression of living as the norm and aim of life, and a hope that may or may not be fulfilled by a particular belief. We are inwardly secure as we hope to be, that is, before the realization of security in a given system of belief.

The distinction between assent and compliance clarifies the primacy of faith over this or that belief. Assent is an expression of our inner moral sense; whereas compliance is always at the expense of our personal way of life. This, on Winnicott's (1963b: 102) estimation at least, is what makes compliance 'immoral'. Thus, viewed in the religious context of this evaluation – 'whatever is not of faith is sin' (Romans 14.23) – compliance remains inimical to the very idea of faith. Assuming an obliging manner or attitude in this way results neither in moral integrity nor in a sense of emotional security. Without the depth of feeling that pervades a genuine culture of civility, self-restraint becomes a form of submission devoid of trust.[6] The same may also be said of mechanisms of self-regulation under similar historical conditions.

Conversely, the primacy of faith ('belief in') is demonstrable in the case of religious experience, precisely where reason yields to basic trust before the institutions of ritual and customary morality.[7] For Winnicott (1963b: 95), 'believing in' is an expression of 'innate morality involving the total personality', as distinct from whatever individuals and society happen to believe at any one time. The argument applies to any system of religious belief. For instance, in the case of Christian belief the doctrines are acceptable only insofar as they issue from the experience of 'believing in a completely trustworthy God' (Williams 2007: viii). The certainty of ultimate security in God proceeds from 'believing in' as the original impulse to believe, a primordial experience which precedes the experience of belief itself. We cannot have any belief at all without a capacity to believe. Nor do we acquire this capacity a posteriori in the enactment of a belief; we do not learn to believe by believing in something. As Winnicott (1963b: 97) put it, the idea of a personal and trustworthy God rests on 'a belief in reliability'; the idea of goodness, on love. It requires faith in what is given for experience to feel good and valuable. This, at least, is the conclusion we came to in our discussion of love as the primary framework for the infant's propensity to believe: faith is an expression of the gifted (*l'adonné*) infant of maternal love. Winnicott elaborated this understanding of faith, accordingly, in the form of what we might call a *maternal Christian figuration*.

Giddens formulates an entirely different view of belief. The reflexive norm of self-regulation does not allow for trust ('belief in') as an amalgam of intuitive understanding and innate potential. To the contrary, Giddens argues that socially recognizable action is generated and reproduced in institutionalized routines. As set out in structuration theory, the sociological account of action is based on the series routine, conduct, and norm. To recall the basic claims of the sociological argument: first, beliefs are recognizable only at the level of practical action; second, the realization of belief as knowledge enables us to go on producing intelligible and coherent accounts of the world; and, third, knowledge organizes our feelings retrospectively as systems of belief. Instead of differentiating primary and secondary forms of awareness, Giddens couples basic trust with two types of consciousness, namely, the realization of belief as 'practical consciousness', and knowledge taken to the second power in the form of 'discursive consciousness'. The innate capacity to believe in the world, to keep faith with gods of our own making, is subsumed by *recognition* and *representation*, respectively.

This is more than an argument about religion. It concerns the nature of belief as such and reveals two entirely different perspectives on the self. For Giddens, faith is valuable according to what knowledge makes of it, while belief assumes coherence only through its realization. The modes of realization comprise daily routines and orders of conduct that are organized, at the level of representation, in the form of norms and values. From a sociological perspective, a belief is essentially something that we exercise. Thus our religious beliefs and moral sentiments, the things that matter to us, become meaningful only through their enactment. Of course we may claim self-knowledge only about the beliefs we practise; this must be the case. There is nothing particularly contentious in this view as far as it goes. Once again Durkheim (1912) set a precedent for this approach in the sociology of religion. But while the criterion of coherence renders the sociological account of belief valid, this is not to say that faith and conduct are one and the same.

The communal world of shared meanings (i.e. the institution of religious worship and its ritual attitudes) accounts neither for the original impulse to believe nor for what Husserl (1907: 54) would describe as its authentic mode of 'givenness' (*Gegebenheit*). To account for the origin and authenticity of belief, indeed for a primordial sense of *commūniō* as distinct from *commūnicāre*, we need to supplement the distinction between private and public life with the two types of awareness mentioned above. Staying with the example of religion, the structure of religious experience, although maintained through the rules of religious life, is nonetheless rooted in the emotional impulses of archaic life. Religion is clearly a human construct, but this does not necessarily account for why we are positively inclined to religion. The experience of prayer, for instance, is more than a sociological exercise; the fact that we keep faith with our feelings through the act of prayer does not mean that religious sentiments are mere artefacts of social life. Our becoming more fully aware of our beliefs at the level of meaning and through daily observance does not render human feeling identical to human society. The unconscious urge in the case of belief, religious or otherwise, remains irreducibly strange as the source of meaning and of co-operative living. At a fundamental level, communion exceeds communal living as a pre-reflective, psychosomatic experience.

The realization of belief as knowledge may well be an adequate sociological account of the constitution and reproduction of society. In this respect, Giddens makes it clear that social life is possible on the condition that forms of cognition provide inner experience with a recognizable coherence at the level of perception. However, the criterion of coherence notwithstanding, the viability of the interpersonal world does not account for its appearance. It is important to be clear, then, what the emotive–cognitive orientation means. To continue with the example of religious experience: in what sense is belief in a 'trustworthy God' sensible? What do we mean by the sensibility of faith and trust? Winnicott continued to trace the growth of the moral sense back to reliable ways of being cared for in infancy. This clearly supports the idea of communion as a psychosomatic experience, where the internalization of maternal love accounts for the emergence of value. Evaluation is seen here, as Lear (1992: 210) puts it, as 'a manifestation of love's developmental thrust'. The development of a secure sense of self may be traced along this trajectory. Similarly, in Christian faith it is primarily God's promise that is to be relied on; most importantly, as Rowan Williams (2007: 92) points out, 'Christianity is a contact before it is a message'. The same holds for Williams as for Winnicott: a sense of contact comes before the ongoing communication it makes possible; initially, at least, feelings of trust, or truths of faith, determine our actions independent of rational reflection. We believe as we feel, not as reason legislates.

Williams confirms the sense of contact that lies at the heart of basic trust. In effect, by pointing to the primacy of contact over content (message) he verifies both the unconscious origins and emotional authenticity of our beliefs as manifestations of archaic mental functioning. Winnicott came to the same conclusion in identifying faith with primary creativity. This is what Meissner (1984: 184) has in mind when he refers to 'the creative moment in the illusion of faith'. Primary creativity and the primacy of faith are necessarily conjoined in the infant's spontaneous gesture, insofar as spontaneity presupposes a belief in one's own creative potential. Furthermore, as regards the archaic sense of contact, Winnicott (1967c: 196) describes a capacity to have faith based on 'the accumulation of introjected reliability'.

By contrast, Giddens (1981: 194) posits 'cognitive beliefs' as types of social action. The recognizable coherence of the world, therefore, becomes the measure of emotional contact, as well as the means for validating truths of faith.[8] Consequently, affectivity is understood as a property of the very thing it is supposed to facilitate. In what amounts to a defining move in Giddens's sociological argument, the inclusion of trust ('belief in') on the axis of cognition blurs the distinction between 'conditions' and 'attributes'. Giddens (1991: 129) claims that the 'substratum of trust is the condition and the outcome' of 'everyday knowledgeability'. From the perspective of sociology, trust is seen as a condition of belief and, at the same time, as an attribute of the knowing subject.

How can an attribute of subjectivity also be the condition of its identity? There seems to be a confusion here over the grounds and predicates of being, which comes about largely as a result of the way in which Giddens defines affectivity. That affects are evidently irreducible to rules is important for the definition of affects as *attributes* of the subject. Thus Giddens (1977a: 126) allows for the identification of affects as 'properties of individuals', as distinct from rules understood as 'structural components of social action'. On the other hand, however, as a *condition* of subjectivity affectivity amounts to a 'meaningful' phenomenon of daily life. What Giddens appears to be saying is that while affects are more 'personal' than rules, at the same time they provide social life with much of its normative content or meaning.

Winnicott continued to emphasize the limitations of human cognition from the standpoint of pre-reflective experience, including the primordial experience of faith and its creative substratum. Alternatively, Giddens emphasizes the extent to which affects are regulated by means of the normative routines of social life. The distinction turns out to be decisive: for it is precisely in terms of what we know about our feelings, how we appropriate our sense of trust, that Giddens addresses the fundamental relationship for sociology between order and meaning. In short, Giddens (1984: 22) upholds the cognitive bias of sociology, by drawing attention to the 'achievement' (*Leistung*) of knowledge in 'the production and reproduction of day-to-day social encounters'. Thus the realization of belief as knowledge underpins the mobilization of daily life.

Normative orders of conduct

Freud (1915a: 177–8) held that emotions cannot be unconscious, that we must be aware of an emotion when it occurs. Taking matters in an entirely different direction, Giddens maintains that the unconscious itself operates along the axis of cognition. He elaborates on this claim with respect to knowledge as well as trust. And having considered the emotive–cognitive schema of security from the perspective of basic trust, in this section we shall address the question of knowledge once again through a comparative reading of Giddens and Winnicott. An initial comment on the concept of 'convention' will indicate what is at stake. Giddens takes the idea of 'agreement' or 'convention' (*Übereinkunft, Konvention*) from Wittgenstein (1953: 113) rather than Hume (1740: 226), a choice that tells us something important about his theory of personal identity, as well as his approach to the normative orders of conduct. Hume and Wittgenstein held different views on the habit of character. Briefly, Hume's concept of convention belongs to a tradition of political thought in which conventions founded on utility are opposed to a set of obligations founded on a contract.[9] Experience takes precedence over representation; the experiential, over the contractual. This idea has direct implications for the relationship between cognition and affect. For Hume, knowledge is possible on condition that the sensation of affect provides ideas with 'associations'; self-knowledge, therefore, is a secondary phenomenon. Primarily, relations and passions are seen as 'kinds of affections' that function in relation to one another. And while relations link ideas in the imagination; at the same time, passions give us a sense of these relations. Convention thus allows for an 'attunement' of the passions prior to the identities of reason.

In accordance with his general emotive–cognitive orientation, Giddens eschews the Humean problem of subjectivity in favour of a sociological version of Wittgenstein's conventionalism. He opts for the latter in an attempt to ground mechanisms of self-regulation in a normative conception of rule-governed behaviour. In an argument that goes back to *New Rules of Sociological Method*, Giddens takes his bearings on grammar and semantics alike from Wittgenstein rather than from Lacan. His account of the instantation of rules is based on the following assumptions: first, that grammatical propositions resemble rules insofar as they 'play the role of norms of description' (Wittgenstein 1937–44: 55); second, that grammatical propositions therefore allow for transformations of empirical propositions; and, third, that 'every action according to the rule is an interpretation' (Wittgenstein 1953: 81). Wittgenstein (1953: 80) himself came to these conclusions in answer to the following question: 'what has the expression of a rule got to do with my actions?'

Wittgenstein indicates the practical character of rule-governed behaviour, where obeying a rule delimits the form and function of social life. Giddens applies this argument to individuals and to social systems alike; to the regulation and maintenance of ego-identity, as well as the regulation of environments of action. Thus, for Giddens (1976: 51) the non-discursive conception of knowledge is derived from the notion of convention as the ground of intelligible action. He describes this form of knowledge as 'practical consciousness', and argues that the knowledgeable use of conventions presupposes a competent actor. Once again, the hypotheses of competency and self-knowledge underpin the concept of a securely founded self. For Giddens (1984: 26) a secure sense of self is founded on the enactment of conventions and routines by 'competent members of society'. Like Parsons (1958: 94), in this respect, Giddens places the cognitive subject and its 'active manipulation of the object-world', in the context of a generalized motivational system of competence. The general competencies of knowledgeability, according to Giddens, provide the motivational source for the normative principle of regulation.

As a mechanism of regulation and integration, the notion of practical consciousness is based on the following sociological propositions. First, constitution and regulation are inextricably linked when it comes to rules or orders of conduct. The coincidence of knowledge and conduct is manifest in the constitutive function of regulatory action. Second, rules generate routines and exercises rather than generalize actions. The idea that routines operate in conjunction with discourse confirms the internal coherence of social life as well as the identity of the subject. Any disruption in either case is seen as anomalous rather than inherent. Third, the logical and grammatical structure of rules is combined with the enactment of rule-governed behaviour in the continuous practice of daily life. The cognitive bias is carried over in these propositions to a theory of motivation and the rationalization of action, where reflexive functions and orders of conduct are seen as everyday activities.

The problem of subjectivity is assimilated to the problem of knowledge, with respect to the exercise of know-how in rule-governed situations. The basic assumption, here, is that competent actors know how to apply rules on the basis of recurrent orders of conduct in systems of social interaction. As a result the propensity of humans to believe is addressed as a problem of knowledge; the value of faith is actually indistinguishable from the value of knowledge. Indeed, Giddens holds that not only propositional beliefs but all belief-claims are subject to the standard of validity/falsity in accordance with the knowledgeability of actors. For Giddens, the problem is not how to believe in the world (cf. Winnicott's act of faith), but rather, how to appropriate belief as knowledge.

The assimilation of subjectivity to knowledge is based on a confusion concerning the distinction between experience and evidence, between the first-personal viewpoint of value and the third-person position of observation and prediction.[10] As a result of which Giddens (1984: 338) assumes that 'beliefs can be shown to be invalid or inadequately grounded' simply by the use of reason. Where beliefs form part of 'the reasons actors have for what they do', the veridical norms of scientific discourse are generalized as mundane accounts of 'good reasons'. The latter become conventions, or norms of conduct, through the 'constant slippage' that Giddens (1984: 374) refers to between science and belief. In which case a reflexive conception of knowledge grounded in reason, is seen to provide an *external* perspective from which 'belief claims' can be measured. On these grounds, it is always possible, as Giddens (1984: 340) argues, 'to demonstrate that some belief claims are false, while others are true'.

This is essentially what we mean by the cognitive bias of sociology: rational reflection arbitrates our actions as well as our belief in the world. Giddens turns to psychoanalysis at this point to substantiate the generalization of motivational systems on the one hand and, on the other, the assimilation of affectivity to cognitive representation through daily routines and norms of conduct. He uses psychoanalysis as a motivational source for the theory of regulatory action. In *Modernity and Self-Identity*, for instance, Winnicott's account of the mother–infant relationship is used to substantiate claims about the routine nature of intuitive management. Giddens (1991: 41) subsumes the Winnicottian notion of primary creativity under the general category of 'early routines'. In Winnicott's (1988: 110) account of the infant's potential, creativity is primitively independent of the environment; the radical import of the argument is that the 'world is created anew by each human being'. The infant makes a singular 'contribution' to the world on the basic assumption that creative potential is inherent in being, in which case the process of individuation proceeds from creativity as from the potentialities of human nature. Primary creativity is seen as an expression of total potentiality in a physiological or psychosomatic sense; while at the same time, being in the world, including the feeling of being at home in the world, is understood as the outcome rather than the origin of creative living.

However, where security takes precedence over creativity, where the antinomy between regulation and freedom is settled in favour of the former, the very idea of potentiality itself is compromised. To state the theoretical disagreement between Winnicott and Giddens at its most basic: the generalized competencies of self-consciousness, personal identity, and regulatory action come into conflict with illusion, spontaneity, and intuitive self-understanding. Winnicott allows for the fact that what the infant creates depends not only on what the mother presents at the moment of creation, but also on how she does so. This is another way of saying that nothing is realized outside of a loving and responsive world (see Chapter 1). The further point, however, is that 'if the creativity of the infant is absent, the details presented by the mother are meaningless' (Winnicott 1988: 110–11). Giddens assumes otherwise on both counts. The cognitive bias of his schema makes things too secure for the 'awakening' of being. For Giddens, the world does not emerge on the basis of a 'spontaneous gesture', but may be cultivated as a reflexive achievement. On the other hand, it is hard to see on the sociological reading how love could fall foul of something like a basic fault in nature. Damaged identities, like other human social phenomena, are understood as social facts.

Further to the reduction of potentials to competencies, Giddens (1991: 39) links transitional objects and transitional phenomena to the 'discipline of routine'. Ostensibly, he sees this as a way of linking faith and convention, or trust and norms. Thus, Giddens (1991: 39) applies Winnicott's notion of the primary maternal frame to 'the reproduction of coordinating conventions' as a means of 'orientation towards aspects of the object-world'. In this context, basic trust amounts to a form of risk management, what Giddens (1991: 39–40) calls 'a screening-off device'. Starting with early mother–infant routines and the use of transitional objects, the discipline of routine is brought to bear on 'cultivated risk', according to Giddens (1991: 133), as among 'the most basic orientations of modernity'. There is a question of how far these routines contribute to a genuine sense of inner security, although Giddens does not confine matters to the immediate intimacies of intuitive management. The combined focus on disciplinary routines and cultivated risks raises an historical question: can we count faith among the authentic orientations of modernity? Giddens gives a conditional response to this question. The emotive–cognitive schema orientates us towards an inner world of security only where trust routinely affects our lives in the form of knowledge. This means that values have to be considered before they are experienced; belief requires reflection in order to become a source of inner security. Intuitive management is reconfigured along sociological lines as a way of conceptualizing the assessment of risk against the reflexive norm of regulatory action.

Through a sociological account of early routines Giddens effectively decouples the Winnicottian configuration of faith and inner security. While this skews his interpretation of psychoanalysis, at the same time it enables him to formulate a reflexive conception of order without recourse to the groundwork of archaic mental functioning. The psychosomatic relation of inner security, which is essential for Winnicott, plays no part in the sociological schema. The main connections set out on Giddens's stratification model between basic security and practical consciousness, account for neither the existence of unconscious affects nor the primacy of faith. The emotive–cognitive orientation does not include the impersonal force relations that precede our identifications with a given order of reality. No matter how far back one takes things in Giddens's schema there is some kind of representation at work. Thus the qualitative distinction between 'believing' and 'knowing' breaks down on two counts. On the one hand, there is no equivalent in the sociological problematic of security to the Freudian idea of undifferentiated unity, or what Winnicott (1962b: 61) calls 'unintegration'. On the other hand, Giddens does not allow for the type of intuitive experience characteristic of the noetic-noematic structure of mental processes in the phenomenological sense (Husserl 1913: 233). Intuitive management and intuitive understanding alike are displaced by normative orders of conduct; indeed, the reduction of belief to a type of knowledge goes hand in hand with the emphasis on conduct as a type of regulatory action.

The coincidence of knowledge and conduct applies precisely to social actors. Giddens generalizes the combined problem of trust and knowledge from the individual to society in a way that effectively undermines the ontological nature of his argument. The constitution of society is explained in terms of an underlying sense of security which extends neither from 'the absolute singularity of the ego' (Husserl 1907: 186), nor yet from the ego's pre-individualized forms of life in the Freudian drives. On the other hand, the positive claim of the sociological argument is clear: we appropriate our belief in the world through the knowledgeable use of norms and conventions. The use of faith is not part of the sociology of reflection for Giddens. To the contrary, Giddens (1991: 127) argues that our investment in social life is realized through the use of practical modes of consciousness; that the cognitively intentional structures of subjectivity connect the 'basic security system' to a wider system of relevancies and competencies at the level of everyday life.

The positive argument is set out as an alternative to the subject/object dualism in classical sociology. For Giddens, the fundamental problem of social theory is how to explain the formation and regulation of everyday life on the model of a securely founded self. The theory of structuration addresses this problem through a critique of the traditional dualisms in social theory, a critique which extends to the conscious/unconscious system in psychoanalysis. For Giddens (1979: 256; emphasis added) '[p]ractical consciousness is not "consciousness" as ordinarily understood in structuralist theories; but it is also easily distinguishable from the unconscious *in any sense* of that term'. This is the central manoeuvre in the sociological revision of psychoanalysis: the reflexive project reduces subjectivity to a problem of self-regulation and the maintenance of identity. Giddens (1984: 25) concludes that 'the structural properties of social systems are both medium and outcome of the practices they recursively organize'. Instead of a framework for the articulation of anxiety, the work of the day is linked to norms and routines as defensive mechanisms of self-regulation.[11]

The sociology of self-identity is invariably concerned with modes of consciousness rather than the essential characteristics of the unconscious as a system. The compatibility that Giddens insists on with regards to identity and the unconscious is possible only to the extent that he incorporates 'unconscious motives', as well as 'unintended consequences', within a general theory of regulatory action. Accordingly, Giddens (1979: 56) presents the coincidence of self-identity and the unconscious in terms of a 'continuous flow of conduct', which includes 'unacknowledged conditions of action' alongside practical and discursive consciousness. Finally, practical consciousness is more properly a type of what Freud called the preconscious (*das Vorbewusste*) rather than the unconscious (*das Unbewusste*). This is already evident in the critique of Lacan and the structuralist theory of the subject, where Giddens (1979: 24; emphasis added) defines practical consciousness as a 'non-discursive, *but not unconscious*, knowledge of social institutions'. The essential bias of structuration theory is clear: inner security is seen as an attribute of the cognitive subject and, therefore, continuous with the societal mechanisms of order and security. For Giddens (1984: 375), while practical consciousness designates all those contents that are not necessarily, or ordinarily available to discursive consciousness, it is nonetheless not screened off by a 'bar of repression', as is the case with the unconscious.

Notes

1 For a recent challenge in social theory to the secularization hypothesis, see Habermas (2008). And for a timely political and sociological debate on the Christian character of contemporary European identity in the secular context of the central European tradition, see Michalski (2006b).
2 For the concepts of 'regulation' (*régulation*) and 'regulator' (*régulateur*) in Comte, see Canguilhem (1974). In this article, Canguilhem discusses the positivist theory of the 'social organism' with reference to the application of the concept of regulation to biological function. For an earlier critical statement on the assimilation of society to the life of the organism, see Canguilhem (1955). Our discussion of self-regulation in sociology is indebted to Canguilhem's identification of the organism and society as two radically heterogeneous domains.
3 While Fournier (2007: 495) underlines the analogy between Durkheim's 'society' and Kant's 'God'; as Lukes (1975: 54) points out, it was the work of Renouvier rather than that of Kant himself that 'exercised the strongest immediate influence' on Durkheim. For a critique of the neo-Kantian origins of Durkheimian sociology, see Rose (1981). Rose identifies the classical origins of sociology in the generation of Kant critics after 1870, the Marburg and Heidelberg schools of neo-Kantianism, who took their philosophical bearings from the previous generation of Bolzano, Lotze, and others.
4 The identity of knowledge and conduct, which is the central argument in Foucault's 1981–2 lectures at the Collège de France (2001; English translation: *The Hermeneutics of the Subject*, 2005) on ancient spiritual exercises, may be reconstructed with

the benefit of these lectures as a modern principle of regulation. As a theoretical reconstruction, however, this does necessarily imply any direct historical influence.
5 See Descartes (1641: 285) for the idea of a type of 'internal awareness [*cognitione illa interna*] which always precedes reflective knowledge'. This distinction has been reworked psychoanalytically, for instance, in terms of 'declarative' and 'procedural' knowledge, a distinction between explicit/verbal awareness and the implicit relational domain (Stern *et al.* 1998).
6 For the decline of civility as another perspective on the crisis of trust, see Elias (2000).
7 For a comment on the religious implications of Winnicott's ideas about the 'capacity to believe', see Hopkins (1997). Meissner (1984: 177–84) provides a more comprehensive commentary on faith as a form of transitional religious experience. He considers Winnicott's 'capacity for faith' as an aspect of religious experience alongside, for instance, the representation of God as a transitional object; the symbolic value of Scripture and liturgical practice; and the experience of prayer.
8 For an alternative attempt in sociological theory to construct a dialogue between the authority of secular reason and truths of faith, see Habermas (2010). However, Habermas's critique of the secularization hypothesis notwithstanding, it could be argued that he uses religion in much the same way as Giddens uses psychoanalysis, extrapolating the moral expressions of religion as the basis of normative principles. Thus religion and psychoanalysis, respectively, provide normative foundations for the project of deliberative democracy.
9 For the idea of 'justice' as 'a kind of convention', see Hume (1740: 228).
10 See Bilgrami (2010) for the distinction between first- and third-person viewpoints, and for a critical comment on the extension of scientism to the social sciences. For a general critique of reason along these lines, see Habermas (2003: 108): 'The scientistic belief in a science which will one day not only supplement, but *replace* the self-understanding of actors as persons by an objectivating self-description, is not science but bad philosophy'.
11 See Kennedy (1993: 134–5) for a critique of Giddens along these lines, and Kennedy (1987) for the 'work of the day' as a means of therapeutic management.

8

THE REGULATED LIFE

Giddens formulates two related problems along the axes of cognition: the problem of trust (how to believe in the world) and the problem of knowledge (how to render trust operational). Trust is defined as an achievement at the level of self-identity, the realization of which as knowledge at the level of practical consciousness is seen as part of the ordinary work of the day. What does rational cognition achieve? What do we accomplish in our daily routines and practical forms of knowing? The main argument is that what actors know (believe) about the social world helps ward off feelings of insecurity. This applies especially to knowledge about the normative conditions of one's own conduct. The realization of belief as knowledge presupposes a sense of inner security that keeps anxiety at bay and, among other things, enables us to achieve our desired goals in life. The cognitive model of self-knowledge assumes, first, that basic trust constitutes the existential conditions of security; second, that our capacity to believe makes us feel safe; and, third, that only a securely founded self is capable of properly rational and competent action. This is essentially a theory of self-regulation; as Giddens (1984: 50) puts it, the 'origins of ontological security are to be found in basic anxiety-controlling mechanisms ... hierarchically ordered as components of personality'.

These mechanisms of self-regulation form the main part of a sociological problematic of security that extends beyond individual psychology to a general theory of action. The latter is seen as the basis of managed society, where the trust–knowledge couple is linked to a further series of problems at the level of social management. Existential anxieties are prioritized here in terms of how we defend and manage our lives in what is seen as an increasingly hazardous and threatening world. This includes ways of managing our satisfactions, achievements, and feelings of well-being as well as our underlying apprehensions and uncertainties. The management of risk remains a central concern and, with respect to the sociology of anxiety, the emphasis turns more directly to the competent management of secure attachment and its social derivatives. Further to the development of a secure sense of self, the defence against anxiety involves the integration and regulation of the self along the related axes of competence and self-governance. Giddens harnesses the ego-ideal of competency to the reflexive imperative of late modernity, where the synthetic acts of self-regulation amount to a new use of individualism. Essentially, self-regulation is institutionalized as a regulated life through the project of reflexive governance.

How does this project work? How is the regulated life meant to relieve or resolve anxiety? Psychoanalysis continues to provide a basic frame of reference for sociological reflection as it extends from 'the core of the self', the cognitive model of self-knowledge, to the governmental aims of 'utopian realism'. In this case, the parallels between structuration theory and attachment theory confirm the revised nature of the psychoanalytic interpretation. Although Giddens does not make explicit use of an attachment-theory framework, there is nonetheless a clear parallel between his problematic of security and the idea of a 'secure base' in the work of Bowlby (1969; 1973; 1980), Ainsworth (1982), and the updated version of attachment theory in the likes of Fonagy *et al.* (2002).

The comparison seems particularly striking to me in the case of Fonagy and his colleagues, whose theory of 'mentalization' is analogous with the reflexive project of the self in Giddens. First, 'mentalization' refers to the understanding of mental states, 'the process by which we realize that having a mind mediates our experience of the world' (Fonagy *et al.* 2002: 3). Second, the process or mechanism by means of which we generate this type of understanding, the knowledge of our own mental conduct, is defined as 'reflective function'. These two concepts in particular mark a decisive shift in the attachment paradigm, namely, from a theory of 'internal working models' based on the mother–infant relationship to the idea of attachment as a developmental condition of 'interpersonal interpretive mechanisms'. The idea of regulating mechanisms comes to the fore through the emphasis on reflective capacity and affective self-control. For Fonagy, as for Giddens, the experience of security presupposes an 'attachment system' that constitutes and maintains the sense of self-agency. Fonagy *et al.* (2002: 37) define this system as 'an open biosocial homeostatic regulatory system'. The reflexive project amounts to a comparable hypothesis, particularly where the basic anxiety-controlling mechanisms of everyday life constitute the conditions of self-conscious governance.[1]

Whereas regulation in the classical Freudian model applies to internal tension caused by physiological needs, there is an increasing emphasis in the post-Freudian development on attachment needs as well as appetitive drive needs. In the present chapter we consider the generalization of this development: concentrating on the implicit comparison between attachment theory and sociology, we approach the re-moralization of the social from the perspective of the regulated life. We attempt to draw out this comparison on three counts. First, Giddens (1994b: 186) poses the problem of management in terms of 'damaged identities'; further to the traditional sociological problem of order, social defence is presented as a therapeutic task in the form of general coping mechanisms. In a further elaboration on the permanent task (see Chapter 2), Giddens's therapeutic argument is underpinned by a post-Freudian concept of anxiety. We focus on the difficulties that arise with the use of this concept in sociology, and the extent to which Giddens compounds these conceptual difficulties through his reading of Heidegger. Second, the parallels with attachment theory are apparent above all in Giddens's (1991: 244) account of the constitution of identity by 'the reflexive ordering of self-narratives'. We consider the management implications of narrative competence as a type of coping mechanism, and consider narrative itself as a means of bridging the two problems of self-awareness and identity through time. Finally, in attempting to make good on the claim that attachment theory is situated in a wider psychosocial tradition (Fonagy *et al.* 2002: 6), we address the governmental problem of security as part of a new 'settlement' between claimants and citizens. Giddens formulates a new rationality of government under the heading of 'utopian realism' which, running in parallel with the tradition of James, Cooley, and Mead in social psychology, comprises a post-Durkheimian theory of order. We discuss the latter in the historical context of advanced liberalism, concentrating on the governmental programme of moral renewal with reference to 'positive welfare' as an example of 'utopian realism' in practice.

Together with the integration of a securely founded self, the re-moralization of the social extends the sociological frame of reference and its therapeutic underpinning from basic trust to wider issues of defence and social management. This necessitates a shift of emphasis in the problematic of security: further to the realization of belief along the axis of cognition, additional techniques and mechanisms of self-regulation are set out along the axes of competence and governance. First, Giddens (1991: 243) underwrites the hypothesis of competency in terms of our capacity to narrate stories 'by means of which self-identity is reflexively understood'. In emphasizing the narrative project of subjectivity, he argues that competence augments a secure sense of self and invests it with personal meaning. Second, under the heading of utopian realism, Giddens emphasizes the generative and positive nature of social governance in what he calls 'post-traditional' society. More than an ideology of late modernity, utopian realism comprises a programme of techniques and mechanisms for managing opportunity and risk. We discuss, in turn, the narrative frame of reference as a supplement to mechanisms of defence and the ethics of regulatory action in Giddens's neo-Durkheimian programme of welfare. Further to the realization of belief as knowledge, we differentiate two further sets of regulatory action in the schema of security: the integration of the self along the axis of competence, and the moralization of the social along the axis of governance.

Coping with anxiety

Trust and anxiety are not seen as discrete analytic problems, even as personal and social defence are treated as complementary tasks. For Giddens (1991: 46), the exercise of 'ontological security' is inextricably linked with the competent defence of oneself; at the same time, self-regulation comes to the fore as a function of the knowledge agents have in the way that 'anxiety is socially managed'. Importantly, the social management of anxiety is linked to the historical crisis of trust. Thus Giddens brings the cognitive bias of the sociological reduction to bear on strategic and administrative problems, combining the trust-knowledge couple with an anxiety-defence couple. This arrangement constitutes a particular domain of intimacy within the wider framework of deliberative democracy, where solutions to the problems of trust and anxiety are sought increasingly beyond the more traditional uses of individualism.

What part does psychoanalysis play in the reconfiguration of intimacy as a social problem of anxiety? Freud's (1926a) views on anxiety developed in line with his attempt to account for repetition, ambivalence, and hatred in the context of the death instinct. Giddens responds to these views on two counts. First, he generalizes the Freudian 'repetition compulsion' (*Wiederholungszwang*) in terms of 'the compulsive character of modernity' (1994a: 90). The same holds for Giddens as for Freud: the compulsion to repeat is a problem of anxiety. However, whereas Freud treated compulsion as a recalcitrant problem of regulation at the level of unconscious structure; Giddens (1994a: 71) sees it as a social formation characteristic of late modernity, 'a "negative index" of the very process of the de-traditionalizing of society'. Freud consistently ground his understanding of anxiety in internal conflict modelled on the drives. For Giddens (1994a: 70) anxiety is essentially an obstacle, a hindrance to further progress, something which 'stands in the way of autonomy'. In particular, Giddens (1994a: 71) argues that anxiety becomes a problem where daily routines are not 'geared to processes of institutional reflexivity'. Like trust, anxiety is seen as a twofold problem of inner security and social order, the solution to which, however, can no longer be found in so-called 'traditional ways of thinking' about the relationship between individuals and society.

Second, Giddens accepts the general distinction Freud (1916–17: 395) makes between 'anxiety' (*Angst*) and 'fear' (*Furcht*), the idea that anxiety has no definite object, but is a diffuse, free-floating phenomenon. In other words, Giddens (1991: 44) accepts the basic Freudian argument that, 'lacking a specific object, [anxiety] can come to be pinned to items, traits or situations which have an oblique (although unconsciously precise) reaction to whatever originally provoked it'. At the same time, he ignores the fundamental shift in Freud's thinking in the early 1920s with the introduction of the structural model. Initially, Freud (1887–1904: 82) maintained that, as opposed to realistic anxiety, 'neurotic anxiety' (*Angstneurose*) was the result of the accumulation of sexual tension, involving the transformation of affect that had not been discharged or successfully repressed. In this case, dammed-up libido is transformed into manifestly felt anxiety, and anxiety is experienced to the extent that repression fails. Freud (1926a) revised the theory of anxiety as damned-up instinctual energy with the later theory of 'signal anxiety'.[2] In the later theory anxiety not only precedes repression, but, more importantly, is seen as a motive for repression.[3]

The later anxiety theory poses a particular problem for sociology. The idea that anxiety is antecedent to subjectivity is incommensurable with the basic sociological assumptions of Giddens's argument. In particular, Giddens (1991: 45) insists that anxiety 'attacks the core of the self once a basic security system is set up'. The source of a persistent confusion in Giddens, anxiousness appears only as a representation and is not otherwise manifest. Reflection, in other words, is set over and against its perturbation, its tendency to be diverted from the psychosocial norm. We have already met with this way of thinking in the case of belief. The confusion arises to the extent that Giddens reduces the feeling of being alive in oneself to the order of representation. The sense of anxiety (the same applies to the sense of basic trust) is confused with the idea of capacity as an intentional structure of subjectivity.

As such, the sociology of anxiety allows neither for the primitive agony of 'unthinkable anxiety' (Winnicott 1963a: 89–90) nor for the post-Kleinian notion of inchoate anxiety that Bion (1970: 46) describes as 'nameless dread'.[4] Once again the radical implications of psychoanalysis are dissipated in the sociological reduction, in this case, with the assimilation of the unthinkable and the unnameable to types of so-called 'ontological insecurity'. The unthinkability of despair is immediately subject to representation. This is hardly unprecedented: the assimilation of the Freudian interpretation to an existentialist perspective is by now a familiar manoeuvre.[5] For his part, Giddens (1990: 100; emphasis in the original) presents anxiety as a personal problem, but also as a problem of being; as a state of mind, but also as a form of 'existential *angst* or *dread*'. But while the phenomenon of anxiety is set out explicitly in ontological terms, it is nonetheless seen as a problem of identity, a risk that presents itself from the perspective of reason. This is the source of a fundamental conceptual muddle: trust and anxiety are subject to the same treatment, where Giddens attempts an ontological understanding of the representational structures of self-identity.

In an attempt to theorize anxiety as a social problem, Giddens (1991: 37) describes the 'chaos that threatens on the other side of the ordinariness of everyday conventions ... the prospect of being overwhelmed by anxieties that reach to the very roots of our coherent sense of "being in the world"'. The possibility of chaos as it appears in our immediate surroundings, in the very fabric of everyday life, is described in terms of psychotic anxiety and defence. Anxiety is seen as a threat to our sense of being and, therefore, as something that needs to be managed in fundamental ways. How does Giddens propose to deal with the *existential* nature of the threat? Concentrating for the moment on the conceptual argument, Giddens attempts to augment the sociological problematic of security by drawing on Heidegger.[6] And yet, far from supporting the sociology of anxiety, the recourse to Heideggerian ontology compounds the problems that beset Giddens's reading of psychoanalysis.

For Heidegger, 'being in the world' (*In-der-Welt-sein*) is more than simply 'belonging to the world' (*weltzugehörig*). It is not simply a matter of existing 'within the world' (*innerhalb der Welt*). The distinction proves decisive for the understanding of anxiety. On the one hand, Giddens counts everyday life, its mobilization through the work of the day, as a bulwark against anxiety. On the other hand, Heidegger (1927: 233) proposes that 'anxiousness is a basic kind of being-in-the world' which, moreover, results in a 'collapse' of the familiar aspect of everyday life. Heidegger (1927: 233; emphasis in the original) draws attention to the 'uncanny' (*unheimlich*) feelings we invariably experience due to anxiety: 'Dasein has been individualized, but individualized *as* being-in-the-world. Being-in enters into the existential "mode" of the "*not-at-home*" [*Un-zuhause*].' From Heidegger's perspective, insofar as we are given to feeling anxious as a matter of course, we are therefore not 'at home' (*zu Hause*) in the world. Of course this is not to say that we have ceased to be in the world, but rather, that the world itself becomes de-centred, that we find it more or less strange, on account of an anxiety that is 'always latent' in our way of being.

The irreconcilable differences between the perspectives of Heidegger and Giddens are immediately apparent. For Heidegger, anxiety is constitutive in its 'uncanny' (*unheimlich*) presence, such that 'homelessness' (*Unheimlichkeit*) is our primordial condition. Heidegger describes us as strangers to ourselves, which allows for strangeness not as a 'social problem', but rather, as a basic phenomenon of being in the world. The sociological reduction proves entirely inadequate in the face of this 'uncanny strangeness', where Freudian thought merges with Heidegger's phenomenology. Indeed, the sociological argument skirts the limits of Freud's own understanding of anxiety and the uncanny.[7] Thus the immanence of the strange within the familiar, the shaking of accepted meaning, exceeds the risks that Giddens calculates for in a societal rather than an existential framework of meaning. On the other hand, as Heidegger (1927: 234) puts it, the threat to 'the at-home of publicness ... can go together factically with complete security and self-sufficiency in one's everyday concern'.

The idea that anxiety comes about in ordinary, harmless situations raises two further points, concerning disclosure and attunement. First, insofar as it goes along with the everyday way of taking care of things, then one does not have to cope with anxiety as something exterior to being.[8] For Heidegger, anxiety is not a problem that befalls us from the outside, a type of deviation from the norm to which we are prone. Rather, it is seen as a disclosure of phenomenal givenness. Thus, for Heidegger (1927: 232) anxiety 'discloses Dasein as *being-possible*' and, as such, extends the reach for meaning beyond our entanglement in the 'tranquilized familiarity' of normative routines and orders of conduct. Far from a threat to everyday life that calls for yet more effective mechanisms of regulation, anxiousness ensures that we are not compliant in our way of being. This, at least, is the gist of Heidegger's argument: as the existential nature of uncanny strangeness confirms, conflicts are not always to be managed.

Second, anxiety comes about in everyday life, according to Heidegger, not only as disclosure but also as 'attunement' (*Befindlichkeit*). For Heidegger (1927: 233), 'attunement makes manifest "how one is" [*Befindlichkeit, so wurde früher gesagt, macht offenbar, "wie einem ist"*]'. This is not primarily a matter of knowledge: while the 'mood' (*Stimmung*) of anxiety reveals how we are; the existential constitution of the 'there' as attunement and disclosure is nonetheless inimical to the cognitive bias of the sociological reduction: 'the possibilities of disclosure which belong to cognition reach far too short a way compared with the primordial disclosure belonging to moods' (1927: 173). Moods reveal 'how one is and is getting along [*wie einem ist und wird*]' (1927: 173). As such, moods bring being to its 'there' not as an objective attribute of cognition, nor yet as a synthetic act of self-reflection; but rather, as 'an existential attribute of the entity which has being-in-the-world as its way of being' (1927: 174). How we are is not something we come across simply by looking, nor can it be fully realized as knowledge. Rather, attunement and disclosure comprise an a priori existential orientation to the world, even as they describe interior disturbance as the very condition of being with others.

From *The Constitution of Society* (1984) onwards, Heidegger does not occupy a significant position in Giddens's thinking. The contrast in their approach to anxiety, however, is important for us insofar as it clarifies the sociological revision of psychoanalysis. Once again, for Giddens (1984: 34–5) order is 'the fundamental question of social theory', where everyday life involves 'coping with the continuity of conduct across time-space'. The ethic of the reflexive project is one of less abandon, a calculative stance towards anxiety as an immoderate feeling of strangeness. Anxiety is seen as yet one more thing we have to 'cope with', an occasion for managing ourselves and coming to terms with the world. The strategic and moral implications of which are clear: contentment means more than anxiety in an attitude towards the inner life that emphasizes the satisfaction in doing things well and, in the process, regulating our feelings. So long as we conduct ourselves in accordance with our capabilities as competent actors, the implication is that we remain free from the burden of anxiety.

While this fails to get at the experience of inwardness in any meaningful sense, the idea is that we are happy doing what we do, rather than anxious being who we are. Thus the criterion of happiness is brought to bear on the problem of risk. The reflexive project operates as a homeostatic regulatory system in which we manage anxiety not as a fundamental mood, but as a risk to ourselves. A risk that Giddens (1991: 196) explains historically in terms of the disintegration of normative routine and the prevalence of doubt concerning 'forms of lifestyle'. The argument that anxieties emerge in a fragmented and increasingly uncertain world implies that society itself gives us something to feel anxious about. For Giddens, we experience anxiety in the form of risk, where risks belong to an already constituted world and, by the same token, even the most angst-ridden events adhere to the core of the self.

What, exactly, are we supposed to experience through the perception of risk? In Giddens's explanation the anxious appear as individuals who are disenchanted with life, a Weberian theme in which anxiety is seen as dissatisfaction, an expression of a discontented lifestyle. Thus, an explanation based on the immediacy of enjoyment and its ruin turns the basic existential mood of anxiety into an estimation of human failure in terms of wasted opportunity. The dialectic of disaster and hope is replaced by a calculation of opportunity and risk. Anxiety amounts to a self-reproach that one is not getting the best out of life. The anxious are seen as unhappy with their lot. In turn, the social management of anxiety becomes a permanent task, a way of coping with some of our most intimate fears and disappointments. We manage anxiety, according to Giddens (1990: 98), as an historical achievement, harnessing the discursive and practical resources of our modernity to the 'continuity of the routines of daily life'. Giddens follows Heidegger in making a connection between daily existence and anxiety; indeed, Heidegger was no less convinced than Giddens about the prevalence of coping mechanisms in conditions of reflexive modernization. The way Heidegger (1989: 139) viewed the matter, however, implicates the sociological attitude itself as a major part of the problem: 'Angst before beyng is as great today as ever. Proof: the gigantic apparatus for shouting down this Angst'.

The narrative frame of reference

There is no equivalent to the sociological concept of anxiety in either Freud or Heidegger. Giddens does not treat anxiety as antecedent to subjectivity nor, properly speaking, as a phenomenon of being in the world. Anxiety is seen as a threat to one's secure sense of attachment, something one has to find ways of coping with as a permanent task. From a governmental perspective, the task is similar in each of the three cases under discussion throughout the book, although it is worth recalling the different emphases. First, whereas the psychiatric argument gravitates to therapeutic supervision in communities of care, Giddens prioritizes the link between regulatory action and lifestyle as the main line of defence against anxiety. Regulation extends in this case from physical and emotional self-control to daily routines and normative modes of conduct, the strategic import of which rests on the generalization of therapeutic values as motivational resources. Second, the psychosomatic perspective of intuitive management, the materiality of sensible–intelligible experience in Winnicott, is subsumed in the sociological model by techniques of intimacy. The argument here is that, in an uncertain world of risks and opportunities, nothing is given that is not immediately subject to calculation.

There may indeed be a crisis of trust, if not a more general crisis of reflection, but not for the reasons Giddens suggests. The social sciences actually contribute to the problem insofar as they endorse calculative norms as the basis of order. Indicative of the self-criticism that the Enlightenment bestows on our modernity, the sociological argument embodies the technological element of enlightened reason and its values. In many ways, the latter have all but exhausted our capacity to believe, and the cognitive–affective orientation towards everyday life is an important part of this process. It is at this point that Habermas (2010: 18) calls for a dialogue between religion and the political reason of the liberal state, in which Christian theology makes available the unspent presence, or *das Unabgegoltene*, of its tradition as a moral resource for modern, secular consciousness.

Although Giddens does not in any way emulate this call, there is nonetheless more to his conception of reflexivity than a posture of self-defence. The critical work one is meant to conduct on oneself cannot be achieved simply by a series of defensive manoeuvres. The adoption of a wholly defensive stance would simply bog things down in a vicious circle of anxiety and insecurity, resulting in a permanently embattled self mired in suspicion. This is not my understanding of the contemporary formation of managed lives. Something more than a defensive stance is required to control and make use of the perpetual self-questioning that Giddens (1994b: 97–103) attributes to situations of 'manufactured uncertainty'. Thus, besides the problem of defence, Giddens focuses on individual *autonomy*, assuming that a securely founded self requires ongoing opportunities to actively reflect on its own competency. Narrative plays a key role here as a supplement to mechanisms of defence. The general problematic of security is extended by linking the therapeutic question of coping mechanisms to a biographical model of self-reflection.[9] The narrative frame of reference thus invests self-regulation with an ideal of autonomy.

In our discussion of Parkes, we came to the conclusion that narrative proves indispensable for the task of self-management in the supervisory field of psychiatric medicine. I shall argue in this section that the same applies to the sociology of managed lives: it is only through the instantiation of reflection in the form of narrative projects that the integration and regulation of the self becomes viable. The stories we tell ourselves about ourselves prove vitally important, insofar as narrative facilitates the reflexive project as a more comprehensive and subtle project of order. Indeed, for Giddens (1991: 243) 'self-identity is reflexively understood' in narrative forms, where the biographical frame of reference consolidates the reflexive project, bridging the phenomena of cognition and competence, articulating the two problems of self-awareness and identity through time, and providing for the transformation of risks into opportunities. The different axes of security (cognition, competence, and governance) are not merely contiguous but conjoined, and the biographical frame is instrumental in establishing this conjunction in the form of narrative projects. Self-criticism becomes something more than self-defence, where the reflexive ordering of self-narratives assumes pivotal status between the intimacies of personal life and the discursive formations of collective meaning. In short, I am proposing that the realization of belief as knowledge is consolidated through the representation of the self in narrative.

The narrative dimension of regulatory action prompts us to take stock of our general argument before turning to the culmination of the sociological argument in the form of self-conscious governance. What Giddens makes of reflective thought at the interface of knowledge and competence, demonstrates the sociological revision of Freud at its most fundamental. As much as anything else, it is the way in which sociology relates to the crisis of reflection that renders it inimical to Freudian psychoanalysis. More pervasive and, consequently, more corrosive than a crisis in trust, the crisis of reflection refers to the kind of difficulty that 'sets us in movement' (Ricoeur 1970: 55). In a critical state of affairs that exists far beyond the social sciences, the task is how to make reflection concrete, how to recover ourselves where we appear deprived of hopes, dispossessed, and disenchanted.

Ricoeur (1969) places psychoanalysis itself in this critical context, which he identifies in terms of rival hermeneutics. The question here is whether reflective philosophy can make sense of Freudian psychoanalysis. What kind of adventure might psychoanalysis be from the standpoint of reflection? In raising this question, Ricoeur presents the philosophical interpretation of Freud as a call for reflection. How should we understand this call? What does the demand for reflection amount to today? Who would assume the task? We have not set out in this book to answer these larger philosophical questions, but focused more specifically on the post-Freudian legacy as a source of motivation for the normative principles of maturity, reflexivity, and regulation. The major fault line in our study of Freud's contested legacy falls between the dialectic of disaster and hope, on the one hand, and the promotion of ethical life-plans on the other.

A further distinction opens up in relation to the sociological schema. Winnicott proposes to manage society on a permanent basis through the criterion of maturity; and Parkes, through the criterion of need. Maturity and need may be seen as criteria of reconciliation in a time of ethical and political difficulty. In managing a range of clinical problems from dissociation and disaffection to vulnerability and trauma, the movement towards disillusionment and realism defines the work of therapy. At the level of intuitive management too Winnicott's thinking stands apart in admitting disillusionment as a figure of love, an integral part of the maternal framework of maturation. Giddens offers a third option from the perspective of sociology. Making no explicit claims on the criteria of maturity or need, and opposed to the Winnicottian version of Cartesian 'inner knowledge' (*cognitione illa interna*) as the groundwork of subjectivity, Giddens emphasizes instead the socially embedded nature of individuals as autonomous subjects of action. Again, the political and moral implications of the argument are evident in the narrative frame of reference.

Politically, the sociological argument gravitates to the question of democracy: for Giddens, as for Winnicott and Parkes, the problem of self-management arises within the sphere of the liberal democratic polity. Giddens, however, is more insistent than either Winnicott or Parkes on the political determination of the self: he makes far-reaching claims for the reflective function of self-narratives, insisting on the positive contribution they provide for the expansion of democratic public life. The political argument rests, to a large extent, on a connection between reflection as a form of narrative and democratic types of civil association. Reflective narratives are seen as paradigmatic expressions of 'dialogic democracy'.[10] Giddens (1994b: 115) identifies the potential for the latter 'in the spread of social reflexivity as a condition both of day-to-day activities and the persistence of larger forms of collective organization'. The assumption here is that the narrative frame facilitates links between the cognitive bias of inner security, the ideal of competence, and the collective life of the polity. As such, dialogic democracy extends its sphere of action from the state to society and, at the same time, from politics to ethics.

The moral reach of narrative discourse is seen as particularly significant; indeed, for Giddens morality subjects the political domain itself to a permanent critique. Giddens (1994b: 111) describes how the reflective use of narrative articulates intimate emotional links that 'cut across the political arena and destabilize the liberal democratic system as much as they reinforce it'. The narrative frame of reference, therefore, is used to advance an important argument concerning the limits of political tradition. What Giddens calls 'emotional democracy' does not simply bypass the formal political sphere. Rather, rejuvenated by the biographical model of self-reflection, liberal democracy itself is furnished with new techniques of intimacy and more effective mechanisms of regulation.

The idea of 'intimacy as democracy' underpins Giddens's account of the transformation or re-invention of personal life in late modernity. Where does narrative come into the argument? There are, Giddens (1994b: 118–19) postulates, 'remarkable parallels between what a good relationship looks like, as developed in the literature of marital and sexual therapy, and formal mechanisms of political democracy'. Essentially, this is what the narrative frame of reference amounts to in the sociological schema of security: the self-help literature on intimacy is presented as an exemplary instance of reflective narrative. The 'ideals of intimacy' discussed in this literature are seen as analogous to the 'ideals of public democracy'. While the biographical turn in the social sciences is aesthetically inconsequential, it is nonetheless assigned an important role in the assimilation of therapeutic thinking to social and political discourse. The manoeuvre is predicated on the notion of dialogue understood as a form of reflection characteristic of democratic personal relationships. Based on the narrative dimension of regulatory action, Giddens applies the democratic ideals of intimacy to the public sphere: 'In a democracy, political life is founded on dialogue rather than on violence, coercion or tradition ... A good relationship is also one in which each party is equal and autonomous, in which issues are discussed rather than driven underground, and which is free from violence' (Giddens and Pierson 1998: 125). The 'discussion' is envisaged as a type of reflexive narrative.

More than the claims themselves, it is the conflation of public and private experience that proves decisive from the point of view of regulation and strategic conduct. Decoupled from its clinical base, the biographical model of the therapeutic self enables Giddens to link the political and moral relations of public life with the idea of a 'good relationship' in intimate situations. The idea here is that public and private relations are managed most effectively through dialogical forms of regulatory action. Once again this does not involve any kind of aesthetic discrimination. Giddens uses the narrative frame of reference strategically in order to draw parallels between the 'good relationship' and the 'good society'. He promotes narrative not as an aesthetic form so much as a linchpin at the interface of auto-regulation and the pursuit of happiness. Autobiography thus involves a particular way of thinking about what it means to be an individual in society, the moral implications of which are of first importance for the sociology of managed lives.

Giddens (1992: 31) assumes the question of 'life values' as an integral part of the reflexive ordering of self-narratives, and the fact that the ideal of autonomy is posed as an ethical question brings the sociological argument directly in line with attachment theory. In elaborating on the reflexive value of autonomy in a post-Freudian context, Giddens does not rely on the criterion of maturity any more than the coincidence of norms and needs; and the emphasis on the market economy notwithstanding, nor is this an argument about the moral impact that markets have under conditions of reflexive modernity (Sandel 2012). Rather, the sociological discriminations of security are comparable above all to the kind of 'narrative competence' that is attributed to securely attached children (Main et al. 1985). The ideal of autonomy thus corresponds to the combined emphasis on representation and security in the understanding of mental states (Fonagy et al. 1991). Giddens is not interested in clinical practice *per se* so much as the augmentation of the therapeutic perspective as a moral resource for the normative principles of autonomy and regulation. Nevertheless, the deployment of narrative competence as an ideal of autonomy is a matter of historical significance in the clinical domain. Holmes (1993: 9) makes the point that 'securely attached children tell coherent stories about their lives', a hypothesis which he places in a decidedly post-Freudian context by arguing that we are entering 'an era of therapeutic co-constructionism – far removed from the *ex-cathedra* interpretations of classical therapy'.

The use of the narrative paradigm as a critique of classical psychoanalysis is entirely germane to the sociological argument. For his part, Giddens identifies the opportunities and risks of social life with the *dramatis personae* of reflexive modernity. For instance, in *The Transformation of Intimacy* the theory of unconscious desire gives way to a representational schema personified by the homosexual couple and anorexic girls. In a discursive formation that extends from 'internally referential' techniques of intimacy to mechanisms of integration and regulation, homosexuality and anorexia are presented as anchorage points for the self-narratives of modern life. Freud is no longer a significant reference for these narratives; psychoanalysis itself becomes a strategic resource for a revised project of social order based on autonomous lifestyles. Thus, Giddens (1991: 54; emphasis in original) concludes that one's 'identity is not to be found in behaviour, nor – important though this is – in the reactions of others, but in the capacity *to keep a particular narrative going*'. Action is privileged over being in a sociological conception of narrative that rests on the idea of competence and the autonomy of the narrator.

Rather than applying a narrative framework to psychoanalysis, Giddens proposes to reverse the trend by assimilating psychoanalysis to the biographical model of self-regulation.[11] The proposal is supported on two counts: first, Giddens (1991: 76) argues that the kind of 'autobiographical thinking' promoted by analytic therapy is constitutive of 'the core of self-identity in modern social life'. Second, Giddens (1991: 34) claims that, as a 'secular version of the confessional', the therapeutic narrative provides 'a means for coping with novel anxieties'. Thus the psychoanalytic narrative, in conjunction with the 'broader institutions of modernity', is appropriated as a moral framework for the permanent critique of oneself. In particular, the integrative function of the post-Freudian narrative is identified with 'innovative social forms' ranging from modern step-parenting to the reflexive appropriation of the body and its pleasures. Again, for Giddens (1991: 218) 'guidebooks and practical manuals to do with health, diet, appearance, exercise, [and] lovemaking' exemplify the therapeutic narrative form in everyday life. As such, the autobiographical model of regulatory action, according to Giddens (1991: 34), 'balances opportunity and potential catastrophe in equal measure'. Self-help literature is conceived as part of a generalized moral therapeutics, where the emphasis is on guiding individuals as autonomous agents towards certain lifestyle options rather than exercising external constraint.

This form of guided living, which represents a type of supervised life, is set out as an alternative to the Freudian life and its tragic overtones. For Freud (1910: 137), the 'first years of our childhood' are combined with 'the "necessities" of our constitution' as the two aspects of human fate. Alternatively, the 'biographical turn' in the social sciences marks a shift from a tragic to a general entrepreneurial order of culture. Giddens exemplifies the trend in promoting 'active attitudes to risk management' (Giddens and Pierson 1998: 216) as opposed to the very idea of fateful inheritance. The tragic fate of the human psyche (what Freud called the Oedipus complex) is displaced by the reflexive values of agency and autonomy on the biographical model of narrative competence. Accordingly, the discussion of modern culture is oriented towards what Giddens (1991: 114–26) calls the 'personal colonizing of future domains'; by which he means the 'reflexive achievements' of risk assessment. For Giddens (1991: 143), insofar as 'fateful moments' arise at all they are seen as opportunities for the narrative 'reconstruction of self-identity'. The sociological argument is constitutive rather than reparative and, in this case, Giddens (1991: 112) reflects a particular line in post-Freudian thought by identifying those moments when we are 'called on to take decisions that are particularly consequential for [our] future lives' not only as 'calculable' in terms of risk, but also as opportunities for opening up 'new fields' of experience.

Giddens (1998a: 81) employs 'therapeutic models', then, as a way of linking biography and society; irrespective of what Freud (1926a) says about the existence of defences prior to repression, Giddens draws on psychoanalysis in support of the claim that 'reflexive biographies' integrate external events and regulate the equilibrium of the system. Transposed from the Freudian drama of unconscious conflict to the sociology of identity, Giddens applies the narrative resources of psychoanalysis to orchestrate the reflexive phenomenon of the self across these two orders of social reality, integrating the worlds of emotional behaviour and self-awareness, and at the same time stabilizing the mundane regime of daily life at the level of representation.

Achievements are not especially dependent on hope in Giddens, who is much closer in this respect to Parkes than he is to Winnicott. A hopeful frame of mind is judged less important than opportune moments, the calculative logic pertaining to which applies across the entire field of personal life from bereavement and illness to divorce and unemployment. For Giddens (1991: 79), managing situations like this means 'running consciously entertained risks in order to grasp the new opportunities which personal crises open up'. Hence 'new lifestyle options' emerge guided by a 'morality of authenticity' in the form of therapeutic narratives. While the latter are articulated more or less at a distance from the clinic, they are nonetheless counted as complementary to psychological counselling and the formation of supervised lives. Thus, further to the developments in therapeutic management and supervision set out in Parts I and II, the sociological problematic of security comprises a loosely defined therapeutic model of everyday life; while at the same time Giddens (1991: 225–6) reworks the traditional sociological problem of order in terms of 'the most intimate human sensibilities'. Let us now turn more directly to the governmental implications of this model.

Utopian realism

Giddens (1998a: 116) addresses the problem of risk management in a particular historical and political context, where risk is construed in terms of 'technological change, social exclusion or the accelerating proportion of one-parent families'. This represents the dark side of lifestyle politics apropos of which two questions present themselves. First, who is at risk? Giddens assumes we form moral ideas about the world by defending our sense of who we are, but holds the view that it is society itself that has to be permanently defended on our behalf. The permanent task falls to individuals, but invariably as stakeholders in society. Calculations are based on the assumption that those who have the least to lose are likely to cause the greatest threat. Winnicott treated the problem quite simply as one of antisocial behaviour; in comparison, Giddens tends to be more circumspect. Nevertheless, in practice the caution is indicative of a more comprehensive calculation of opportunity and risk, as the antisocial tendency gives way to a culture of disaffection.

Second, how do we manage ourselves politically? Again the political question turns on the problem of risk rather than dangerousness.[12] Giddens (1998a: 107–8) does not advocate extensive state provision of unconditional entitlements, but rather, the reclamation of the public sphere as a form of civic liberalism. The latter is envisaged in ethical and political terms rather than economic terms, namely, as 'a common morality of citizenship'. This does not involve an investment in the moral and civic goods of the market so much as an ideological commitment, albeit in the context of a market economy, to individual responsibility and self-conscious governance. Giddens does not approach risk as an accountancy problem, nor is the general schema of security set out as an argument for a self-regulating market economy.[13] The principal aim is to defend society by redefining the relationship between risk and security, and while this turns out to be perfectly consistent with an increasingly austere economic climate, the argument is nonetheless based on the moral principles of autonomy and agency. An eye for risk is harnessed to a more systematic approach to risk taking through an ethics of regulatory action. For Giddens, managing ourselves means developing a society of 'responsible risk takers' rather than welfare recipients, the argument for which is set out in terms of the moral and emotional attributes of the reflective citizen.

Giddens conceives of 'welfare society' without recourse to the founding principles of the welfare state, including the basic principle of assistance. Instead, he advances a psychosocial perspective on two counts: on the one hand, Giddens (1998a: 100) argues that individuals 'need protection when things go wrong, but also the material and moral capabilities to move through major periods of transition in their lives'. The ideal of competency is elaborated along governmental lines through a focus on psychosocial transitions. On the other hand, Giddens (1998a: 117) insists that '[w]elfare is not in essence an economic concept, but a psychic one, concerning as it does well-being'. The question of a fiscal policy is therefore passed over in the preoccupation with psychosocial norms. A primary investment in human social capital is the defining characteristic of the social investment state, which, to underline the strategic import of the argument, includes the acquisition of psychological skills and capacities over and above the provision of economic benefits.

It is this 'skills and capacities' model rather than the traditional welfare state that provides the political underpinning of welfare society.[14] Giddens's (1998a: 117) claim that psychological counselling is often 'more helpful than direct economic support', a claim that complements the narrative dimension of regulatory action, may be seen as emblematic of his version of welfare society. It is also indicative of the therapeutic thinking that supports the problematic of security, where the aim as Giddens (1998a: 94) puts it is to secure 'a balance of autonomy and responsibility in which positive forms of encouragement go along with other sanctions'. As the argument for dialogic democracy demonstrates, the therapeutic model of civic culture lends weight to the idea that morality is essentially about individuals coming to terms with themselves in increasingly uncertain times. Well-being is seen as the outcome of a securely founded individual guided by this model of social order; reflective citizenship, the outcome of the secure self.

How does Giddens arrive at this view of well-being? We began in the previous chapter with his attempt to rework the Durkheimian project of rational ethics as a general theory of security. To understand what Giddens means by a society of 'positive welfare' we need to expand on the Durkheimian legacy as a project of order. In Durkheim, the sociological preoccupation with order is inextricably linked to the problem of morals. Durkheim (1893) sought to identify in the 'moral realities' of the modern world a cohesive type of individualism. He saw the 'cult of the individual' as a morality of co-operation which, distinct from the pursuit of self-interest, could provide a bulwark against the decline of moral authority and the breakdown of solidarity in everyday life. In turn, the state was seen as responsible for securing the values of 'moral individualism' as the form of authority appropriate to a modern industrial order. While Giddens inherits this sociological understanding of modernity, at the same time he attempts to update the Durkheimian project of rational ethics as a reflexive project of order. The latter is set out in Giddens (1994b: 81) in 'the context of a globalizing, cosmopolitan order, [where] traditions are constantly brought into contact with one another and forced to "declare themselves"'.

The critical confrontation with the notion of tradition has far reaching implications for our understanding of the moral life. Giddens conceives the project of order as a generalized moral therapeutics comprising a coherent post-Freudian narrative coupled with a neo-Durkheimian programme of welfare. This is not to say that Giddens takes morality for granted. On the contrary, he turns to Durkheim on the assumption that the culture of morality is currently in a state of disorder and that, in the process of advanced industrialization, society has undergone changes requiring a new, constitutive morality. However, Giddens (1991: 123) follows Durkheim only so far, emphasizing instead 'the generalized "climate of risk" characteristic of late modernity'. The morally autonomous subject is seen as a reflexive agent operating in historical circumstances of 'manufactured risk'. The ideal of autonomy that extends from Kant to Durkheim is reworked as a mechanism of regulatory action; most importantly, morality itself is taken up in the context of risk. Focusing on the problem of 'impoverished morality' in terms of the integral relation between modernity and uncertainty, Giddens views contemporary individuals as more heteronomous and more self-interested than Durkheim envisaged.

Although implicit in Durkheim's sociology of modern life, there is a far more pronounced sense of disenchantment in Giddens. He occupies the other end of the spectrum to Winnicott in our comparative study of the culture of therapeutic values. For Giddens, as for Durkheim, disenchantment is an inherent phenomenon of modernity and its immanent framework. The disengaged rational agent, the 'buffered self' in Taylor's (2007: 37–42) description, is no longer affected by the uncanny or the world of spirits, but rather, embodies the philosophically enlightened self-understanding of modernity. Giddens thus reworks the traditions of Durkheim and Freud in support of our disillusioned sense of reality; in doing so, however, he generalizes Durkheim's concern with the antinomies of social control as an altogether more pervasive problem of security. Traditional fears about the fate of the soul are replaced by anxieties over our sense of security; on the other hand, there is more to contend with here than the encroachments of antisocial behaviour. The threat that Giddens would have us defend ourselves against, and against which he would have us defend society, amounts to a kind of inner moral paralysis. Starting with the social problems of trust and anxiety, the imperative of defence is set out against a perceived crisis in the power of action, where the sociology of morals combines an ideal of self-reflection with an active type of risk management.

What is to be done about the threat of moral paralysis? How is society to be mobilized? The project of reform yields an ideal after Thomas More's sixteenth-century political satire *Utopia*, which is seen as no less subject to reality than the problem of disenchantment itself. Thus the Durkheimian 'spirit of attachment' is found wanting not only with respect to the diagnosis of our discontents, but also in terms of the reformation of moral authority. In short, Giddens updates Durkheim's rational ethics with a psychosocial perspective of secure attachment based on the coincidence of identity and the unconscious. Together with his critical stance towards the Durkheimian version of autonomy, and at the same time distinct from what he sees as the 'formulaic truth' of tradition, Giddens (1994a: 100–2) posits a 'discursive defence' of tradition as grounds for moral renewal. His argument relies explicitly on Oakeshott's (1975) notion of human relations in the form of civil association. The secular consciousness of risk society, which Giddens sees as a defining characteristic of reflective citizenship, is coupled with the reinvention of tradition along the lines of philosophical conservatism. This combination forms the basis of 'utopian realism'. To summarize schematically what Giddens means by the latter, the problematic of security is 'utopian' in that it aspires to be a new ethic of social and personal well-being, and 'realistic' in that it supposedly accords with our sense of ourselves and how we live as securely founded selves.

Utopia is a place one can live in, after all. For Giddens (1994b: 184) utopian realism constitutes a 'new ethic of individual and collective responsibility'; far from a spontaneous phenomenon of modernity, however, this new ethic requires a 'programme of renewed political radicalism'. As we shall see in a moment, 'positive welfare' exemplifies what Giddens means by the programme of utopian realism. The programme itself, however, is inextricably linked with Giddens's theoretical critique of functionalism.[15] These are two sides of the same argument. The attempt to bring the sociology of morals up to date as a programme of moral individualism presupposes a break with the functionalist model of order. As we have already covered some of this ground above, a brief word will suffice here to indicate the shift in sociological perspective from functionalism to a version of attachment theory.

In the first volume of *A Contemporary Critique of Historical Materialism* (1981), Giddens presents the problematic of 'time-space distanciation' as an alternative to progressive evolutionary schemes of historical development. Functionalism is rejected as a deficient explanation of intentionality; at the same time, Giddens remains critical of the external analysis of moral and cultural norms as well as the assimilation of the notions of system and structure. Here, as elsewhere, Giddens (1981: 150) argues that the 'continuity of daily life is not a "directly motivated" phenomenon, but assured in the routinization of practices'. Social life is understood neither as a natural phenomenon nor as an expression of internalized normative commitments. The exercise of daily routines is seen as necessary to make good the supposed motivational deficit of practical consciousness under the demoralized conditions of late modernity. From the auto-regulation of everyday coping mechanisms to forms of calculated risk, routine thus offsets the endemic problem of deficient motivation. In particular, the Parsonian hypothesis of 'system needs' is replaced by the concepts of reflexive function and regulatory action; the attribution of empirical needs to social systems, by the skilled accomplishment of everyday life on the part of social actors.

The key concepts of reflexivity and regulation presuppose a new orientation in sociology based not on the externality of social norms, but rather, on the achieved norms of structure in action. Whereas Parkes attempted something similar *contra* psychoanalysis; Giddens, on the other hand, advances the normative theory of reflective citizenship through the sociological appropriation of psychoanalysis. Once again Fonagy initiates a comparable development in post-Freudian psychology by employing 'dynamic skills theory' as a framework for the concepts of 'reflective function' and 'affect regulation'. Thus, in Giddens and Fonagy alike, reflexivity is seen 'not simply as a property of the person, but of the person and situation together' (Fonagy *et al.* 2002: 60), the situated nature of self-identity comes to the fore in the form of everyday social interaction.

We have kept in view the fact that Giddens (1984: 35) takes it for granted order is 'the fundamental question of social theory'. The problem of order, however, is reworked as a project of order, the aim of which is not to impose regulations on individuals but to enable them to regulate themselves. This is consistent with the main hypotheses of attachment theory: security of attachment is understood as a phenomenon of psychosocial interaction; order and meaning are seen as inextricably linked; and internalization is conceived from the perspective of self-regulation. Giddens adopts this framework as an explicit alternative to the functionalist perspective of 'reproduction'. For Giddens (1981: 215; emphasis in original) the 'concept "reproduction" explains nothing at all in and of itself, but always refers to circumstances that have *to be* explained'. Attachment, then, is a way of explaining social reproduction as the achievement of securely founded individuals.

Starting from the conscious phenomenon of self-identity, Giddens approaches the task of defence in terms of the enactment of basic security in tacit as well as discursive forms of knowledge. The task is not seen as merely 'defensive' in the passive sense, but involves the application of calculative reason and practical consciousness to the order of daily life. The sociology of security is ultimately an argument about reflexive projects and psychosocial mechanisms, underpinned by a comprehensively defined conception of psychosocial interaction. Most importantly, in *The Constitution of Society* (1984) Giddens proposes resolving the problem of order in terms of the continuity of projects unfolding in time and space: the problem is how to turn what we believe into knowledge about what we do or are capable of doing. The project is conceived without recourse to the functionalist hypotheses of system needs, functional prerequisites, and the reproduction of normative sanctions and concomitant motivational commitments. Instead, Giddens elaborates the idea of homeostatic processes along post-Freudian lines: situating the *telos* of these processes in agency itself, he uses psychoanalysis to support the link between reflexive function and self-regulating systems.

The re-moralization of the social

In rejecting the problematic of reproduction as an inadequate model of social order, Giddens formulates an alternative account based on the concepts of reflexivity and regulation. Through an eclectic reading of psychoanalysis, he presents a more systematic account than either Winnicott or Parkes of the relationship between the reflexive project of the self and the welfare of society. In this section, we focus on 'positive welfare' as a form of moral renewal, an example of what utopian realism means in practice. To be clear, utopian realism is not a theoretical critique so much as a particular rationality of government; set out at length in *Beyond Left and Right* (1994b) as a political expression of the general problematic of security, it provides a distinctive framework for political thinking. More than an ideology, then, and not intended as a philosophy, utopian realism may be thought of rather as a 'project'.

Giddens (1994b: 78) argues that late modernity presents an unprecedented series of political and social problems, the solutions to which can no longer be found in the conventional strategies of left and right; indeed, for Giddens 'each political perspective is in its own way exhausted'. Once again the problem of belief as a motivational source for normative principles is at the heart of the matter. Giddens (1991: 21) suggest that the 'integral relation between modernity and radical doubt' is profoundly unsettling and, in an age where the so-called 'formulaic truth' of traditional beliefs is discredited, he posits an alternative view of political and social problems couched in moral terms. The Freudian notion of repression comes into play in Giddens's (1991: 145) description of the sequestration of moral experience, that is, the 'evaporation of morality' at the level of everyday life. As Giddens (1991: 156) put it, 'the ontological security which modernity has purchased, on the level of day-to-day routines, depends on an institutional exclusion of social life from fundamental existential issues which raise central moral dilemmas for human beings'.

The Durkheimian legacy is evident in the idea that security is maintained at the cost of 'moral impoverishment', that modernity simultaneously promotes and represses the conditions of our well-being. That security is won at a cost to our freedom is also a familiar theme in the post-Freudian narrative of modernity. Giddens (1994b: 12) brings these strands together with the idea that we live in a world of 'damaged solidarities', precisely on account of 'the lapsed moralities of everyday life'. The perceived crisis in trust becomes more explicable in a situation where the moral fabric of daily life no longer provides the basis of social cohesion. Thus, for Giddens (1991: 224) the problem is how to found a bonded social body on 'a renewed sensitivity to questions that the institutions of modernity systematically dissolve'. Giddens (1991: 224) sees this as a 'conservative problem', but suggests that 'it does not admit of conservative solutions'. The alternative argument is advanced through a critical engagement with the idea of tradition. Giddens attempts to wrest the democratic argument for solidarity or moral cohesiveness from fundamentalism, but also from the yoke of tradition itself, this includes avoiding any reference to religion and its traditions. Further to the Durkheimian project of rational ethics, Giddens (1994b: 12) conceives the sociology of morals as an inherently complex task comprising a series of related problems: the reparation of social bonds; the mobilization of everyday life; and 'the selective preservation, or even perhaps re-invention, of tradition'.

Giddens's ethical argument rests on the proposal to manage 'damaged solidarities' through the use of tradition in non-traditional ways. What does the non-traditional use of tradition mean? And how does this affect the moral life? Most importantly, while the preservation and renewal of tradition is considered as a *condition* of moral solidarity, tradition itself is not seen as a moral *criterion*. To the contrary, Giddens (1994b: 49) insists that 'we have to decide about the tradition', and that any such decision cannot be made on the grounds of tradition. Far from a standard or means of judging what to save and what to discard, tradition itself is repeatedly called into question. Some other criterion is required to ground tradition as a necessary condition of social life. Thus the 'transformation of tradition' poses something of a dilemma. Lifestyle decisions are increasingly placed centre stage by the sociology of morals, together with what looks like a philosophical quandary about how to live well. It is incumbent on Giddens, then, to reconcile the idea of tradition as a general source of solidarity with the claim that tradition is no longer a privileged 'horizon' of social action.

In a more or less explicit dialogue with psychoanalysis, the three main thinkers under discussion in this book have come up against the normative problem of value. Faced with a similar predicament in the management of self and others, Winnicott posits the criterion of maturity; and Parkes, the criterion of need. Giddens (1994b: 180) represents a third option: arguing for the reflexive use of tradition in the name of social solidarity, he proposes that 'the aim of good government should be to promote the pursuit of happiness'. Basically, for Giddens the non-traditional use of tradition as a means of solidarity depends on the criterion of happiness. Giddens uses tradition in the same way that Durkheim used faith, namely, as a means of adherence to the social facts of belief rather than pious assent. Durkheim (1961: 115) identified the use of faith as 'enlightened assent' beyond religious tradition:

> What prompts the faithful to see that the world is good in principle because it is the work of a good being, we can establish a posteriori to the extent that science permits us to establish rationally what faith postulates a priori.

An emphasis on the instrumental role of collective religious sentiment, the idea that religion binds individuals together and invests their lives with meaning, is comparable to Freud's critical view on religion and morality.

The argument that traditional religious beliefs have no validity or value in themselves, taken to its logical conclusion, amounts at best to a kind of moral pragmatism. This is essentially how Giddens views the task of re-moralization, safeguarding traditions for the defence of society rather than defending tradition *as* tradition. Tradition itself therefore becomes an object of government, and the re-invention of tradition may be seen as yet one more instance of regulatory action. It is hard to see here, in spite of the explicit emphasis on active self-understanding, how Giddens avoids lapsing into a functionalist perspective on social order.[16]

Nevertheless, the demand for innovatory uses of tradition proceeds not from tradition itself, but from the alternative perspective of utopian realism. We can see more clearly now what is at stake in this perspective. Giddens (1994b: 249–50) argues for an understanding of 'actual social processes' combined with the imaginative construction of alternatives, in a world where 'possible futures' assume a constitutive function. Utopian realism is a framework of excellence not on the Aristotelian model of *areté*, but as a psychosocial perspective for assessing the quality of our life-plans. The non-traditional use of tradition, for Giddens at least, involves conducting politics under the auspices of ethical life-plans. The commitment to 'flexible futures' invests moral individualism with a new set of projects in the form of 'life politics' and 'generative governance'. While Giddens shares Durkheim's fidelity to the real as a social phenomenon, the argument is nonetheless utopian to the extent that the underlying continuity of morals and security renders social justice as a regulative ideal.[17] This is essentially what the reflexive project of order amounts to as a form of experience: the framework of programmatic goals, combined with the self-conscious application of moral ideals, assigns the future of 'radical politics' to a regulative, normative horizon of expectation.

There is clearly a utopian aspect to the reflexive use of tradition. Giddens (1994b: 13) describes a 'radically damaged world' in need of 'conservation, restoration and repair'. At the same time, he highlights new conditions of possibility for generating a sense of solidarity and moral cohesiveness. It is the world of possibilities and opportunities, alongside the doubts and uncertainties of modern life, which underwrites the utopian aspect of the argument; hence an administered world of social resources coupled with the implementation of emotional skills and capacities. While Giddens (1998a: 107) accepts that 'welfare systems do and should influence resource distribution'; the emphasis is nonetheless on the underlying conditions of social attachment. He envisages a generative model of solidarity and well-being predicated on a 'new pact' between different economic groups in society. This involves what Giddens (1994b: 194) calls an 'effort bargain' on the part of all social classes aimed at 'common' risks. Again, the argument does not rely on the moral impact of markets as such. For Giddens, it requires something more fundamental than the link between economy and society if we are to manage our lives as reflective citizens.

Does the utopian alternative address the problem? How far is positive welfare a solution to demoralization? Are life-plans the solution? We are certainly on new ground as far as sociology is concerned. The idea of self-consciousness and its synthetic acts of reflection railing against tradition in the name of social reparation and the common good, takes us beyond the Durkheimian tradition of moral thinking. In this sense, at least, utopian realism forms part of the late-twentieth-century revival of normative ethics.[18] But the schema of security also marks a radical break with some of the more basic political assumptions of the modern sociological imagination. Most importantly, the perspective of utopian realism breaks decisively with the idea of welfare as extensive state provision of unconditional entitlements. Rather than revenue and taxation, Giddens addresses the problems of the welfare state consistently in terms of risk management, reflective engagement, and the mechanisms of self-regulation. The re-invention of tradition proceeds from the renewal of utopianism as a combined work of reparation and re-moralization. This dual goal is evident above all in what Giddens (1998b: 99–128) calls 'the social investment state, operating in the context of a positive welfare society'. While the re-invention of tradition serves the aims of the latter, at the same time it upholds a conception of generative politics, as Giddens (1994b: 18) puts it, by 'connecting autonomy with personal and collective responsibilities'.

The intrinsic tie between state and welfare is called into question along the related axes of generative governance and life politics. Let us conclude our critique of sociological reason by considering these two aspects of reflective citizenship, first, active risk management, and second, the pursuit of happiness. Welfare is no longer seen as a mechanism for the alleviation of inequality and hardship in Giddens. This is presented as an historical as well as a moral argument. The reformist ideal of social justice associated initially in the post-war period with Beveridge (1942), T. H. Marshall (1949), and others is rendered synonymous with the idea of the welfare state as a 'passive-risk system'. Giddens (1994b: 150) identifies the latter as 'part of a now lapsed historical endeavour'. The humane aspirations of the welfare state, together with the idea that our happiness presupposes the virtue of just-generosity, are considered anachronistic.

Positive welfare is at odds with the notion of a virtue-based model of welfare. This marks a definitive break in the British context with the tradition of ethical socialism.[19] That we answer to the claimant in direct proportion to his or her claim is not part of the calculation of risk and opportunity. The virtues of egalitarianism, self-restraint, public service, and neighbourliness are no longer held together by the underlying criterion of need. Unlike the kind of 'reconstruction' that Tawney (1921: 10) proposes, which is more in line with the original Durkheimian argument of moral individualism, Giddens describes a society of positive welfare based on an insurance system. The latter is seen as 'positive' largely to the extent that it enables individuals, understood as rational agents, to take calculated risks. The relationship between risk and security is redefined in terms of what Giddens (1998b: 100) sees as a society of 'responsible risk takers'. Welfare claimants themselves are displaced by responsible citizens, and claimants' demands by the moral underpinnings of dialogic democracy. The sentiment of charity is expunged from the rationality of government, together with the promise of donation, in a 'world with no others' where, as Giddens (1994b: 243) puts it, 'we all share common interests, just as we face common risks'.

On Giddens's reckoning, a needs-based mechanism of welfare is no longer credible or adequate. The ideal of human welfare is formulated without the notion of gifts, without a moral justification for unconditional entitlements in the public sphere. The idea that we should give to claimants who are in need without first reckoning their contribution, or that claimants are in need before they are in any way responsible, is ruled out by the calculative rationale of positive welfare. Before their needs are met, individuals are contracted to society not only in the event of injury; but also, more importantly, in terms of their contributions and achievements. The ideal of competency is finally realized as an administrative goal, where risk takes precedence over vulnerability, and the criterion of secure attachment is posited over and above the criterion of need. This represents a distinctive use of human social welfare as a mode of moral life. The underlying assumption here is that, by managing the risks and uncertainties manufactured by modern society, moral agents invest in their own well-being before the promise of benefits to others. Active risk management is promoted, accordingly, as part of the wider project of order, an investment in one's own security as an essential corollary to economic investment.

The argument for welfare society rests on a new use of individualism and, as such, demonstrates the extent to which the defence of society is conceived from the standpoint of the reflective citizen. Social solidarity and individual security are seen as two sides of the same problem, the solution to which is sought in the techniques of intimacy and the mechanisms of self-regulation that underpin the programme of utopian realism. Once again the biographical frame is linked to the aim of good government, augmenting the narrative dimension of regulatory action. While insisting on the fact that '[p]eople have to "construct their own biographies" in order to sustain a coherent sense of self-identity'; at the same time, Giddens (1994b: 126–7) argues that intimacy itself is a means of solidarity, 'the very medium whereby a sense of the communal is generated and continued'. Individualism is presented, then, as a condition of social cohesion supported by the mechanisms of active trust that are seen as characteristic of positive welfare.

Closer in this respect to Crosland's (1956) pronouncements on 'post-capitalist' society than Tawney's ongoing commitment to egalitarianism and economic redistribution, Giddens makes it perfectly clear that a society of positive welfare is predicated on the reflexive values of agency and autonomy rather than any kind of attachment through debt. Crosland, however, held to the criterion of need as a justification for welfare entitlements, arguing for the rights of individuals against society. By contrast, Giddens assumes that generating active trust in defence of society takes precedence over the fulfilment of whatever is promised to others. In the related but distinct traditions of ethical and liberal socialism, solidarity and attachment remain common problems, an essential part of the human ethical predicament. In seeking a solution to this predicament through the re-moralization of the social, Giddens comes to new conclusions about the future of radical politics. Most importantly, perhaps, in the case of positive welfare we are urged to face the future as a problem of continuity and cohesion irrespective of what we owe one another.

This brings us to a central manoeuvre in the therapeutic version of the sociology of morals. Giddens (1994b: 217) describes a 'world with no others', a world in which we are all subject to the same anxieties, risks and uncertainties, even as we defend ourselves through the 'positive appropriation of the moral character of life'. In conjunction with a neo-Durkheimian programme of welfare, the general re-moralization of the social may be seen as a radical reworking of Freud's (Breuer and Freud 1893–5: 305) ethic of 'common unhappiness'. The notion of commonality clearly applies to a global citizenry under conditions of manufactured risk. Unlike Freud, however, Giddens (1994b: 261n18) views the 'basic existential problem areas in social life' as an opportunity for the pursuit of happiness. Through the 'positive appropriation' of the moral life, welfare society provides an institutional framework that enables us to calculate on being happy with the way we live.

While making a case for human welfare based on the criterion of 'happiness'; nonetheless, Giddens continues to address the question of how one should live without reference to the Aristotelian tradition of 'moral virtue' (*ethiké areté*) as the groundwork for the life of 'happiness' (*eudaimonia*).[20] Arguing along similar lines to Williams (1995), Giddens (1994b: 180) is yet more dismissive of Aristotelian ethics as implausible under conditions of late modernity: 'Aristotle's "virtuous activity of the soul" linked happiness to the attractions of sedimented tradition; happiness as both the means and object of emancipation is a much later development.' Thus the pursuit of happiness is seen as continuous with the reflexive or non-traditional use of tradition. And while matters turn decisively to moral psychology, the argument remains focused on social management and its therapeutic underpinnings. For Giddens (1994b: 181), a securely founded sense of well-being 'depends less on controlling the outer world than controlling the inner one'. In a society of positive welfare, the criterion of happiness extends the practice of self-management to the control of the internal world.

The emphasis on self-control as a primary activity of inner security exemplifies the difference between the sociological ethics of regulation and Aristotelian virtue ethics. For Aristotle, as Cottingham (1996: 61) points out, 'self-control [*enkrateia*] is a second best virtue, rescuing (but in no sense transfiguring or validating) the life of the individual whose emotional and behavioural habits have not been properly and harmoniously laid down'. As an alternative formulation of the ethics of reason, Giddens presents the argument for a social investment state by extending self-actualization as a form of self-control under the heading of 'life politics'. Again, Giddens (1991: 214) emphasizes the psychosocial nature of 'life-political issues' in a situation 'where globalizing influences intrude deeply into the reflexive project of the self, and conversely where processes of self-realization influence global strategies'. In this case, coping with risk remains an essential part of the permanent task of social defence; more systematically than Winnicott or Parkes, Giddens constructs an ethics of regulatory action based on self-control and mechanisms of defence.

Nevertheless, as we saw in the case of the narrative frame, defence is not the whole of what Giddens means by well-being. On the contrary, happiness is valued as part of a more comprehensive attitude towards the present state of our existential condition. The pursuit of happiness is seen as yet another, albeit fundamental, part of the critical reflection on ourselves and others. As such, Giddens posits happiness as a criterion of well-being, which may be seen alongside maturity and need as among the main criteria of managed lives. Together with his more explicit pronouncements on reflexive governance, Giddens presents us with a sociological theory of morals the utopian nature of which links the pursuit of happiness to the thematic of late modernity. Under the heading of utopian realism, then, the renewal of the social bond is taken up as a governmental problem beyond the traditions of ethical and liberal socialism, but more generally at 'the limits of modernity'.

The criterion of happiness consolidates the reflexive project of order by extending the scope of welfare society to the administration of life. This is the single most far-reaching objective in the sociological problematic of security. The problem of government is defined in terms of the management of risk; the aim of government, as the pursuit of happiness. Security remains the basic problem, but only insofar as its maintenance promotes happiness; indeed, Giddens (1994b: 180) assumes that security itself, be it personal or social, is based on the fact that 'human beings strive for happiness above everything else'. The critical encounter between sociology and psychoanalysis comes to a head over the question of moral values. Giddens rejects Freud's attempt to ground a regulatory principle of psychological life on pleasure rather than happiness. This is coupled with a rejection of a needs-based mechanism of welfare and, by the same token, an object relations model of infantile satisfaction in the post-Freudian tradition of Balint, Winnicott, and Fairbairn. As a criterion of the secure self, happiness is promoted over and above the pleasures of infantile sexuality, on the one hand, and the satisfaction of infantile needs on the other.

Finally, the sociological problematic of security incorporates the coincidence of dysfunction and identity as a defining characteristic of the reflexive norm. As both an ethical and a political formation, utopian realism thus extends the supervised life further in the direction of self-regulation. On the one hand, the negative value of welfare society is aimed exclusively at the claimant. Once again, Giddens (1994b: 180–1) eschews the economic argument: 'the current problems of the welfare state should not be seen as a fiscal crisis ... happiness and its opposite bear no particular relation to either wealth or the possession of power'. Construed as a problem of internal control, it is argued that the problem of welfare dependency may be managed by fostering a 'desire to work' on the part of the claimant. The latter is targeted as a new figure of disaffection in a society of self-control. Giddens presented this argument alongside New Labour's 'welfare to work' policy, in which claimants received means-tested income assistance on condition that they were actively seeking employment and/or readily participating in programmes of counselling and psychotherapy. Thus, Giddens (1994b: 187) argues that if 'good government is about facilitating the pursuit of happiness, it certainly has to be concerned with the psychic states of its citizenry'. Based on the so-called 'damaged identities' of disaffected welfare recipients, Giddens (1994b: 187) concludes that government can and should influence the 'psychic states' of individuals.

On the other hand, the reflexive imperative of secure attachment applies to the population as a whole. The connection between 'good government' and 'the good relationship' is predicated on the idea of democracy as a kind of 'inner dialogue'. Techniques of intimacy are institutionalized as techniques of moral management aimed at the responsible citizen, and realized in the form of emotional communication. Giddens (1994b: 119) invests moral individualism with a new set of values along the lines of emotional democracy: 'Individuals who have a good understanding of their own emotional make-up, and who are able to communicate effectively with others on a personal basis, are likely to be well prepared for wider tasks of citizenship.' As well as a rationale for the management of claimants and the culture of disaffection, the criterion of happiness promotes the moral life itself as an emotional tie.

Notes

1 See Canguilhem (1974) on the history of the concept of regulation and its application as a social mechanism (governing a state) as well as a biological function. As regards 'homeostatic regulatory systems', the term and concept 'homeostasis' was first used by the American physiologist Walter Cannon in 1926 in his article 'Physiological regulation of normal states: Some tentative postulates concerning biological homeostasis'. Canguilhem (1955) views the concept in the historical context of organic regulation, beginning with the physiology of Claude Bernard and the idea that the organism's stable states are obtained by conserving the 'internal milieu'. More importantly for us, Canguilhem (1955: 72) underlines the fact that where the organism *qua* organism resolves an inherent tension between stability and modification, this requires 'terms whose significance is at once physiological and moral'.
2 Rangell (1955) proposes to unite these two theories of anxiety on the grounds that together they form the very basis of Freudian psychoanalysis.
3 The revised theory of anxiety was decisive for the Kleinian development: insofar as the causal distinction between 'real fear' and 'neurotic anxiety' is put into question, anxiety is therefore seen as 'one of the mainsprings of human endeavour' (Britton 1998: 6).
4 See Samuel Taylor Coleridge, 'The rime of the Ancient Mariner' (Part VI, l. 450), for the 'frightful fiend' as the original of Bion's psychotic figure.
5 See the attempts at synthesis, for instance, in the form of existential psychoanalysis (Sartre 1943) and Dasein analysis (Binswanger 1975).

6   See Craib (1998: 64–5) for a critical comment on Giddens's treatment of Heidegger in *Central Problems in Social Theory* (1979) and the first volume of *A Contemporary Critique of Historical Materialism* (1981).
7   Kristeva (1991: 189) elaborates on the point made by Yvon Brès that 'Freud's recourse to aesthetic works in order to set up the notion of uncanny strangeness was an admission that psychoanalysis could not possibly deal with it'.
8   Anticipating the phenomenological analysis of 'factical' Dasein in *Being and Time* (Heidegger 1927), 'factical life' (*faktisches Leben*) is already equated with Dasein in the 1923 Freiburg lectures, *Ontologie (Hermeneutik der Faktizität)* (1988). In *Being and Time*, 'existentiality', 'facticity', and 'falling' are presented as the three basic constituents of Dasein; hence, being-ahead-of-itself (existence), being-already-in-a-world (facticity), and being-alongside entities within the world (falling). The idea that an entity within the world already has being-in-the-world, recalls the earlier formulation of the being there of facticity, as Heidegger (1988: 29) puts it, 'in its *temporally particular "there"*, its being *"there" for a while* [*in seinem* jeweiligen "Da"]'.
9   For the 'biographical turn' in the social sciences, see Rustin (2001). For the combination of biography and psychotherapy in narrative research see, for instance, White and Epston (1990); Freedman and Combs (1996); Chamberlayne et al. (2000); Speedy (2000); White (2004); Payne (2006); Emerson and Frosh (2009).
10 Cf. the dialogical dimension of reason in Habermas's (1984; 1987) reflexive framework of communicative action.
11 On the narrative paradigm in contemporary psychoanalysis, see Spence (1982) and Schafer (1992).
12 See Castel (1984; 1991) for the distinction between 'dangerousness' and 'risk' in the preventive technologies and strategies of social governance.
13 See Congdon (2011) for the defence of monetarism in the face of the financial crisis following the 'benign outcomes' of the 20 years up to mid-2007.
14 For a critical comment on the secular reduction of order and meaning to a 'skills and capacities' model of welfare, see Williams (2004). In his Romanes Lecture on Etty Hillesum, Williams (2004: 321) differentiates the 'religious life', understood as 'a responsibility for God's appearing on earth', from 'the deployment of skills to settle and assure the self'. The egocentric orientation of the latter in the form of the 'selective modern' psyche, defines the type of generative governance and lifestyle politics that Giddens promotes as the basis of managed societies.
15 See the critique of Merton, Nagel, and Stinchcombe in Giddens (1977a).
16 Cf. the re-moralization of the social in Giddens, with the evolutionary perspective of Durkheimian utilitarianism in Haidt's (2012) moral foundations theory.
17 The concept of 'justice' has played a central role in the revival of normative moral philosophy since the 1970s, most notably in the work of John Rawls (1971). However, as Cottingham (1998: 20) points out, insofar as it 'specifies the most effective social arrangements for individuals to pursue their goals – whatever those goals eventually turn out to be', the Rawlsian project is not comparable to earlier philosophical ethics. On the other hand, as we shall see, the 'committee ethics' of Rawls's actors, indeed 'deliberating about the arrangements for society', may be compared with Giddens's ethics of regulatory action. Starting from a different vantage point to both Giddens and Rawls, Canguilhem (1955: 77) concludes that justice does not come from society but from elsewhere: 'the supreme regulation of social life, namely, justice, does not figure in the form of an apparatus produced by society itself, even if there exist in society institutions of justice'.
18 For the renewed interest in ethics in late-twentieth-century Anglophone philosophy, see Crisp (1996); and for a comparable renewal of ethics in recent Continental philosophy, see Rose (1993).

19 For the British tradition of ethical socialism, see Richard Tawney (1921), William Temple (1926), and John Macmurray (1949). Rowan Williams called attention to the tradition of 'the un-secular socialist voice' in his Raymond Williams Lecture, given on 1 June 2002 at the Hay-on-Wye Festival. Symington (2004) draws on Macmurray's *The Structure of Religious Experience* (1936) in his account of psychoanalysis as a 'scientific religion'; the close affinity between Symington and Winnicott, from an ethical as well as an analytic perspective, has yet to be explored.
20 Cf. MacIntyre (1985) on the moral formation of modern society.

CONCLUSION
The difficult task

What can we make of the good life after Freud? Is it simply a case of being armed against 'a sea of troubles'? This is clearly one reading of our human predicament: we achieve our potential, as best we can, through managed lives. There are grounds for thinking that, in a modern, post-Freudian world of common unhappiness, the ethical question of how to live has become a technical problem of management. It seems safe to say the traditional philosophical task of helping people to achieve happy and fulfilled lives has fallen only sporadically to contemporary moral philosophers. Besides which we experience the reach for meaning in secular culture without 'the naïve acknowledgement of the transcendent, or of goals or claims which go beyond human flourishing' (Taylor 2007: 21). On the other hand, however, psychoanalysts and psychotherapists are among a growing body of practitioners ready to take on the burden of life-management as a permanent task, providing managerial resolutions of one kind or another to personal disaffection as well as social disorder.

But is the analyst in a position to assume this task? Articulating the call to inwardness on the authority of unconscious mentality, the psychoanalyst thereby threatens to undermine the reasonable conception of the good life on the Classical model, as well as its Christian analogue. To set security at odds with free will, albeit as an interior predicament, strikes at the heart of our grandiose self-regard, while at the same time casting doubt on reason as the ground of moral understanding and progress. Under no illusion of what was at stake, Freud (1916–17: 285) acknowledged the disapproval that would follow his looking inward from the perspective of 'what is going on unconsciously in the mind', thereby demonstrating 'to the ego that it is not even master in its own house'. It is precisely for this reason that we count Freud among the main architects of the secularized or secularizing culture of our modernity. The disenfranchised ego reflects a disenchanted world, where self-identity no longer grounds security and we neither fully control nor grasp our lives.

In each of the three cases we discuss in the book, there is an implicit response to the challenge that Freud presented to the traditional paradigms of moral philosophy: Aristotelian, Kantian, and utilitarian.[1] Winnicott, Parkes, and Giddens represent contrasting options in post-Freudian ethics. We have examined these different options in terms of life-management and, in conclusion, we can see how the conflict of interpretations after Freud turns on the question of how to live our lives to the full. The question is subject to a dividing line that separates the reflexive project and the spontaneous gesture. An attempt to recoup the rationally ordered life after Freud, to reinstate the intellectualization of ethics, is evident in the work of Parkes and Giddens along the lines of supervision and regulation, respectively. Parkes presents reflexive medicine as an alternative to psychoanalysis. From the perspective of the supervised life a world of sickness and health remains fully accessible, in principle at least, to rational scrutiny. And, in what may be seen as a complementary manoeuvre, Giddens appropriates psychoanalysis to the reflexive project as the basis of a regulated life. On both counts, we live meaningful, coherent lives insofar as we lay claim to experience through the use of reason, be it in the form of a life-plan or through the exercise of practical consciousness.

To take the proposal of supervision, on the basic assumption that there is no morally correct way to mourn, the grieving process is therefore open to any number of rationally articulated plans for emotional conduct. The psychological and social sciences continue to exploit this area of possibility. For his part, Parkes proposes an inclusive model of medical rationality in the form of psychosocial management, a proposal that renders the 'community' itself as an administrative object and mechanism. In his attempt to formulate this new model, Parkes was faced with two main obstacles, the sociological obstacle of moral hygiene, and the medical obstacle of health surveys. The progress of reflexive medicine, we argued, was hindered by the explanation of social facts as 'things', on the one hand, and by the symptomological rationale of pathological medicine on the other.

In overcoming these obstacles, Parkes has advanced a reasonable conception of the good life beyond the immediate confines of psychiatric medicine. It is possible to extrapolate an account of how best to live, how to reorganize a life of one's own, from Parkes's description of the process of grieving. The bereaved self may be seen as a paradigmatic example of the reflective citizen: the feeling that life itself has lost its meaning affords the bereaved an opportunity to renegotiate how to live. The plight of loss, by its very nature, is seen as a moral quandary. An acknowledgement of the moral dimension of grief calls for a particular shift of emphasis in the order of rational reflection. The therapeutic supervision of bereavement does not amount to a meditation on death; the supervised life in this case does not involve an examination of oneself from the personal viewpoint of death and dying.[2] A greater emphasis is placed on the self as a responsible member of the community, someone who, at one remove from his or her own death, is able to exercise self-control and a degree of personal insight in managing feelings of grief. Accordingly, Parkes sets out the supervised life as an ethics of identity rather than an ascetic exercise in self-transformation. Psychic change amounts to no more or less than a coherent and unified process of psychosocial transition, a process that involves coming to terms with loss.

For Parkes, grief is not a set of symptoms that occur following a loss and then gradually subside. To the contrary, types of symptoms are replaced with modes of reaction on the grounds that norms proceed from needs. We mourn each of us as our needs dictate and, according to Parkes, only in this way pass through the phases of grieving. While this allows for a considerable degree of variation from one person to another as regards the experience of grief, the humane acknowledgement of difference in hard plight is nonetheless coupled with a wider concern. The essential question is not 'What is grief?' but 'Who is at risk?' A managerial resolution is implied in the question. Modes of reaction are thus linked to the management of risk at the level of personal and social security, while the governmental argument is set out in terms of a combined therapeutic and familial strategy. The institutionalization of mourning and the medical treatment of the family are seen as part and parcel of the same process. In particular, Parkes argues for a family-centred mental health service in the form of the hospice–home couple. But this is only one aspect of the supervised life; at the same time, Parkes extends the therapeutic argument to the wider community of friends and associates. AIDS-related bereavement lends momentum to an extended application of supervision, where the strategic conjunction of psychiatric and domestic space is set alongside a generalized conception of risk. Parkes offers a managerial approach to the treatment of bereavement based on the categorization of 'special-risk' and 'at-risk' groups. Aimed primarily at self-understanding under supervision, these categories are not confined to grief-prone individuals, but apply to the population as a whole.

The therapeutic supervision of bereavement operates primarily as a form of risk management, on the assumption that vulnerability and trauma are the two major determinants of grief. The quantification of risk yields predictive hypotheses that are seen as adequate to the task of self-management only when combined with the act of disclosing. It is disclosure above all that highlights the confrontation between bereavement studies and psychoanalysis. Whereas Freud continued to adhere to a tragic interpretation of mourning, Parkes sets aside the basic psychoanalytic assumption that there are ideas in one's mind that are not present to consciousness. The radical heterogeneity of the Freudian psyche is replaced by a 'ratiocentric' conception of self-identity. The outpourings of grief are not seen as symptomatic of unconscious conflict, but rather, as an opportunity for the bereaved to manage themselves under therapeutic supervision. In short, Parkes establishes the supervised life through the application of a set of coping mechanisms. The argument is that we cope with grief, understood as a stressful experience, by putting our feelings into words, and that only what goes into words is manageable. The coincidence of identity and speech links the moral norm to our age of confession, and yet without recourse to the Freudian interpretation. As a result of which we can plan for the days to come and, in the face of loss, rebuild our lives on the ground of reason.

Following Parkes, Giddens generalizes the reflexive norm through the sociological category of 'everyday life', while at the same time attempting to reconcile psychoanalysis and the ethics of identity. Once again the problem of how to live our lives is addressed primarily in terms of risk. Giddens consolidates the conscription of therapeutic understanding through a preoccupation with the 'manufactured risks' of late modernity. Psychoanalysis is included here as part of a calculative attitude towards the positive and negative possibilities of living in a so-called 'risk society'. Considered useful in this context, precisely to the extent that it renders self-identity as a technical problem of management, psychoanalysis thereby augments the sociology of self-knowledge. Psychoanalytic ideas about basic trust are used to explain the transformation of what we believe into knowledge about what we do, or are capable of doing as moral agents and good citizens. By 'good citizens' Giddens means entrepreneurial citizens and, through an eclectic use of post-Freudian psychoanalysis, ranging from Lacan and ego-psychology to a selective adaptation of British object-relations theory, he consolidates the managerial standards of the reflexive norm as a reflexive project. The project is essentially twofold, involving a combination of self-knowledge and self-management; and, while Parkes privileges rational life-plans as the basis of therapeutic supervision, the 'ratiocentric' orientation is yet more pronounced in Giddens's realignment of self-identity, inner security, and moral norms. The general tendency to intellectualize ethics, which Cottingham (1998) identifies in the Classical model, is updated in Giddens as a neo-Durkheimian project of rational ethics.

Giddens derives an ethical *system* from his sociological theory of personal identity, which is applied under the heading of 'utopian realism' as a *programme* of political and moral reform. The programme incorporates the epistemological proposition of cognition (the cognitive bias) as well as the normative objectives of self-mastery and rational control. We discussed 'positive welfare' as an example of utopian realism in practice. Defined primarily in terms of solidarity and happiness, the object and activities of self-conscious governance are predicated on a knowing subject who is also a skilled actor replete with a repertoire of social competencies. In Giddens, skills and capacities take precedence over needs; this includes the skilled use of self-narratives as constitutive of regulatory action. Here, as elsewhere, the use of narrative goes to the heart of therapeutic forms of experience; and our comments on the role of disclosure, in the case of therapeutic supervision, are applicable to the reflexive order of self-narratives in everyday life. The stories, by means of which Giddens claims we understand ourselves, are incommensurate with the Freudian theory of subjectivity and language. Indeed, the narrative frame of reference, as conceived on the cognitive model of self-knowledge, articulates two contrasting modes of *conscious* awareness, as opposed to the dynamic unconscious. If, as we argued, Parkes deliberately dismantles the Freudian interpretation, Giddens does so by default.

The reflexive project of self-management, in Giddens and Parkes alike, emerges in the historical and political context of administrative decentralization. Giddens, however, is more explicit than Parkes in establishing the regulated life on a therapeutic model of civic culture. Where Parkes refers to moral and civic obligation more or less by implication; Giddens assimilates the Freudian legacy to the future of 'radical politics', assuming that traditional political institutions no longer provide a horizon of intelligibility for the moral life. Psychoanalysis augments the sociological account of basic security; but also, more importantly, it provides Giddens with a framework for the re-moralization of the social along managerial lines. Alongside the moral implications of the therapeutic aim in the case of bereavement, we can extrapolate a complementary account from the sociological perspective of the regulated life. Practical consciousness delivers us the means of working out how best to live by weighing our opportunities against an inherently unstable climate of risk. Again, the moral argument turns on the question of risk, what Giddens refers to as the secular consciousness of risk. Continuous with inner security, the good life amounts to a life regulated by risk assessment in a world bereft of moral certainties.

The Freudian interpretation, in many ways, underwrites the reflexive project of self-understanding. We can see that, with respect to the augmentation of ego-function, Freud clearly linked the therapeutic aim to the use of reason. For instance, in *The Question of Lay Analysis*, Freud (1926b: 205) describes the principal reason for conducting an analysis as follows: 'We try to restore the ego, to free it from its restrictions, and to give it back the command over the id which it has lost owing to its early repressions ... our whole technique is directed to this aim'. We find a similar line of argument, concerning the aim and technique of psychoanalysis, in the second part of *An Outline of Psycho-analysis*, where Freud focuses directly on the practical task. Freud (1940: 177) values self-knowledge here as an initial stage in the analytic process:

> The method by which we strengthen the weakened ego has as a starting-point an extending of its self-knowledge ... the first part of the help we have to offer is intellectual work on our side and encouragement to the patient to collaborate in it.

Thus reason provides grounds for hope, as far as the analytic encounter is concerned, in terms of 'the transcendentalist association of the unconscious with rationality' (Gardner 2012: 47). How far the post-Kantian model of the subject may be developed along psychoanalytic lines is a matter for debate. In any case, Freud (1940: 177) went on to say that self-knowledge, under the impetus of 'transcendental reflection' as it were, was only a 'preliminary stage', a first step that was meant to facilitate 'another, more difficult, task'. Although this does not necessarily amount to a repudiation of the transcendental image of mind, once he had moved beyond the fitful efforts in *Studies in Hysteria*, Freud saw the cognitive model of self-knowledge as fundamentally inadequate to the task of analytic therapy; conscious knowledge was not seen as the main vehicle of psychic change.

Freud's 'difficult task' divides reflection and reclamation, and our conclusions are based on this distinction. Thus, while psychosocial studies and sociology come down decidedly on the side of self-knowledge; the Winnicottian typology of management exemplifies the inherent tension in the post-Freudian development between regulation and spontaneity. The tension is evident in the different meanings of 'environment' that underpin the Winnicottian typology: ranging from the maternal environment and its clinical analogue to the social environment and various types of residential management. Winnicott proposed residential management for the treatment of 'difficult children' and, applying his war-time experience in maintaining the peace, his ideas on deprivation and delinquency are consistent with the familial strategy of social normalization. On his own estimation, Winnicott counted social management as an essential part of society's permanent task, by which he meant the containment of antisocial elements through the fostering of social maturity. Some of our most intimate intuitions and hopes, therefore, are exposed to management as a type of 'social provision'.

As an apologist for a social order supposedly under attack from the more recalcitrant and disruptive elements in the society, Winnicott presented himself, during the Cold War, as a conservative exponent of English liberal-mindedness. The terms of political engagement have been redefined since the 1950s: the post-war preoccupation with children deprived of normal affective lives has become more entrenched as the 'antisocial tendency' has given way to a thoroughgoing culture of disaffection. Against this background, we have traced the post-war calculus of security as a continuous political trajectory from the problem of antisocial behaviour to demoralization; from the permanent task of social defence through supervisory control to the regulated life; and from post-war liberal humanism, a characteristic strain of English psychoanalysis exemplified by Winnicott, to the governmental programmes of advanced liberal democracies. The prevalence of conflicting interpretations within psychoanalysis, however, means there are more fundamental conclusions to draw about Winnicott than a critique of liberal disillusionment would allow. Winnicottian management is more than a harbinger of control society. The problem of how to be fully alive was far more important to Winnicott than the managerial problem of order. The social administration of life was not his main concern; he was more interested in the moral contours of inner security in the earliest relationship. Alongside his singular contribution to our understanding of primitive emotional development, the reflections on society are comparatively modest.

The critical conclusion does not cover the more important things Winnicott had to say about life. The originality of his contribution to psychoanalysis rests on the idea of intuitive management as the model of therapeutic reclamation. The former is understood as the pre-reflective ground of creative living; the latter, as the imaginative recovery of a life. The hoped-for is not a calculation, however. Winnicott credits the irreducibility of what Williams (2002: 16) calls 'unmanageable times'. Thus, without endorsing a tragic view of failure, the developmental and clinical arguments allow for the fallible nature of human striving. And unlike Freud, who was a consistently dualistic thinker, Winnicott presented the different types of management from a dialectical perspective. We set out in the first part of the book, with this perspective in mind, to reconstruct the dialectic of disaster and hope as the basis of Winnicott's clinical thinking. A central part of therapy as a vocation, the tendering of hope may also be seen as the groundwork of Winnicottian ethics. Alongside maternal love and the idea of life as an act of faith, hope epitomizes the Christianized understanding of values that sustains this calling. The deep optimism that runs through Winnicott's thought is based on an understanding of human nature as inherently good. For Winnicott, the moral life is commensurate with the nature of reality; and where a failure of life dictates, redemption reworks the difficult task of Freud's wager regarding the disenfranchised ego. In the name of the 'true self', psychoanalysis assumes the task of 'discovering how to live our lives in the way that is truest to our human nature' (Cottingham 1998: 152). Basically, for Winnicott the task is to believe in the potentials of a life.

Again, while a rationally articulated plan for the conduct of life is not the actuating force of this worldview, the Winnicottian figure of hope is nonetheless subject to the tension between spontaneity and reflexivity. Winnicott identified two types of hope, including, reclamation ('reliving') as the equivalent of memory and the institutional management of disaffection. The former applies in the case of early trauma; the latter, in the case of deprivation. We can see how hope is therefore open to different meanings and may include instrumental as well as imaginative uses. On both counts, however, the difficult task of therapeutic treatment is modelled on the movement from primitive to mature love. The basic intuition in intuitive management is love. Far from a cognitive model of self-understanding, the criterion of maturity is derived from the convergence of understanding and love. This remains the case even though the idea of 'social maturity' may be seen as a precursor of the regulated life.

Winnicott envisaged hope in terms of the unconscious sense of having been born for nothing, or the feeling that one's life has come to nothing. The analyst responds to latent and manifest expressions of hope, respectively. *I hope there was a beginning so that I may finally become someone. I hope something can be done about this dreadful mess so that I may yet find a way to be who I am.* The former is an expression of the latent hope of pre-reflective intuition; a primordial, somatic expectation inscribed in encapsulated mnemonic impressions rather than repressed memories. The latter is an expression of the moment of hope embodied in the child's antisocial imagination; a manifestation of the disaffected imaginary, it is the kind of hope that may be heard when, in the course of treatment, a patient tells us he is getting used to being himself. They are both types of unconscious communication and, in responding to dissociation and disaffection as such, the analyst is not trying to make the unconscious conscious – 'where id was, there ego be [*Wo Es war, soll Ich warden*]' (Freud 1933a: 80) – so much as helping patients to be more alive, those who are deprived of life as well as those for whom life seems to have failed.

Winnicott invented radically new ways of thinking about elemental failure, as well as the emotional and moral mess of deprived lives. If these disastrous situations require in response from us a mature attitude to reality, the response itself is hopeful only to the extent that it is sourced in vitality and creative wholeness. In doing psychoanalysis Winnicott aimed at surviving and at being himself; and in attending to failure, ultimately, he was expressing his innate passion for *believing in* and *living on*.

Notes

1 For the challenge psychoanalytic theory poses to 'ratiocentric' ethics, the traditional project of moral philosophy, see Cottingham (1998). The term 'ratiocentrism' is used by Cottingham (1998: 36) to suggest 'a number of distinct though often crisscrossing and overlapping strands' in the history of philosophy; it is not meant to be taken as 'a simple, monolithic idea'. I am indebted to Cottingham, whose arguments on morals and the emotions inform my own conclusions on psychoanalytic ethics. There is of course a large body of literature, outside the Anglophone philosophical tradition, on the possibilities of a spiritual life: the work of Blanchot, Levinas, Ricoeur, Derrida, Marion, Walter Benjamin and others includes not only theistic considerations in regard to the moral life, but also the possibilities of leading an ethical life in the absence of God.
2 Cf. Foucault's 1981–2 lectures at the Collège de France (2001; English translation: *The Hermeneutics of the Subject*, 2005) on practices of the self in Greco-Roman ethics, where the meditation on death (*meletē thanatou*) is viewed in the context of Hellenistic and Roman ascetics. Linking the practice of this meditation to an ethics of old age, Foucault emphasizes the objective in Stoic ascetics on freedom from oneself.

REFERENCES

Winnicott

Winnicott, D. W. (1935) 'The manic defence', in *Through Paediatrics to Psychoanalysis*, London: Hogarth Press, 1978, pp. 129–44.

Winnicott, D. W. (1939a) 'Letter to the *British Medical Journal*', in C. Winnicott, R. Shepherd and M. Davis (eds) *Deprivation and Delinquency*, London and New York: Tavistock Publications, 1984, pp. 13–14.

Winnicott, D. W. (1939b) 'Aggression and its roots', in C. Winnicott, R. Shepherd and M. Davis (eds) *Deprivation and Delinquency*, London and New York: Tavistock Publications, 1984, pp. 84–99.

Winnicott, D. W. (1940) 'Discussion of war aims', in C. Winnicott, R. Shepherd and M. Davis (eds) *Home Is Where We Start From*, Harmondsworth: Penguin Books, 1986, pp. 210–20.

Winnicott, D. W. (1941) '*Review of* the Cambridge Evacuation Survey: a wartime study in social welfare and education', in C. Winnicott, R. Shepherd and M. Davis (eds) *Deprivation and Delinquency*, London and New York: Tavistock Publications, 1984, pp. 22–4.

Winnicott, D. W. (1945) 'Primitive emotional development', in *Through Paediatrics to Psychoanalysis*, London: Hogarth Press, 1978, pp. 145–56.

Winnicott, D. W. (1946) 'Some psychological aspects of juvenile delinquency', in C. Winnicott, R. Shepherd and M. Davis (eds) *Deprivation and Delinquency*, London and New York: Tavistock Publications, 1984, pp. 113–19.

Winnicott, D. W. (1947) 'Hate in the countertransference', in *Through Paediatrics to Psychoanalysis*, London: Hogarth Press, 1978, pp. 194–203.

Winnicott, D. W. (1948) 'Children's hostels in war and peace', in C. Winnicott, R. Shepherd and M. Davis (eds) *Deprivation and Delinquency*, London and New York: Tavistock Publications, 1984, pp. 73–7.

Winnicott, D. W. (1950a) 'The deprived child and how he can be compensated for loss of family life', in C. Winnicott, R. Shepherd and M. Davis (eds) *Deprivation and Delinquency*, London and New York: Tavistock Publications, 1984, pp. 172–88.

Winnicott, D. W. (1950b) 'Some thoughts on the meaning of the word "democracy"', in C. Winnicott, R. Shepherd and M. Davis (eds) *Home Is Where We Start From*, Harmondsworth: Penguin Books, 1986, pp. 239–59.

Winnicott, D. W. (1950–5) 'Aggression in relation to emotional development', in *Through Paediatrics to Psychoanalysis*, London: Hogarth Press, 1978, pp. 204–18.

REFERENCES

Winnicott, D. W. (1952) 'Anxiety associated with insecurity', in *Through Paediatrics to Psychoanalysis*, London: Hogarth Press, 1978, pp. 97–100.

Winnicott, D. W. (1953) 'Transitional objects and transitional phenomena: a study of the first non-me possession', *International Journal of Psychoanalysis*, 34: 89–97.

Winnicott, D. W. (1954a) 'The depressive position in normal emotional development', in *Through Paediatrics to Psychoanalysis*, London: Hogarth Press, 1978, pp. 262–77.

Winnicott, D. W. (1954b) 'Metapsychological and clinical aspects of regression within the psychoanalytical set-up', in *Through Paediatrics to Psychoanalysis*, London: Hogarth Press, 1978, pp. 278–94.

Winnicott, D. W. (1956a) 'Primary maternal preoccupation', in *Through Paediatrics to Psychoanalysis*, London: Hogarth Press, 1978, pp. 300–5.

Winnicott, D. W. (1956b) 'The antisocial tendency', in C. Winnicott, R. Shepherd and M. Davis (eds) *Deprivation and Delinquency*, London and New York: Tavistock Publications, 1984, pp. 120–31.

Winnicott, D. W. (1957) 'The mother's contribution to society', in C. Winnicott, R. Shepherd and M. Davis (eds) *Home Is Where We Start From*, Harmondsworth: Penguin Books, 1986, pp. 123–27.

Winnicott, D. W. (1958) 'The psychology of separation', in C. Winnicott, R. Shepherd and M. Davis (eds) *Deprivation and Delinquency*, London and New York: Tavistock Publications, 1984, pp. 132–5.

Winnicott, D. W. (1960a) 'The theory of the parent-infant relationship', in *The Maturational Processes and the Facilitating Environment: Studies in the Theory of Emotional Development*, London: Hogarth Press, 1985, pp. 37–55.

Winnicott, D. W. (1960b) 'The family and emotional maturity', in *The Family and Individual Development*, London: Tavistock, 1965, pp. 88–94.

Winnicott, D. W. (1961) 'Psychoanalysis and science: friends or relations?' in C. Winnicott, R. Shepherd and M. Davis (eds) *Home Is Where We Start From*, Harmondsworth: Penguin Books, 1986, pp. 11–18.

Winnicott, D. W. (1962a) 'Providing for the child in health and crisis', in *The Maturational Processes and the Facilitating Environment: Studies in the Theory of Emotional Development*, London: Hogarth Press, 1985, pp. 64–72.

Winnicott, D. W. (1962b) 'Ego integration in child development', in *The Maturational Processes and the Facilitating Environment: Studies in the Theory of Emotional Development*, London: Hogarth Press, 1985, pp. 56–63.

Winnicott, D. W. (1963a) 'Fear of breakdown', in C. Winnicott, R. Shepherd and M. Davis (eds) *Psycho-analytic Explorations*, London: Karnac Books, 1989, pp. 87–95.

Winnicott, D. W. (1963b) 'Morals and education', in *The Maturational Processes and the Facilitating Environment: Studies in the Theory of Emotional Development*, London: Hogarth Press, 1985, pp. 93–105.

Winnicott, D. W. (1963c) 'From dependence towards independence in the development of the individual', in *The Maturational Processes and the Facilitating Environment: Studies in the Theory of Emotional Development*, London: Hogarth Press, 1985, pp. 83–92.

Winnicott, D. W. (1963d) 'The development of the capacity for concern', in *The Maturational Processes and the Facilitating Environment: Studies in the Theory of Emotional Development*, London: Hogarth Press, 1985, pp. 73–82.

Winnicott, D. W. (1963e) 'D. W. W's dream related to reviewing Jung', in C. Winnicott, R. Shepherd and M. Davis (eds) *Psycho-analytic Explorations*, London: Karnac Books, 1989, pp. 228–30.

REFERENCES

Winnicott, D. W. (1963f) 'Communicating and not communicating leading to a study of certain opposites', in *The Maturational Processes and the Facilitating Environment: Studies in the Theory of Emotional Development*, London: Hogarth Press, 1985, pp. 179–92.

Winnicott, D. W. (1964a) *The Child, the Family, and the Outside World*, Harmondsworth: Penguin Books, 1957.

Winnicott, D. W. (1964b) 'Youth will not sleep', in C. Winnicott, R. Shepherd and M. Davis (eds) *Deprivation and Delinquency*, London and New York: Tavistock Publications, 1984, pp. 156–8.

Winnicott, D. W. (1965a) 'Introduction', in *The Maturational Processes and the Facilitating Environment: Studies in the Theory of Emotional Development*, London: Hogarth Press, 1985, pp. 9–10.

Winnicott, D. W. (1965b) 'The psychology of madness: a contribution from psychoanalysis', in C. Winnicott, R. Shepherd and M. Davis (eds) *Psycho-analytic Explorations*, London: Karnac Books, 1989, pp. 119–29.

Winnicott, D. W. (1966) 'The ordinary devoted mother', in *Babies and their Mothers*, Reading, MA: Addison-Wesley, 1987, pp. 3–14.

Winnicott, D. W. (1967a) 'Delinquency as a sign of hope', in C. Winnicott, R. Shepherd and M. Davis (eds) *Home Is Where We Start From*, Harmondsworth: Penguin, 1986, pp. 90–100.

Winnicott, D. W. (1967b) 'The location of cultural experience', in *Playing and Reality*, Harmondsworth: Penguin, 1974, pp. 112–21.

Winnicott, D. W. (1967c) 'The concept of clinical regression compared with that of defence organisation', in C. Winnicott, R. Shepherd and M. Davis (eds) *Psycho-analytic Explorations*, London: Karnac Books, 1989, pp. 193–9.

Winnicott, D. W. (1967d) 'Mirror-role of mother and family in child development', in *Playing and Reality*, Harmondsworth: Penguin, 1974, pp. 130–8.

Winnicott, D. W. (1967e) 'D. W. W. on D. W. W.', in C. Winnicott, R. Shepherd and M. Davis (eds) *Psycho-analytic Explorations*, London: Karnac Books, 1989, pp. 569–82.

Winnicott, D. W. (1968a) 'The use of an object and relating through identifications', in C. Winnicott, R. Shepherd and M. Davis (eds) *Psycho-analytic Explorations*, London: Karnac Books, 1989, pp. 218–27.

Winnicott, D. W. (1968b) 'Communication between infant and mother, and mother and infant, compared and contrasted', in *Babies and their Mothers*, Reading, MA: Addison-Wesley, 1987, pp. 89–103.

Winnicott, D. W. (1968c) 'Comments on my paper "The use of an object"', in C. Winnicott, R. Shepherd and M. Davis (eds) *Psycho-analytic Explorations*, London: Karnac Books, 1989, pp. 238–40.

Winnicott, D. W. (1969) 'The mother-infant experience of mutuality', in C. Winnicott R. Shepherd and M. Davis (eds) *Psycho-analytic Explorations*, London: Karnac Books, 1989, pp. 251–60.

Winnicott, D. W. (1970a) 'On the basis for self in body', in C. Winnicott, R. Shepherd and M. Davis (eds) *Psycho-analytic Explorations*, London: Karnac Books, 1989, pp. 261–83.

Winnicott, D. W. (1970b) 'Living creatively', in C. Winnicott, R. Shepherd and M. Davis (eds) *Home Is Where We Start From*, Harmondsworth: Penguin, 1986, pp. 37–54.

Winnicott, D. W. (1971a) 'Creativity and its origins', in *Playing and Reality*, Harmondsworth: Penguin, 1974, pp. 76–100.

Winnicott, D. W. (1971b) 'The place where we live', in *Playing and Reality*, Harmondsworth: Penguin, 1974, pp. 122–9.
Winnicott, D. W. (1984) *Deprivation and Delinquency*, C. Winnicott, R. Shepherd and M. Davis (eds) London and New York: Tavistock Publications.
Winnicott, D. W. (1986) *Home Is Where We Start From*, C. Winnicott, R. Shepherd and M. Davis (eds) Harmondsworth: Penguin Books.
Winnicott, D. W. (1987a) *Babies and their Mothers*, Reading, MA: Addison-Wesley.
Winnicott, D. W. (1987b) *The Spontaneous Gesture: Selected Letters of D. W. Winnicott*, F. R. Rodman (ed.) Cambridge, MA: Harvard University Press.
Winnicott, D. W. (1988) *Human Nature*, London: Free Association Books.
Winnicott, D. W. and Britton, C. (1944) 'The problem of homeless children', *New Era*, September–October, 155–61.
Winnicott, D. W. and Britton, C. (1947) 'Residential management as treatment for difficult children', in C. Winnicott, R. Shepherd and M. Davis (eds) *Deprivation and Delinquency*, London and New York: Tavistock Publications, 1984, pp. 54–72.

Parkes

Parkes, C. M. (1964) 'The effects of bereavement on physical and mental health: a study of the case records of widows', *British Medical Journal*, 1964 (2): 274.
Parkes, C. M. (1965) 'Bereavement and mental illness, Part I: a clinical study of the grief of bereaved psychiatric patients; Part II: a classification of bereavement reactions', *British Journal of Medical Psychology*, 38: 1–26.
Parkes, C. M. (1970) 'The first year of bereavement: a longitudinal study of the reaction of London widows to the death of their husbands', *Psychiatry*, 33: 444–67.
Parkes, C. M. (1972) 'Components of the reaction to loss of a limb, spouse or home', *Journal of Psychosomatic Research*, 16: 343–49.
Parkes, C. M. (1973) 'Factors determining the persistence of phantom pain in the amputee', *Journal of Psychosomatic Research*, 17: 97–108.
Parkes, C. M. (1976) 'The psychological reaction to loss of a limb: the first year after amputation', in J. Howells (ed.) *Modern Perspectives in the Psychiatric Aspects of Surgery*, New York: Brunner Mazel, pp. 515–32.
Parkes, C. M. (1981) 'Evaluation of a bereavement service', *Journal of Preventive Psychiatry*, 1: 179–88.
Parkes, C. M. (1991) 'Planning for the aftermath', *Journal of Royal Society of Medicine*, 84: 22–5.
Parkes, C. M. (1993) 'Bereavement as a psychosocial transition: processes of adaptation to change', in M. S. Stroebe, W. Stroebe and R. O. Hansson (eds) *Handbook of Bereavement*, Cambridge: Cambridge University Press, pp. 91–101.
Parkes, C. M. (1996) *Bereavement: Studies of Grief in Adult Life*, 3rd edn, London: Routledge.
Parkes, C. M. and Weiss, R. S. (1983) *Recovery from Bereavement*, New York: Basic Books.
Parkes, C. M., Laungani, P. and Young, B. (eds) (1997) *Death and Bereavement across Cultures*, London: Routledge.

References

Giddens

Giddens, A. (1976) *New Rules of Sociological Method*, London: Hutchinson.
Giddens, A. (1977a) 'Functionalism: *après la lutte*', in *Studies in Social and Political Theory*, London: Hutchinson, pp. 96–134.
Giddens, A. (1977b) 'The "individual" in the writings of Émile Durkheim', in *Studies in Social and Political Theory*, London: Hutchinson, pp. 273–91.
Giddens, A. (1979) *Central Problems in Social Theory*, London: Macmillan.
Giddens, A. (1981) *A Contemporary Critique of Historical Materialism*, vol.1, London: Macmillan.
Giddens, A. (1982) *Profiles and Critiques in Social Theory*, London: Macmillan.
Giddens, A. (1984) *The Constitution of Society: Outline of the Theory of Structuration*, Cambridge: Polity Press.
Giddens, A. (1990) *The Consequences of Modernity*, Cambridge: Polity Press.
Giddens, A. (1991) *Modernity and Self-Identity*, Cambridge: Polity Press.
Giddens, A. (1992) *The Transformation of Intimacy*, Cambridge: Polity Press.
Giddens, A. (1994a) 'Living in a post-traditional society', in U. Beck, A. Giddens and S. Lash (eds) *Reflexive Modernisation: Politics, Tradition and Aesthetics in the Modern Social Order*, Cambridge: Polity Press, pp. 56–109.
Giddens, A. (1994b) *Beyond Left and Right: The Future of Radical Politics*, Cambridge: Polity Press.
Giddens, A. (1998a) *The Third Way: The Renewal of Social Democracy*, Cambridge: Polity Press.
Giddens, A. (1998b) 'The politics of risk society', in A. Giddens and C. Pierson, *Conversations with Anthony Giddens*, Cambridge: Polity Press, pp. 204–17.
Giddens, A. and Pierson, C. (1998) *Conversations with Anthony Giddens*, Cambridge: Polity Press.

General

Ablon, J. (1973) 'Reactions of Samoan burns patients and families to severe burns', *Social Science and Medicine*, 7: 167–78.
Abraham, K. (1924) 'A short study of the development of the libido, viewed in the light of mental disorders', in *Selected Papers on Psychoanalysis*, London: Maresfield Reprints, pp. 418–501.
Abram, J. (2008) 'Donald Woods Winnicott (1896–1971): a brief introduction', *International Journal of Psychoanalysis*, 89: 1189–1217.
Abram, J. (2012) 'D. W. W.'s notes for the Vienna Congress 1971: a consideration of Winnicott's theory of aggression and an interpretation of the clinical implications', in J. Abram (ed.) *Donald Winnicott Today*, London: Routledge, 2013, pp. 302–30.
Abram, J. (ed.) (2013) *Donald Winnicott Today*, London: Routledge.
Ainsworth, M. (1982) 'Attachment: retrospect and prospect', in C. M. Parkes and J. Stevenson-Hinde (eds) *The Place of Attachment in Human Behaviour*, London: Tavistock, pp. 3–30.
Aldritch, C. K. (1963) 'The dying patient's grief', *Journal of the American Medical Association*, 184: 329–31.
Alexander, F. (1950) 'Analysis of the therapeutic factors in psychoanalytic treatment', *Psychoanalytic Quarterly*, 19: 482–500.

REFERENCES

Alexander, F. and French, T. M. (1946) *Psychoanalytic Therapy: Principles and Applications*, New York: Ronald.
Alvarez, A. (1992) *Live Company: Psychoanalytic Psychotherapy with Autistic, Borderline, Deprived and Abused Children*, London: Routledge.
Anderson, R. (ed.) (1992) *Clinical Lectures on Klein and Bion*, London: Routledge.
Anzieu, D. (1985) *Le Moi-peau*; trans. C. Turner (1989) *The Skin Ego: A Psychoanalytic Approach to the Self*, New Haven, CT: Yale University Press.
Applegate, J. S. and Bonovitz, J. M. (1995) *The Facilitating Partnership: A Winnicottian Approach for Social Workers and Other Helping Professionals*, Northvale, NJ and London: Jason Aronson.
Ariès, P (1976) *Western Attitudes towards Death: From the Middle Ages to the Present*, London: Marion Boyars.
Ariès, P. (1983) *The Hour of Our Death*, London: Peregrine Books.
Armstrong, D. (1983) *Political Anatomy of the Body: Medical Knowledge in Britain in the Twentieth Century*, Cambridge: Cambridge University Press.
Athill, D. (2009) *Somewhere Towards the End*, London: Granta.
Bachelard, G. (1951) *L'activité rationaliste de la physique contemporaine*, Paris: Presses Universitaires de France.
Bachelard, G. (1984) *The New Scientific Spirit*, Boston, MA: Beacon Books.
Badio, A. (1993) 'Is there a theory of the subject in the work of Georges Canguilhem?' in *The Adventure of French Philosophy*, London: Verso, 2012, pp. 39–52.
Balint, M. (1952) *Primary Love and Psychoanalytic Technique*, London: Hogarth Press.
Balint, M. (1968) *The Basic Fault: Therapeutic Aspects of Regression*, London: Tavistock.
Barbalet, J. M. (1998) *Emotion, Social Theory, and Social Structure: A Macrosociological Approach*, Cambridge: Cambridge University Press.
Bartlett, P. and Wright, D. (1999) *Outside the Walls of the Asylum: The History of Care in the Community 1750–2000*, London: The Athlone Press.
Bartrop, R. W., Luckhurst, E., Lazarus, L., Kiloh, L. G. and Penny, R. (1977) 'Depressed lymphocyte function after bereavement', *Lancet*, 97: 834–36.
Bate, J. (2003) *John Clare: A Biography*, London: Picador.
Beck, U. (1992) *Risk Society: Towards a New Modernity*, London: Sage Publications.
Benjamin, J. (1988) *The Bonds of Love: Psychoanalysis, Feminism, and the Problem of Domination*, New York: Pantheon.
Benjamin, J. (1995) *Like Subjects, Love Objects: Essays on Recognition and Sexual Difference*, New Haven, CT: Yale University Press.
Beveridge, W. H. (1942) *Social Insurance and Allied Services*, London: Allen and Unwin.
Bick, E. (1968) 'The experience of the skin in early object relations', *International Journal of Psychoanalysis*, 49: 484–86.
Bilgrami, A. (2010) 'What is enchantment?' in M. Warner, J. VanAntwerpen and C. Calhoun (eds) *Varieties of Secularism in a Secular Age*, Cambridge, MA: Harvard University Press, pp. 145–65.
Binswanger, L. (1975) *Being-in-the-world: Selected Papers of Ludwig Binswanger*, London: Souvenir Press.
Bion, W. R. (1970) *Attention and Interpretation*. London: Maresfield Reprints.
Blanchot, M. (1993) 'The narrative voice (the "he", the neutral)', in *The Infinite Conversation*, Minneapolis, MN: University of Minnesota Press, pp. 379–87.
Bollas, C. (1987) *The Shadow of the Object: Psychoanalysis of the Unthought Known*, London: Free Association Books.

REFERENCES

Bollas, C. (1989) *Forces of Destiny: Psychoanalysis and Human Idiom*, London: Free Association Books.
Bollas, C. (1995) *Cracking Up: The Work of Unconscious Experience*, London: Routledge.
Bollas, C. (2009) *The Evocative Object World*, London: Routledge.
Bollas, C. (2012) 'The psychoanalytic passage', *Psychoanalysis in Europe Bulletin*, 66: 75–85.
Botella, C. and Botella, S. (2005) *The Work of Figurability: Mental States without Representation*, Hove and New York: Brunner-Routledge.
Botella, S. (2010) 'De la mémoire du ça', in *L'Inconscient freudien: Monographies et débats de psychanalyse*, Paris: PUF, pp. 161–70.
Bowlby, J. (1940) 'Psychological aspects', in R. Padley and M. Cole (eds) *Evacuation Survey: A Report to the Fabian Society*, London: Routledge.
Bowlby, J. (1951) *Maternal Care and Mental Health*, Geneva: World Health Organization.
Bowlby, J. (1961) 'Processes of mourning', *International Journal of Psychoanalysis*, 44: 317.
Bowlby, J. (1963) 'Pathological mourning and childhood mourning', *Journal of the American Psychoanalytical Association*, 11: 500.
Bowlby, J. (1969) *Attachment and Loss*, vol. 1, *Attachment*, London: Hogarth Press.
Bowlby, J. (1973) *Attachment and Loss*, vol. 2, *Separation: Anxiety and Anger*, London: Hogarth Press.
Bowlby, J. (1980) *Attachment and Loss*, vol. 3, *Loss: Sadness and Depression*, London: Hogarth Press.
Bowlby, J. and Parkes, C. M. (1970) 'Separation and loss within the family', in *The International Yearbook for Child Psychiatry and Allied Disciplines*, vol. 1, pp. 197–216; reprinted in E. J. Anthony (ed.) *The Child in his Family*, New York: Wiley.
Box, K. and Thomas, G. (1944) 'The war-time social survey', *Journal of the Royal Statistical Society*, 107.
Brandchaft, B., Doctors, S. and Sorter, D. (2010) *Towards an Emancipatory Psychoanalysis: Brandchaft's Vision*, London: Routledge.
Braudel, F. (1972/3) *The Mediterranean and the Mediterranean World in the Age of Philip II*, New York: Harper & Row.
Braudel, F. (1980) 'History and the social sciences. The *longue durée*', in *On History*. Chicago, IL: Chicago University Press.
Brenman Pick, I. (1985) 'Working through in the counter-transference', in E. Spillius (ed.) *Melanie Klein Today. Developments in Theory and Practice*, vol. 2, *Mainly Practice*, London and New York: Routledge, 1988, pp. 34–47.
Breuer, J. and Freud, S. (1893–5) *Studies on Hysteria. The Standard Edition of the Complete Psychological Works of Sigmund Freud*, trans. J. Strachey, London: Hogarth Press, vol. 2.
Britton, R. (1998) *Belief and Imagination: Explorations in Psychoanalysis*, London: Routledge.
Bromberg, P. (1979) 'Interpersonal psychoanalysis and regression', *Contemporary Psychoanalysis*, 15: 647–55.
Bromberg, P. (1995) 'Psychoanalysis, dissociation, and personality organization: reflections on Peter Goldberg's essay', *Psychoanalytic Dialogues*, 5: 511–28.
Bromberg, P. (1998) *Standing in the Spaces: Essays on Clinical Process, Trauma and Dissociation*, Hillsdale, NJ: The Analytic Press.

REFERENCES

Bromberg, P. (2006) *Awakening the Dreamer: Clinical Journeys*, Hillsdale, NJ: The Analytic Press.

Burgoine, E. (1988) 'A cross-cultural comparison of bereavement among widows in New Providence, Bahamas, and London, England', Paper read at an International Conference on Grief and Bereavement in Contemporary Society, London, July 12–15.

Burnham, J. (ed.) (2012) *After Freud Left: A Century of Psychoanalysis in America*, Chicago, IL: University of Chicago Press.

Byatt, A. S. (2009) *The Children's Book*, London: Chatto and Windus.

Canguilhem, G. (1955) 'The problem of regulation in the organism and in society', in *Writings on Medicine*, New York: Fordham University Press, 2012, pp. 67–78.

Canguilhem, G. (1966) *Le normal et le pathologique*; trans. C. R. Fawcett (1989) *The Normal and the Pathological*, New York: Zone Books.

Canguilhem, G. (1974) 'The development of the concept of biological regulation in the eighteenth and nineteenth centuries', in *Ideology and Rationality in the History of the Life Sciences*, Cambridge, MA: MIT Press, 1988, pp. 81–102.

Canguilhem, G. (1977) *Idéologie et rationalité dans l'histoire des sciences de la vie*; trans. A. Goldhammer (1988) *Ideology and Rationality in the History of the Life Sciences*, Cambridge, MA: MIT Press.

Cannon, W. (1926) 'Physiological regulation in normal states: some tentative postulates concerning biological homeostasis', reprinted in L. L. Langley (ed.) *Homeostasis: Origins of the Concept*, Stroudsburg: Dowden, Hutchinson and Ross, 1973.

Cartwright, A. (1983) *Health Surveys in Practice and in Potential: A Critical Review of their Scope and Methods*, London: King Edward's Hospital Fund for London.

Castel, R. (1984) *La gestion des risques: De l'anti-psychiatrie à l'après psychanalyse*, Paris: Editions de Minuit.

Castel, R. (1991) 'From dangerousness to risk', in G. Burchell, C. Gordon and P. Miller (eds) *The Foucault Effect: Studies in Governmentality*, Hemel Hempstead: Harvester Wheatsheaf, pp. 281–98.

Castel, R., Castel, F. and Lovell, A. (1979) *La societé psychiatrique avancée*, Paris: Editions Grasset.

Chamberlayne, P., Bornat, J. and Wengraf, T. (2000) *The Turn to Biographical Methods in Social Science*, London: Routledge.

Clarke, P. (2007) *The Last Thousand Days of the British Empire*, London: Allen Lane.

Clayton, P. J. (1979) 'The sequelae and nonsequelae of conjugal bereavement', *American Journal of Psychiatry*, 136: 1530–34.

Coltart, N. (1986) 'Slouching towards Bethlehem ... or thinking the unthinkable in psychoanalysis', in *Slouching Towards Bethlehem and Further Psychoanalytic Explorations*, London: Free Association Books, 1993, pp. 1–14.

Commission on Social Justice (1994) *Social Justice: Strategies for National Renewal*, London: Vintage Books.

Congdon, T. (2011) *Money in a Free Society: Keynes, Friedman, and the New Crisis in Capitalism*, New York: Encounter.

Cottingham, J. (1996) 'Partiality and the virtues', in R. Crisp (ed.) *How Should One Live? Essays on the Virtues*, Oxford: Clarendon, pp. 57–76.

Cottingham, J. (1998) *Philosophy and the Good Life: Reason and the Passions in Greek, Cartesian and Psychoanalytic Ethics*, Cambridge: Cambridge University Press.

Council of the Royal Medico-Psychological Association (1944) *Memorandum on Social Insurance and Allied Services in Their Bearing on Neurotic Disorder*, London: RMPA.

REFERENCES

Craib, I. (1998) *Experiencing Identity*, London: Sage.
Crisp, R. (ed.) (1996) *How Should One Live? Essays on the Virtues*, Oxford: Clarendon.
Crosland, C. A. R. (1956) *The Future of Socialism*, London: Jonathan Cape.
Dante (1315–21) *La Divina Commedia*; trans. P. Dale (1996) *The Divine Comedy*, London: Anvil Press Poetry.
Defert, D. (1991) '"Popular life" and insurance technology', in G. Burchell, C. Gordon and P. Miller (eds) *The Foucault Effect: Studies in Governmentality*, Hemel Hempstead: Harvester Wheatsheaf, pp. 211–33.
Deleuze, G. (2001) 'Immanence: a life', in *Pure Immanence: Essays on a Life*, New York: Zone Books, pp. 25–33.
Denzin, N. K. (1984) *On Understanding Emotion*, San Francisco: Jossey-Bass Publishers.
Descartes, R. (1641) *Meditationes de Prima Philosophiae*; trans. J. Cottingham, R. Stoothoff and D. Murdoch (1984) *Meditations on First Philosophy*, Cambridge: Cambridge University Press.
Didion, J. (2005) *The Year of Magical Thinking*, London: Faber and Faber.
Doka, K. (1989) *Disenfranchised Grief*, Lexington, MA: Lexington Books.
Donzelot, J. (1979) *The Policing of Families: Welfare versus the State*, London: Hutchinson.
Donzelot, J. (1991) 'The mobilization of society', in G. Burchell, C. Gordon and P. Miller (eds) *The Foucault Effect: Studies in Governmentality*, Hemel Hempstead: Harvester Wheatsheaf, pp. 169–79.
Donzelot, J. (1993) 'The promotion of the social', in M. Gane and T. Johnson (eds) *Foucault's New Domains*, London: Routledge, pp. 106–38.
Durkheim, É. (1893) *De la division du travail social*; trans. G. Simpson (1964) *The Division of Labour in Society*, New York: The Free Press.
Durkheim, É. (1895) *Les Règles de la méthode sociologique*; trans. W. D. Halls (1982) *The Rules of Sociological Method*, Basingstoke: Macmillan Press.
Durkheim, É. (1897) *Le Suicide*; trans. J. A. Spaulding and G. Simpson (1970) *Suicide: A Study in Sociology*, London: Routledge and Kegan Paul.
Durkheim, É. (1912) *Les formes élèmentaires de la vie religieuse*; trans. J. W. Swain (1976) *The Elementary Forms of the Religious Life*, London: George Allen and Unwin.
Durkheim, É. (1961) *Moral Education*, Glencoe, IL: Free Press.
Eigen, M. (1993) 'The area of faith in Winnicott, Lacan, and Bion', in *The Electrified Tightrope*, Northvale, NJ and London: Jason Aronson, pp. 109–38.
Elias, N. (1985) *The Loneliness of the Dying*, Oxford: Blackwell.
Elias, N. (2000) *The Civilizing Process*, Oxford: Blackwell.
Elias, N. (2001) *The Society of Individuals*, London: Continuum.
Eliot, T. S. (1927) 'A note on poetry and belief', *Enemy* I (January 1927).
Eliot, T. S. (1928) *The Sacred Wood: Essays on Poetry and Criticism*, 2nd edn, London: Faber and Faber.
Eliot, T. S. (1929) 'Dante', in *Selected Essays*, London: Faber and Faber, 1932, pp. 237–77.
Eliot, T. S. (1933) *The Use of Poetry and the Use of Criticism*, London: Faber and Faber.
Eliot, T. S. (1934) *After Strange Gods: A Primer of Modern Heresy*, London: Faber and Faber.
Eliot, T .S. (1948) *Notes towards a Definition of Culture*, London: Faber and Faber.
Eliot, T. S. (1964) *Knowledge and Experience in the Philosophy of F. H. Bradley*, London: Faber and Faber.

REFERENCES

Eliot, T. S. (1969) *The Complete Poems and Plays of T. S. Eliot*, London: Faber and Faber.

Emerson, P. and Frosh, S. (2009) *Critical Narrative Analysis in Psychology: A Guide to Practice*, 2nd edn, Basingstoke: Palgrave.

Engel, G. L. (1961) 'Is grief a disease? A challenge for medical research', *Psychosomatic Medicine*, 23: 18–22.

Erikson, E. H. (1946) 'Ego development and historical change – clinical notes', *Psychoanalytic Study of the Child*, 2: 359–96.

Erikson, E. H. (1950) *Childhood and Society*, London: Vintage, 1995.

Ewald, F. (1991) 'Insurance and risk', in G. Burchell, C. Gordon and P. Miller (eds) *The Foucault Effect: Studies in Governmentality*, Hemel Hempstead: Harvester Wheatsheaf, pp. 197–210.

Fagin, L. and Little, M. (1984) *The Forsaken Families*, Harmondsworth: Penguin Books.

Faimberg, H. (1981) '"Listening to listening": an approach to the study of narcissistic resistances', in *The Telescoping of Generations: Listening to the Narcissistic Links between Generations*. London: Routledge, 2005, pp. 19–30.

Feifel, H. (1959) *The Meaning of Death*, New York: McGraw-Hill.

Fonagy, P., Steele, H., Moran, G., Steele, M. and Higgitt, A. (1991) 'The capacity for understanding mental states: the reflective self in parent and child and its significance for security of attachment', *Infant Mental Health Journal*, 13: 200–17.

Fonagy, P., Leigh, T., Steele, M., Steele, H., Kennedy, R., Mattoon, G., Target, M. and Gerber, A. (1996) 'The relation of attachment status, psychiatric classification, and response to psychotherapy', *Journal of Consulting and Clinical Psychology*, 64: 22–31.

Fonagy, P., Gergely, G., Jurist, E. L. and Target, M. (2002) *Affect Regulation, Mentalization, and the Development of the Self*, New York: Other Books.

Foucault, M. (1961) *Folie et Déraison: Histoire de la folie à l'âge classique*; trans. J. Murphy and J. Khalfa (2006) *History of Madness*, London and New York: Routledge.

Foucault, M. (1963) *Naissance de la Clinique*; trans. A. Sheridan (1976) *The Birth of the Clinic: An Archaeology of Medical Perception*, London: Tavistock Publications.

Foucault, M. (1966) *Le Mots et les choses*; trans. A. Sheridan (1974) *The Order of Things: An Archaeology of the Human Sciences*, London: Tavistock Publications.

Foucault, M. (1975) *Surveiller et punir: Naissance de la prison*; trans. A. Sheridan (1979) *Discipline and Punish: The Birth of the Prison*, Harmondsworth: Penguin Books.

Foucault, M. (1976) *La Volonté de savoir*; trans. R. Hurley (1978) *The History of Sexuality*, vol. 1, *An Introduction*, London: Allen Lane.

Foucault, M. (1980) 'The politics of health in the eighteenth century', in C. Gordon (ed.) *Power/Knowledge: Selected Interviews and Other Writings 1972–1977*, Brighton: Harvester Press, pp. 166–82.

Foucault, M. (1982) 'The subject and power', in H. L. Dreyfus and P. Rabinow *Michel Foucault: Beyond Structuralism and Hermeneutics*, Chicago, IL: University of Chicago Press, pp. 208–26.

Foucault, M. (1989) 'Introduction', in G. Canguilhem *The Normal and the Pathological*, New York: Zone Books, pp. 7–24.

Foucault, M. (1991) 'Governmentality', in G. Burchell, C. Gordon and P. Miller (eds) *The Foucault Effect: Studies in Governmentality*, Hemel Hempstead: Harvester Wheatsheaf, pp. 87–104.

Foucault, M. (1997) *Il faut défendre la société: Cours au Collège de France*; trans. D. Macey (2003) *Society Must Be Defended: Lectures at the Collège de France, 1975–1976*, London: Allen Lane.

Foucault, M. (2000a) 'The birth of social medicine', in J. D. Faubion (ed.) *Power*, vol. 3, *Essential Works of Foucault 1954–1984*, New York: The New Press, pp. 134–56.

Foucault, M. (2000b) 'Governmentality', in J. D. Faubion. (ed.) *Power*, vol. 3, *Essential Works of Foucault 1954–1984*, New York: The New Press, pp. 201–22.

Foucault, M. (2000c) 'The subject and power', in J. D. Faubion (ed.) *Power*, vol. 3, *Essential Works of Foucault 1954–1984*, New York: The New Press, pp. 326–48.

Foucault, M. (2001) *L'Herméneutique du sujet: Cours au Collège de France*; trans. G. Burchell (2005) *The Hermeneutics of the Subject: Lectures at the Collège de France, 1981–1982*, Basingstoke: Palgrave Macmillian.

Foucault, M. (2004) *Sécurité, Territoire, Population: Cours au Collège de France*; trans. G. Burchell (2007) *Security, Territory, Population: Lectures at the Collège de France, 1977–1978*, Basingstoke: Palgrave Macmillian.

Fournier, M. (2007) *Émile Durkheim*; trans. D. Macey (2013) *Émile Durkheim: A Biography*, Cambridge: Polity Press.

Freedman, J. and Combs, G. (1996) *Narrative Therapy: The Social Construction of Preferred Realities*, New York: W. W. Norton.

Freud, S. (1887–1904) *The Complete Letters of Sigmund Freud to Wilhelm Fliess*; trans. J. Masson (1985), Cambridge, MA: The Belknap Press of Harvard University.

Freud, S. (1892–4) 'Preface and footnotes to the translation of Charcot's *Tuesday Lectures*', *The Standard Edition of the Complete Psychological Works of Sigmund Freud*, trans. J. Strachey, London: Hogarth Press, 1953–74 (hereafter '*Standard Edition*'), vol. 1: 127–43.

Freud, S. (1895) *Project for a Scientific Psychology. Standard Edition*, vol. 1: 281–397.

Freud, S. (1900) *The Interpretation of Dreams. Standard Edition*, vols 4 and 5.

Freud, S. (1905) *Three Essays on the Theory of Sexuality. Standard Edition*, vol. 7: 121–245.

Freud, S. (1910) *Leonardo da Vinci and a Memory of His Childhood. Standard Edition*, vol. 11: 55–137.

Freud, S. (1911a) 'Formulations on the two principles of mental functioning', *Standard Edition*, vol. 12: 210–26.

Freud, S. (1911b) 'Psychoanalytic notes on an autobiographical account of a case of paranoia (dementia paranoides)', *Standard Edition*, vol. 12: 1–82.

Freud, S. (1911c) 'The handling of dream-interpretation in psychoanalysis', *Standard Edition*, vol. 12: 87–96.

Freud, S. (1913) 'The disposition to obsessional neurosis: a contribution to the problem of choice of neurosis', *Standard Edition*, vol. 12: 311–26.

Freud, S. (1914) 'Remembering, repeating and working-through', *Standard Edition*, vol. 12: 145–56.

Freud, S. (1915a) 'The unconscious', *Standard Edition*, vol. 14: 159–215.

Freud, S. (1915b) 'Thoughts for the times on war and death', *Standard Edition*, vol. 14: 273–302.

Freud, S. (1916–17) *Introductory Lectures on Psycho-Analysis. Standard Edition*, vols 15–16.

Freud, S. (1917) 'Mourning and melancholia', *Standard Edition*, vol. 14: 237–60.

Freud, S. (1920) *Beyond the Pleasure Principle. Standard Edition*, vol. 18: 7–64.

Freud, S. (1921) *Group Psychology and the Analysis of the Ego. Standard Edition*, vol. 18: 65–143.

Freud, S. (1923) *The Ego and the Id. Standard Edition*, vol. 19: 12–66.

REFERENCES

Freud, S. (1926a) *Inhibitions, Symptoms and Anxiety. Standard Edition*, vol. 20: 75–175.
Freud, S. (1926b) *The Question of Lay Analysis. Standard Edition*, vol. 20: 176–258.
Freud, S. (1927) *The Future of an Illusion. Standard Edition*, vol. 21: 1–56.
Freud, S. (1930) *Civilization and Its Discontents. Standard Edition*, vol. 21: 57–145.
Freud, S. (1933a) *New Introductory Lectures on Psychoanalysis. Standard Edition*, vol. 22: 1–182.
Freud, S. (1933b) 'Why war?' *Standard Edition*, vol. 22: 197–215.
Freud, S. (1937) 'Constructions in analysis'. *Standard Edition*, vol. 23: 255–69.
Freud, S. (1940) *An Outline of Psychoanalysis. Standard Edition*, vol. 23: 139–207.
Fulgencio, L. (2007) 'Winnicott's rejection of the basic concepts of Freud's metapsychology', *International Journal of Psychoanalysis*, 88: 443–61.
Fulton, R. (1963) *The Sacred and the Secular: Attitudes of the American Public Toward Death*, Milwaukee, WI: Bulfin Printers.
Furedi, F. (2004) *Therapy Culture: Cultivating Vulnerability in an Uncertain Age*, London: Routledge.
Gardner, H. (1949) *The Art of T. S. Eliot*, London: Cresset Press.
Gardner, H. (1978) *The Composition of Four Quartets*, London: Faber and Faber.
Gardner, S. (2012) 'Psychoanalytic theory: a historical reconstruction', in *Proceedings of the Aristotelian Society Supplementary Volume*, 86: 41–60.
Garfinkel, H. (2002) *Ethnomethodology's Program: Working out Durkheim's Aphorism*, Lanham, MD: Rowan & Littlefield Publishers.
Girard, M. (2010) 'Winnicott's foundation for the basic concepts of Freud's metapsychology?' *International Journal of Psychoanalysis*, 91: 305–24.
Glaser, B. G. and Strauss, A. L. (1965) *Awareness of Dying*, Chicago, IL: Aldine.
Glick, I. O. Weiss, R. S. and Parkes, C. M. (1974) *The First Year of Bereavement*, New York: Wiley.
Golan, N. (1975) 'Wife to widow to woman', *Social Work*, 20: 369–74.
Goldberg, P. (1995) '"Successful" dissociation, pseudovitality, and inauthentic use of the senses', *Psychoanalytic Dialogues*, 5: 493–510.
Goldman, D. (1993) *In Search of the Real: The Origins and Originality of D. W. Winnicott*, Northvale, NJ: Jason Aronson.
Goldman, D. (2012) 'Vital sparks and the form of things unknown', in J. Abram (ed.) *Donald Winnicott Today*, London: Routledge, 2013, pp. 331–57.
Goldstein, K. (1933) 'L'analyse de l'aphasie et l'étude de l'essence du langage', *Journal de Psychologie*, 30: 430–96.
Gordon, C. (1980) 'Afterword', in C. Gordon (ed.) *Michel Foucault: Power/Knowledge: Selected Interviews and Other Writings 1972–1977*, Brighton: Harvester Press, pp. 227–58.
Gorer, G. (1965) *Death, Grief, and Mourning in Contemporary Britain*, London: Cresset.
Green, A. (1966–7) 'Primary narcissism: structure or state?', in *Life Narcissism Death Narcissism*, London: Free Association Books, 2001, pp. 48–90.
Green, A. (1975) 'Potential space in psychoanalysis: the object in the setting', in *On Private Madness*. London: Hogarth Press, 1986, pp. 277–96.
Green, A. (1983) 'The dead mother', in *On Private Madness*, London: Hogarth Press, 1986, pp. 142–73.
Green, A. (1999) 'The Greening of psychoanalysis: André Green in dialogues with Gregorio Kohon', in G. Kohon (ed.) *The Dead Mother: The Work of André Green*, London: Routledge, pp. 10–58.

REFERENCES

Green, A. (2001) *Life Narcissism Death Narcissism*, London: Free Association Books.

Green, A. (2002) *Time in Psychoanalysis: Some Contradictory Aspects*, London: Free Association Books.

Green, A. (2005) *Psychoanalysis: A Paradigm for Clinical Thinking*, London: Free Association Books.

Green, A. (2012) 'On constructions in Freud's work', *International Journal of Psychoanalysis*, 93: 1238–48.

Grinberg, L. (1964) 'Two kinds of guilt: their relationship with normal/pathological aspects of mourning', *International Journal of Psychoanalysis*, 45: 366.

Groarke, S. (2003) 'A life's work: on Rodman's *Winnicott*', *Free Associations*, 10 (4): 472–97.

Groarke, S. (2010a) 'Making contact', *The International Journal of Infant Observation and its Applications*, 13 (2): 209–22.

Groarke, S. (2010b) 'Unthinkable experience: Winnicott's ontology of disaster and hope', *American Imago*, 67 (3): 399–429.

Gurevich, H. (2008) 'The language of absence', *International Journal of Psychoanalysis*, 89: 561–78.

Habermas, J. (1984) *The Theory of Communicative Action*, vol. 1, *Reason and the Rationalization of Society*, Boston, MA: Beacon Press.

Habermas, J. (1987) *The Theory of Communicative Action*, vol. 2, *Lifeworld and System: A Critique of Functionalist Reason*, Boston, MA: Beacon Press.

Habermas, J. (2003) 'Faith and knowledge', in J. Habermas, *The Future of Human Nature*, Cambridge: Polity Press, pp. 101–15.

Habermas, J. (2008) *Between Naturalism and Religion*. Cambridge: Polity Press.

Habermas, J. (2010) *An Awareness of What is Missing: Faith and Reason in a Post-Secular Age*, Cambridge: Polity Press.

Hacking, I. (1975) *The Emergence of Probability*, Cambridge: Cambridge University Press.

Hacking, I. (1990) *The Taming of Chance*, Cambridge: Cambridge University Press.

Haidt, J. (2012) *The Righteous Mind: Why Good People Are Divided by Politics and Religion*, London: Allen Lane.

Harding, D. W. (1963) *Experience into Words*, London: Chatto and Windus.

Heaney, S. (1995) *The Redress of Poetry: Oxford Lectures*, London: Faber and Faber.

Heaney, S. (1996) 'Keeping going', in *The Spirit Level*, London: Faber and Faber, pp. 10–12.

Heidegger, M. (1919) *Zur Bestimmung der Philosophie*; trans. T. Sadler (2000) *Towards the Definition of Philosophy*, London: Athlone Press.

Heidegger, M. (1927) *Sein und Zeit*; trans. J. Macquarrie and E. Robinson (1962) *Being and Time*, Oxford: Basil Blackwell.

Heidegger, M. (1962) 'Preface', in W. J. Richardson, SJ, 3rd edn, *Heidegger: Through Phenomenology to Thought*, The Hague: Martinus Nijhoff, 1974, pp. vii–xxiii.

Heidegger, M. (1988) *Gesamtausgabe*, vol. 63, K. Bröcker-Oltmanns (ed.) *Ontologie (Hermeneutik der Faktizität)*, Frankfurt am Main: Klostermann.

Heidegger, M. (1989) *Gesamtausgabe*, vol. 65, F.W. von Hermann (ed.) *Beiträge zur Philosophie (Vom Ereignis)*, Frankfurt am Main: Klostermann.

Hilliard, C. (2012) *English as a Vocation: The 'Scrutiny' Movement*, Oxford: Oxford University Press.

Hirst, P. (1975) *Durkheim, Bernard and Epistemology*, London: Routledge.

REFERENCES

Hirst, P. and Woolley, P. (1982) *Social Relations and Human Attributes*, London: Tavistock Publications.

Hochschild, A. R. (1983) *The Managed Heart: Commercialization of Human Feeling*, Berkeley, CA: University of California Press.

Hoffman, M. (2004) 'From enemy combatant to strange bedfellow: the role of religious narratives in the work of W. R. D. Fairbairn and D. W. Winnicott', *Psychoanalytic Dialogues*, 14: 769–804.

Holmes, J. (1993) *John Bowlby and Attachment Theory*, London: Routledge.

Honneth, A. (1995) *The Struggle for Recognition: The Moral Grammar of Social Conflicts*, Cambridge: Polity Press.

Honneth, A. (2012) *The I in We: Studies in the Theory of Recognition*, Cambridge: Polity.

Hopkins, B. (1989) 'Jesus and object-use: a Winnicottian account of the resurrection myth', *International Review of Psycho-Analysis*, 16: 93–100.

Hopkins, B. (1997) 'Winnicott and the capacity to believe', *International Journal of Psychoanalysis*, 78: 485–97.

Houghton, P. and Houghton, D. (1977) *Unfocused Grief: Responses to Childlessness*, Birmingham: The Birmingham Settlement.

Howell, E. (2005) *The Dissociative Mind*, Hillsdale, NJ: The Analytic Press.

Hughes, J. (1989) *Reshaping the Psychoanalytic Domain: The Work of Melanie Klein, W. R. D. Fairbairn, and D. W. Winnicott*, Berkeley, CA: University of California Press.

Hume, D. (1740) *A Treatise of Human Nature*, Books II and III, London: Fontana, 1972.

Husserl, E. (1907) *Die Idee der Phänomenologie*; trans. L. Hardy (1999) *The Idea of Phenomenology*, Dordrecht: Kluwer Academic Publishers.

Husserl, E. (1913) *Idee zu einer reinen Phänomenologie und phänomenologischen Philosophie, I. Buch*; trans. F. Kersten (1983) *Ideas Pertaining to a Pure Phenomenology and to Phenomenological Philosophy, First Book*, Dordrecht: Kluwer Academic Publishers.

Isaacs, S. (ed.) (1941) *The Cambridge Evacuation Survey: A Wartime Study in Social Welfare and Education*, London: Methuen.

Janet, P. (1889) *L'automatisme psychologique*, Paris: Alcan.

Janet, P. (1892) *Névroses et idées fixes*, Paris: Alcan.

Janet, P. (1893–4) *Etat mental des hystériques*, 2 vols, Paris: Bibliothèque medical Charcot-Delbove.

Janet, P. (1903) *Les obsessions et la psychasthénie*, 2 vols, Paris: Alcan.

Kahr, B. (1996) *D. W. Winnicott: A Biographical Portrait*, London: Karnac Books.

Kaminer, H. and Lavie, P. (1993) 'Sleep and dreams in well-adjusted and less adjusted Holocaust survivors', in M. S. Stroebe, W. Stroebe and R. O. Hansson (eds) *Handbook of Bereavement*, Cambridge: Cambridge University Press, pp. 331–4.

Kearl, M. C. (1989) *Endings: A Sociology of Death and Dying*, Oxford: Oxford University Press.

Kemper, T. D. (1978) *A Social Interactional Theory of Emotion*, New York: John Wiley.

Kennedy, R. (1987) 'Work of the day: aspects of work with families at the Cassel Hospital', in R. Kennedy, A. Heymans and L. Tischler (eds) *The Family as In-patient: Families and Adolescents at the Cassel Hospital*, London: Free Association Books, pp. 27–48.

Kennedy, R. (1993) *Freedom to Relate: Psychoanalytic Explorations*, London: Free Association Books.

Khan, M. (1979) *Alienation in Perversions*, London: Hogarth Press.

REFERENCES

Khan, M. (1981) *The Privacy of the Self*, London: Hogarth Press.
Khan, M. (1983) *Between Theory and Practice in Psychoanalysis*, London: Hogarth Press.
King, P. and Steiner, R. (1991) *The Freud-Klein Controversies 1941–45*, London: Routledge.
Kirschner, S. (1996) *The Religious and Romantic Origins of Psychoanalysis: Individuation and Integration in Post-Freudian Theory*, Cambridge: Cambridge University Press.
Kitson, G. (1982) 'Attachment to the spouse in divorce: A scale and its application', *Journal of Marriage and the Family*, May: 379–93.
Klein, M. (1940) 'Mourning and its relation to manic-depressive states', in *Love, Guilt and Reparation and Other Works 1921–1945*, London: Hogarth Press, 1981, pp. 344–69.
Kleinman, A. (2012) 'Culture, bereavement, and psychiatry', *The Lancet*, 379: 608–9.
Kristeva, J. (1991) *Strangers to Ourselves*, New York: Harvester Wheatsheaf.
Krystal, H. (1968) *Massive Psychic Trauma*, New York: International Universities Press.
Kübler-Ross, E. (1973) *On Death and Dying*, London: Tavistock Publications.
Kuipers, L. and Bebbington, P. (1991) *Working in Partnership: Clinicians and Carers in the Management of Long-Term Mental Illness*, London: Heinemann.
Kynaston, D. (2007) *Austerity Britain, 1945–1951*, London: Bloomsbury.
Lacan, J. (1949) 'The mirror stage as formative of the *I* function as revealed in psychoanalytic experience', in *Écrits*, New York: W. W. Norton, 2006, pp. 75–81.
Lacan, J. (1953) 'The function and field of speech and language in psychoanalysis', in *Écrits*, New York: W. W. Norton, 2006, pp. 197–268.
Lacan, J. (1954) 'Response to Jean Hyppolite's commentary on Freud's "*Verneinung*"', in *Écrits*, New York: W. W. Norton, 2006, pp. 318–33.
Lacan, J. (1959) 'On a question prior to any possible treatment of psychosis', in *Écrits*, New York: W. W. Norton, 2006, pp. 445–88.
LaFarge, L. (2012) 'The screen memory and the act of remembering', *International Journal of Psychoanalysis*, 93: 1249–65.
Lear, J. (1992) *Love and Its Place in Nature*, London: Faber and Faber.
Leavis, F. R. (1932) *New Bearings in English Poetry: A Study of the Contemporary Situation*, reprinted with 'Retrospect 1950' 1950, Harmondsworth: Penguin Books, 1972.
Lewis, A. (1935) 'Neurosis and unemployment', *The Lancet*, 2: 293–97.
Lewis, A. (1942) 'Incidence of neurosis in England under war conditions', *The Lancet*, 2: 175–83.
Lewis, A. (1943a) 'Social effects of neurosis', *The Lancet*, 2: 167–70.
Lewis, A. (1943b) 'Mental health in war-time', *Public Health*, 57: 27–30.
Lewis, A. (1945a) 'Psychiatric investigations in Britain', *American Journal of Psychiatry*, 101 (4): 486–93.
Lewis, A. (1945b) 'The industrial resettlement of the neurotic', *Labour Management*, 27: 40–3.
Lewis, A. (1945c) 'Psychiatric advice in industry', *British Journal of Industrial Medicine*, 2: 41–2.
Lewis, A. (1951) 'Social aspects of psychiatry', *Edinburgh Medical Journal*, LVIII: 214–47.
Lewis, A. (1957) 'Social psychiatry', in *Lectures on the Scientific Basis of Medicine*, London: Athlone Press.
Lewis, A. (1962) 'Ebb and flow in social psychiatry', *Yale Journal of Biology and Medicine*, 35: 62–83.

REFERENCES

Lewis, A. and Goldschmidt, H. (1943) 'Social causes of admissions to a mental hospital for the aged', *Sociological Review*, 35: 86–98.
Lewis, A. and Goodyear, K. (1944) 'Vocational aspects of neurosis in soldiers', *The Lancet*, 2: 105–9.
Lewis, A. and Slater, E. (1942) 'Neurosis in soldiers: a follow-up study', *The Lancet*, 1: 496–8.
Lewis, J. (1980) *The Politics of Motherhood, Child and Maternal Welfare in England 1900–1939*, London: Croom Helm.
Little, M. (1986) *Transference Neurosis and Transference Psychosis: Towards Basic Unity*, London: Free Association Books and Maresfield Library.
Little, M. (1990) *Psychotic Anxieties and Containment: A Personal Record of an Analysis with Winnicott*, Northvale, NJ: Jason Aronson.
Loewald, H. W. (1966) 'Review: Max Schur, *The Id and the Regulatory Principles of Mental Function*', in *The Essential Loewald: Collected Papers and Monographs*, Hagerstown, MD: University Publishing, 2000, pp. 58–68.
Logan, W. P. D. and Brooke, E. M. (1957) *The Survey of Sickness 1943 to 1952*, General Register Office Studies in Medical and Population Subjects, no. 12, London: HMSO.
Longuenesse, B. (2012) 'Kant's "I" in "I ought to" and Freud's superego', *Proceedings of the Aristotelian Society Supplementary*, 86: 19–39.
Lovell, D. M., Hemmings, G. and Hill, A. B. (1993) 'Bereavement reactions of female Scots and Swazis: a preliminary comparison', *British Journal of Medical Psychology*, 66 (3): 259–74.
Lukes, S. (1975) *Émile Durkheim: His Life and Work*, Harmondsworth: Penguin Books.
MacIntyre, A. (1985) *After Virtue*, 2nd edn, London: Duckworth.
Macmurray, J. (1936) *The Structure of Religious Experience*, London: Faber and Faber.
Macmurray, J. (1949) *Conditions of Freedom*, London: Faber and Faber.
Main, M., Kaplan, N. and Cassidy, J. (1985) 'Security in infancy, childhood and adulthood: a move to the level of representation' in 'Growing points of attachment theory and research', I. Bretherton and E. Waters (eds) *Monographs of the Society for Research in Child Development*, 50: 66–104.
Maker, E. L. (1982) 'Anomic aspects of recovery from cancer', *Social Science and Medicine*, 16: 907.
Marion, J.-L. (1998) *Reduction and Givenness: Investigations of Husserl, Heidegger, and Phenomenology*, Evanston, IL: Northwestern University Press.
Marion, J.-L. (1999) *Cartesian Questions: Method and Metaphysics*, Chicago: The University of Chicago Press.
Marion, J.-L. (2011) *The Reason of the Gift*, Charlottesville, VA: University of Virginia Press.
Marshall, T. H. (1949) 'Citizenship and Social Class', in *Sociology at the Crossroads, and other essays*. London: Heinemann, 1963, pp. 67–127.
Martin, J. (1988) 'Psychological consequences of AIDS-related bereavement among gay men', *Journal of Consulting and Clinical Psychology*, 56: 856–62.
Martin, J. and Dean, L. (1993) 'Bereavement following death from AIDS: unique problems, reactions, and special needs', in M. S. Stroebe, W. Stroebe and R. O. Hansson (eds) *Handbook of Bereavement*, Cambridge: Cambridge University Press, pp. 217–30.
Marty, P. (1976) *Les mouvements individuels de vie et de mort*, Paris: Payot.
Matthiessen, F. O. (1947) *The Achievement of T. S. Eliot: An Essay on the Nature of Poetry*, Oxford: Oxford University Press.

REFERENCES

McGinley, E. (2012) 'Mourning or melancholia?' *New Associations*, 10: 2–3.

Meissner, W. W. (1984) *Psychoanalysis and Religious Experience*, New Haven, CT: Yale University Press.

Mellor, P. A. (1993) 'Death in high modernity: the contemporary presence and absence of death', in D. Clark (ed.) *The Sociology of Death: Theory, Culture, Practice*, Oxford: Blackwell/Sociological Review, pp. 11–30.

Mellor, P. A. and Shilling, C. (1993) 'Modernity, self-identity and the sequestration of death'. *Sociology*, 27, 3: 411–31.

Menand, L. (2007) *Discovering Modernism: T. S. Eliot and His Context*, 2nd edn, Oxford: Oxford University Press.

Merleau-Ponty, M. (1945) *Phenomenology of Perception*, London: Routledge, 1962.

Michalski, K. (ed.) (2006a) *Conditions of European Solidarity*, vol. 1, *What Holds Europe Together?* Budapest and New York: Central European University Press.

Michalski, K. (ed.) (2006b) *Conditions of European Solidarity*, vol. 2, *Religion in the New Europe*, Budapest and New York: Central European University Press.

Miller, P. and Roes, N. (1990) 'Governing economic life', *Economy and Society*, 25 (3): 327–56; reprinted in P. Miller and N. Rose (2008) *Governing the Present*, Cambridge: Polity Press.

Milner, M. (1972) 'Winnicott and the two-way journey', in *The Suppressed Madness of Sane Men: Forty-Four Years of Exploring Psychoanalysis*, London: Tavistock Publications, 1987, pp. 246–52.

Milner, M. (1977) 'Winnicott and overlapping circles', in *The Suppressed Madness of Sane Men: Forty-Four Years of Exploring Psychoanalysis*, London: Tavistock Publications, 1987, pp. 279–86.

Ministry of Health (1944) *Hostels for 'Difficult' Children*, London: HMSO.

Mitchell, S. (1993) *Hope and Dread in Psychoanalysis*, New York: Basic Books.

Mitford, J. (1963) *The American Way of Death*, New York: Simon and Schuster.

Morris, J. N. (1957) *Uses of Epidemiology*, Edinburgh and London: E. and S. Livingston.

Munoz, L. (1980) 'Exile as bereavement: socio-psychological manifestations of Chilean exiles in Britain', *British Journal of Medical Psychology*, 53: 227–32.

Oakeshott, M. (1975) *On Human Conduct*, Oxford: Oxford University Press.

Oates, J. C. (2011) *A Widow's Story: A Memoir*, New York: Ecco Press.

Ogden, T. (1986) *The Matrix of the Mind: Object Relations and the Psychoanalytic Dialogue*, Northvale, NJ: Jason Aronson.

Ogden, T. (1989) *The Primitive Edge of Experience*, Northvale, NJ: Jason Aronson.

Ogden, T. (1992) 'The dialectically constituted/decentred subject of psychoanalysis: II. The contributions of Klein and Winnicott', *International Journal of Psychoanalysis*, 73: 613–26.

Ogden, T. (2001) 'Reading Winnicott', in *Conversations at the Frontier of Dreaming*, London: Karnac Books, pp. 203–35.

Ogden, T. (2004) 'On holding and containing, being and dreaming', *International Journal of Psychoanalysis*, 85: 1349–64.

Osborne, T. (1994) 'On anti-medicine and clinical reason', in G. Jones and R. Porter (eds) *Reassessing Foucault: Power, Medicine and the Body*, London: Routledge, pp. 28–47.

Parker, S. E. (2012) *Winnicott and Religion*, Northvale, NJ: Jason Aronson.

Parsons, M. (2000) *The Dove that Returns, The Dove that Vanishes: Paradox and Creativity in Psychoanalysis*, London: Routledge.

REFERENCES

Parsons, T. (1958) 'Social structure and the development of personality: Freud's contribution to the integration of psychology and sociology', in *Social Structure and Personality*, New York: The Free Press, 1964, pp. 78–111.

Parsons, T., Shils, E. A. and Kluckhohn, C. (1951) *Towards a General Theory of Action*, Cambridge, MA: Harvard University Press.

Payne, M. (2006) *Narrative Therapy: An Introduction for Counsellors*, London: Sage.

Phillips, A. (1988) *Winnicott*, London: Fontana Press.

Prior, L. (1989) *The Social Organisation of Death*, London: Macmillan.

Rangell, L. (1955) 'On the psychoanalytic theory of anxiety: a statement of a unitary theory', *Journal of the American Psychoanalytic Association*, 55: 3–12.

Raphael, B. (1977) 'Preventive intervention with the recently bereaved', *Archives of General Psychiatry*, 34: 1450–4.

Rawls, J. (1971) *A Theory of Justice*, Cambridge, MA: Harvard University Press.

Ricoeur, P. (1969) *The Conflict of Interpretations*, Evanston, IL: Northwestern University Press, 1974.

Ricoeur, P. (1970) *Freud and Philosophy: An Essay on Interpretation*, New Haven, CT: Yale University Press.

Ricoeur, P. (2005) *The Course of Recognition*, Cambridge, MA: Harvard University Press.

Riley, D. (1983) *War in the Nursery: Theories of the Child and Mother*, London: Virago.

Rizzuto, A. M. (1979) *The Birth of the Living God*, Chicago, IL: University of Chicago Press.

Robertson, J. and Bowlby, J. (1952) 'Responses of young children to separation from their mothers', *Courier of the International Children's Centre, Paris*, II: 131–40.

Rodman, F. R. (2003) *Winnicott: Life and Work*, Perseus Publishing.

Rose, G. (1981) *Hegel contra Sociology*, London: Athlone.

Rose, G. (1993) *Judaism and Modernity: Philosophical Essays*, Oxford: Blackwell.

Rose, N. (1989) *Governing the Soul: The Shaping of the Private Self*, London: Routledge.

Rose, N. (1994) 'Medicine, history and the present', in C. Jones and R. Porter (eds) *Reassessing Foucault: Power, Medicine and the Body*, London: Routledge, pp. 48–72.

Rose, N. (1996a) 'The death of the social? Refiguring the territory of government', *Economy and Society*, 25 (3): 327–56; reprinted in P. Miller and N. Rose (2008) *Governing the Present*, Cambridge: Polity Press.

Rose, N. (1996b) 'Governing "advanced" liberal democracies', in A. Barry, T. Osborne and N. Rose (eds) *Foucault and Political Reason: Liberalism, Neo-Liberalism and Rationalities of Government*, London: UCL Press, pp. 37–64; reprinted in P. Miller and N. Rose (2008) *Governing the Present*, Cambridge: Polity Press.

Rose, N. and Miller, P. (1992) 'Political power beyond the state: problematics of government', *British Journal of Sociology*, 43 (2): 173–205; reprinted in P. Miller and N. Rose (2008) *Governing the Present*. Cambridge: Polity Press.

Rosenblatt, P. C. (1993) 'Grief: the social context of private feelings', in M. S. Stroebe, W. Stroebe and R. O. Hansson (eds) *Handbook of Bereavement*, Cambridge: Cambridge University Press, pp. 102–11.

Rosenblatt, P. C., Walsh, R. P. and Jackson D. A. (1976) *Grief and Mourning in Cross-cultural Perspective*, New York: HRAF Press.

Rosenblatt, P. C., Spoentgen, P., Karis, T. A., Dahl, C., Kaiser, T. and Elde, C. (1991) 'Difficulties in supporting the bereaved', *Omega*, 23 (2): 119–28.

Roussillon, R. (2010) 'Winnicott's deconstruction of primary narcissism', *International Journal of Psychoanalysis*, 91: 821–37.

Roussillon, R. (2011) *Primitive Agony and Symbolization*, London: Karnac.
Royal Commission on the National Health Service (Merrison Commission) (1979) Cmnd. 7615, London: HMSO.
Rudnytsky, P. (2011) *Rescuing Psychoanalysis from Freud and Other Essays in Re-vision*, London: Karnac.
Rustin, M. (2001) 'A biographical turn in social science?' in *Reason and Unreason: Psychoanalysis, Science and Politics*, London: Continuum, pp. 88–109.
Rycroft, C. (1955) 'On idealization, illusion, and catastrophic disillusion', in *Imagination and Reality*, London: Maresfield Library, 1987, pp. 29–41.
Rycroft, C. (1966) 'Causes and meaning', in P. Fuller (ed.) *Psychoanalysis and Beyond*, London: Chatto and Windus, 1985, pp. 41–51.
Ryle, J. A. (1948) *Changing Disciplines*, London: Oxford University Press.
Sandel, M. (2012) *What Money Can't Buy: The Moral Limits of the Market*, London: Allen Lane.
Sartre, J.-P. (1943) *Being and Nothingness: An Essay on Phenomenological Ontology*, London: Methuen, 1958.
Schafer, R. (1992) *Retelling a Life*, New York: Basic Books.
Schene, A., Tessler, R. and Gamache, G. (1994) 'Instruments measuring family or care giver burden in severe mental illness', *Social Psychiatry and Psychiatric Epidemiology*, 29: 228–40.
Seale, C. (1998) *Constructing Death: The Sociology of Dying and Bereavement*, Cambridge: Cambridge University Press.
Sebald, W. G. (1998) *Logis in einem Landhaus*; trans. J. Catling (2013) *A Place in the Country*, London: Hamish Hamilton.
Selye, H. (1954) 'D'une révolution en pathologie', *La nouvelle revue française*, 1 March.
Selye, H. (1955) 'Stress and disease', *Science*, 122: 625–31.
Selye, H. (1956) *The Stress of Life*, New York: McGraw-Hill.
Selye, H. and Horava, A. (1950) *Annual Reports on Stress*. Montreal: Acta.
Sennett, R. (2012) *Together: The Rituals, Pleasures and Politics of Cooperation*, London: Allen Lane.
Sheldon, A. R., Cochrane, J., Vachon, M. L. S., Lyall, A. W., Rogers, J. and Freeman, S. J. J.(1981) 'A psychological analysis of risk of psychological impairment following bereavement', *Journal of Nervous and Mental Disease*, 169: 253–5.
Shepherd, M. (1979) 'From social medicine to social psychiatry: the achievement of Sir Aubrey Lewis', in C. Rosenberg (ed.) *Healing and History: Essays for George Rosen*, New York: Science History Publications, pp. 191–204.
Slater, P. (1947) *Survey of Sickness, October 1943 to December 1945: A Report on a Series of Surveys on the Health of the Civilian Population...Made for the Ministry of Health*, Great Britain: Central Office of Information, Social Survey Division.
Slochower, J. (1996) *Holding and Psychoanalysis: A Relational Approach*, Hillsdale, NJ: The Analytic Press.
Slochower, J. (2006) *Psychoanalytic Collisions*, Hillsdale, NJ: The Analytic Press.
Speedy, J. (2000) 'The "storied" helper: an introduction to narrative ideas in counselling and psychotherapy', *European Journal of Psychotherapy, Counselling and Health*, 3, 3: 361–75.
Spence, D. (1982) *Narrative Truth, Historical Truth*, New York: Norton.

REFERENCES

Spillius, E. B. (1988) 'Developments in technique: introduction', in *Melanie Klein Today: Developments in Theory and Practice*, vol. 2, *Mainly Practice*, London: Routledge, pp. 5–16.
Spurling, L. S. (2008) 'Is there still a place for the concept of "therapeutic regression" in psychoanalysis?' *International Journal of Psychoanalysis*, 89: 523–40.
Stern, D. B. (1997) *Unformulated Experience: From Dissociation to Imagination in Psychoanalysis*, Hillsdale, NJ: The Analytic Press.
Stern, D. N., Sander, L. W., Nahum, J. P., Harrison, A. M., Lyons-Ruth, K., Morgan, A. C., Bruschweilerstern, N. and Tronick, E. Z. (1998) 'Non-interpretive mechanisms in psychoanalytic therapy: the "something more" than interpretation', *International Journal of Psychoanalysis*, 79: 903–21.
Stocks, P. (1949) *Sickness in the Population of England and Wales 1944–1947*, General Register Office, Studies on Medical and Population Subjects, no. 2, London: HMSO.
Stolorow, R. (2011) *World, Affectivity, Trauma: Heidegger and Post-Cartesian Psychoanalysis*, London: Routledge.
Stroebe, M. S., Stroebe, W. and Hansson, R. O. (eds) (1993) *Handbook of Bereavement: Theory, Research, and Intervention*, Cambridge: Cambridge University Press.
Sudnow, D. (1967) *Passing On*, Upper Saddle River, NJ: Prentice Hall.
Suttie, I. (1935) *The Origins of Love and Hate*, London: Free Association Books, 1988.
Symington, N. (2004) *The Blind Man Sees: Freud's Awakening and Other Essays*, London: Karnac Books.
Symington, N. (2007) 'The patient makes the analyst', in *Becoming a Person through Psychoanalysis*, London: Karnac, pp. 27–49.
Symington, N. (2012a) *The Psychology of the Person*, London: Karnac.
Symington, N. (2012b) 'The essence of psycho-analysis as opposed to what is secondary', *Psychoanalytic Dialogues*, 22 (4): 395–409.
Szmukler, G. and Bloch, S. (1997) 'Family involvement in the care of people with psychosis', *British Journal of Psychiatry*, 171: 401–5.
Tauber, A. (2010) *Freud, the Reluctant Philosopher*, Princeton, NJ: Princeton University Press.
Tawney, R. H. (1921) *The Acquisitive Society*, London: Fontana, 1966.
Taylor, C. (2007) *A Secular Age*, Cambridge, MA: Harvard University Press.
Temple, W. (1926) *Personal Religion and the Life of Fellowship*, London: Longmans, Green & Co. Ltd.
Thornicroft, G. and Tansella, M. (1999) *The Mental Health Matrix: A Manual to Improve Services*, Cambridge: Cambridge University Press.
Titmuss, R. M. (1950) *Problems of Social Policy*, London: HMSO.
Titmuss, R. M. (1968) *Commitment to Welfare*, London: Allen and Unwin.
Tomalin, C. (2006) *Thomas Hardy: The Time-Torn Man*, London: Viking.
Tustin, F. (1985) 'The rhythm of safety', in *Autistic Barriers in Neurotic Patients*, London: Karnac Books, 1986, pp. 268–85.
Tustin, F. (1986) *Autistic Barriers in Neurotic Patients*, London: Karnac Books.
Virgil (29–19 BCE) *The Aeneid*; trans. R. Fitzgerald (1985), Harmondsworth: Penguin Books.
Walter, T. (1991) 'Modern death: taboo or not taboo?' *Sociology*, 25 (2): 293–310.
Welshman, J. (1999) 'Rhetoric and reality: community care in England and Wales, 1948–74' in P. Bartlett and D. Wright (eds) *Outside the Walls of the Asylum: The History of Care in the Community 1750–2000*, London: Athlone Press, pp. 204–26.

REFERENCES

Welshman, J. (2010) *Churchill's Children: The Evacuee Experience in Wartime Britain*, Oxford: Oxford University Press.

White, M. (2004) *Narrative Practice and Exotic Lives: Resurrecting Diversity in Everyday Life*, Adelaide: Dulwich Centre Publications.

White, M. and Epston, D. (1990) *Narrative Means to Therapeutic Ends*, New York: W. W. Norton.

Widlöcher, D. (2012) 'Winnicott and the acquisition of a freedom of thought', in J. Abram (ed.) *Donald Winnicott Today*, London: Routledge, 2013, pp. 235–49.

Williams, B. (1995) 'Replies', in J. Altham and R. Harrison (eds) *World, Mind, and Ethics: Essays on the Ethical Philosophy of Bernard Williams*, Cambridge: Cambridge University Press, pp. 185–224.

Williams, P., Keene, J. and Dermen, S. (eds) (2012) *Independent Psychoanalysis Today*, London: Karnac.

Williams, R. (2002) 'Has secularism failed?', in *Faith in the Public Square*, London: Bloomsbury, 2012, pp. 11–22.

Williams, R. (2004) 'Religious lives', in *Faith in the Public Square*, London: Bloomsbury, 2012, pp. 313–25.

Williams, R. (2007) *Tokens of Trust: An Introduction to Christian Belief*, London: Canterbury Press.

Williams, R. (2012) *Faith in the Public Square*, London: Bloomsbury.

Willmott, H. (2000) 'Death. So what? Sociology, sequestration and emancipation', *The Sociological Review*, 48 (4): 649–65.

Wilson, E. (1980) *Halfway to Paradise: Women in Post-war Britain 1945–1968*, London: Tavistock Publications.

Winnicott, C. (1980) 'Child care in Oxfordshire: an interview with Alan Cohen', in J. Kanter (ed.) *Face to Face with Children: The Life and Work of Clare Winnicott*, London: Karnac, 2004, pp. 127–41.

Wittgenstein, L. (1937–44) *Remarks on the Foundations of Mathematics*, Oxford: Basil Blackwell, 1978.

Wittgenstein, L. (1953) *Philosophical Investigations*, Oxford: Basil Blackwell, 1978.

Worden, J. (1991) *Grief Counselling and Grief Therapy: A Handbook for the Mental Health Practitioner*, London: Routledge.

Worden, J. and Silverman, P. (1989) 'Predicting grief responses', paper presented at the NHO Conference on Hospice Bereavement Care, Denver, August.

Wright, K. (1991) *Vision and Separation: Between Mother and Baby*, London: Free Association Books.

Wright, K. (2009) *Mirroring and Attunement: Self-Realization in Psychoanalysis and Art*, London: Routledge.

Yeats, W. B. (1921) 'The Second Coming', in Richard J. Finneran (ed.) *W. B. Yeats: The Poems*, London: Macmillan, 1984, p. 187.

Zaretsky, E. (2004) *Secrets of the Soul: A Social and Cultural History of Psychoanalysis*, New York: Alfred Knopf.

INDEX

abreaction 139–40, 144
absolute dependence 23
accommodation 33, 163
accountability of action 156, 157
adaptation 33, 61, 167
affectivity 160, 174–5, 177
agency 149, 158, 168, 194, 204
AIDS-related bereavement 115, 136, 212
Ainsworth, Mary 183
Alexander, Franz 35
Alvarez, Anne 21
America, history of psychoanalysis 79
American Psychiatric Association 111
amnesic memory 35
anal stage of development 167–8
anomie, and suicide 91, 92
anorexia 193
antisocial behaviour 5, 23, 24, 64, 65–6, 215; management of 68–74
anxiety 32; coping with 182–3, 184–9
Anzieu, Didier 52
Aristotle 205
Armstrong, David 102, 109, 110
Arnold, Matthew 43
Athill, Diana 6
attachment theory 90, 91, 92, 183–4, 199, 204–5
attunement 187
Auden, W. H. 43
autonomy 149, 150, 158, 190, 193, 194, 197, 198; and bereavement 123; in development 167–8; and welfare 204

Badio, Alain 2
Balint, Michael 51
basic trust 167, 168, 169, 170, 178
belief, and knowledge 171–5, 177

bereavement: categorization of 111; factors affecting outcome 127–8; traumatic 135–45; *see also* grief; mourning
Bereavement (Parkes) 86, 87, 88–9, 115
bereavement counselling 88, 129, 131
Bereavement Risk Index 131–2
bereavement studies 79, 84–5, 110, 132; *see also* Parkes, Colin Murray
Bethlem Royal and Maudsley Hospitals 87
Bethlem Study of bereavement 87–8, 119
Beveridge Report 104
Bick, Esther 52
biological psychiatry 82
Bion, Wilfred R. 186
Bollas, Christopher 19–20, 34, 37, 142
Bowlby, John 24–5, 72, 85, 89–90, 93, 121, 183
Braudel, Fernand 3
breakdown, fear of 34–5, 39, 52
Breuer, Josef 138, 139, 205
Britain: history of psychoanalysis 79; post-war 3, 4–5
Browning, Robert 43
Byatt, A. S. 59

Canguilhem, Georges 2–3, 33, 34, 35, 86, 94, 103, 157, 163
Caring for People (1989) 115
Cartwright, Ann 101
Castel, Robert 133
catastrophic disillusionment 21–4, 32–5, 40–1, 47, 52–6
Celtic Christianity 45
childhood, management of 6
Childhood and Society (Erikson) 165–7
children: deprived 6, 24–5, 68–74, 215; wartime evacuation of 8, 24–5, 67; *see also* infants

239

INDEX

Children Act (1948) 26, 67
civic liberalism 195
civilizing process 59
Commission on Social Justice (1994) 115
communication, patient and analyst 47–8
communion 17, 19, 47, 48, 58, 77, 173
community care 81, 85, 90, 92, 114–16, 130–1
community mourning 80, 90
community psychiatry 79, 114
competency 163, 164, 168, 176, 178, 182–3, 184; and welfare 196, 204
compliance 172
concern, capacity for 65
conduct, normative orders of 175–80
control society 158
convention 175–6
co-operation, decline of in modern life 161
Cottingham, John 205, 216, 217
Craib, Ian 85, 95
creativity 43–4; primary 7, 8, 42, 174, 177–8
crisis of trust 161–5, 184–5, 200
criterion of maturity: and evaluation of war 61–3; and poetry 42–3
Crosland, Anthony 204
culture, Freud's critique of 11–12, 13–14, 15
Curtis Committee 26, 67

daily life, deskilling of 161
daily routines 167, 170, 173, 176, 177, 189, 198
Dante 55
death, preoccupation with 79–80
death drive 13, 15, 59, 144
debt, to mother 75–6
deferred action *see* Nachträglichkeit
delinquency 25, 72
democracy 61, 62, 64–7, 165, 191–2; dialogic 191, 196, 203; emotional 192
democratic personal relationships 192
demoralization 202, 215
dependence: acceptance of 75–6; infant's on mother 18; levels of 23
depression 82, 111
deprivation 23, 24, 68, 69
deprived children 6, 24–5, 68–74, 215
destructiveness 62–3
detraditionalization 164–5
development, Erikson's schema 167–9
Diagnostic and Statistical Manual of Mental Disorders (DSM) 111, 113

dialectic of disaster and hope 5–9, 37, 191; *see also* failure of life; reclamation
dialogic democracy 191, 196, 203
Didion, Joan 129
disability, and grief 112
disaster: infant's 21–4, 32–5, 40–1, 47, 52–6; *see also* dialectic of disaster and hope
disclosure, intimate 136, 145, 187–8, 212
disenchantment 197–8
disenfranchised grief 136
disillusionment, catastrophic 21–4, 32–5, 40–1, 47, 52–6
doctors, role in bereavement 117–18, 129, 130
Donzelot, Jacques 6, 91, 116
duality of structure 156, 160
Durkheim, Émile: and Giddens 152–3, 155, 156, 158–9, 161, 173, 196–7, 201; and Parkes 86, 91–3, 97–100, 103, 109–10
dwelling 16, 17, 18
dying, and grief 112

early routines 177–9
early trauma 21–4, 32–5, 40–1, 47, 52–6
Ego and the Id, The (Freud) 10, 11, 13
ego-identity 165–9, 170
egoism, and suicide 91
Eigen, Michael 41
Elias, Norbert 155
Eliot, T. S. 32, 39, 40, 41–2, 43, 45, 47; purgatorial process 54–6; social criticism 64–5, 66
emotional development 15–20, 21; *see also* maternal love
emotional discharge 139–40
encapsulated memory 35, 36, 53–4
English literature 7
English Romanticism 32, 39, 43, 45, 46
entitlements, unconditional 195, 203, 204, 207
environment, importance of 8
environment mother 15, 17, 35
environmental failure 20–4, 27, 32–5, 52
environmental provision 69, 70–1, 72–4
epidemiology 100–5
Erikson, Erik H. 165–70
escape, therapeutic 144–5
ethical life, Freud's critique of 13–14, 62
ethical life-plans 191, 202
ethical socialism 203, 204–5
evacuation of children, wartime 8, 24–5, 67

240

INDEX

facial recognition 18
failure–dissociation model 32–5
failure of life 21–4, 32–5, 40–1, 47, 52–6
faith 6–7, 8, 20, 201; and knowledge 171–5, 177; therapy as an act of 35–9
family: and bereavement 90, 114–16, 212; leaving and returning 77
family doctors, role in bereavement 117–18, 129, 130
fathers 16, 76
fear of breakdown 34–5, 39, 52
fear of women 74–5
Fonagy, Peter 154, 155, 183, 193, 199
forgiveness 24
foster homes 25
Foucault, Michel 2, 98, 102, 108, 116, 132–3; disciplinary society 158; nature of war 3; power 4, 5, 26–7
free association 37
freedom 61, 62, 200
freezing 33, 34
Freud, Sigmund 35, 46, 135, 194, 210; anxiety 185; bereavement 119–20, 121–3; common unhappiness 205; critique of culture 11–12, 13–14, 15; critique of morality 13–14, 62; critique of religion 11–12, 13, 171; Erikson's revision of 165–6, 167–9; and Kant 160; memories 53, 138; Nachträglichkeit 31; psychological trauma 137, 138–41, 143–5, 212; psychosexual development 76, 167–8, 169; remembering 48, 49; self-knowledge 214; sociological themes 10–11, 59–60; unconscious 162–3; view of psychosis 53; war 59–60
Furedi, Frank 96
Future of an Illusion, The (Freud) 11, 13

Gardner, Helen 41, 47
Gardner, Sebastian 160, 214
general practitioners, role in bereavement 117–18, 129, 130
generative governance 202–7
genital stage of development 168
Giddens, Anthony 93, 149–53, 154–5, 182–4, 211, 212–14; coping with anxiety 184–9; and Erikson 167, 168–70; faith and knowledge 171, 173, 174–5; narrative frame of reference 189–95, 213; normative orders of conduct 175–80; political argument 164–5, 191–2, 195–207;

social facts and reflexive norms 155–61; sociological appropriation of psychoanalysis 160, 161–4, 177–80, 199; structuration 150, 156, 160, 179–80, 183; utopian realism 183, 184, 198–9, 200, 202–7, 213; and Winnicott 177–9
globalization 164
Goffman, Erving 170
Goldstein, Kurt 34
good-enough mother 20, 22
good life 210
government intervention 26–8, 67, 91
grammatical propositions 176, 177
Green, André 35, 37, 38, 40, 49
grief 22, 79–80, 211–12; active and passive responses 94–5; biological theory of 89–90; calculation of risk 131–5; categorization of 111–13; disenfranchised 136; as emotional reaction to loss 82; expression of 135; normal and pathological 87–8, 95, 113, 117–19, 129; prediction of pathological 127–35; psychosocial model of 85–6, 89–91, 96–7; as psychosocial transition 112, 123–4, 140, 141, 145; traumatic 135–45; *see also* mourning
Group Psychology and the Analysis of the Ego (Freud) 10
guilt: and bereavement 119, 122, 123; sense of 13–14, 65
Gurevich, Hayuta 36

Habermas, Jürgen 44, 171, 189
happiness 75–6, 188, 201, 205, 206–7
Harding, Denys W. 55
Hardy, Thomas 6–7, 65
hate, and death drive 15
health surveys 100–5, 107, 109
Heaney, Seamus 39, 40, 46
Heidegger, Martin 160, 186–8, 189
Henry (case study) 143, 144
Herald of Free Enterprise 143
historical reconstruction 36
holding 18, 51–2
Holmes, Jeremy 193
home, leaving and returning 77
homosexuality 193
hope 5–9; and antisocial behaviour 68–74; utopian use of 8–9
Hopkins, Brooke 38
hospice–home couple 116, 212
hospice movement 80–1, 89

hostels *see* residential care
Human Nature (Winnicott) 1–2
Hume, David 175–6
Husserl, Edmund 151, 160, 173, 179
hysterical amnesia 53

illness, as survived destruction 34
illusion 11–13, 171; *see also* catastrophic disillusionment
imagination 36–7; antisocial 67–74, 216; as memory 40, 48
impingement 23, 33; *see also* failure of life
individual responsibility 195; *see also* positive welfare
individualism 183, 185, 196; moral 196, 198, 202, 203, 204
infantile amnesia 53
infants: catastrophic disillusionment 21–4; Erikson's developmental schema 167–9; illusion in relationship with mother 12; importance of maternal love 15–20; inability to mourn 22–3; mother–infant relationship 12, 27, 75–6, 167, 177–8
inherent deficiencies 104
initiative 168, 169
innate morality 7
insecurity, ontological 157, 186
institutional care: bereaved 114; deprived children 6, 25, 68, 69, 73–4, 215
integration, and suicide 91
intimate disclosure 136, 145
intuitive management 8, 12, 15–20, 26, 35, 51–2, 177–9, 215–16
Isaacs, Susan 8, 25

Kahr, Brett 42
Kant, Immanuel 160
Keynesian economics 5
King James Bible 32, 44
Kirschner, Suzanne R. 38
Klein, Melanie 15, 22, 38
knowledge: and conduct 176–7; and faith 171–5, 177
Korn, Eric 45
Kübler-Ross, Elisabeth 93, 120

Lacan, Jacques 31, 54, 162–3, 176
language 163, 176
Lawrence, D. H. 65
Lear, Jonathan 56
leave-taking 77

Leavis, F. R. 42–3, 47
Lewis, Aubrey 93, 103–5, 107
liberal socialism 204–5
life cycle, Erikson's model of 167–9
life-plans 202, 211; ethical 191, 202; reconstruction after bereavement 140, 145
life politics 149, 202–7
lifestyle politics 195
listening 21
literary memoirs of bereavement 126
Little, Margaret 36, 50, 51
London Study of bereavement 88, 90, 93, 94, 119
Longuenesse, Béatrice 160
lost time 40
love: Freud's thoughts on 14; Winnicott's thoughts on 18; *see also* maternal love

Main, Mary 193
Major Depressive Disorder 111
managed hope 68–70, 73
market economy 195, 202
maternal love 15–20, 26, 27, 178; failures of 20–4, 52; and illusion 12; and morality 174
maturity: calculation of 65–6; as psychological process 62; social 64–7; *see also* criterion of maturity
Meissner, William W. 20, 174
memory 40–1; encapsulated 35, 36, 53–4
Menand, Louis 65
Mental Health Act (1959) 87, 115
mental illness: bereavement as 85; pharmacological treatment of 82
mentalization 183
Merleau-Ponty, Maurice 19
Miller, Emanuel 24–5
Miller, Peter 97, 116
Milner, Marion 42, 58
mirroring response 18, 19
moods 187–8
moral argument for war 60–2
moral impoverishment 200
moral individualism 196, 198, 202, 203, 204
morality 196–7; Freud's critique of 13–14, 62
moral paralysis 197
More, Thomas 197
Morris, Jeremy N. 102
mother–infant relationship 12, 27, 75–6, 167, 177–8

INDEX

mothers 15–20; absent 24–5; failures of maternal love 20–4, 52; fathers' protection of 76; search for lost relationship with 71–3; targets of government intervention 27; *see also* maternal love

mourning: active and passive modes 94–5; changes in 80; customs of 90; infant's inability 22–3; process of 120–3, 124–5; as process of normalization 81–2; and reclamation 47; reconstruction of life-plans 140, 145; *see also* grief

Nachträglichkeit 31, 36, 46
narcissism 10
narrative frame of reference 189–95, 213
negative illusion *see* catastrophic disillusionment
New Labour 207
non-interpretive interventions 38
normalization ix, 3, 4, 26, 67, 82, 87, 94, 96, 99, 110, 113, 118, 215; *see also* reflexive norms
normative orders of conduct 175–80

Oakeshott, Michael 198
Oates, Joyce Carol 126
object-relations theory 16–17, 26, 165
object-seeking 72
Oedipus complex 10–11, 194
Ogden, Thomas H. 36, 48
ontological insecurity 157, 186
ontological security 7, 8, 159, 161, 170, 184, 200
oral stage of development 167

parents: fathers 16, 76; professional help for 67; *see also* maternal love; mothers
Parkes, Colin Murray 80–1, 211–12; bereavement studies 85–9, 92–6; calculation of risk 131–5; comparison with Winnicott 95, 119, 128, 129, 141; concept of grief 111–13; concept of mourning 81–2, 120–3, 124–5; criticism of findings 87; epistemological aspects 108–10; family-centred care 114–15, 212; and Freud 119–20, 121–3, 135, 137, 138–41, 143–5, 212; obstacles to reflexive models 97–8; predictive–preventive strategy 127–35; psychosocial model of grief 85–6, 89–91, 96–7; therapeutic argument 117–25; traumatic bereavement 135–45

Parsons, Michael 21
Parsons, Talcott 149, 157–8, 159, 176
paternal function 76
paternal identification 10–11
perseverance of being 39
Persistent Complex Bereavement Related Disorder 111, 112, 113
personal disclosure 136, 145
personalization 16, 17
pharmacological treatment of mental illness 82
Phillips, Adam 25
poetic thinking 6–7
poetry: and criterion of maturity 42–3; English Romanticism 32, 39, 43, 45, 46; The Tree (Winnicott) 44; *see also* Eliot, T. S.
positive welfare 203–7, 213
post-traumatic memories 138–9, 140, 141, 144
post-traumatic stress disorder (PTSD) 137, 143
practical consciousness 176–7, 179, 180, 198, 211, 214
prayer 173
prediction of pathological grief 127–35; calculation of risk 131–5
pre-reflective intuition 35, 37, 38, 41, 51
primary creativity 7, 8, 42, 174, 177–8
primary intuition 35, 37, 41
primary trauma 33; *see also* early trauma
probability 132–4, 137
Prolonged Grief Disorder 111
Protestant values 167
psychosexual development 76, 167–8, 169
psychosocial predictors of pathological grief 127–8
psychosocial transitions 112, 123–4, 140, 141, 145, 211
psychotic illness 23; as defence 53
public hygiene 97–100
purgatorial process 55–6

reality, Freud's emphasis on 13, 15
reclamation: and mourning 47; paradox of 49–51; *see also* therapeutic management
recognition 18–19
reflective citizenship 196, 198, 199, 202, 204

243

reflexive medicine 113, 211; Durkheimian obstacles to 97–100; health surveys as obstacles to 100–5
reflexive norms 163–4, 170; and social facts 155–61
reflexivity 149, 199
regression: to dependence 38, 48, 50–1; normal and catastrophic types 33–4; not remembrance 50
regulation, and suicide 91
rehabilitation, deprived children 68–74
relative dependence 23
reliable experience, importance of 8, 16, 18, 69, 73, 174
religion 189, 201; Freud's critique of 11–12, 13, 171; in Giddens' thinking 173; sociology of 173; in Winnicott's thinking 7–8, 12, 15, 19–20, 38–9, 44–6, 171, 172–3
religious experience 6–7
remembering 48, 49, 50
re-moralization ix, 200, 214
repeated recollection 138–9, 140, 141, 144
repetition compulsion 185
repression 33, 34, 50, 53, 54, 200; and anxiety 185; and psychological trauma 138, 139, 143
residential care 6, 25, 68, 69, 73–4, 215
responsible risk takers 196, 203
Ricoeur, Paul 75, 191
risk management: basic trust 178; calculation of risk 131–5; predictive–preventive strategy 127–35, 212; and welfare 204
Robertson, James 121
Rodman, Robert F. 44, 45, 46
Rose, Nikolas 97, 104, 105, 116
Roussillon, René 34, 37
routines: of daily life 167, 170, 173, 176, 177, 189, 198; disciplinary 178; early 177–9
Royal Commission on Mental Health (1957) 87, 115
Royal Commission on the National Health Service (1979) 115
Royal Medico-Psychological Association 103–4
rule-governed behaviour 176–7
Rycroft, Charles 120
Ryle, John A. 102, 103

St. Christopher's Hospice 80–1, 131–2
satisfaction of need 76

Saunders, Cicely 80
secondary trauma 33
secure sense of self 165–9, 172, 174, 176, 182
security 3, 8; calculus of 63–7, 215; and freedom 200; ontological 7, 8, 159, 161, 170, 184, 200; problematic of 150, 151, 157, 160–1, 170, 182, 184, 206
Segal, Hanna 38
self, sense of: deprived child's search for 72; development of secure 165–9, 172, 174, 176, 182; infant's 16
self-conscious governance 183, 190, 195
self-control 205
self-criticism 189, 190
self-governance 182–3
self-help literature 194
self-identity 154, 162, 163, 170, 180, 199, 213; and bereavement 85, 92, 122, 135, 142–3; explanation of crisis of 166–7; formation of 165–9; and restructuring of medicine 82
self-knowledge 111, 154, 170, 176, 182, 183, 213, 214–15
self-management: bereaved 82, 86–9, 94–5, 107, 116, 130, 145; positive welfare 205
self-reflection 81, 82, 190
self-regard, and bereavement 122, 123
self-regulation 159, 160, 163–4, 167, 182–3, 184, 190, 199
self-reproach: anxiety as 188; and bereavement 119, 122, 123
self-restraint 172
Sennett, Richard 161
separation 8, 26
shame 167–8
Shepherd, Michael 104
silence 47
social facts and reflexive norms 155–61
social governance 164, 184
social inclusion 68–70
social justice 112–13, 116, 202, 203
social management 24–8, 64, 215; of anxiety 188–9; deprived children 68–74
social maturity 64–7
social medicine 102–3
social networks, and bereavement 90
social provision 26–7
social psychiatry *see* Lewis, Aubrey; Parkes, Colin Murray

social sense 65
social solidarity 91, 92, 161, 201, 204–5
social welfare 4–5, 91, 92; *see also* welfare society
sociological appropriation of psychoanalysis 149, 155, 160, 161–4, 177–80, 199
sociology, Durkheimian 109–10, 152–3, 155; obstacle to reflexive medicine 97–100
sociology of anxiety 186–9
sociology of modernity 196–7
sociology of morals 198, 200–7
solidarity, social 91, 92, 161, 201, 204–5
sorrow, expression of 89
special needs 88, 89, 98, 108–10, 112, 113
special risk 86, 136–41, 212
Spillius, Elizabeth Bott 38
Spinoza, Benedict de 160
spontaneity 8, 178; as welcome 21; as a virtue 46
stealing 71–2
stigmatization, avoiding 128, 130
Stocks, Percy 102
Stolorow, Robert D. 41
strategic argument for war 60–2
structuration 150, 156, 160, 179–80, 183
Studies on Hysteria (Breuer and Freud) 138, 139, 214
suicide 91–2, 130–1
superego 11, 13–14, 168
supervision, psychiatric 80, 86, 116, 117, 122, 124
Survey of Sickness 101–2
survival, Winnicott's notion of 62
Suttie, Ian 18
Symington, Neville 37

tactile experiences 47–8
Tavistock Institute of Human Relations 89
Tawney, R. H. 203, 204
Taylor, Charles 155, 197, 210
theft 71–2
therapeutic management 21, 24, 47–8, 52–6; deprived children 68–74; failure–dissociation model 32–5; paradox of reclamation 49–51; therapy as an act of faith 35–9
therapeutic narrative 193–5
therapeutic supervision 80, 82, 110, 112, 117–18, 130–1, 211–12
Thomas, Edward 47

time 31–2, 46; redemption of 46
Titmuss, Richard M. 102
Tomalin, Claire 6
tradition: end of in daily life 164–5; non-traditional use of 200–4, 205
transcendence 11, 13, 20
transference-countertransference 36
transformation of intimacy 164–5, 168
trauma: early 21–4, 32–5, 40–1, 47, 52–6; Freud's views 137, 138–41, 143–5, 212; repeated recollection of 138–9, 140, 141, 144; Winnicott's theory of 33
traumatic bereavement 135–45
traumatic neuroses, external vs internal aetiology 140, 143–4
Tree, The 44–6
trust 182; crisis of 161–5, 184–5, 200
Tustin, Frances 52

uncanny 49, 187
unconditional entitlements 195, 203, 204, 207
unconscious 162–3, 175, 180; analytic voice of 37
unemployment 104
unhappiness, and morality 13–14
unthinkable loss 21–4, 32–5, 40–1, 47, 52–6
utopian longing 34, 35, 37, 41
utopian realism 183, 184, 198–9, 200, 202–7, 213

Virgil 55
vital normativity 35, 60, 155, 172
vulnerability, identification of 127–35
vulnerable widow category 126, 127

Walter, Tony 96
war 59–60; nature of 3–4, 5; strategic and moral arguments for 60–2; Winnicott's evaluation of 60–3
Wartime Social Survey 104
wasted opportunity 188
Waste Land, The (Eliot) 32, 42
welfare dependency 195, 203, 204, 207
welfare society 196, 202–5, 206–7
welfare state 91, 92, 196, 203, 206–7
welfare to work policy 207
widows 84, 86–7, 117–18, 124; London Study 88, 90, 93, 94, 119; memoirs of bereavement 126; suicide 92; vulnerable widow category 126, 127

Williams, Bernard 205
Williams, Rowan 174, 215
Winnicott, Donald 1–2, 5–9, 215–17; child evacuation 8, 24–5; comparison with Erikson 166, 167; comparison with Parkes 95, 119, 128, 129, 141; creativity 43–4; Curtis Committee 26, 67; and Eliot 32, 39, 41–2, 45, 47, 54–6, 64–5; evaluation of war 60–3; failure–dissociation model 32–5; failures of maternal love 20–4, 52; faith and knowledge 171–3, 174; Giddens' use of ideas 177–9; holding 51–2; illusion 11–13, 171; management of deprived children 68–74; maternal love 15–20, 26, 27; memory 40–1; paradox of reclamation 50–1; psychosis as defence 53; reclamation 31–2; religion 7–8, 12, 15, 19–20, 38–9, 44–6, 171, 172–3; social management 24–8; social maturity 64–7; therapy as an act of faith 35–9; The Tree 44–6; view of managed life 74–7
Wittgenstein, Ludwig 175, 176
women, fear of 74–5
Worden, J. William 126, 136
Wordsworth, William 46, 50, 54
working-through 46, 144–5; infant's inability 22–3
Wright, Kenneth 18–19, 20

For Product Safety Concerns and Information please contact our EU representative GPSR@taylorandfrancis.com
Taylor & Francis Verlag GmbH, Kaufingerstraße 24, 80331 München, Germany

www.ingramcontent.com/pod-product-compliance
Lightning Source LLC
Chambersburg PA
CBHW070029010526
44117CB00011B/1759